Meeting Jesus in the Sacraments

Meeting Jesus in the Sacraments

AVE MARIA PRESS AVE Notre Dame, Indiana

The Subcommittee on the Catechism, United States Conference of Catholic Bishops, has found this catechetical text, copyright 2010, to be in conformity with the *Catechism of the Catholic Church*.

Imprimatur: Most Reverend John M. D'Arcy
                 Bishop of Fort Wayne-South Bend

Nihil Obstat: The Reverend Michael Heintz
                 Censor Liborum
                 Given at Fort Wayne, Indiana, on 11 February 2009.

Founded in 1865, Ave Maria Press is a ministry of the United States Province of Holy Cross.

Engaging Minds, Hearts, and Hands for Faith® is a trademark of Ave Maria Press, Inc.

www.avemariapress.com

ISBN-10 1-59471-143-7 ISBN-13 978-1-59471-143-5

Project Authors and Editors: Michael Amodei and Janie Gustafson, PhD.

Theological Consultant: Reverend Paul Turner
                          Former President of the North American Academy of Liturgy
                          Facilitator for International Commission on English in the Liturgy

Cover design by Andy Wagoner.

Text design by Brian C. Conley.

Printed and bound in the United States of America.

ENGAGING MINDS, HEARTS, AND HANDS FOR FAITH

"An education that is complete is one in which the hands and heart are engaged as much as the mind. We want to let our students try their learning in the world and so make prayers of their education."

Blessed Basil Moreau
Founder of the Congregation of Holy Cross

In this text, you will find:

 intellectually challenging exercises and projects designed to stimulate you to know more about the sacraments and their relationship to the Paschal Mystery of Christ.

 presentations and activities that promote a prayerful study of Scripture and connect you to the Church's liturgy.

 hands-on applications that encourage you to live the sacraments through witness, charity, and service.

Contents

The Sacramental Nature *of the* Church

WHAT IS THE MEANING OF THE SACRAMENTS?

While you are likely familiar with the names of the Seven Sacraments of the Church, Unit 1 provides a fuller definition of *sacrament* and defines Jesus himself as a sacrament and his Church as both the Body of Christ and the sacrament of Christ.

The *Catechism of the Catholic Church* defines sacraments in the following way:

> The sacraments are **efficacious** signs of grace, instituted by Christ and entrusted to the Church, by which divine life is dispensed to us. The visible rites by which the sacraments are celebrated signify and make present the graces proper to each sacrament. They bear fruit in those who receive them with the required dispositions. (*CCC* 1131)

The next sections briefly elaborate on this definition.

Efficacious Signs of Grace

St. Thomas Aquinas wrote that sacraments "have efficacy from the incarnate Word himself." In a related way, the sacraments themselves are efficacious symbols, meaning they effect what they symbolize and symbolize what they effect. Further, as "efficacious signs of grace," each sacrament confers a grace that is proper to it.

The *Catechism of the Catholic Church* defines *grace* as "a participation in the life of God" (*CCC* 1997). Grace is the "free and undeserved help that God gives us" so that we can respond to his call (*CCC* 1996).

It is important to understand that grace is not some *thing* that is outside of the relationship we have with God. Rather, grace is a gift that helps us participate in a relationship with him as the Three Persons of the Holy Trinity are in relationship with one another. Grace is first and foremost a gift of the Holy Spirit himself, but grace also includes the ability God gives us to participate in and collaborate with his work.

sacrament

An outward (visible) sign of an invisible grace. An "efficacious" symbol brings about the spiritual reality to which it points. This term applies to Christ Jesus, the great sign of God's love for us; to the Church, his continuing presence in our world; and to the Seven Sacraments.

efficacious

A term that means "capable of producing a desired effect." This means that the sacraments actually confer the grace they signify.

God gives us his grace in many ways and through many opportunities in our lives. The Seven Sacraments are guaranteed moments of encountering Father and Son, through the grace of the Holy Spirit. Sacraments strengthen and deepen our relationship with Jesus and our brothers and sisters in the Church and the world. They draw us into the wonder and completeness of the divine life.

Instituted by Christ

The sacraments are rooted in Jesus and traceable to him. His ongoing presence in the Church through the gift of the Holy Spirit has helped the Church know and understand the Seven Sacraments as times when Christ is with us. The same Jesus who in his earthly ministry healed the sick, forgave the sinner, celebrated marriage with his friends, and fed thousands with his bread and with his words is present today in the Seven Sacraments. As St. Leo the Great put it, "What was visible in our Savior has passed over to his mysteries."

Commemorations of the Paschal Mystery

The sacraments celebrate the Paschal Mystery—the Life, Passion, Death, Resurrection, and Ascension of Christ—that brought about our Salvation. In each sacrament, the saving actions of Christ are made present. The way Christ dispenses the fruits of the Paschal Mystery until he comes again is known as the **sacramental economy**. The term originates from Greek words that mean "management of the household." The sacramental economy refers to the way Christ cares for his household, the Church.

Of course, the actual historical events of the Paschal Mystery occurred only once, but by the power of the Holy Spirit the liturgy makes the events present for us today. It brings us into communion with the Blessed Trinity and with one another. More information about this unity is shared in Chapter 1. How the Blessed Trinity works in the liturgy is explored in Chapter 2.

SACRAMENTS ARE THE MASTERWORKS OF GOD

In the sacraments, God really becomes present to us. No created object, no spoken word, or no ritualized action can ever "force" God to be present. Nothing we do or say can control what God does. Pouring water over someone's head or saying certain words doesn't produce God "on demand." Instead, God comes to us in the sacraments because he chooses to communicate with us during these times and places, through these rituals. The *Catechism of the Catholic Church* teaches that sacraments are powers that emanate from the Body of Christ. They are actions of the Holy Spirit at work in the Church. They are the "masterworks of God" (*CCC* 1116).

In a sacrament, God acts first, and then we act in response. God takes the initiative of being present, of offering us a share in his own life and love. We, in turn, open our hearts to the divine, giving God worship and accepting God's Word as the truth on which to base our lives. In other words, every sacrament is an *encounter*, a dialogue, a two-way street. A sacrament always involves a relationship between God and humanity.

This understanding means that a definition of *sacrament* can now read:

DID YOU KNOW?

In the twelfth century, theologian Peter Lombard wrote that a sacrament is "an outward sign of invisible grace." He meant that a sacrament is both a sign and a cause of grace.

sacramental economy

An expression that means the communication or dispensation of the fruits of Christ's Paschal Mystery through the celebration of the sacramental liturgy.

"a visible sign that points to and *makes real* God's presence; God invites us to enter into communion with him and with all those who are celebrating with us." But even this definition falls short of what a sacrament truly is. We also need to realize that each sacrament fills us with grace and *transforms* us. Each sacrament works to make us completely whole and holy. We start to live more fully; we grow in God's likeness through our participation in the sacraments. Each sacrament empowers us to come alive in the Holy Spirit, so that our every thought and action can praise God and give witness to Christ's saving power.

In summary, every sacrament has four aspects or dimensions. It is a

1. *memorial*—a remembering that God is present with us now and has always acted for our benefit in the past;
2. *celebration*—a Church-approved ritual (involving objects, words, and actions) that gives worship and thanks to God for our Salvation in Christ;
3. *communion*—a real encounter of oneness between God and humanity, and oneness between Church members; and
4. *transformation*—an empowerment to become more holy and to minister to others through the gift of God's grace.

It is important to realize that these four aspects or dimensions are not like stages or steps. One does not happen necessarily before the other, nor is there any particular order. Rather, each sacrament—in its entirety—is a memorial, a celebration, a communion, and a transformation.

From Catholic Bloggers

SACRAMENTS ARE GOD'S CLEAR GIFT

I believe that all the tools God gives us through his Church work so well for one reason. What they all have in common is that they bring us grace. I'm certainly not saying non-Catholic Christians don't receive grace because they don't have all the tools. God cannot be put in a box, he is not tied to the sacraments, he can give grace where he sees fit. But, the sacraments and other tools are God's clear gift and promise to us, they are an assurance that when we need grace to overcome sin, he is there waiting in the sacraments to give it to us.

—from Stephanie, Austin, Texas

SOME REASONS TO ATTEND MASS (FROM MY RELIGION CLASS)

- Grace
- The Mass is Calvary continued
- Holy Mass is the world's most powerful atonement for your sins
- At the hour of death, the Masses you have heard will be your greatest consolation
- One Mass heard during life will be of more benefit to you than many heard for you after your death
- Every Mass wins for you a higher degree of glory in Heaven
- You receive the priest's blessing which our Lord ratifies in Heaven
- You kneel amidst a multitude of holy angels, who are present at the adorable Sacrifice with reverential awe
- You are blessed in your temporal goods and affairs

—from Elm

The Church *and the* Sacramental Economy *of* Salvation

The Incarnation
God loves us and wants to be near to us.

Jesus Christ Is the Sacrament of God
Jesus himself is the way to God the Father. He is the prime, or primordial, sacrament.

The Church, the Universal Sacrament of Salvation
The saving work of Christ is revealed and communicated through the Church.

The Mission of the Church, the Body of Christ
The Church completes the work of Christ and brings us into unity with the Blessed Trinity and with one another.

The Church, the Channel of Grace
As the sacrament of Christ, the Church has the power to transform us.

THE INCARNATION

The June sky was rumbling with thunder. The little girl's room lit up with the aftermath of the bright lightning strikes that followed in proximity. Finally, she had enough. She removed her covers and dashed down the hall to her parents' bedroom.

Her sleepy mother spoke to the girl as she peered into her eyes, the mother prone, the girl standing near the edge of the bed.

"Honey, you can go back to your room. You aren't alone. Jesus is with you," the mother gently told her.

"Mommy, I know Jesus is with me," the girl said in return. "But I want someone with skin."

The message of this story of the little girl on the night of a storm is that we want to be close to the ones who know us, protect us, and most of all, love us. This is why God, who is Spirit, took on flesh and became a human being:

> And the Word became flesh
> and made his dwelling among us,
> and we saw his glory,
> the glory of the Father's only Son,
> full of grace and truth. (Jn 1:14)

God's becoming man, entering human history as a fellow human, and becoming flesh like us is the mystery of the **Incarnation**. St. Augustine described the sacraments as

Incarnation
A word that means "taking on human flesh." Jesus is the Incarnation of God. In Jesus, God took human form.

"visible signs of invisible grace." This means that to understand the sacraments we must make the invisible visible. To understand how Christ is the ever-present Sacrament of God, we must also understand how the Church is the Universal Sacrament of Jesus Christ.

For Reflection

What is your experience of loving someone who isn't physically present with you? How is that different from loving someone who is in physical proximity to you?

JESUS CHRIST IS THE SACRAMENT OF GOD

liturgy

The official public worship of the Church. The sacraments and the Divine Office constitute the Church's liturgy. Mass is the most important liturgical celebration.

Simply put, we meet Jesus, our Redeemer and High Priest, in the **liturgy**. *Liturgy* traditionally meant a "public work" or "people's work." More properly, it refers to the participation of God's people through prayer and celebration in the fruits of the Paschal Mystery—that is, our Salvation. The sacraments and liturgy—known as the "sacramental economy"—are the system Christ uses to make himself and his saving graces present on earth.

Because of his love for us, Jesus simply cannot remain separated from his members, the Church. He communicated this fact to his disciples while he lived on earth: "I am the vine, you are the branches. Whoever remains in me and I in him will bear much fruit, because without me you can do nothing" (Jn 15:5). St. Paul also understood this connection. He wrote to the Galatians:

I have been crucified with Christ; yet I live, no longer I, but Christ lives in me; insofar as I now live in the flesh, I live by faith in the Son of God who has loved me and given himself up for me. (Gal 2:19–20)

Likewise, we too have a deep longing for Christ that our participation in the sacraments satisfies. While this longing often becomes staid and taken for granted, it was not always so. For example, you might remember your great desire for Jesus at the time of your First Communion. St. Thérèse of Lisieux recalled her First Communion as the "most wonderful day of my life" in her autobiography, *Story of a Soul*:

I can remember every tiny detail of those heavenly hours: my joyous waking up at dawn, the tender, reverent kisses of the mistresses and older girls, the room where we dressed—filled with the white "snowflakes" in which one after another we were clothed—and above all, our entry into chapel and the singing of the morning hymn: "O Altar of God, Where the Angels Are Hovering." I would not tell you everything, even if I could, for there are certain things which lose their fragrance in the open air, certain thoughts so intimate that they cannot be translated into earthly language without losing at once their deep and heavenly meaning. How lovely it was, that first kiss of Jesus in my heart—it was truly a kiss of love.

Today, Jesus' desire to be with us remains strong. Jesus longs to share your life, both the tragedies and joys. The sacramental economy is the way the fruits of Christ's Redemption are given to us. This is accomplished in the Church's liturgy through the work of the Holy Trinity.

Christ, the Prime Sacrament

One of the definitions of *sacrament* is that it is a mystery. This tells us that sacraments cannot be fully explained or understood. This description fits Jesus as well. To say that Jesus is a sacrament is to say that he too is a mystery that cannot be fully explained or understood. Jesus is truly human, like us in all ways, "yet without sin" (Heb 4:15). Jesus also is truly divine, the Second Person of the Holy Trinity—without beginning and without end.

We do not understand *how* Jesus can be fully man yet fully divine at the same time. This mystery is known as the **hypostatic union**. This doctrine of faith, first expressed by St. Cyril of Alexandria (d. 444), says that in Jesus there are two natures—one human and the other divine—in one Person. These natures are united in such a way that Jesus was human like every human. He was born as a baby, grew as a child, experienced adolescence, and finally became an adult. He needed to eat, sleep, drink, breathe, bathe, and learn—just as we do. He laughed, cried, and felt real pain. And because he had a real human body, he was subject to death just as we are.

Along with his humanity, Jesus is fully and completely divine. As the Son of God, Jesus is the equal of God the Father and God the Holy Spirit. Jesus is all-knowing, all-powerful, all-good, and all-loving. As God, he is not limited in any way by time or space. He is everywhere, in all places at once. He is with us always.

The four Gospels in the New Testament give us a glimpse into the historical life of Jesus. We know that Jesus was born of a young Jewish woman in Bethlehem during the reign of Herod the Great (sometime before 4 BC). He grew up in Nazareth. Then he worked throughout Palestine as a spiritual teacher and healer for one to three years before his Death in Jerusalem under Pontius Pilate (around AD 30). The Gospels never tell us what Jesus looked like. Nor do they methodically describe his personality or temperament. The **evangelists** were more concerned about proclaiming the Good News of Salvation that Jesus taught by his words and actions.

In addition to being a mystery, Jesus fulfills the definition of *sacrament* in many other ways. For example, he is a *sign of something hidden*—the divine presence. He is also an *efficacious sign*. Instead of simply pointing to or revealing God's love for us, Jesus actually

hypostatic union
The doctrine of faith that recognizes two natures (one human and one divine) in the one divine Person of Jesus Christ.

evangelists
The writers of the four Gospels in the New Testament. According to tradition, the four evangelists are Matthew, Mark, Luke, and John.

Jesus

A Hebrew name that means "God saves." This name explains the purpose of Jesus' life—to save all people from sin.

Christ

A Greek name that means "anointed one." This name, when applied to Jesus, means he is the Son of the living God.

Messiah

The long-prophesied Savior that God would send to save people from their sins. Some Jews in the time of Jesus thought this Messiah would be a political figure, someone who would rescue them from domination by the Romans.

primordial sacrament

A reference to Jesus as the "prime sacrament" because he points to God's love while at the same time he is God's love for us as he reconciles the world to his Father.

brings us this love, this saving grace. He makes communion with the divine possible because he is God.

Jesus is a sacrament because he is the perfect, most complete visible sign of the Father's presence. A person may witness God in the beauties of creation or in a relationship filled with love. But there is no greater expression of God's presence than Jesus, the Second Person of the Trinity. As he told his disciples the night before his Death, "Whoever has seen me has seen the Father. . . . I am in the Father and the Father is in me" (Jn 14:9–10). The name *Jesus* means "God saves." The name *Christ* means "anointed one." Jesus is the anointed one of God, the promised **Messiah** who came to save all people from sin. But even more important, as the Second Person of the Holy Trinity, he is the visible expression of the Father's eternal being and love. God became man in the historical Jesus.

Think about it. When the Apostles heard Jesus speak, they were hearing God's actual words to them. When they saw Jesus, they were really looking upon the face of God. When they witnessed the healing miracles of Jesus, they were seeing God's love in action. And when Jesus touched them, it was God himself touching them.

Throughout the Gospels, Jesus tells people in many different ways that he is *the* sign of God's love. He doesn't just talk about water or use it as a sign of God's love. He *himself* is the living water of eternal life. "Whoever drinks the water I shall give will never thirst; the water I shall give will become in him a spring of water welling up to eternal life" (Jn 4:14).

Jesus doesn't just bake bread for his disciples or multiply bread as visible proof of God's love. He *himself* is the living bread come down from Heaven. "I am the bread of life; whoever comes

to me will never hunger" (Jn 6:35). "I am the living bread that came down from heaven; whoever eats this bread will live forever; and the bread that I will give is my flesh for the life of the world" (Jn 6:51).

Likewise, Jesus doesn't merely talk about light in his parables as a way to explain the absence of darkness (see Luke 11:33–36). He presents *himself* as God's light to a world darkened by sin. "I am the light of the world. Whoever follows me will not walk in darkness, but will have the light of life" (Jn 8:12).

Jesus is called the prime sacrament, or **primordial sacrament**. To put it more simply, Jesus himself is our only way to God the Father. "I am the way and the truth and the life. No one comes to the Father except through me" (Jn 14:6).

Jesus, an Efficacious Sign

Recall from the unit opener that a sacrament is an efficacious sign. It not only points to God's presence, it makes his presence an experienced reality in the here and now. Jesus is similarly an efficacious sign. Jesus is not only a sign of God's love, he effects that love and makes it present. During his life on earth, Jesus brought people into direct contact with God through his words and actions.

And the Word became flesh and made his dwelling among us, and we saw his glory, the glory as of the Father's only Son, full of grace and truth. . . . From his fullness we have all received. . . . No one has ever seen God. The only Son, God, who is at the Father's side, has revealed him. (Jn 1:14, 16, 18)

After his Resurrection, Jesus appeared to his disciples in the same body that had been tortured and crucified;

yet at the same time had new properties of a glorious body that would eventually take his place "at the right hand of God" (see Acts 7:55–56). Christ gave the Apostles the power (through the gift of the Holy Spirit) to form the Church and establish the Seven Sacraments so that he would remain present to them always. Through the Seven Sacraments, the Church continues Christ's work of perfectly worshiping the Father and of making redeeming grace available to humanity.

To say that Jesus is the Sacrament of God or the primordial sacrament does not mean he is an eighth sacrament, on top of the Church's Seven Sacraments. Rather, Jesus Christ is the reason for, the basis of, all Seven Sacraments.

For Review

1. What is meant by the "sacramental economy"?
2. How is Christ, like the sacraments, a mystery?
3. How is Jesus an efficacious sign?
4. Explain why saying Jesus is the "primordial sacrament" is different from saying he is the "eighth sacrament."
5. What is the saving effect of the Paschal Mystery?

For Reflection

- What are your memories of your own First Communion?

- How would you describe your personal longing for Christ?

New Life in Christ

We believe that Jesus came into the world to bring us full, abundant life (see John 10:10). St. Irenaeus, a second-century bishop who was killed for his faith in Jesus, said it brilliantly: "The glory of God is the human person fully alive." Think about it: God actually rejoices when we are fully, abundantly alive! God's will is that we should live forever. The saving effect of the Paschal Mystery of Christ is a vibrant new life in the Blessed Trinity. We participate in this new life through the sacraments. The sacraments, in turn, empower us to share our God-fulfilled life with others.

Read the following Scripture passages. For each one, reflect in your journal about what you think this aspect of new life is like. Then write down a specific plan to bring new life to someone you know—at home, at school, or in your local community. Carry out your plan sometime this week.

- We are to be bread to others (see John 21:15-17).
- We are to be life-giving water in the desert (see Matthew 10:42).
- We are to be light in the darkness (see Matthew 5:14-16).
- We are to be salt to those who feel flat or depressed (see Matthew 5:13).
- We are to be yeast to everyone (see Matthew 13:33).
- We are to be good soil that nurtures the seeds of faith (see Matthew 13:23).
- We are to bear fruit that will last (see John 15:16).

THE CHURCH, THE UNIVERSAL SACRAMENT OF SALVATION

The saving work of Christ's entire life is the sacrament of salvation; this work is "revealed and active in the Church's sacraments" (*CCC* 774). The Church's sacraments have meaning only in and through Jesus. Each sacrament is primarily and fundamentally a personal act of Christ himself acting through his Mystical Body, the Church. Each sacrament is the saving action of Christ in visible form; it is the act of Christ the High Priest who "entered once for all into the sanctuary, not with the blood of goats and calves but with his own blood, thus obtaining eternal redemption" (Heb 9:12). In the words of the *Catechism*, "it really is Christ who acts in the sacraments through the Holy Spirit for the Church" (*CCC* 1120).

In the Church, especially in her Seven Sacraments, Jesus continues to live and work among us. "Christ now acts through the sacraments he instituted to communicate his grace" (*CCC* 1084). "[The sacraments] are *efficacious* because in them Christ himself is at work; it is he who baptizes, he who acts in his sacraments in order to communicate the grace that each sacrament signifies" *(CCC* 1127). The Church is the "universal sacrament of salvation" because she is the visible channel of grace to the whole human race. Cardinal Joseph Bernardin of Chicago once explained, "As Christ is the sacrament of God—the visible and incarnate, efficacious and gratuitous bestowal of divine grace and life—so the Church is the sacrament of Christ in human history." The Church makes Christ present in today's world.

The relationship between the Church and Christ is much like the relationship between the moon and the sun. The moon has no light of its own, but it shines in the night sky because it reflects the light of the sun. In the same way, the Church is a light to the world because she reflects the light of Christ. She makes this light—the grace of Salvation and new life—available to all people.

To understand further how the Church is the sacrament of Christ, we need to see how the Church herself meets the definition of *sacrament*.

First, a sacrament is a mystery.

Second, it is also a visible sign of the unseen divine reality.

Third, a sacrament is an efficacious sign—something that makes real what it signifies. The Church also has these same three dimensions, explained in the following sections.

The Church as Mystery

St. Paul spoke of the Church as a great mystery—something we cannot fully explain or understand (see Ephesians 5:32). For this reason, he and the other writers of the New Testament described the Church in symbolic language. They used images that would help people understand the Church as mystery. Some of the images for the Church found in the New Testament are included in the following table:

Symbols for Church	New Testament Reference
Sheepfold (a fenced enclosure with Christ as the gate)	John 10:1–18
Flock of sheep	John 21:15–19
Cultivated field or vineyard	John 15:1–10
Building of God	Ephesians 2:19–22
Bride of Christ and Mother	Ephesians 5:25–27
New Jerusalem (Kingdom of God)	Revelation 21:9–27

The last image is perhaps the most difficult to comprehend. On the one hand, the Church is the New Jerusalem, the Kingdom of God, and "the kingdom of Christ already present in mystery" (*Lumen Gentium* [Dogmatic Constitution on the Church] 3). At the same time, however, the Church is not yet perfect. As the *Catechism* teaches, the Church is "the seed and beginning of the Kingdom" (*CCC* 764). The Church is indeed holy, but she is a pilgrim Church. The Church "grows visibly in the world through the power of God" (*Lumen Gentium* 3). In addition,

the Church, to which we are all called in Christ Jesus, and in which by the grace of God we attain holiness, will receive its perfection only in the glory of heaven, when the time for the renewal of all things will have come (Acts 3:21). (*Lumen Gentium* 48)

The Church as Visible Sign

A sacrament is a visible sign of an unseen divine dimension. The same is true for the Church. The Church is the visible sign of Jesus Christ, who is the perfect sign of the Father's saving love. In more detail:

The Church is both human and divine, visible but endowed with invisible realities, zealous in action and dedicated to contemplation, present in the world, yet a migrant, so constituted that in it the human is directed toward and subordinated to the divine, the visible to the invisible, action to contemplation, and this present world to that city yet to come, the object of our quest (see Hebrews 13:14). (*Sacrosanctum Concilium* [The Constitution on the Sacred Liturgy] 2)

As *the* visible sign of Christ's presence in today's world, the Church has four distinguishing characteristics, or marks. The **marks of the Church** are one, holy, catholic, and apostolic. Here is what we mean when we use these words.

1. The Church is a visible sign of *oneness.* Each individual parish is part of a larger diocese, which is part of the universal Church. These local communities share the same faith received from the Apostles. All local communities share the same Mass and sacraments. In other words, all local churches within the one universal Church are united to one another. "All those, who in faith look towards Jesus, the author of salvation and the source of unity and peace,

marks of the Church
Four essential signs or characteristics of Christ's Church that mark her as his true Church. The Church is one, holy, catholic, and apostolic.

MARKS OF THE CHURCH

Review the meaning of the marks of the Church described on pages 13–14. Then do one of the following:

- Research several periods in Church history when each mark of the Church was especially influential.
- Research and report on the words of St. Paul, St. Ignatius of Antioch, and St. Irenaeus of Lyon on the importance of unity in the Church.
- Read and summarize the meaning of *catholicity* from the New Catholic Encyclopedia: www.newadvent.org/cathen/03449a.htm.

God has gathered together and established as the Church, that it may be for each and everyone the visible sacrament of this saving unity" (*Lumen Gentium* 9).

2. The Church is a visible sign of *holiness*. The Holy Spirit "dwells in the Church and in the hearts of the faithful, as in a temple" (*Lumen Gentium* 4). The presence of the Holy Spirit in the Church is seen most clearly in the lives of Mary and numerous saints throughout the centuries. Following their example, we grow in holiness by participating in the Church's sacraments and mission of charity.

3. The Church is a visible sign of *catholicity*. The word *catholic* means "universal." The Church is catholic in a double sense. First, she is catholic because Christ is present in her. As St. Ignatius of Antioch wrote: "Where there is

Christ Jesus, there is the Catholic Church" (quoted from *CCC* 830). The Church offers the fullness of the means of Salvation, the fullness of faith, the sacraments, and ordained ministry by apostolic succession. Second, the Church is universal because her mission is to everyone. (See pages 16–20.)

4. The Church is a visible sign of *apostolicity*. The Church is a hierarchical community, under the supervision of leaders who are authorized to act in the name of Christ. The Church is founded on the Apostles, whom Jesus himself chose. The Church hands on the Apostles' own teaching and faith through the Sacrament of Holy Orders. The pope and bishops can trace their authority back to the Apostles and their successors.

The Church as Efficacious Sign

A sacrament is more than a visible sign. It is also efficacious. A sacrament makes the real, saving action of the Risen Christ present to us through the work of the Holy Spirit. The Church, too, is a visible sign of Christ. The Church is both the means and goal of God's plan—prefigured in creation, prepared for in the Old Covenant, and instituted by the words and actions of Jesus. On the other hand, the Church is the Mystical Body of Christ, continuing to bring God's saving love to people throughout the world. The Holy Spirit makes the Church "the temple of the living God" (*CCC* 797).

The power of the Church to effect what she signifies was given by Christ to Peter and the Apostles when he said, "I will give you the keys to the kingdom of heaven. Whatever you bind on earth shall be bound in heaven; and

whatever you loose on earth shall be loosed in heaven" (Mt 16:19; 18:18). "And behold, I am with you always, until the end of the age" (Mt 28:20). Further, Jesus instructed:

> "Amen, amen, I say to you, whoever believes in me will do the works that I do, and will do greater ones than these, because I am going to the Father. And whatever you ask in my name, I will do, so that the Father may be glorified in the Son. If you ask anything of me in my name, I will do it." (Jn 14:12–14)

Because of the power Jesus gave her, "the Church, then, both contains and communicates the invisible grace she signifies. It is in this analogical sense that the Church is called a 'sacrament'" (*CCC* 774). "The church, in Christ, is a sacrament—a sign and instrument, that is, of communion with God and of the unity of the entire human race" (*Lumen Gentium* 1). This was the reason the Fathers of the Second Vatican Council called the Church "the universal sacrament of salvation" (*Lumen Gentium* 48).

DID YOU KNOW?

The Holy Spirit works so intimately within the Church that he inspires the Magisterium (the college of bishops in union with the pope) to teach on the truth, the will of God for today's world.

For Review

1. What are three dimensions of the Church that are similar to three dimensions of the sacraments?
2. What biblical symbols have been used to describe the Church as mystery?
3. Name and explain the four marks of the Church.
4. How is the Church an efficacious sign?

For Reflection

Use another analogy (besides the sun and the moon) to explain the relationship between Jesus and the Church.

THE MISSION OF THE CHURCH, THE BODY OF CHRIST

BUILDING THE BODY OF CHRIST

Read what St. Paul wrote about the Church as a body with many parts (1 Cor 12:14-26) and the Church as a community (Rom 12:9-18). Then check the following websites or others like them for practical ideas on how you can be a witness to the faith by serving others both in and out of the Catholic Church. Write a proposal for your plan of service in this area. Incorporate some of St. Paul's words into your plan. Enact the plan. Write a summary of your actions. Sample websites for service:

- **Catholic Relief Services:** www.crs.org/act/participate.cfm
- **Urban Youth Ministry:** www.dirtyvagabond.com/live/

The Church, which is the Body of Christ, completes the mission of Christ and the Holy Spirit. This mission is to bring us into communion with the Three Persons of the Holy Trinity: Father, Son, and Holy Spirit. "Through the Church's sacraments, Christ communicates his Holy and sanctifying Spirit to the members of his Body" (*CCC* 739). How this is specifically done in the individual sacraments is the subject of Chapters 3 to 9 of this textbook. For now, it is important to introduce the image of Church as the Body of Christ and point out ways Christ and the Spirit animate her members through the sacraments to engage in and live out their mission.

The origins of this image come from the Epistles of St. Paul. In the First Letter to the Corinthians, Paul wrote: "As a body is one, though it has many parts, and all the parts of the body, though many, are one body, so also Christ. For in one Spirit we were all baptized into one body" (1 Cor 12:12–13a).

The Second Vatican Council also expressed the importance of this description of the Church very clearly:

> Rising from the dead (see Rom 6:9) [Christ] sent his life-giving Spirit upon his disciples and through him set up his body which is the Church as the universal sacrament of salvation. Sitting at the right hand of the Father he is continually active in the world in order to lead people to the church and through it to join them more closely to himself; by nourishing them with his own Body and Blood, he makes them sharers in his glorious life. (*Lumen Gentium* 48)

As members of the Body of Christ, we are united not only to Christ but also to one another. Our participation in the sacraments—especially in the Eucharist—strengthens this unity and helps us to live morally. Also, we participate in the Body of Christ, the Church, with the understanding that Christ is the Head. Part of a prayer in the Letter to the Colossians reads:

> [Christ] is the head of the body, the church.
> He is the beginning, the firstborn from the dead,
> that in all things he himself might be preeminent. (Col 1:18)

An understanding of the Church as the Body of Christ has several implications that involve our communion with the Blessed Trinity as well as our communion with other Catholics, locally and universally, with all people throughout the world, and with the **communion of saints**. Each of these implications of the Church as the Body of Christ is discussed in the sections that follow.

Communion with Christ and the Church

Through our participation in the Church and particularly due to the graces of the sacraments, we find communion with Christ and the Church. The *Catechism of the Catholic Church* describes the intimacy of this communion:

- "The comparison of the Church with the body casts light on the intimate bond between Christ and his Church. Not only is she gathered *around him*; she is united *in him*, in his body" (*CCC* 789).
- "[The Church] draws her life from the word and the Body of Christ and so herself becomes Christ's Body" (*CCC* 752).
- "The Church . . . is the visible sign of the communion in Christ between God and men" (*CCC* 1071).

Pope John Paul II, in his encyclical *Redemptor Hominis* (Redeemer of Man), wrote that communion with Christ is the Church's main purpose for existing—that "each person may be able to find Christ, in order that Christ may walk with each person the path of life" (13). That is why we can say the Church is "the sacrament of unity" (*CCC* 1140). She is the "sign

and instrument . . . of communion with God" (*Lumen Gentium* 1).

We also encounter Christ and delve more deeply into a relationship with the Holy Trinity *whenever* we come together as Church. This means that when we do the things Christ did and in his name—visit the sick, attend a Bible study class, volunteer in a soup kitchen, sort clothes for a St. Vincent de Paul thrift shop, or even have fun at a church social event—we grow in communion with Christ and the Church. *Whatever* we do as Catholics, we act as the Body of Christ, as Christ himself in today's world.

Communion with Other Catholics

A second type of communion the Church makes possible is unity with other Catholics. Just as the human body has many parts, so we need everyone in the Church to make up the Body of Christ. We form community in local parishes with other Catholics in two ways. First, we try to welcome everyone—even those we disagree with politically, those in a different economic bracket, those who may not like us,

communion of saints
The unity in Christ of all those he has redeemed: the Church on earth, in Heaven, and in Purgatory.

or those of other races. Second, we realize that every person has something positive to add to the Church. Whether that person is a priest, an altar server, a member of the choir, a catechumen, or a family member sitting in the pews, each person is important and needed in Christ's Body.

Catholics share communion with the Church worldwide. The "particular churches" (a diocese under the leadership of a bishop) are fully Catholic through their communion with the Church of Rome. This means that the universal Church is not a loosely gathered federation of particular churches, each doing its own thing. Rather, its vocation and mission connect the particular local churches with the universal Roman Catholic Church.

Communion with People Throughout the World

The Church is the universal sacrament of salvation. Christ gave the Church the mission of witnessing to the Gospel and baptizing in his name. The Second Vatican Council taught that "the church, in Christ, is a sacrament . . . of the unity of the entire human race" (*Lumen Gentium* 1). Such unity can be understood by understanding catholicity, a mark of the Church. This mark has several implications for a Catholic's participation in the world and communion with others. This applies to the relationship of Catholics with other members of the Church, with others who believe in Christ, and finally with all of humankind who are called by God's grace to Salvation.

The Church is joined, albeit imperfectly, to those who are baptized Christians but do not profess the Catholic faith in its entirety or have not remained united under the pope. With Orthodox churches the communion is profound and, in the words of Pope Paul VI, "lacks little to attain the fullness that would permit a common

celebration of the Lord's Eucharist" (quoted in *CCC* 838).

Non-Christians, too, share a unity with the Church in different ways. Jewish people hold a special place of honor because Jews first received God's covenant. Because of a shared belief in one God, Muslims also are related to the Church. Even many non-believers distinguish between right and wrong and experience something transcendental in their lives.

The Church has a missionary mandate to proclaim the Gospel to all peoples. This is a requirement of the mark of catholicity. This mission originates with Christ's commandment to the Apostles:

> "Go, therefore, and make disciples of all nations, baptizing them in the name of the Father, and of the Son, and of the holy Spirit, teaching them to observe all that I have commanded you. And behold, I am with you always, until the end of the age." (Mt 28:19–20)

The Church's message expresses the eternal love that the Holy Trinity has for all people. "The ultimate purpose of mission is none other than to make men share in the communion between the Father and the Son in their Spirit of love" (*CCC* 850). The message preached by those who undertake this missionary charge directed by the Holy Spirit is that God wills the Salvation of all through the knowledge of truth.

The task requires missionaries and all who witness the Gospel to live a life of penance, accept the cross, and

abide in a deep respect for others by building on their religious beliefs. We must see everyone as our brother or sister in Christ. We are interconnected. Because God is the Father of all people, we care about everyone as we care about the members of our own family. Like members of the same human body (e.g., arms, legs, vital organs), "if (one) part suffers, all the parts suffer with it; if one part is honored, all the parts share its joy" (1 Cor 12:26). If people in another part of the world are suffering from famine, a natural disaster, or oppression, we suffer with them and try to help. We call such concern for others **human solidarity**.

Also, we try to treat everyone fairly and equally. We try to protect the rights and needs of everyone, especially those who are most vulnerable and in danger of being exploited or abused. We work together to try to bring about just laws that are good for everyone. This is known as **social justice**. As the *Catechism* explains,

> Society ensures social justice when it provides the conditions that allow associations or individuals to obtain what is their due, according to their nature and their vocation. Social justice is linked to the common good and the exercise of authority. (*CCC* 1928)

The Church is called to be both a sign of social justice and an instrument of that justice. Catholics are to regard all people throughout the world as "neighbors" and to follow Jesus' command to love these neighbors as themselves (cf. Luke 10:25–37).

Finally, in working toward communion with others, we live in peace with all people. As the Risen Jesus said to his Apostles, "Peace be with you. As the Father has sent me, so I send you" (Jn 20:21), so we are to be peacemakers in today's world. Not only do Catholics work to avoid war, but the Church also tries to improve communication, understanding, and cooperation between countries. "For all of you who were baptized into Christ have clothed yourselves with Christ. There is neither Jew nor Greek, there is neither slave nor free person, there is not male and female; for you are all one in Christ Jesus" (Gal 3:27–28).

Communion of Saints

Another type of communion in the Church is among the communion of saints; that is, of all the living faithful and all the deceased faithful—those being purified after death and those already in Heaven. The *Catechism of the Catholic Church* teaches that "the communion of saints is the Church" (*CCC* 946). This statement has two meanings.

First, everyone in the Church shares a communion in spiritual goods. Among these goods are the following:

- *Communion in the faith.* The faith we share among Catholics today is the same faith inherited from the Apostles.
- *Communion of the sacraments.* The sacraments of the Church unite us to the communion of saints because they unite us to God in Christ. The name "communion" is applicable to all of the sacraments, but it "is better suited to the Eucharist than to any other, because it is primarily the Eucharist that brings this communion about" (*CCC* 950).
- *Communion of charisms.* A **charism** is a special gift, talent, or ability given to each Church member by the Holy Spirit. Charisms are intended to help build up the Church; they are for the good of all. The Church collectively shares the charisms she has received individually.

human solidarity
The virtue of social charity, friendship, and responsible sharing whereby we recognize our interdependence on others and that we are all brothers and sisters of one family under a loving Father.

social justice
A form of justice that treats all people fairly and equally, according to their due. Social justice involves fair treatment of individuals. It also involves the structures of society that protect or oppress the rights of certain people.

charism
A God-given talent, gift, skill, or ability that is given to each person for the good of everyone in the Church.

YOUR COMMUNION OF SAINTS

Make a prayer card as a reminder of your personal "communion of saints." Cut an equilateral triangle out of construction paper or card stock. On the front at one corner, list one or more names of living people who are pilgrims with you in the journey of faith. In the second corner, list one or more names of people who have died but are not known officially as saints. In the third corner, list one or more names of saints in Heaven to whom you have a particular attachment. Finally, put your own name in the center of the triangle. On the back, write your own prayer of communion with these people. Pray for their spiritual well-being and also ask them to help you be a better Church member. Be prepared to share all or part of your prayer at the prayer service at the end of this chapter.

- *Communion of goods.* The early Christians held everything in common. So too, "all Christians should be ready and eager to come to the help of the needy" (*CCC* 952).
- *Communion in charity.* Every act of charity performed by Catholics benefits the entire Body of Christ. Every sin harms this communion.

Second, there is a communion of all holy people—between the Church of Heaven and the Church of earth. The saints in Heaven intercede for those who are living and for the dead who are still being purified. Likewise, the living can receive strength and aid from the saints in Heaven. And living members of the Church can pray for those who have died. "Our prayer for them is capable not only of helping them, but also of making their intercession for us effective" (*CCC* 958).

For Review

1. What are four types of communion to which the image of the Body of Christ refers?
2. What are two ways we form community with other Catholics?
3. How does human solidarity relate to the Church's mission?
4. What are two meanings of the *communion of saints*?
5. What does the *Catechism* mean when it says the Church is a communion in spiritual goods and a communion of all holy people?

For Reflection

- How do you understand the ultimate purpose of the Church's mission: to come into unity with the Holy Trinity?
- Describe a charism with which you have been gifted. How can this charism help build up the Church?

THE CHURCH, THE CHANNEL OF GRACE

As the universal sacrament of salvation, the Church first affects the inner union of people with God. Second, the Church is also the sacrament of the unity of the human race. In both of these ways, the Church, as the sacrament of Christ, has the power to transform us. While the transformation has already begun, the Church is also a sign and an instrument of the unity that has yet to be realized.

Christ uses the Church as his instrument of salvation for all. Through the Church we are transformed into the Body of Christ. We ourselves become the Church, the sign and instrument of Christ's presence in the world today. This understanding is detailed in the New Testament: "Do you not know that you are the temple of God, and that the Spirit of God dwells in you?" (1 Cor 3:16). "Like living stones, let yourselves be built into a spiritual house to be a holy priesthood to offer spiritual sacrifices acceptable to God through Jesus Christ" (1 Pt 2:5).

The Second Vatican Council summarized much of how the sacraments transform us into the Church, and hence how the Church herself is transforming. Examples from each sacrament follow:

- *Baptism.* Our faith and participation in this sacrament make us members of the Church and the People of God. We are "reborn as sons and daughters of God" (*Lumen Gentium* 11).
- *Confirmation.* Our union with Christ and the Church is strengthened. We are "endowed with the special strength of the holy Spirit" so that we may act "as true witnesses of Christ," spreading and defending the faith (*Lumen Gentium* 11).
- *Eucharist.* "Strengthened by the body of Christ in the Eucharistic communion, [we] manifest in a concrete way that unity of the people of God which this most holy sacrament aptly signifies and admirably realizes" (*Lumen Gentium* 11).
- *Penance and Reconciliation.* Every sin is not only an offense against God; it is also an offense against the Church. Sin separates us from the Church. This sacrament forgives sin and restores our unity with God and with the Church (cf. *Lumen Gentium* 11).
- *Anointing of the Sick.* This sacrament strengthens the sick and suffering members of the Church

to "contribute to the good of the people of God by freely uniting themselves to the passion and death of Christ" (*Lumen Gentium* 11).
- *Holy Orders.* This sacrament enables bishops, priests, and deacons to "nourish the church with the word and grace of God in the name of Christ" (*Lumen Gentium* 11).
- *Matrimony.* As a sign of oneness between Christ and the Church, this sacrament strengthens married couples to help one another attain holiness in their lives together and to build up the Church by "accepting and educating their children" in the faith (*Lumen Gentium* 11).

As Church, we join in carrying out the mission of Christ in today's world. Just as Jesus had a threefold mission as priest, prophet, and king, so "the whole People of God participates in these three offices of Christ and bears the responsibilities for mission and service that flow from them" (*CCC* 783). These next sections consider how participating in the Church transforms us into priests, prophets, and royalty.

Our Mission as Priests

Baptism transforms us into a spiritual house and a holy priesthood. This common priesthood differs from the hierarchical priesthood of bishops and priests. On the basis of our Baptism, we are to act as Christ. We are to offer ourselves to God in worship, become holy, and

sacramental grace

A participation in the life and love of the Trinity that comes to us through the sacraments. Each sacrament brings us a different dimension of God's life and love.

theological virtues

Three important virtues bestowed on us at Baptism that relate us to God: faith (belief in and personal knowledge of God), hope (trust in God's Salvation and his bestowal of graces needed to attain it), and charity (love of God and love of neighbor).

laity

All the members of the Church who have been initiated into the Church through Baptism and who are not ordained (the clergy) or in consecrated life. The laity participate in Jesus' prophetic, priestly, and kingly ministries.

help others grow in holiness. Duties of the common priesthood include:

- *Spiritual sacrifices to God.* Catholics have a responsibility and duty to worship God at all times and in all places by their holy actions. "All [the laity's] works, prayers, and apostolic undertakings, family and married life, daily work, relaxation of mind and body, if they are accomplished in the Spirit—indeed even the hardships of life if patiently born—all these become spiritual sacrifices acceptable to God through Jesus Christ" (*CCC* 901).

- *Personal holiness.* Through the Church, God sanctifies us, transforming us with his presence and grace through the Holy Spirit. Grace is not a particular thing or a quantifiable amount. Rather, grace is a sharing in the actual life and love of the Trinity. We become holy because we are united with God in grace. Each sacrament enables us to share God's life in a particular way. In other words, each sacrament brings us **sacramental grace**, a different aspect of God's life and love. For example, the Sacrament of the Anointing of the Sick brings us the healing dimension of God's life and love. The Sacrament of Penance and Reconciliation offers us the forgiving dimension of God's life and love. All sacraments also dispense sanctifying grace (a sharing in God's life that transforms us into the divine, or makes us holy) and actual grace (divine help to perform some good action we would not ordinarily be able to do on our own such as forgiving an enemy, avoiding a habitual sin, or remaining faithful to Jesus despite

torture or death). Grace is never something we "earn." Our holiness is God's wonderful and generous gift to us.

- *Helping others grow in holiness.* In making us holy, the sacraments transform us into a community of faith, hope, and charity. These three **theological virtues** not only permeate our lives. They also help us form a community of faith, hope, and charity with others.

Our Mission as Prophets

A prophet is someone who speaks God's Word to others, witnesses to the truth about Jesus Christ, and reminds people to persevere in the true faith—not a person who predicts the future, as is commonly understood. Jesus was a prophet because he spoke the truth about God's infinite saving love. He called people to repent of their sins and turn back to God's covenant of love. As Church, we share in the prophetic mission of Christ whenever we give witness to him through our words, actions, or example. We also act as prophets whenever we encourage others in the Church to persevere in faith despite times of discouragement, disillusionment, and confusion.

The Church's sacraments transform us into evangelists—people who spread the message of Christ throughout the world. We become "God's co-workers," "God's field," and "God's building" (1 Cor 3:9). We help proclaim the faith to others *in* the Church through discussions, religious education classes, Bible study groups, and the use of communications media. Furthermore, we help proclaim the Good News of Jesus Christ to those outside the Church by our every word and action.

While ordained bishops and priests work as prophets mainly within the Church, the **laity** carry their prophetic mission primarily *outside* the Church, in the secular world—in neighborhoods, workplaces, shopping malls, schools, hospitals, and so forth. The Second Vatican Council clarified that laypeople have "the special vocation" to help build God's Kingdom "by engaging in temporal affairs and directing them according to God's will. . . . They are called by God to contribute to the sanctification of the world from within, like leaven" (*Lumen Gentium* 31). "In faith, hope and charity they manifest Christ to others" (*Lumen Gentium* 31). We act as salt of the earth and light to the world. We help bring all people to Christ.

Think about it: Everywhere you go, you can bring Christ's presence and love to others. In everything you do—whether it is working in a grocery store, chatting on the Internet, counseling a friend, competing in sports against a rival school, or talking with your parents—you can be Christ to others. As St. Augustine once said, "Let us rejoice then and give thanks that we have become not only Christians, but Christ himself."

Our Royal Mission

Christ offered us the gift of "royal freedom" so that we might overcome our own sinfulness and encourage the world at large—institutions and individuals—to do the same. Those who embrace the royal mission do not let themselves be, as St. Ambrose wrote, "imprisoned by sin, or thrown headlong into wickedness." Laypeople can cooperate with priests in this royal mission by participating in various ministries to which they are called and in which they are gifted.

Many people equate royalty with worldly power and riches. However, the true role of those in power is to serve the people they are charged to protect and provide welfare for. True royalty—as Jesus lived—does not seek to be served, but rather seeks to serve others, especially the poor and the suffering. Just as Jesus came "to bring glad tidings to the poor" (Lk 4:18), and "to seek and to save what was lost" (Lk 19:10), so we participate in his royal mission whenever we work for justice and peace and serve others in charity. "The Church encompasses with its love all those who are afflicted by human infirmity and it recognizes in those who are poor and who suffer, the likeness of its poor and suffering founder. It does all in its power to relieve their need" (*Lumen Gentium* 8).

One way the Church carries out her royal mission is by establishing and maintaining foreign missions. In addition to spreading the Good News of Jesus throughout the world, these missions serve people in many other ways—by providing food, clothing, shelter, and education. The Church also carries out her royal mission by serving needy people in local areas. For example, the Church operates hospitals; St. Vincent de Paul thrift stores; centers for the blind and deaf; homes for the care of cancer patients; rehabilitation facilities for substance abuse (alcohol and other drugs); prison ministries; dining rooms for the poor; shelters for runaways, the abused, the exploited, and the homeless; facilities for retired and aged people; facilities for children and adults with disabilities; houses of retreat and renewal; elementary schools; high schools; colleges and universities; and Catholic newspapers, magazines, and newsletters, as well as radio, television, film, and theater programs. In all these services, Catholics seek to treat others as Christ would treat them—with love, patience, understanding, and genuine caring.

Catholics who involve themselves in the Church's priestly, prophetic, and royal mission become a sign and an instrument of Christ's presence in every part of today's world. As sacrament, the Church brings the healing, forgiving, and comforting love of God to all those in need. Whenever we act as Church—even in small, ordinary ways—we are a type of sacrament. We are the Church, the sacrament of Christ.

For Review

1. How does each of the Seven Sacraments transform us as Church?
2. How do Catholics carry out the priestly, prophetic, and royal missions of Christ?
3. Explain the difference between sacramental grace, sanctifying grace, and actual grace.
4. What are the theological virtues?

For Reflection

Describe a person your age you consider to be holy.

Famous Catholics and the Sacraments:

BL. JOHN PAUL II

Near the end of his long reign and just a year before his death, Pope John Paul II declared 2004 to be a "Year of the Eucharist," when the Church would recognize the Eucharist as the very center of her life. Recalling the teaching of the Second Vatican Council, which called the Eucharist "the source and summit of the Christian life" (*Lumen Gentium* 11), the Pope remembered several places and occasions where he had celebrated Mass during his priesthood:

I remember the parish church of Niegowić, where I had my first pastoral assignment, the collegiate church of St. Florian in Krakow, Wawel Cathedral, Saint Peter's Basilica and so many basilicas and churches in Rome and throughout the world. I have been able to celebrate Holy Mass in chapels built along mountain paths, on lakeshores and seacoasts; I have celebrated it on altars built in stadiums and in city squares. . . . This varied scenario of celebrations of the Eucharist has given me a powerful experience of its universal and, so to speak, cosmic character. Yes, cosmic! Because even when it is celebrated on the humble altar of a country church, the Eucharist is always in some way celebrated *on the altar of the world*. It unites heaven and earth. It embraces and permeates all creation. The Son of God became man in order to restore all creation, in one supreme act of praise, to the One who made it from nothing. He, the Eternal High Priest who by the blood of his cross entered the eternal sanctuary, thus gives back to the Creator and Father all creation redeemed. He does so through the priestly ministry of the Church, to the glory of the Most Holy Trinity. (*Ecclesia de Eucharistia* 8)

Karol Wojtyla was ordained a priest in 1946, just after World War II. The war had deeply influenced the future pope. The Nazis closed the university in Kraków, Poland, where he had studied, and Karol was forced to work in a quarry and later in a chemical plant. During this dark time, he was introduced to the writings of St. John of the Cross and St. Teresa of Avila. He began to study for the priesthood in secret.

After he was ordained, Karol Wojtyla served as a parish priest and chaplain for university students in Poland. He was a university teacher, and he mentored the youth who were growing in dissatisfaction over the Communist influence in Poland. When he was only thirty-eight, Fr. Wojtyla was named a bishop by Pope Pius XII. He attended the Second Vatican Council.

Named Archbishop of Kraków in 1963 and honored as a cardinal in 1967, Karol Wojtyla proved a master at defending the faith while operating in an atheistic country. He was able to ordain several priests during this time to serve clandestinely in Communist-controlled Czechoslovakia.

When Pope John Paul I died after only thirty-three days as pope, Karol Wojtyla was elected the 263rd successor of St. Peter. He was the first Polish pope in history and the first non-Italian pope since the sixteenth century. His nearly twenty-seven-year reign was the third longest in history.

The pope expressed his love of the liturgy and sacraments over and over. In several Holy Thursday addresses, he spoke of the gift of the priesthood. His general audiences from which his "Theology of the Body" developed were rooted in the sanctity of the Sacrament of Matrimony. He envisioned worship of the Holy Trinity permeating the Sacrament of the Eucharist. Pope John Paul II explained how the mission of God the Father through the Son and the Holy Spirit is present in the sacraments. He wrote:

> What else are the sacraments (all of them!), if not the action of Christ in the Holy Spirit? When the Church baptizes, it is Christ who baptizes; when the Church absolves, it is Christ who absolves; when the Church celebrates the Eucharist, it is Christ who celebrates it: "This is my body." And so on. All the sacraments are an action of Christ, the action of God in Christ. (*Crossing the Threshold of Hope*)

Pope John Paul II died on April 2, 2005. At his funeral Mass, many in the vast crowd outside St. Peter's Basilica took up the chant "Magnus, Magnus, Magnus," meaning "Great, Great, Great." It was a public proclamation that Pope John Paul should take the title Pope John Paul the Great and should be remembered as a man who had great influence in the twentieth century while helping usher in the new millennium. On May 1, 2011, Pope John Paul II was beatified, a step to sainthood. He is now rightly called Blessed Pope John Paul the Great.

- Report on the early life of the priesthood of Karol Wojtyla.
- Research and share more of Pope John Paul II's role in contributing to the end of Communism.
- Share three quotations of Pope John Paul II on the importance of the liturgy and sacraments. Write your own commentary on their meanings.

BL. JOHN PAUL II

CHAPTER QUICK VIEW

Main Ideas

- St. Augustine described the sacraments as "visible signs of invisible grace." (pp. 7-8 and pp. 13-14)

- Christ makes himself known in the sacraments and liturgy, known as the "sacramental economy." (p. 2 and pp. 8-11)

- Christ is both true man and true God; this mystery is a characteristic of sacraments and enables him to be described as the "primordial sacrament." (pp. 7-10)

- Jesus is an efficacious sign because not only is he a sign of God's love, he effects that love and makes it present. (pp. 10-11)

- In the Seven Sacraments, Jesus continues to live and work among us. (pp. 8-11)

- The Church is the "universal sacrament of salvation." (pp. 12-13)

- The Church has four distinguishing characteristics or marks: one, holy, catholic, and apostolic. (pp. 13-14)

- The Church is an efficacious sign because it makes the saving actions of the Risen Christ present to us through the work of the Holy Spirit. (pp. 14-15)

- The Church completes the mission of Christ, which is to bring us into communion with the Holy Trinity. (pp. 16-17)

- An understanding of the Church as the Body of Christ has other implications: that Catholics will achieve communion with other Catholics, with all other people of the world, and with the communion of saints. (pp. 16-20)

- The Church is the source of God's grace, offering the power to transform us. (pp. 21-23)

TERMS, PEOPLE, PLACES

Complete each sentence by choosing the correct answer from the list of terms below. You will not use all of the terms.

Incarnation	Messiah	social justice
liturgy	primordial sacrament	charism
hypostatic union	marks of the Church	sacramental grace
evangelists	communion of saints	Theological Virtues
Jesus	human solidarity	laity
Christ		

1. The _____ were concerned with proclaiming the Good News of Salvation, not recording a biographical account of Jesus' life.

2. A _____ is a special gift given by the Holy Spirit to an individual, but meant to be collectively shared for the good of the Church.

3. Collectively sharing in the suffering, honors, and joys of other members of the Body of Christ is a function of _____.
4. _____ refers to the participation of God's People through prayer and celebration in the fruits of the Paschal Mystery; that is, our Salvation.
5. _____ means "God saves."
6. The _____ refers to our sharing in spiritual goods and the unity between the Church in Heaven and the Church on earth.
7. The _____ are faith, hope, and charity.
8. The _____ are the baptized who are not ordained or in consecrated life.

ONGOING ASSIGNMENTS

As you cover the material in this chapter, choose and complete at least three of these assignments.

1. Read the following Scripture passages: Matthew 18:20 and Matthew 25:40. How can each be considered a way of meeting the Lord?

2. In a poem, a drawing, or a short video, offer your own impression of the Incarnation.

3. Secure a copy of the autobiography of St. Thérèse of Lisieux, *Story of a Soul*. Read and share several passages that describe St. Thérèse's belief in and love of the sacraments.

4. Write a short report explaining in more detail the meaning of *hypostatic union*.

5. Read the following Scripture passages: Matthew 3:1–17; Matthew 21:12–13; Mark 2:15; Luke 6:27–30; and Luke 12:6–7. Write a sentence for each telling what it reveals about Jesus.

6. Read Chapter 1 of *Lumen Gentium*. Write five quotations that describe for you how Christ lives in the Church.

7. Write definitions clarifying the differences between sacramental grace and sanctifying grace.

8. Research the connection between sacraments and mystery. Refer to ways that St. Paul used the term *mystery* to refer to Christ, apostolic preaching, things that are spoken of in the Spirit, and the relationship between Christ and the Church.

PRAYER SERVICE

Theme: We Are the Church, the House of God

First Reading: 2 Corinthians 4:5-6

All: The Lord is God, our maker to whom we belong, whose people we are, God's well-tended flock. (Psalm 100:3)

Side 1: I rejoiced when they said to me,
    "Let us go to the house of the Lord."
And now our feet are standing
    within your gates, Jerusalem.
Jerusalem, built as a city,
    walled round about.

Side 2: Here the tribes have come,
    the tribes of the Lord,
As was decreed for Israel,
    to give thanks to the name of the Lord.
Here are the thrones of justice,
    the thrones of the house of David.

Side 1: For the peace of Jerusalem pray:
    "May those who love you prosper!
May peace be within your ramparts,
    prosperity within your towers."

Side 2: For family and friends I say,
    "May peace be yours."
For the house of the Lord, our God, I pray,
    "May blessings be yours." (Psalm 122)

All: The Lord is God, our maker to whom we belong, whose people we are, God's well-tended flock. (Psalm 100:3)

Second Reading: Ephesians 2:19-22

Spontaneous Prayers: Pray using the reflections written as part of the "Your Communion of Saints" activity on page 20.

Closing Prayer (All):

Lord, you saw fit to call the people of God a Church; grant that the baptized, gathered together in your name, may respect, love, and follow you as you lead them to their promised reward. May the Lord bless us, deliver us from all evil, and bring us to everlasting life. Amen.
(Morning Prayer, *Dedication of a Church*)

What Happens
in the Sacraments

Celebrating Our Redemption
The liturgy transforms us so that our entire lives are patterned after the life of Christ.

Christ Acts through the Sacraments
By the power of the Holy Spirit, the events of Christ's life—especially the Paschal Mystery—are present and real for us today in the liturgy.

Introducing the Seven Sacraments
The Seven Sacraments have several doctrinal elements in common with one another and can be described as Sacraments of Christ, Sacraments of the Church, Sacraments of Faith, Sacraments of Salvation, and Sacraments of Eternal Life.

Celebrating the Church's Liturgy
All Catholics have a role in celebrating the liturgy; signs and symbols along with proper matter and form play a role in the celebration.

CELEBRATING OUR REDEMPTION

The Church's liturgy celebrates the Paschal Mystery of Christ. It is in the Paschal Mystery—especially Christ's Passion, Death, Resurrection, and Ascension—that Jesus redeemed the world.

What is *redemption*? One definition of the term is "to recover ownership by paying a sum." Another meaning of redemption is "to set free or ransom." For Christians, Redemption is the action of Jesus Christ whereby he paid the price of his own Death on the cross to save us from sin and thus return us to new, eternal life in union with God: Father, Son, and Holy Spirit.

In the liturgy—particularly in the Eucharist—we proclaim the mystery of our Redemption. But we don't only remember the events that accomplished our Redemption, as if watching a rerun of a past event. Rather, in the liturgy ("work of the people") we actually *participate* in the events of the Paschal Mystery. We are present to those events. More, we celebrate Christ's continuing his work of our Redemption in the Church, by the Church, and through the Church.

Really, the liturgy transforms us so that our entire lives—not just at the time we are at Mass or participating in any of the other sacraments—take up the pattern of Jesus' very life: from the time of his Incarnation, infancy, and hidden life in Nazareth, to the saving events of the Paschal Mystery.

Blessed Dom Columba Marmion, O.S.B. (1858–1923), prayed and reflected on how the pattern of Christ's life should make up our own. Dom Columba Marmion was an Irish diocesan priest in Dublin who changed the course of his vocation at the age of thirty and entered a Benedictine monastery in Belgium. Pope John Paul II beatified him in 2000. From Columba's experience of leading retreats came a body of spiritual writing that is preserved. A central theme of his writings is "divine adoption"; that is, because God became man, men and women today can become adopted children of God. This theme is reflected in how he understood the Paschal Mystery and how the liturgy allows us to participate in the Paschal Mystery and to imitate the life of Christ:

> You will perhaps now ask how can we strengthen this Paschal grace within us. First of all, by contemplating the mystery with great faith. . . . Faith places us in contact with Christ; if we contemplate this mystery with faith, Christ produces in us the grace which he gave to his disciples when, as their Risen Lord, he appeared to them. Jesus lives in our souls; ever living, he unceasingly acts in us, according to the degree of our faith and in accordance with the grace proper to each of his mysteries. . . .

> It is above all by sacramental Communion that we now assimilate the fruits of this mystery. What indeed do we receive in the Eucharist? We receive Christ, the Body and Blood of Christ. . . . We receive Christ such as he is now, that is to say glorified in the highest heavens and possessing, in its fuller expansion, the glory of his Resurrection. He whom we thus really receive is the very fount of holiness. He cannot fail to give us a share in his "holy" Resurrection; here as in all things, it is of his fullness that we are all to receive.

> Still in our days, Christ, ever living, repeats to each soul the words that he said to his disciples when at the time of the Pasch, he was about to institute his sacrament of love: "With desire I have desired to eat this pasch with you" (Lk 22:15). Christ Jesus desires to effect in us the mystery of his Resurrection. He lives entirely for his Father above all that is earthly; he wills, for our joy, to draw us with him into this divine current. If, after having received him in Communion, we leave him full power to act, he will give to our life, by the inspirations of the Holy Spirit, that steadfast orientation towards the Father in which all holiness

is summed up; so all our thoughts, all our aspirations, all our activity will refer to the glory of our Father in heaven. (Dom Columba Marmion, O.S.B., *Spiritual Writings*)

The liturgy, particularly the Eucharist, is the way Christ communicates the fruits of the Paschal Mystery, our Redemption, until he comes again. It helps us move our lives into the course of the "divine current," as Bl. Dom Columba Marmion termed the process. With this attitude, which we increase through faith and our participation in the sacraments, every facet of our lives—from misery to joy—becomes intertwined with the life of Jesus as we grow in union with the Blessed Trinity. How this takes place in the sacramental economy—what happens in the sacraments—is the subject of this chapter.

For Reflection

- What do you think Columba meant by the term "divine current"?
- How do you imagine the divine current is present in your life?

CHRIST ACTS THROUGH THE SACRAMENTS

Before his Ascension, Jesus told his Apostles to teach and baptize people of all nations (see Matthew 28:16–20). They were not actually empowered to begin this mission until the Jewish Feast of **Pentecost**. On that day, the **Paraclete** that Jesus had promised came to them:

> When the time for Pentecost was fulfilled, they were all in one place together. And suddenly there came from the sky a noise like a strong driving wind, and it filled the entire house in which they were. Then there appeared to them tongues as of fire, which parted and came to rest on each one of them. And they were all filled with the holy Spirit and began to speak in different tongues, as the Spirit enabled them to proclaim. (Acts 2:1–4)

The experience forever changed the Apostles. Before Pentecost, they were lost, despondent, and afraid. After the Holy Spirit came to them, they became enlivened, rejuvenated, and filled with courage. They no longer hid in fear; they spoke openly to the "Jews from every nation" who had come to Jerusalem to celebrate Pentecost. "Those who accepted his message were baptized, and about three thousand persons were added that day" (Acts 2:41). The Church of Jesus, prepared for from the beginning of time, had been born.

The Holy Spirit continued to be present in the Apostles, just as Jesus had promised. The Apostles became "sacramental signs of Christ" (*CCC* 1087), bringing the grace of Jesus to the members of the early Church. Before the Apostles died, they realized they would need to appoint others to carry on their work of teaching, baptizing, serving, and building up the Church. By the power of the Holy Spirit, they entrusted this power and authority to their replacements (see *CCC* 1087). Through an unbroken chain of this **apostolic succession**, today's Church can trace a continuous line of leadership back to the days of the Apostles and the first Christians.

From a historical perspective, the events of our Salvation—Jesus' Passion, Death, Resurrection, and Ascension, and the coming of the Holy Spirit at Pentecost—occurred only once. But by the power of the Holy Spirit, the liturgy makes these events present and real for us today. The liturgy brings us into communion with God and with one another. The liturgy also allows us to participate in Christ's prayer to the Father, made in the Holy Spirit.

The distinct roles of the Three Persons—Father, Son, and Holy Spirit—help us understand the work of the Blessed Trinity in the liturgy and how Christ acts through the sacraments.

God the Father: Source and Goal of the Liturgy

In the same way that God the Father is the source of all creation, he is the source of the **blessings** we receive from the liturgy. From the beginning of the world to the end of time, all of God's work is a blessing. We return the blessings we receive to the Father when we respond to his grace.

Initially our response involves recognizing God's blessings in the story of creation, in the covenants God established with the Chosen People of the Old Testament, and finally in the coming of Christ.

Throughout human history, people have seen visible signs of God's blessings. As St. Paul reminds us, "Ever since the creation of the world, [God's] invisible attributes of eternal power and divinity have been able to be understood and perceived in what he has made" (Rom 1:20). Many people have noticed or experienced God's majesty,

Pentecost
A Greek word that means "fiftieth day." On this day, the Church celebrates the descent of the Holy Spirit upon Mary and the Apostles. It is often called the "birthday of the Church."

Paraclete
Another name for the Holy Spirit that means advocate, defender, or consoler.

apostolic succession
An unbroken chain of power and authority connecting the pope and bishops to St. Peter and the Twelve Apostles of Jesus.

blessings
Divine life-giving actions that originate from God the Father. His blessing is both word and gift.

power, and greatness in things like the roar of an ocean's waves, an erupting volcano, a hurricane or an earthquake, or in a flood or a lightning bolt. Others have sensed God's beauty in the dawn, in a mountain stream, in a newborn

colt, or in a field of wildflowers. Many ancient peoples mistakenly confused their experiences of creation with God. They began to worship the sun, mountains, oceans, and various trees as gods in themselves. But, as God's Chosen People, the Israelites gradually learned that these visible signs of creation merely point to the divine; they aren't the same as the God who created them.

"In the Church's liturgy the divine blessing is fully revealed and communicated" (*CCC* 1082). It took the Israelites more than 2,000 years to understand that while creation can point to the sacred, creation is not a sacrament in itself. In a way, that is part of its mystery: A true sacrament *makes real* the spiritual dimension it signifies.

A sacrament not only points to God's existence; it also makes God truly present to us.

In a sacrament, God acts first, and then we act in response. As the source of the liturgy, God the Father takes the initiative of being present, of offering us a share in his own life and love. In the liturgy, the Father's blessing is fully revealed to us and communicated. The Father is the source and the end of all blessings. As the priest raises the Body and Blood of Christ at Mass, he prays on behalf of the Church:

Through him,
with him,
in him,
in the unity of the Holy Spirit,
all glory and honor is yours,
Almighty Father,
for ever and ever.
Amen.

We respond to God by giving him worship and accepting his Word as the truth on which to base our lives.

The Work of Christ in the Liturgy

Jesus Christ instituted the sacraments through his words and actions while on earth. Now, "seated at the right hand of the Father," he pours out his blessings on the Church and acts through the sacraments to communicate his grace. In the liturgy, he primarily makes present his own Paschal Mystery.

Jesus is God-in-the-flesh. His entire life reveals God the Father. The Paschal Mystery transcends time and place. Because Jesus brought about our Redemption through the saving actions of the Paschal Mystery, he remains present in the sacraments—"perceptible signs (words and actions) accessible to our human nature" (*CCC* 1084).

A Place for the Blessed Sacrament

Throughout the centuries, some of the Body of Christ under the species of unleavened bread or hosts reserved from Mass has been placed in a tabernacle in the church building. The word *tabernacle* means "tent." The ancient Israelites believed that God was really present in the tabernacle they carried with them. In the early Church, there were no tabernacles in Roman church buildings. By the Middle Ages, the tabernacle was a small receptacle (*pyx*) kept in the sacristy. During the Catholic Reformation, the tabernacle became bigger and had a prominent place in church. Nowadays the tabernacle is located in either the sanctuary or some suitable chapel.

The consecrated species of bread "reserved" in the tabernacle is called the **Blessed Sacrament**. This is the Body of Christ, the Real Presence of Christ. It is used for Communion that is brought to the sick and dying. It is also used by the Church for two other purposes: during the Rite of Eucharistic Exposition and Benediction when the Body of Christ is adored, and for private prayer when people come to the church building to pray before the tabernacle.

Among the saints in America who have had great personal devotion to Jesus in the Blessed Sacrament are St. John Nepomucene Neumann (1811-1860), bishop of Philadelphia; St. Elizabeth Ann Bailey Seton (1774-1821), widow and founder of the Sisters of Charity; St. Katharine Drexel (1858-1955), founder of the Sisters of the Blessed Sacrament, who ministered to African Americans and Native Americans in the United States; and Blessed Damien de Veuster (1840-1889), a priest who ministered to the lepers of Molokai, Hawaii.

Christ is always present in the Church. When Jesus gave his Apostles a worldwide mission to share the Gospel, he added: "And behold, I am with you always, until the end of the age" (Mt 28:20). By giving the Holy Spirit to the Apostles and their successors, he gave them the power to make his work of Salvation present in the sacraments, most especially in the Eucharist. Christ's presence is clearly seen in the liturgy in the following ways:

- *Jesus is present in the minister of the sacrament.* Through the Sacrament of Holy Orders, Christ is present in the ordained minister who baptizes, hears confession, anoints, marries, and offers the Sacrifice of the Mass. In point of fact, Christ is the minister of the sacrament. The priest only acts in his name.

- *Jesus is present in the Word, since it is Christ who speaks when the Scriptures are read at the liturgy.* Jesus is the Word of God made flesh (see John 1:14). As the complete Word of God, Jesus alone has "the words of eternal life" (Jn 6:68).

- *Jesus is present when the Church prays and sings and is gathered in his name.* He told his disciples, "For where two or three are gathered together in my name, there I am in the midst of them" (Mt 18:20).

- *Jesus is especially present in the Eucharistic species, his own Body and Blood.* We call this mystery the **Real Presence** of Christ in the Eucharist because it is Jesus' presence in the fullest sense: "it is a *substantial* presence by which Christ, God and man,

Blessed Sacrament
The consecrated species of bread from Mass that is reserved in the tabernacle in church. The Blessed Sacrament is the Real Presence of Jesus.

Real Presence
The doctrine that Jesus Christ is truly present in his Body and Blood under the form of bread and wine in the Eucharist.

transubstantiation

What happens at the consecration of the bread and wine at Mass when their entire substance is turned into the entire substance of the Body and Blood of Christ, even though the appearances of bread and wine remain. The Eucharistic presence of Christ begins at the moment of consecration and endures as long as the Eucharistic species subsist.

? DID YOU KNOW?

The tabernacle is to be situated in churches in places of the greatest honor. This location is preferably either in the sanctuary or in a separate chapel.

makes himself wholly and entirely present" (*CCC* 1374). The Church uses the term *transubstantiation* to express how the reality (substance) of bread and wine changes into the reality of Jesus' risen and glorified Body and Blood.

Besides these ways that Christ is present in the earthly liturgy, he is also present in the heavenly liturgy that is celebrated with the angels and saints. We hope to one day share in the heavenly liturgy and share in some way Christ's glory. Jesus' miracle of the multiplication of the loaves and fishes is a foretaste of the heavenly liturgy we will one day experience (see Matthew 14:13–21, 15:32–39; Mark 6:30–44, 8:1–10; Luke 9:10–17; John 6:1–13). As the bishops of the Second Vatican Council stated,

> In the earthly liturgy we take part in a foretaste of that heavenly liturgy which is celebrated in the holy city of Jerusalem toward which we journey as pilgrims, where Christ is sitting at the right hand of God, minister of the sanctuary and of the true tabernacle (see Apoc 21:2; Col 3:1; Heb 8:2). With all the hosts of heaven we sing a hymn of glory to the Lord; venerating the memory of the saints, we hope to share their company; we eagerly await the Savior, Our Lord Jesus Christ, until he our life shall appear and we too will appear with him in glory (Phil 3:20; Col. 3:4).
> *(Sacrosanctum Concilium* 8)

DEVOTION TO THE REAL PRESENCE

The Church uses two traditional prayers to honor the Real Presence of Jesus during Eucharistic processions on the Solemnity of the Most Holy Body and Blood of Christ (Corpus Christi), on Holy Thursday, and during the Rite of The Eucharistic Exposition and Benediction. St. Thomas Aquinas supposedly wrote the first text, from a song known as "Tantum Ergo," in the thirteenth century. The second text is a prayer found in the "Holy Communion and Worship of the Eucharist Outside Mass" section of *The Roman Ritual*.

Read and pray over both of these prayers. Then write your prayer, poem, or song lyrics to express your thoughts and feelings about the Real Presence of Jesus in the species of consecrated bread and wine. Be prepared to share what you have written at the prayer service at the end of this chapter.

Tantum Ergo
Come adore this wondrous presence
Bow to Christ the source of grace.
Here is kept the ancient promise
Of God's earthly dwelling place.
Sight is blind before God's glory,
Faith alone may see his face.
Glory be to God the Father,
Praise to his coequal Son,
Adoration to the Spirit,
Bond of love, in Godhead one.
Blest be God by all creation
Joyously while ages run.

Prayer for Benediction
Lord our God,
In this great sacrament
We come into the presence of Jesus Christ, your Son
Born of the Virgin Mary
And crucified for our salvation.
May we who declare our faith in this fountain of love
    and mercy
Drink from it the water of everlasting life.
We ask this through Christ our Lord. Amen.

The Holy Spirit Prepares Us to Meet Christ in the Liturgy

The Holy Spirit is the Teacher of faith, the one Christ promised. The Holy Spirit's role in dispensing the graces of the sacraments is to prepare the Church to encounter Jesus. The Holy Spirit desires that we might live the life of the Risen Christ. When we cooperate with the Holy Spirit in this desire, he brings about unity in the Church. This common work of the Holy Spirit and the Church takes place in the liturgy.

Christ is the center of the liturgy, and every dimension of it points to him. The *Catechism of the Catholic Church* teaches that "every liturgical action, especially the celebration of the Eucharist and the sacraments, is an encounter between Christ and the Church" (*CCC* 1097). The Holy Spirit prepares us for Christ in several ways. First, he enables the Church to understand the Old Testament as the preparation for the New Testament. In the liturgy this is accomplished by:

- reading the Old Testament;
- praying the psalms; and
- recalling how the saving events and significant realities of the Old Covenant have been fulfilled in the mystery of Christ.

Rereading these events with the inspiration of the Holy Spirit and in light of the life of Christ reveals their new meaning. For example, Salvation by Baptism was prefigured by the flood and Noah's ark and by the crossing of the Red Sea. Water from the rock in the Sinai desert prefigured the spiritual gifts of Christ, and the reception of manna in the desert prefigured the Eucharist, "the true bread from heaven" (Jn 6:32).

The Holy Spirit prepares us to be properly disposed to encounter Jesus in the liturgy. The Holy Spirit also uses the liturgy—especially the Eucharist—to forge a unity between Christ and the Church. The Holy Spirit helps us see Christ in one another and gather into one Body of Christ that goes beyond all racial, cultural, social, and other human similarities.

Also, the Holy Spirit serves as the "living memory" of the Church, helping us understand the words of the liturgy, including the inspired Word of Scripture. The "remembering of" (e.g., the events detailed in the Old Testament) is known by a Latin word, *anamnesis*. The Liturgy of the Word recalls all that God has done for us. You will note that at Sunday Mass, the Scripture

readings are typically taken from the Old Testament, a New Testament Epistle, and the Gospel. The Holy Spirit awakens our memory in this story of our faith. Anamnesis is also central to the Liturgy of the Eucharist. The Church fulfills the memorial of Christ ("Do this in memory of me") by recalling his Paschal Mystery in the Eucharistic Prayer.

The liturgy, of course, is more than just remembering the events of our Salvation. It also makes them present to us today. By the outpouring of the Holy Spirit, we are present today to the saving actions of Christ. This *epiclesis* or "invocation prayer" is the intercessory prayer the priest makes at Mass in which he begs the Father to send the Spirit so that the offers of bread and wine can become the Body and Blood of Christ. Then, when we receive them, we become a living offering to God. The Spirit is called upon in the liturgy to come and sanctify the elements used in the liturgy—besides bread and wine, water and chrism in Baptism, for example.

The epiclesis is also the prayer for the full effect of the Church's communion with the mystery of Christ. The fruit we receive of the Spirit, described in Galatians 5:22–23, is love, joy, peace, patience, kindness, generosity, faithfulness, gentleness, and self-control.

For Review

1. When were the Apostles empowered to begin the mission of Jesus?
2. How did the Apostles ensure that the sacraments would continue to be celebrated after they died?
3. How do we return God the Father's blessings to him?
4. How is the Father the source and the goal of the liturgy?
5. How does the Paschal Mystery transcend time and place in the sacraments?
6. Name four ways that Jesus is present in the sacraments.
7. Explain the Holy Spirit's role in the *anamnesis* and *epiclesis* at the liturgy.

For Reflection

• Describe an experience when Jesus was present to you in the Blessed Sacrament.

• Use art, music, a poem, or a short story to describe how you imagine the heavenly liturgy.

INTRODUCING THE SEVEN SACRAMENTS

The Church's entire liturgical life revolves around the Sacrifice of the Eucharist and the other sacraments. Recall again that through the power of the Holy Spirit, the sacraments not only help us remember the saving events of the Paschal Mystery, but also make these events present to us today. The Seven Sacraments are Baptism, Confirmation (or Chrismation), Eucharist, Penance and Reconciliation, Anointing of the Sick, Holy Orders, and Matrimony. Several doctrinal elements are common to the Seven Sacraments. Some of these are detailed in the sections that follow.

The Sacraments of Christ

The sacraments can be called Sacraments of Christ because Christ instituted each of them while he was on earth. This doesn't mean that Jesus, during his human life, literally celebrated all Seven Sacraments in the form we know them today. However, it does mean that the Church's sacraments begin and end through Christ's words and actions. Christ is present and acting in all the sacraments. Each sacrament is rooted in and based in his Paschal Mystery. As mentioned, they are "powers that come forth" (cf. Lk 5:17, 6:19, 8:46) from the Body of Christ.

The Sacraments of the Church

Before his Ascension, Christ entrusted his Apostles, and hence, his Church, with the power of the Holy Spirit. Christ gave his Church the power to make God's grace available through the sacraments. Specifically, Christ gave the Church authority to determine which rituals would be sacraments and what the rituals themselves would consist of. The sacraments are of the Church because they bring us into communion with God and form us into a holy people, the Body of Christ (see *CCC* 1117–1121).

How does this work? Through Baptism and Confirmation, the priestly people are enabled to celebrate the liturgy, while the Sacrament of Holy Orders appoints those who have been ordained "to nourish the Church with the word and grace of God in the name of Christ" (*Lumen Gentium*, quoted in *CCC* 1119). This teaching points out how the **ministerial priesthood** is at the service of the **common priesthood**. The ordained priesthood guarantees that it is really Christ who ministers in the sacraments through the Holy Spirit for the Church. This teaching also points out why these three sacraments—Baptism, Confirmation, and Holy Orders—confer an indelible **sacramental character** by which a Christian shares in the priesthood of Christ according to different states and functions.

The Sacraments of Faith

Christ gave the Church the mission to **evangelize** others. It was always a sacramental mission—to "make disciples of all nations" and "to baptize" (see Matthew 28:19). Before a person can be baptized, he or she must assent or "say yes" to God's Word. The assent is the meaning of faith. The faith of the Church comes before the faith of the believer. That is why the Church baptizes infants, for example. That is also why sacraments are celebrated communally. They are rooted not in the individuals who participate in them, whether the minister of the sacraments or the recipients, but in the faith of the whole Church. In celebrating the sacraments, the Church confesses the faith she received from the Apostles. The sacraments are Sacraments of Faith because the faith of the Church has preserved them in the Church's history.

The particular words the Church prays in the sacramental rites express our faith. This statement is the origin of the ancient saying *"lex orandi, lex credendi,"* which means "the law of praying is the law of believing." It can also

ministerial priesthood
The priesthood of Christ received in the Sacrament of Holy Orders. Its purpose is to serve the common priesthood by building up and guiding the Church in the name of Christ.

common priesthood
The priesthood of the faithful. Christ has made the Church a "kingdom of priests" who share in his priesthood through the Sacraments of Baptism and Confirmation.

sacramental character
An indelible spiritual mark which is the permanent effect of the Sacraments of Baptism, Confirmation, and Holy Orders. The mark is a permanent configuration to Jesus Christ and a specific standing in the Church. The reception of these sacraments is never repeated.

evangelize
To bring the Good News of Jesus Christ to others.

Sacred Tradition
The living transmission of the Church's Gospel message found in the Church's teaching, life, and worship. It is faithfully preserved, handed on, and interpreted by the Church's Magisterium.

Holy Trinity
The central mystery of the Christian faith and of Christian life that there are three Divine Persons in one God. God alone can make it known to us by revealing himself as Father, Son, and Holy Spirit.

be expressed in reverse: *lex credendi, lex orandi*. In this order, it expresses the role the liturgy and prayer have in shaping and nurturing our faith. The words of the liturgy, like the words of the creeds, are a foundational element of the Church's **Sacred Tradition**. For this reason no sacramental rite may be modified or manipulated by an ordained minister or by the will of the community. Even the pope cannot change the words of the liturgy arbitrarily.

The Sacraments of Salvation

The sacraments are Sacraments of Salvation because they confer the grace they signify. They are efficacious *ex opere operato* ("by the very fact of the action's being performed"). What follows is that the grace of a sacrament is not dependent on the worthiness of either the celebrant or the recipient. Rather, whenever the sacrament is celebrated in accordance with the intention of the Church, the power of Christ and the Holy Spirit acts in and through it, independently of the holiness of the minister. Still, the fruits of the sacrament depend on the disposition of the one who receives them.

In this life, the sacraments help us avoid sin and live as disciples of Jesus. They bring us healing and forgiveness. As the *Catechism* explains, through the sacraments, "the Spirit heals and transforms those who receive him by conforming them to the Son of God" (*CCC* 1129). This definition helps us understand why the sacraments, like faith, are necessary for Salvation.

The Sacraments of Eternal Life

An ancient prayer of the Church was *Marana tha*, an Arabic expression that means "O Lord, come!" This prayer expresses the ultimate meaning of the sacraments and of all Christians—eternal life.

Defining the sacraments as Sacraments of Eternal Life reminds us that the sacraments are celebrated in anticipation of the divine life and assures us the graces necessary to enter eternal life. The sacraments unite us with the **Holy Trinity** in an everlasting experience of oneness, communion, and joy. This life, which we will experience fully only after death, begins to live in us now through the sacraments. Through them we are made holy; we

For Review
1. Write the names of the Seven Sacraments.
2. What does it mean to say that the sacraments are "Sacraments of Christ"?
3. Explain the roles of the ministerial priesthood and common priesthood in celebrating the liturgy.
4. What is the meaning of the ancient saying *lex orandi, lex credendi*?
5. Why is the grace of a sacrament not dependent on the worthiness of either the celebrant or the recipient?
6. How does *Marana tha* express the ultimate meaning of the sacraments and of all Christians?

become "partakers of the divine nature" (*CCC* 1721; see 1130).

CELEBRATING THE CHURCH'S LITURGY

It is proper to say we "celebrate" the sacraments because the sacraments are acts of divine worship and the Church is involved in them through her participation in the liturgy. Sacraments are celebrations that are "woven from signs and symbols" (*CCC* 1145). Signs and symbols, along with their proper matter and form, play a role in their celebration. This section addresses particulars of how the sacraments are celebrated, specifically:

• Who celebrates the liturgy?
• How is the liturgy celebrated?
• When is the liturgy celebrated?
• Where is the liturgy celebrated?

Celebrating the liturgy and the sacraments is essential to Catholic belief. Reflecting on these questions allows for a deeper understanding and appreciation of the sacraments.

Who Celebrates the Liturgy?

In the broadest sense, the liturgy is an action of the "whole Christ" (*Christus totus*)—Head and Body. As High Priest of the liturgy, Christ celebrates with the Church in Heaven and on earth. The heavenly liturgy is celebrated by the hosts of angels and saints, including those of both the Old Testament and the New Testament, especially Mary, the Mother of God, the Apostles, the martyrs, and the great multitude of Heaven.

We, the pilgrim Church on earth, participate in the heavenly liturgy whenever we participate in the sacramental liturgy on earth, including keeping the memorials of the saints—first those of Mary the Mother of God, then, the Apostles, martyrs, and other saints on fixed days in the liturgical year. It is the whole *community* united with its Head that celebrates. This means that liturgical services are best celebrated communally, the people of the Church organized under the bishop, as expressions of the Church's unity.

The celebration of the liturgy involves all members of the Body of Christ, each according to his or her calling. Those of the common priesthood of the baptized offer themselves in spiritual sacrifice. God calls bishops, priests, and deacons in and through the Church to special service in the liturgy. The Sacrament of Holy Orders enables these men to act in the Person of Christ in the sacraments for the service of all the Church. This is most evident in the Eucharist, where the bishop and the priests in communion with him offer the Sacrifice of the Mass.

Other particular ministries, not consecrated by the Sacrament of Holy Orders, may exist and assist at liturgy; for example, servers, readers, commentators, and members of the choir.

How Is the Liturgy Celebrated?

The sacraments are celebrated with signs and symbols. They are words, actions, and objects that express the meaning of each sacrament. They are drawn from our human experience, where God speaks to us through visible creation.

Jesus instituted the sacraments and he gave the Apostles and their successors the authority to determine the physical matter, words, and gestures of the sacraments. In the sacraments, the Church uses elements from creation and human culture to make God's grace available to us. For example, the Church may use signs of creation, such as water and fire. The Church may use signs of human social life, such as washing, anointing, or breaking bread. Or she may use historical signs of Salvation, such as the Jewish rites of Passover.

The celebration of each sacrament also involves solemnity. These ceremonies include traditional words, elements, and/or gestures. Jesus himself did not tell us exactly what to do and say for each sacrament. Rather, he gave his Church authority to determine which words, elements, and gestures would be used in each sacramental celebration. The traditional words said for each sacrament are called the *form* of the sacrament. When we hear these words, we know for sure that the sacrament is taking place. God is truly present, filling us with his love and grace. The traditional physical element(s) and/or gesture(s) used in each sacrament are called the *matter* of the sacrament.

Listed below is a summary of the traditional form and matter of each of the Seven Sacraments:

Sacrament	Form	Matter
Baptism	"I baptize you in the name of the Father, and of the Son, and of the Holy Spirit."	*Element*: immersion in water or water *Gesture*: threefold pouring of water over one's head
Confirmation (or Chrismation)	"Be sealed with the Gift of the Holy Spirit."	*Element*: oil (Sacred Chrism) *Gesture*: anointing with oil
Eucharist	"This is my Body. This is my Blood."	*Elements*: wheat bread and grape wine *Gestures*: eating the consecrated species of bread; drinking the consecrated species of wine
Penance and Reconciliation	"Through the ministry of the Church may God give you pardon and peace, and I absolve you from your sins in the name of the Father, and of the Son, and of the Holy Spirit."	the penitent's contrition, confession, and satisfaction for sin
Anointing of the Sick	"Through this holy anointing may the Lord in his love and mercy help you with the grace of the Holy Spirit."	*Element*: oil (Oil of the Sick) *Gesture*: anointing with oil
Holy Orders	"Grant, we pray, Almighty Father, to these your servants, the dignity of the Priesthood; renew deep within the spirit of holiness; may they henceforth possess this office which comes from you, O God, and is next in rank to the office of Bishop; and by the example of their manner of life, may they still instill right conduct."	*Element*: the laying on of the hands (Sacred Chrism) *Gestures*: laying on of the bishop's hands on the head and anointing the hands of the person being ordained
Matrimony	"I, N., take you, N., to be my wife/ husband. I promise to be true to you in good times and in bad, in sickness and in health. I will love you and honor you all the days of my life."	consent of the man and woman

The words spoken and the actions performed by the assembly are other signs at the liturgy. The fact that people say and do the same thing at the same time is a sign of unity, which the liturgy establishes and strengthens.

In particular, the liturgy makes use of the Word of God, given to the Church in Sacred Scripture. The Church has a three-year cycle of Sunday Scripture readings and a two-year cycle of weekday Scripture readings so that Catholics at Mass can hear a selection from all of the books of the Old Testament and the New Testament over that period. All of the readings are read in the vernacular, the common language of the people. The **Liturgy of the Word** at Sunday Masses usually consists of a reading from the Old Testament, a responsorial from the Book of Psalms, a New Testament reading, and a Gospel reading. During the Easter season the first reading comes from the Acts of the Apostles, or the Book of Revelation. The following signs accompany the Liturgy of the Word:

- Scripture is contained in a special book—the lectionary or book of Gospels.
- Scripture is venerated with a procession, incense, and candles.
- Scripture is proclaimed from a special place—the ambo.
- Scripture is read audibly and intelligibly.
- Scripture's proclamation is extended by the minister's **homily**.
- The assembly participates with responsorial psalms, acclamations, intercessions and a profession of faith.

Liturgical singing and music are also essential to celebrating the liturgy. The Second Vatican Council called music "a necessary or integral part of the solemn liturgy" (*Sacrosanctum Concilium* 112). Music allows us to express what is in our hearts. Songs chosen for the liturgy should conform to Catholic doctrine in their texts and should be drawn primarily from Scripture and liturgical sources. Songs and music at the liturgy should encourage all the faithful to sing. As St. Augustine once put it, "He who sings, prays twice."

Sacred images, called **icons**, are also a significant part of celebrating the liturgy. Representations of Christ, the Blessed Virgin, and saints in sculptures or paintings help those participating in the liturgy understand more deeply the truths of faith and inspire them to a devotion to Christ, Mary, the angels, and the saints.

Since apostolic times the Church's liturgy has been one with the Paschal Mystery, though it has been celebrated in a variety of forms. The mystery of Christ is so rich that it is celebrated by several liturgical traditions. The criterion that assures that there is unity amidst the diversity of liturgical rites is that they are each faithful to apostolic tradition, that is the communion in the faith and the sacraments received by the Apostles and passed on and guaranteed through apostolic succession. Besides the Latin rite (principally the Roman rite, but also rites of other local churches), five Eastern rites are faithful to the Church. They are:

Liturgy of the Word
The part of the Mass that includes the "writings of the prophets" (the Old Testament reading and psalm) and the "memoirs of the Apostles" (the New Testament Epistles and the Gospel), the homily, the profession of faith, and the intercessions for the world.

homily
A reflection given by a bishop, priest, or deacon that reflects on the Scripture readings during Mass or the sacraments. The homily helps us hear God's Word and apply it to our lives today.

icons
From a Greek word meaning "image," icons are religious images or paintings.

DID YOU KNOW?

In the Western Church, the approved rites for the Mass and the other sacraments are found in books called *The Roman Missal* and *The Roman Ritual*. The Church recently updated *The Roman Missal* and translated it into English.

GOD'S WORD IN THE SACRAMENTS

Listed to the right are some of the Scripture readings often proclaimed for each sacrament. Choose one sacrament and read the Scripture passages for it. Write a short essay explaining (1) what the Bible passages recall and (2) what reality is made present to us in these readings (how God is acting the same way in our lives today). Be prepared to summarize your ideas with the class.

- the Byzantine Rite, which developed out of the Church in Constantinople;
- the Alexandrian or Coptic Rite, which developed out of the Church in Alexandria (Egypt);
- the Antiochene or Syriac Rite, which developed out of the Church in Antioch (Syria);
- the Armenian Rite, which developed out of the Church in Armenia; and
- the Chaldean Rite, which developed out of the Church in Iraq and eastern Syria.

While there are unchangeable elements in the liturgy that have been instituted by God, there are also elements subject to change by the Church in order to adapt to the cultures of diverse peoples. "The mystery of Christ is so unfathomably rich that it cannot be exhausted by its expression in any single liturgical tradition" (*CCC* 1201). "It is fitting that liturgical celebration tends to express itself in the culture of the people" (*CCC* 1207).

Sacrament	Scripture Readings
Baptism	Exodus 17:3-7; John 4:5-14
Confirmation (or Chrismation)	Isaiah 11:1-4a; Luke 4:16-22a
Eucharist	Exodus 16:2-4, 12-15; Luke 9:11b-17
Penance and Reconciliation	Isaiah 1:10-18; Matthew 3:1-12
Anointing of the Sick	Acts 3:1-10; Matthew 8:1-4
Holy Orders	Deuteronomy 1:9-14; Mark 1:14-20
Matrimony	Genesis 2:18-24; John 2:1-11

Earthly Signs Used by Jesus

Jesus, too, used earthly signs from creation to tell us about the Father's love and bring us into greater communion with him. He did this in both his sermons and his actions. For example, when he wanted to tell people how much God the Father cared for them, Jesus told of the Father's constant love for the birds of the air and the wildflowers in the fields (see Matthew 6:26-30). When he explained what God's Kingdom was like, he used three-dimensional daily necessities—water, bread, wine, oil, and human touch and acceptance. Jesus took these essentials of human life and gave them a sacramental dimension. He showed people how these signs could reveal something important about God's love. For example:

Water. In the desert environment of Galilee, water was both scarce and essential. It was essential to human life—for drinking, for cleansing or bathing, for irrigation, and as a source of food (such as fish from a lake or sea). The following Gospel accounts include some of the times Jesus used water to reveal God's love:

- He turned water into wine at a wedding in Cana (see John 2:1-12).
- He walked on water (see John 6:16-21).
- He used water to wash the feet of his disciples (see John 13:1-15).

Bread. Bread was a staple in the diet of all ancient peoples. Without it, humans would have faced malnourishment. Some of the occasions Jesus used bread and other food to reveal God's love are listed here:

- He multiplied fish and loaves of bread to feed the crowds (see Matthew 14:13-21).
- He described God's Kingdom as the yeast used to make bread (see Matthew 13:33).
- He served a breakfast of bread and fish to his Apostles (see John 21:1-14).

Oil. Oil had many essential purposes in Old Testament daily life. It was used for anointing a chosen leader (especially a prophet or king) and for anointing the dead. It was also used for cooking, for healing the sick, to soothe dry irritated skin, and as a source of fuel for lamps. Jesus used oil to reveal God's love in the following ways:

- He talked about the oil needed for lamps in his Parable of the Ten Bridesmaids (see Matthew 25:1-13).
- He showed how oil could heal wounds in his Parable of the Good Samaritan (see Luke 10:29-37).
- He allowed a sinful woman to anoint his feet with perfumed oil (see Luke 7:36-50).

Human touch and acceptance. People are social beings who need human touch and acceptance in order to flourish and be happy. In the days of Jesus, part of the tragedy of the various skin diseases called leprosy in the Bible was that they made a person "untouchable," someone who could no longer enjoy human contact or physical touch. Jesus often used human touch to accept and heal others, as shown in the following Gospel passages:

- He healed sick people at Gennesaret (see Mark 6:53-56).
- He hugged little children and blessed them (see Mark 10:13-16).
- He cured a leper (see Matthew 8:1-4).

Jesus' use of these ordinary daily necessities made them sacramental—signs of God's love. "He gives new meaning to the deeds and signs of the Old Covenant, above all to the Exodus and the Passover, for he himself is the meaning of all these signs" (*CCC* 1151).

When Is the Liturgy Celebrated?

When God entered human history through the Incarnation, he made history and time sacred. Our celebration of the saving work of Jesus is therefore set in time, on certain days and weeks throughout the course of the year. The liturgy is structured around daily, weekly, and yearly schedules that all take root around Sunday, the first day of the week. This was the day Jesus rose from the dead, and it has become for Christians "the first of all days, the first of all feasts, the Lord's Day" (*CCC* 2174). Church Father St. Jerome wrote:

> The Lord's day, the day of the Resurrection, the day of Christians, is our day. It is called the Lord's day because on it the Lord rose victorious to the Father. If pagans call it the "day of sun," we willingly agree, for today the light of the world is raised, today is revealed the sun of justice with healing in his rays. (quoted from *CCC* 1166)

Sunday fulfills the Jewish **Sabbath** but is distinguished from the Sabbath that occurs on the seventh day of the week. For Christians, Sunday replaces the obligations of the Sabbath. This understanding did not come right away in the early Church. The Jewish Christians continued to keep the Sabbath on Saturday while commemorating Christ's Resurrection on Sunday through the sharing of Eucharist. The New Testament refers to the special meal shared by Christians as an *agape*, or a love meal. The Eucharist was usually shared in "house churches."

Also, in the first three centuries, Sunday continued to be a day of work while Christians with Jewish origins continued to keep Saturday as a day of rest. In 321 the Emperor Constantine declared Sunday to be a day of rest for people who lived and worked in urban areas. Farmers were still permitted to work on Sundays.

Today the Sunday Eucharist remains the foundation and heart of the Church's celebration of the Paschal Mystery. Sunday "fulfills the spiritual truth of the Jewish sabbath and announces man's eternal rest in God" (*CCC* 2175). Sunday is the foremost **holy day of obligation** in the Church. Catholics are obliged to participate in the Eucharist on Sundays and other holy days unless excused for a serious reason (e.g., illness, care of an infant) or dispensed from the obligation by their pastor. Deliberately missing Sunday Mass (without a serious reason) is a grave sin.

Liturgical celebrations are "not private functions but are celebrations of the Church" (*Sacrosanctum Concilium* 26). The *Catechism of the Catholic Church* teaches further:

> Participation in the communal celebration of the Sunday Eucharist is a testimony of belonging and of being faithful to Christ and to his Church. The faithful give witness by this to their communion in faith and charity. Together they testify to God's holiness and their hope of salvation. They strengthen one another under the guidance of the Holy Spirit. (*CCC* 2182)

There is a word that describes the Church's celebration of the mystery of Christ in her liturgy. The word is *today*! For even though days and weeks and months are marked and history is remembered, when we celebrate the liturgy, we are brought into the present of those saving moments in the life of Christ. We become present to these events as if they were happening today. This understanding is true not only

---

Sabbath

From the Hebrew word *Shabbat*, "to cease," the Sabbath is a weekly day of rest and worship in the Jewish faith. Jews observe the Sabbath on the seventh day of the week. Christians have replaced the Sabbath with observance of the Lord's Day on Sunday, the first day of the week and the day Christ rose from the dead.

holy day of obligation

One of several special days in the Church Year when all Catholics are obliged to participate in Mass.

for our commemoration of the Sunday feast but for all the holy seasons and days of the **Church Year**. How the Church makes present the life of Jesus throughout the Church Year, from his conception and birth to the events of the Paschal Mystery, is described in the next sections.

Readying for the Incarnation of Jesus Christ

Although the mystery of the Incarnation is celebrated in every liturgy throughout the year, the Church has a special time for celebrating these particular events. The Incarnation is marked during the seasons of Advent and Christmas. Advent takes place in the four weeks before Christmas. The Christmas season begins with vigil Masses on December 24 and continues through the Feast of the Baptism of the Lord in January.

The word *advent* means "coming." This season begins the Church Year and starts with the First Evening Prayer of the Sunday that falls on or closest to November 30. During Advent, the Church celebrates the coming of the Messiah in two main ways. First, we remember the centuries of people who waited with faith and hope that God's promise to send a savior would one day be fulfilled. We especially recall the ministry of St. John the Baptist, who prepared people to receive Jesus as the Messiah. And we also recall the response of Mary to the announcement that she would be the Mother of God. Second, we celebrate our own anticipation of the Second Coming of Christ at the end of time. At his coming, Christ will reward the faithful and punish the unjust. He will bring about God's Kingdom in its fullness. The Revelation to John describes the Second Coming:

Then I saw a new heaven and a new earth. The former heaven and the former earth had passed away, and the sea was no more. I also saw the holy city, a new Jerusalem, coming down out of heaven from God, prepared as a bride adorned for her husband. I heard a loud voice from the throne saying, "Behold, God's dwelling is with the human race. He will dwell with them and they will be his people and God himself will always be with them (as their God). He will wipe every tear from their eyes, and there shall be no more death or mourning, wailing or pain, (for) the old order has passed away." (Rev 21:1–4)

We do not know for sure what these words mean or when this new Heaven and new earth will become a reality. But we look forward in faith and hope that we will one day enjoy eternal peace in God's loving presence in Christ.

The Bible does not tell us the exact date of the birth of Jesus, but ever since the fourth century, the Church has celebrated his birth on December 25. Some historians note that this date was originally celebrated by the Romans to honor a Syrian sun god. By choosing this day as the birthday of

Transfiguration

The occasion when Jesus revealed his glory before Peter, James, and John on a high mountain. His face "shone like the sun and his clothes became white as light" (Mt 17:2).

Easter Triduum

The three-day liturgy that is the Church's most solemn celebration of the Paschal Mystery. It begins with the Mass of the Lord's Supper on Holy Thursday, continues through the Good Friday service, and concludes with the evening prayer on Easter Sunday. Although it takes place over three days, the Triduum is considered one single liturgy.

Christ, the Church was perhaps counteracting pagan belief by stating that Jesus is the true "sun god," the Son of God and Light of the World.

The Christmas season includes several other feasts of Christ. On the Sunday between Christmas and New Year's Day, the Church celebrates the Feast of the Holy Family—Jesus, Mary, and Joseph. On the Sunday after New Year's Day, the Church celebrates the Feast of the Epiphany—the revelation of Jesus' universal mission as the Messiah. On the following Sunday, the Church celebrates the Baptism of the Lord. These days are joyous feasts for Christians as we thank God for the gift of his own Son.

Focusing on the Paschal Mystery

During the season of Lent, which begins on Ash Wednesday and ends on Holy Thursday, the Church especially recalls and celebrates the Paschal Mystery of Christ. The word *lent* means "springtime." The Church saw Lent not only as a time of new life, but also as a time of "spring cleaning" and personal renewal. Originally, Lent was when catechumens began their immediate preparation to receive the Sacraments of Baptism, Confirmation, and First Eucharist at the Easter Vigil service. Over the centuries, Lent was extended to the forty days before Easter (excluding Sundays) as a period of penance, fasting, and prayer. This period recalls the forty years the Israelites spent wandering in the desert before God led them into the Promised Land. Lent also recalls the forty days Jesus spent in the desert immediately after his Baptism—praying, fasting, and being tempted—in preparation for his public ministry.

Like Jesus, who is the New Adam who does not give in to temptation, we are called throughout Lent to conquer our own temptations and discipline ourselves spiritually in preparation for Easter. During this time, the Church proclaims the Gospel of the **Transfiguration** of Jesus (see Matthew 17:1–9; Mark 9:2–10; Luke 9:28–36), Jesus' discourse about living water with a Samaritan woman at the well (see John 4:5–42), Jesus' cure of a blind man (see John 9:1–41), and Jesus' raising of Lazarus from the dead (see John 11:1–45).

The last Sunday of Lent, known also as Passion Sunday or Palm Sunday, celebrates Jesus' triumphal entry as King into Jerusalem (see Luke 19:28–40). On this day, the entire Passion of Jesus (suffering, Death on a cross, and burial) is read at Mass. We thank God for the great gift of Jesus, who became "obedient to death, even death on a cross" (Phil 2:8). Palm Sunday marks the beginning of Holy Week, the week before Easter.

On Holy Thursday, the Church celebrates an evening Mass called the Mass of the Lord's Supper. This Mass commemorates Jesus' institution of the Eucharist at his Last Supper, as well as his washing of the Apostles' feet (see John 13:1–15). The liturgy focuses on Jesus as the Lamb of God, as the Suffering Servant, who willingly went to death so that our sins may be forgiven. The Mass of the Last Supper also begins the **Easter Triduum**, the three most sacred days in the Church Year, which include Good Friday and Holy Saturday and conclude with the Evening Prayer on Easter Sunday.

On Good Friday, the Church has a solemn service recalling the Passion and Death of Jesus. This is the only day of the Church Year when Mass is not celebrated. The Passion account from the Gospel of John is read (see John 18:1–19:42). We reflect on how much Jesus sacrificed for us and how much his Death on the cross reveals to us God's immense love. We take time to appreciate the enormity of the gift Jesus gave us—the gift of Salvation and eternal life. On Holy Saturday there are no Masses during the day. The Church observes a period of quiet, recalling the time Jesus spent in the tomb.

Then, on Holy Saturday evening after sundown, the Church celebrates her glorious Easter Vigil. We light the new fire and the Easter Candle. We listen to the Scripture stories that recount our history since the beginning of creation. We welcome catechumens into the Church through Baptism, Confirmation, and First Eucharist. And we rejoice in the central proclamation of faith: Christ is indeed risen from the dead!

The Easter Vigil is the first celebration of Easter, a word that means "passover." On Easter, we celebrate the Resurrection of Jesus to new life. Just as God saved the Israelites by helping them pass safely through the Red Sea to freedom from the Egyptians, so Easter celebrates the passover of Jesus. He passed through death, once and for all, and entered into new life—a new life we will also one day enjoy as his faithful followers. As the *Catechism* states,

> *Easter* is not simply one feast among others, but the "Feast of feasts," the "Solemnity of solemnities," just as the Eucharist is the "Sacrament of sacraments" (the Great Sacrament). St. Athanasius calls Easter "the Great Sunday" and the Eastern Churches call Holy Week "the Great Week." The mystery of the Resurrection, in which Christ crushed death, permeates with its powerful energy our old time, until all is subjected to him. (*CCC* 1169)

The date of Easter changes from year to year. This is because the feast, which was determined at the Church Council of Nicaea in 325, follows the lunar calendar rather than the solar calendar. According to the bishops at Nicaea, Easter is to be celebrated on the Sunday following the first full moon after the spring equinox. Because the date of the full moon continually changes, the date of Easter changes as well.

The Easter season lasts for fifty days. During this time, the Church reads accounts of the Resurrection appearances of Christ. This time is sometimes called *mystagogia*, because it is when the **neophytes** first immerse themselves in the divine mysteries (the sacraments). The neophytes participate in the entire Mass (instead of being dismissed at the end of the Liturgy of the Word). They are encouraged to participate fully in the life of the Church.

The Church celebrates Jesus' Ascension on a Thursday, the fortieth day

mystagogia

A Greek term that means "unfolding of the mystery." It is named for the period following the Baptism of adults. During this time, the newly baptized are to open themselves more fully to the graces received in Baptism.

neophytes

Those newly received into the Church through the Sacraments of Initiation at the Easter Vigil.

after Easter. (The United States Conference of Catholic Bishops recently allowed the option of celebrating

DID YOU KNOW?

Even though the Church has set the date of Easter as the first Sunday after the first full moon after the spring equinox, the Western and Eastern Churches celebrate Easter at different times, usually one or two weeks apart. This discrepancy occurs because the Western Church follows the Gregorian calendar from the sixteenth century. The Eastern Church follows the older Julian calendar. As the *Catechism* notes, "The [Western and Eastern] Churches are currently seeking an agreement in order once again to celebrate the day of the Lord's Resurrection on a common date" (*CCC* 1170).

JESUS IS RISEN!

Read the Gospel passage of the Risen Jesus' appearance to his disciples from John 20:19-29. Then work with a group of classmates to act out the scene in pantomime as a narrator reads the passage. Choose several venues to perform the pantomime; for example, for a class of younger children, at a retirement home, or for a parent/teacher meeting. Write your reflection of the experience and at least one lesson you gleaned from the passage.

Ascension on the seventh Sunday of Easter.) On this day we celebrate our belief that Jesus Christ lives on in eternal presence with the other divine Persons, Father and Holy Spirit.

On the fiftieth day after Easter, the Church celebrates Pentecost, the coming of the Holy Spirit to Mary and the Apostles (see Acts 2:1–42). Just as Jesus had promised, he sent his own Spirit, the third Person of the Blessed Trinity, to be with his disciples forever. That very day Christ's Church was born. The disciples preached to people of every nation who were gathered in Jerusalem. And they baptized thousands of people as new followers of Jesus.

Marking Ordinary Time

After Pentecost, the Church returns to Ordinary Time. The season gets its name from the word *ordinal*, meaning "numbered," as all the Sundays of Ordinary Time are designated numerically. The season has always existed; however, it was not until the liturgical reforms of the Second Vatican Council that "Ordinary Time" was used to express the period between the Baptism of the Lord and Lent, and between Pentecost and Advent. Prior, those times were called "Season After Epiphany" and "Season After Pentecost." Today, Ordinary Time continues to consist of two separate periods. The first is the five to eight weeks between Epiphany and Ash

Wednesday. The second is the twenty-three to twenty-eight weeks between Pentecost and Advent.

A purpose of Ordinary Time is to teach Christians how to follow Jesus in everyday, ordinary life. During Ordinary Time, the Scripture readings focus on how we should relate to family members, the poor, people we may not like (represented as tax collectors and sinners), and those for whom we work. We learn more about the teachings and miracles of Jesus and how we are to keep the two greatest commandments: "You shall love the Lord, your God, with all your heart, with all your soul, and with all your mind," and "You shall love your neighbor as yourself" (Mt 22:37, 39).

During Ordinary Time, the Church celebrates several solemn feasts of Christ, including the Presentation of the Lord (February 2), the Feast of the Transfiguration (August 6), and the Feast of Christ the King (on the last Sunday of Ordinary Time).

As it was celebrated with the Gospel reading on the Second Sunday of

Lent, on the Feast of the Transfiguration we celebrate not only Christ's Transfiguration on the mountain, but also our own future transfiguration in Christ when God the Father will say to each of us, "You are my beloved child."

In 1925, Pope Pius XI established the Feast of Christ the King to remind people that Christ, rather than any political leader or government, is our supreme Ruler and King. On this day we look forward to the Second Coming of Christ, when he will rule as King and invite the faithful to enter his Kingdom. The celebration reminds us to serve God first in our lives and to work tirelessly to help build God's Kingdom in everyday life.

Mary and the Sanctoral Cycle

Though the Church Year is basically structured around the Incarnation and Paschal Mystery of Jesus Christ, it also prominently includes the feasts of Mary, the Mother of God. The *Catechism* explains why this is so:

> In celebrating this annual cycle of the mysteries of Christ, Holy Church honors the Blessed Mary, Mother of God, with a special love. She is inseparably linked with the saving work of her Son. In her the Church admires and exalts the most excellent fruit of redemption and joyfully contemplates, as in a faultless image, that which she herself desires and hopes wholly to be. (*CCC* 1172 quoting *Sacrosanctum Concilium* 103)

Mary is the perfect model of Christian discipleship. "By her complete adherence to the Father's will, to his Son's redemptive work, and to every prompting of the Holy Spirit, the Virgin Mary is the Church's model of faith and charity" (*CCC* 967). We honor her not only as a symbol of the Church, but as the Mother of the Church (see *CCC* 967–968).

Mary is included in the Church's official rites for the Mass and the sacraments. Throughout the year, the Church also celebrates a number of feasts in her honor, including Mary, Mother of God (January 1), Our Lady of Lourdes (February 11), Annunciation (March 25), Visitation (May 31), Immaculate Heart of Mary (Saturday following the Second Sunday after Pentecost), Our Lady of Mount Carmel (July 16), Assumption into Heaven (August 15), Queenship of Mary (August 22), Birthday of Mary (September 8), Our Lady of Sorrows (September 15), Our Lady of the Rosary (October 7), Presentation of Mary (November 21), Immaculate Conception (December 8), Our Lady of Guadalupe (December 12), Christmas (December 25), and Holy Family (Sunday after Christmas).

The Church has an unparalleled devotion to Mary and invokes her under the titles of "Advocate," "Helper," "Benefactress," and "Mediatrix." It is important to realize, however, that "this . . . is understood in such as way that it neither takes away anything from, nor adds anything to, the dignity and efficacy of Christ the one Mediator" (*Lumen Gentium* 62).

In addition to celebrating feasts of Jesus and feasts of Mary, the Church honors numerous saints throughout the year. This calendar of saints—role models of holiness and charity—is called the **sanctoral cycle**. The Church honors these deceased Church members because they "have suffered and have been glorified with Christ" (*CCC* 1173 quoting *Sacrosanctum Concilium* 104). In their lives, they courageously lived and proclaimed the Paschal Mystery of Christ. Among the honored saints are popes, bishops, martyrs, pastors, Apostles, doctors of the Church,

sanctoral cycle
The feasts of saints found throughout the year on the Church's liturgical calendar.

virgins, and holy men, women, and children. The Church honors all the saints, known and unknown, on November 1. This Feast of All Saints is a holy day of obligation, a day when all Church members are required to participate in Mass.

The Liturgy of the Hours

The Divine Office or **Liturgy of the Hours**, an official public prayer of the Church, extends the mystery of Christ, which we celebrate in the Eucharist, through the hours of each day. The Liturgy of the Hours is the prayer of Christ, intended to become the prayer of the whole People of God. The Church celebrates this prayer, in its complete form, seven times each day, in response to St. Paul's exhortation to "pray without ceasing" (1 Thes 5:17). During the Middle Ages, these hours came to signify and commemorate events in the life of Christ.

Priests and consecrated religious typically pray from the Liturgy of the Hours each day. Many Catholics today pray a shortened form of the Divine Office, which includes an Office of Readings, Morning and Evening Prayer, Daytime Prayer, and Night Prayer. Those who pray the Liturgy of the Hours say they have a heightened awareness of the sacraments at all times, as well as an increased anticipation of the coming of God's Kingdom in its fullness.

Where Is the Liturgy Celebrated?

Jesus told the Samaritan woman that "God is Spirit, and those who worship him must worship in Spirit and truth" (Jn 4:24). This worship Jesus described is not limited to any one place. The whole earth is consecrated to Jesus. What is important is that the faithful gather in one place and make themselves the "temple of the living God" (2 Cor 6:16).

However, when they are free to do so, Catholics construct buildings for divine worship. These buildings are called churches; that is,

> a house of prayer in which the Eucharist is celebrated and reserved, where the faithful assemble, and where is worshipped the presence of the Son of God our Savior, offered for us on the sacrificial altar for the help and consolation of the faithful—this house ought to be in good taste and a worthy place for prayer and sacred ceremonial (*Presbyterorum Ordinis* [Decree on the Ministry and Life of Priests] quoted in *CCC* 1181).

The first church buildings constructed after the practice of worship in house churches ceased were based on the floor plan of the Roman government assembly halls. Known as a **basilica**, this type of building was long and narrow. The altar was at one end, usually on an elevated platform. Because there were no pews or chairs, the

Liturgy of the Hours
The public prayer of the Church that makes holy the entire course of the day and night. It is also called the Divine Office.

basilica
A long, narrow church building based on the architecture of public Roman assembly halls. The term is also an honorary one to describe churches that have special importance.

The Church at Prayer

The liturgy is a participation in Christ's prayer to the Father in the Holy Spirit. Similarly, when we pray personally, we continue to share in the graces of our Redemption and in the Father's great love for us that we receive in the liturgy.

What is prayer? St. John Damascene described prayer as "the raising of one's mind and heart to God or the requesting of good things from God." **Humility** is the foundation of prayer. St. Augustine wrote: "Man is a beggar before God" (quotations from *CCC* 2559).

Where does prayer come from? "God has always called people to prayer" (*CCC*, 2569). Subsequently prayer unfolds as a reciprocal call between God and people. Prayer comes from the heart. The *Catechism of the Catholic Church* describes the heart as our "hidden center . . . the place of decision . . . the place of truth . . . the place of encounter . . . the place of covenant." (*CCC* 2563) "Christian prayer is a covenant relationship between God and man in Christ" (*CCC* 2564). Prayer is essential for the believer. Paul's First Letter to the Thessalonians teaches that we should "pray without ceasing" (1 Thes 5:17). Prayer is an ongoing relationship between God and ourselves. It is always possible to pray. Prayer is the habit of being in the presence of the Blessed Trinity.

There are many ways to pray and several Christian prayer expressions, including the following:

- *Vocal prayer* is when by words our prayer takes flesh. When you express your prayer by words, you are doing as Jesus did when he taught his disciples the Our Father. Vocal prayer is necessary because we have bodies. We are not angels. God wants us to honor him with all our faculties.
- *Meditation* involves a search or a quest. You actively use your thoughts, emotions, imagination, and desires to think about God's presence in the world and in your life. To be fruitful, meditation must be done regularly. And you must be convinced of the necessity of meditation. Christian prayer mainly involves meditating on the mysteries of Christ as in *lectio divina* or the Rosary.
- *Contemplative prayer* or mental prayer is a simple gaze upon God in silence and in love. In mental prayer, you converse with Jesus or reflect on one of the mysteries of his life. This contemplation, a form of silent, wordless prayer, can lead you to rest in the presence of God's all-encompassing love. Again, you should always reserve a set time and duration for mental prayer. You can engage in mental prayer any time you open your heart to God and offer him the chance to open himself to you.

people stood in the nave, or main body of the building, while the celebration was in progress.

Eventually, church buildings became larger and more elaborate, culminating in the huge Gothic cathedrals of Europe. These buildings, many stories high and often shaped as a cross, were decorated with intricate sculptures, woodcarvings, pointed arches, and stained-glass windows. It was not unusual for such cathedrals to be under construction for hundreds of years.

When you walk into any Catholic church today, you will most likely find the following furnishings:

- Altar table which serves for the Sacrifice of the Mass and the Eucharistic Communion
- Tabernacle (sometimes located in a "chapel of reserve"), which contains the Blessed Sacrament,

humility
The virtue by which Christians acknowledge that God is the author of all that is good.

lectio divina
Literally, "divine reading." This is a prayerful way to read the Bible or any other sacred reading.

eschatological

A term to describe the "last things" (death, judgment, Heaven, Hell, Purgatory, the Second Coming of Christ, and the resurrection of the body).

 **DID YOU KNOW?**

Popular piety refers to a great number of devotions and religious practices of the faithful that are not strictly liturgical or sacramental, yet are approved by the Church. These include the veneration of relics, sanctuaries, pilgrimages, processions, Stations of the Cross, the rosary, and medals. These liturgical practices extend the liturgical life of the Church but do not replace it. Rather, they help to enrich the liturgy.

the consecrated species of bread from Mass
- Chair (*cathedra*) of the bishop or priest (the presider of the sacraments)
- Ambo, for proclaiming the Word of God
- Aumbry, a niche or container for storing the Sacred Chrism, the Oil of Catechumens, and the Oil of the Sick, all of which are used in Sacramental anointings
- Baptistery with a font or pool for celebrating the Sacrament of Baptism and receptacles for holy water to recall our Baptism
- Reconciliation room for celebrating the Sacrament of Penance

Even though the architecture of modern-day church buildings has become simplified in several ways, the buildings themselves remain consecrated ground, holy places that "signify and make visible the Church living in this place, the dwelling of God with men reconciled and united in Christ" (*CCC* 1180).

Churches also have an **eschatological** significance. The threshold we pass when entering a Catholic church symbolizes the passing from this world to the everlasting Kingdom of God.

For Review

1. Why is the liturgy best celebrated communally?
2. Explain what *form* and *matter* regarding the sacraments mean.
3. How are words and actions signs at the liturgy?
4. Why does the word *today* describe the Church's celebration of the mystery of Christ in her liturgy?
5. What are the main seasons of the Church Year?
6. Name three feasts that honor Mary.
7. Explain the format of the Liturgy of the Hours.
8. Name three furnishings that are a part of most Catholic churches.
9. Name and describe three common Christian prayer expressions.

For Reflection

- Name a particular ministry you have participated in or would like to participate in at the liturgy. What did you learn or would you like to learn about this ministry?

- Describe or draw a religious icon that is meaningful to you. Explain why this is so.

CHAPTER QUICK VIEW

Main Ideas

- We proclaim our Redemption—the saving action of Jesus Christ—in the liturgy. (pp. 31-32)

- At Pentecost, the Holy Spirit came upon the Apostles, making them "sacramental signs of Christ" (*CCC* 1087). (pp. 32-33)

- The Blessed Trinity works in the liturgy through distinctive roles of Father, Son, and Holy Spirit. (pp. 33-37)

- God the Father is the source of the liturgy; he takes the initiative of being present. (pp. 33-34)

- Jesus instituted the sacraments through his words and actions. (p. 34)

- Jesus is present in the liturgy in several ways, most especially in the Eucharistic species, his own Body and Blood. (pp. 35-36)

- The Holy Spirit dispenses the graces of the sacraments and prepares us to encounter Jesus in them. (p. 37)

- The Spirit helps us both "remember the faith" (*anamnesis*) and make the saving actions of Christ present to us today (*epiclesis*). (p. 37)

- The Seven Sacraments have several doctrinal elements in common and can be called by these names: Sacraments of Christ, Sacraments of the Church, Sacraments of Faith, Sacraments of Salvation, and Sacraments of Eternal Life. (pp. 38-40)

- Sacraments can be called "celebrations" because they are acts of divine worship and the Church is involved in them through her participation. (p. 41)

- The celebration of the liturgy involves all members of the Church; the ministerial priesthood are called to a special role of service in the liturgy while the common priesthood offer themselves in spiritual sacrifice. (p. 41)

- The liturgy is celebrated with signs and symbols, words and gestures. (pp. 42-45)

- The words for each sacrament are called the *form* of the sacrament; the physical elements are called the *matter* of the sacrament. (p. 42)

- Liturgical singing and sacred images known as icons also have a significant role in the liturgy. (p. 43)

- The liturgy is structured around worship on Sunday, the first day of the week, when Christ rose from the dead. (p. 46)

- Seasons of the Church Year also make up the liturgical calendar and include Advent, Christmas, Lent, Easter, and Ordinary Time. (pp. 47-50)

- Mary and the saints have a special place of honor in the Church Year. (pp. 51-52)

- The Liturgy of the Hours, or Divine Office, is the official public prayer of the Church and helps extend the Eucharist through the hours of each day. (p. 52)

- While the celebration of the liturgy is not limited to any one place, Catholics typically construct churches for divine worship. (pp. 52-54)

- Personal prayer helps us share in the graces of our Redemption and in the Father's love for us that we receive in the liturgy. (p. 53)

- Among several ways to express Christian prayer are vocal prayer, meditation, and contemplative prayer. (p. 53)

Famous Catholics and the Sacraments:

ST. KATHARINE DREXEL

When the Drexel family of 1503 Walnut Street in Philadelphia took a trip out west in 1884, the life course of the Drexels' third daughter, Katharine, and the fortunes of thousands of mistreated and impoverished Americans took a dramatic, if not unusual, turn.

The Drexels were extremely wealthy. The father, Francis, was a banker and an exchange broker. By the time of his death, he would amass a $15.5 million estate. But it wasn't the monetary wealth that influenced the Drexels. Francis and his second wife, Emma, were devout Catholics who lived their faith as a "manner of life." Twice per week Emma distributed clothing and rent assistance to widows or single women, always without attracting attention that would embarrass the recipients. Emma Drexel told her daughters, "Kindness may be unkind if it leaves a sting behind."

Katharine was twenty-six years old when she went with her father on the trip west to a Native American mission in Montana. She couldn't believe what she encountered. The poverty was severe; schools were barely funded, and without supplies and teachers. Before she left the mission, she purchased an expensive statue of the Blessed Mother from a catalog and had it shipped there. Her father was hardly upset; rather, he praised Katharine for her generosity.

After Francis Drexel's death in 1885, he left $1.5 million to charities and the rest of his $14 million to his three daughters—a sum of about $1,000 per day for each girl. Katharine immediately began sending her money to support the Native Americans. Her funding established St. Catherine Indian School in Santa Fe, New Mexico, in 1887.

The Drexel sisters vacationed in Europe about the same time. The trip climaxed with a private audience with Pope Leo XIII. Katharine told the Pope the plight of the Native Americans and about her financial sponsorship, and asked him to send missionaries to staff the schools. Pope Leo answered with a question: "But why not be a missionary yourself, my child?"

Within two years, after prayerful reflection, Katharine left for the Sisters of Mercy Convent in Pittsburgh to begin her life as a religious, taking the name Sr. Mary Katharine Drexel. A headline in a Philadelphia newspaper read: "Miss Drexel Enters a Catholic Convent—Gives Up Seven Million."

Katharine Drexel's decision was not based on founding a civil rights movement. Rather, after taking her vows of poverty, chastity, and obedience, she added a fourth promise: "To be mother and servant of the Indian and Negro races." The Archbishop of Philadelphia who heard her vows asked her if she had personal ambitions for her life ahead. She said that "Yes, in a way," she did. Sr. Mary Katharine described them as:

Ambition to work among the poor and neglected, to work in obscurity. An even truer answer is that God calls some souls to a higher life than others. How beautiful the mission of this child who comes to devote her life, her heart, her future, to the suffering races, as when Jesus said to the rich young man, "Sell all thou hast and give it to the poor, and follow me."

Katharine Drexel founded her own religious order, the Sisters of the Blessed Sacrament, to work especially among the Native American and African American peoples in the United States. By the time she died in 1955, Katharine and her religious community had founded sixty schools, including Xavier University in New Orleans, the only African American Catholic college in the United States.

The name Sr. Mary Katharine chose for her religious community—Sisters of the Blessed Sacrament—belies her true mission to the Native Americans and African Americans: to evangelize them into the Catholic Church for the Salvation of their souls. Katharine's love for Jesus in the Blessed Sacrament grew from a very early age. She took great pleasure in building a tabernacle and locating the Blessed Sacrament in her schools and missions, in places where Christ's Real Presence in the Eucharist had never been. On many nights, after everyone was asleep, Katharine would sit before the Blessed Sacrament, kneeling with her arms outstretched. She wrote of the experience:

> My sweetest joy is to be in the presence of Jesus in the Holy Sacrament. I beg that when obliged to withdraw in body, I may leave my heart before the Holy Sacrament. How I would miss Our Lord if he were to be away from me by his presence in the Blessed Sacrament!

After a heart attack and other health problems, Katharine Drexel spent the last eighteen years of her life almost completely immobile. She told her doctors, "Nobody is necessary for God's work. God can do the work without any of his creatures." Katharine spent these years in prayer and devotion to the Blessed Sacrament in a little room in her community's motherhouse near Philadelphia. She recorded several of her middle-of-the-night meditations and adorations. She wrote:

The Eucharist is a never-ending sacrifice. It is the sacrament of love, the supreme love, the act of love. . . . Christ wishes the Christian community to be a body that is perfect because we work together toward a single end, and the higher the motive which actuates this collaboration the higher, no doubt, will be the union. Now the end in question is supremely exalted: the continuous sanctification of the Body for the glory of God and the Lamb that was slain—Jesus in the Most Blessed Sacrament.

A Native American man who knew Katharine Drexel and had been educated in one of her schools said, "She never mixed two religions together. She always stressed the Catholic." Katharine desired that everyone come to a love of the Blessed Sacrament as she had. The Salvation of souls was her ultimate goal.

Pope John Paul II canonized St. Mary Katharine Drexel on October 1, 2000.

- Research the mission of Xavier University in New Orleans. Explain how the dreams and goals of St. Katharine Drexel live on at the university.
- Write a report on a Native American or an African American who was influenced by St. Katharine Drexel and her missions.
- Write a letter to a Sister of the Blessed Sacrament. Ask her how her vocation and ministry have drawn inspiration from St. Katharine Drexel.

TERMS, PEOPLE, PLACES

Match the following definitions with the terms from the list below.

Pentecost
Paraclete
apostolic succession
blessings
Real Presence
transubstantiation
Blessed Sacrament
ministerial priesthood
common priesthood

evangelize
Sacred Tradition
Liturgy of the Word
homily
icons
Sabbath
holy day of obligation
Church Year
Transfiguration

Easter Triduum
neophytes
sanctoral cycle
Liturgy of the Hours
basilica
eschatological
humility
lectio divina

1. has as its mission to build up and guide the Church in the name of Christ
2. advocate, consoler, defender
3. a name for the Real Presence of Christ in the Eucharist
4. divine, life-giving actions that come from God the Father
5. divine reading
6. known as the "birthday of the Church"
7. the living transmission of the Church's Gospel message that is cared for by the Magisterium
8. to bring the Good News of Jesus to others
9. religious images or paintings
10. the priesthood of the faithful

ONGOING ASSIGNMENTS

As you cover the material in this chapter, choose and complete at least three of these assignments.

1. In addition to the Seven Sacraments, the Church has numerous *sacramentals*—smaller sacred signs that prepare Church members "to receive the chief effect of the sacraments, and various occasions in life are rendered holy" (*CCC* 1677). Examples of sacramentals include holy water, ashes, palms, candles, rosaries, medals, and blessings. Among the sacramentals, blessings are most important. They include blessings of persons, meals, objects, and places. Read about the Church's teaching on sacramentals. Write a report on the definition of *sacramentals*, their origins, and beliefs about them.

2. Because "the Lord is near" (Phil 4:5), St. Paul told the Philippians, "Rejoice in the Lord always. I shall say it again: rejoice!" (Phil 4:4). Certainly such rejoicing should be found in each sacrament, where God is present to us. Select a sacred song, hymn, or psalm that you think expresses Christian joy at being loved and saved by God. In your journal, explain what the lyrics mean to you and why they help you rejoice in the Lord today. *Alternative:* Write a song or poem or choreograph a dance that expresses your joy at being loved and saved by God. Present this song, poem, or dance to the class.

3. Keep a diary for one week in which you write down the opportunities you have each day to live as a sacramental person (as the hands, feet, and eyes of Christ). Describe a situation you encountered (at home, at work, at school, or in your neighborhood) and how you think Christ would want to you to respond.

4. Draw a cyclical calendar that highlights the seasons and some of the feast days of the Church Year. Use liturgical colors to differentiate the seasons. Choose other symbols, words, and pictures to depict some important days in the year.

5. Even though the Church has set the date of Easter as the first Sunday after the first full moon after the spring equinox, the Western and Eastern Churches celebrate Easter at different times, usually one or two weeks apart. Research and report on why this is so. Also, find out if there are any recent discussions between West and East to arrive at a common date to celebrate Easter.

6. Read 1 John 1:1–3. Write several paragraphs in your journal relating this passage to the Church's Seven Sacraments.

7. Read what St. Paul had to say about different ministries in the Church (1 Cor 3:5–9; 12:4–11, 27–31). Then make a list of the ministries available to you in your parish. Decide which parish ministry might suit your interests, talents, and charisms. Then research how to get involved in one or two ministries. Write about your plan.

8. Research and write a report that details the devotion to the Blessed Sacrament of one of the following:

   • St. John Nepomucene Neumann

   • St. Elizabeth Ann Bailey Seton

   • Blessed Damien de Veuster

PRAYER SERVICE

Theme: Blessed be God, the Holy One.

All: Blessed are you, O Lord, praiseworthy and exalted above all for all ages.

Side 1: Sun and moon, bless the Lord.
Stars of heaven, bless the Lord.
Every shower and dew, bless the Lord.
All you winds, bless the Lord.

All: Praise and exalt him above all forever.

Side 2: Fire and heat, bless the Lord.
Cold and chill, bless the Lord.
Nights and days, bless the Lord.
Lightning and clouds, bless the Lord.

All: Praise and exalt him above all forever.

Side 1: Let the earth bless the Lord.
Mountains and hills, bless the Lord.
Everything growing from the earth, bless the Lord.
You springs, bless the Lord.

All: Praise and exalt him above all forever.

Side 2: Seas and rivers, bless the Lord.
You dolphins and all water creatures, bless the Lord.
All you birds of the air, bless the Lord.
All you beasts, wild and tame, bless the Lord.

All: Praise and exalt him above all forever.

All: Blessed are you, O Lord, praiseworthy and exalted above all for all ages.

(Based on Daniel 3:52, 62-81)

Reading: Ephesians 1:3–10

Spontaneous Petitions

Share prayers from the "Devotion to the Real Presence" activity

Concluding Prayer: Heavenly Father, transform us into your sons and daughters through the sacraments. Help us see all of creation as a visible sign of your presence. May our every thought, word, and action praise you. May each day of our lives be filled with acts of selfless charity and courageous witness to the saving power of your Son, Jesus Christ. We ask this in union with your life-giving Spirit. Amen.

The Sacraments *of* Christian Initiation

MORE THAN A NEW BEGINNING

Most people use the word *initiation* synonymously with "a new beginning." However, that is not exactly what Christian initiation means. Christian initiation is more like a process of *realignment*—a transformation of something that already exists. That something is a loving relationship between God the Father and his children. On one side of the relationship is the Father, the one who "initiates," who invites us to friendship with him. On the other side of the relationship is the person, a finite creature, made in God's image and likeness.

As the *Catechism of the Catholic Church* teaches: "The sacraments of Christian initiation—Baptism, Confirmation, and the Eucharist—lay the *foundations* of every Christian life" (*CCC* 1212). The *General Introduction to Christian Initiation* outlines the importance of each of the three sacraments.

Baptism Incorporates Us into Christ

Through Baptism, we are formed into God's People. We obtain forgiveness for all of our sins. We are raised from the natural human condition through water and the Holy Spirit to the dignity of God's children. The *Roman Catechism* taught that "Baptism is the sacrament of regeneration through water and in the word."

Confirmation Fills Us with the Holy Spirit

The *General Introduction* says: "Signed with the gift of the Spirit in Confirmation, Christians more perfectly become the image of their Lord and are filled with the Holy Spirit." The Holy Spirit brings Confirmation candidates into conformity with Christ and enables them to spread Christ's presence to all. The Holy Spirit is the source of holiness and love in the Church, and the bond of unity among all Christians.

DID YOU KNOW?

The Church has set aside January 18-25 each year as Christian Unity Week. During this time, members of all Christian churches pray that they may work toward building oneness among them.

Eucharist Brings Eternal Life

The Holy Eucharist completes Christian initiation. We come to the table of the Lord to eat the Body and drink the Blood of Jesus Christ so that we can have eternal life and show forth the unity of God's People. The Eucharist contains the Church's spiritual treasury, who is Christ himself. All of the sacraments are directed to the Eucharist, and the Mass is already the heavenly liturgy by anticipating eternal life.

TWO RITES FOR THE SACRAMENTS OF INITIATION

Because Jesus is the primordial sacrament and the Church is the foundational sacrament, it follows that the Church's Seven Sacraments have to be rooted in Jesus and grounded in the Church. Outside of Jesus and the Church, the sacraments have no meaning. Baptism, Confirmation, and Eucharist initiate us *into* Jesus and into the Church. The Sacraments of Initiation make us the adopted sons and daughters of God the Father. We become the brothers and sisters of Jesus, freed from sin because of his loving sacrifice on the cross. We become temples of the Holy Spirit, the place where God's presence may be found.

The Second Vatican Council reemphasized the early practice of celebrating Baptism, Confirmation, and Eucharist as Sacraments of Initiation and celebrating these sacraments on the evening of the Easter Vigil. This process of complete initiation is for adults and children of catechetical age—the Rite of Christian Initiation of Adults (RCIA). The Church continues to celebrate the rite of Baptism for younger children in which catechesis for the sacraments and usually reception of Confirmation and Eucharist take place at times separate from Baptism.

This unit provides an overview of the Sacraments of Christian Initiation, focusing particularly on an *understanding* of the sacraments, ways the sacraments are *celebrated*, the *graces* of the sacraments, and several ways the sacraments *empower* us to lead lives in unity with Christ and his Church.

From Catholic Bloggers

TEN PRISON INMATES BECOME CATHOLICS

Ten inmates at Lebanon Correctional Institution in Ohio experienced the sense of hope and promise of new life that accompanies the Easter season when they were welcomed into the Catholic Church.

Archbishop Daniel E. Pilarczyk presided at a Mass at the close-security prison during which the men received the Sacraments of Initiation. Prison Chaplain Christine Shimrock, a member of St. Susanna Parish in Mason, Ohio, said the opportunity to develop and share their faith is significant for the inmates on several levels. "Society is so quick to judge people for their mistakes, but God doesn't work that way. It's important restoratively for the inmates to recognize that we're all forgiven. More than 85 percent of the inmates will return to society and, as a citizen, I would like someone to return having repented. This ministry enables the inmates to return full of faith and with some spiritual goals."

The ten men petitioned Archbishop Pilarczyk to celebrate Easter Mass at the prison and confer the sacraments by writing letters and, along with the volunteers and LeCI staff, were thrilled to welcome him. In his homily, Archbishop Pilarczyk spoke of the joy of the Easter season saying, "Easter is the celebration of new life and Jesus' return to the living. In Baptism, we begin to live a new life—the life of the Risen Jesus."

Wearing crisp white shirts, the elect were then called forward to be baptized and confirmed. After the archbishop conferred the sacraments, the assembly welcomed the new members of the Catholic Church with resounding applause. The men later received the Eucharist for the first time. Eric Harmon, who attended a Catholic high school, said he decided to participate in RCIA because "It was time to put myself spiritually where I needed to be and that is being a member of the Catholic family." Being Catholic in prison is a challenge, Harmon acknowledged. "The pettiness goes to the extreme at times, and it's rough to keep on the right path with the corruption going on around you, so I pray a lot," he said.

His fellow inmate, Bernard Perfetto, said what drew him to Catholicism is "the message of love, forgiveness and hope—three things that are in short supply in prison. It (becoming Catholic) really gives me the feeling that I'm a servant of God and that means a lot when you're confined in a place like this."

—quoted from the *Catholic Telegraph*

MORE THAN MEANS TO AN END

The Sacraments of course must not be solely seen as mere means to an end that offers us a solution to whatever problems that may assail us. But in being able to receive them, we proclaim ourselves Catholics who are able to have recourse to these great channels of grace, and whilst I await a long wait to receive them, I only pray that I will be made a worthy recipient of what will be able to further enrich me and mold me in the image of Our Lord.

—from a catechumen in anticipation of the Easter Vigil

The Sacrament *of* Baptism

Pompa Diaboli
In the Sacrament of Baptism, our triple "no" to sin is followed with our affirmative belief in God the Father, God the Son, and God the Holy Spirit.

Understanding the Sacrament of Baptism
Baptism is prefigured in the Old Testament and clarified by its connection with the Paschal Mystery of Jesus Christ; it has always been the way to membership in the Church.

Celebrating the Sacrament of Baptism
There are separate rites for the initiation of adults and children; however, the essential rite of Baptism for each is the same and involves an immersion in or pouring of water and the pronouncement of words in the name of the Father, the Son, and the Holy Spirit.

The Grace of Baptism
Two primary graces or effects of the sacrament are forgiveness of sins and a rebirth to new life.

Loving God More Deeply
The sanctifying grace of justification given at Baptism helps us live a virtuous life; the theological virtues of faith, hope, and charity are infused into our souls.

POMPA DIABOLI

In the Sacrament of Baptism, a series of six questions is asked of the parents and godparents, or in the case of adults, the **catechumens**. Three of the questions really require "no" for answers; they involve things to reject: sin, evil, and Satan, the "father of sin and prince of darkness."

Pope Benedict XVI, in a homily on the Feast of the Baptism of the Lord in 2006, explained that in the ancient Church the three responses rejected the *pompa diaboli*, which referred to the promise of what appeared to be life in abundance from the pagan world of the day; that is, permissiveness, corruption of joy, love of deceit

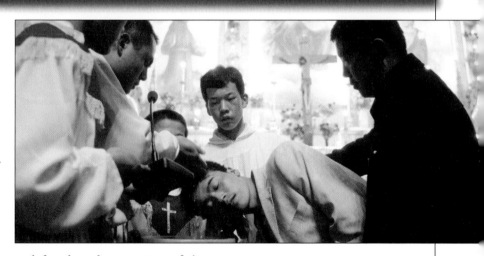

and fraud, and perversion of the true meaning of life.

In those earlier times, this *pompa diaboli* or "anti-culture" exposed itself in actions like those that took place in the Roman Colosseum, where people were set on fire and tortured as a sport.

catechumens
Unbaptized people who are preparing to receive all of the Sacraments of Christian Initiation.

THE CULTURE OF LIFE

Baptism makes real the new life that Christ won for us. In Baptism, we join with Christ in saying "no" to sin and "yes" to moral goodness. In other words, we say "yes" to the culture of life. In doing so, we obey each of the Ten Commandments.

Listed below are examples that Pope Benedict XVI gave of saying "yes" to life in today's world. Think about each example. Then write one or two practical ways you will try to carry out each example this week. Follow through on your plan.

- Say "yes" to a God who gives meaning to life (Commandments 1-3).
- Say "yes" to the family (Commandment 4).
- Say "yes" to life (Commandment 5).
- Say "yes" to responsible love (Commandment 6).
- Say "yes" to social responsibility and justice (Commandment 7).
- Say "yes" to the truth (Commandment 8).
- Say "yes" to respect for others and their belongings (Commandments 9 and 10).

Today, at Baptism the three rejections of sin, evil, and Satan are really a condemnation of the prevalent culture we live in today and its apparent promises of joy, satisfaction, and happiness. The sinfulness in our own pagan world rears itself in actions like sexual pro-

miscuity, cruelty, violence, drug abuse, atheism, and so much more. Pope Benedict, in addressing those who had come for Baptism and to accompany them, said:

> Let us say "no" to this promise of apparent happiness, to this "pompa" of what may seem to be life but is in fact merely an instrument of death, and to this "anti-culture," in order to cultivate instead the culture of life.

In the Sacrament of Baptism, this "no" to the popularity of sinful culture rings out loud and clear for all to hear. Concurrently we also respond affirmatively to life when we, or those answering for us, respond "yes" when asked if we believe in God: Father, Son, and Holy Spirit.

What do we expect when we are baptized in the Church? The Pope also explained in simple words:

> We hope for a good life, the true life . . . and also for happiness in a future that is still unknown. We are unable to guarantee this gift for the entire span of the unknown future, so we turn to the Lord to obtain this gift from him.

The *Catechism of the Catholic Church* teaches that "Through Baptism we are freed from sin and reborn as sons of God; we become members of Christ, are incorporated into the Church and made sharers in her mission" (*CCC* 1213). What happens at Baptism that sets these wheels of new life in motion? What are the effects of the sacrament? How do we who are baptized become the fruits of what we have experienced?

These are some of the main questions that will be addressed in this chapter.

For Reflection

- What are some sinful elements of popular culture that you have rejected?
- By word or action, how do you affirm your baptismal promise of belief in God?

UNDERSTANDING THE SACRAMENT OF BAPTISM

The Sacrament of Baptism takes its name from its central rite; "to baptize" comes from the Greek word *baptizein*, which means "to plunge" or "immerse." The plunging of the catechumens into water represents being buried with Christ; when they emerge they rise up with Christ as a "new creature." St. Paul wrote:

> Or are you unaware that we who were baptized into Christ Jesus were baptized into his death? We were indeed buried with him through baptism into death, so that, just as Christ was raised from the dead by the glory of the Father, we too might live in newness of life. (Rom 6:3–4)

The sacrament is also known by other names. It is called *the washing of regeneration and renewal by the Holy Spirit* because it actually brings about the rebirth of a person by water and Spirit that Jesus spoke of: "Amen, amen, I say to you, no one can enter the kingdom of God without being born of water and Spirit" (Jn 3:5).

St. Justin Martyr called the sacrament *enlightenment*, "because those who receive this [catechetical] instruction are enlightened in their understanding." Jesus is the light of the world who enlightens everyone. St. Gregory of Nazianzus wrote that "Baptism is God's most beautiful and magnificent gift" (both quotes from *CCC* 1216).

Baptism's place in the sacramental economy is remembered in the liturgy of the Easter Vigil, in which several events of the Old Testament prefigure Baptism. Christ's own baptism reveals more of the sacrament's meaning. Finally, the history of Baptism in the Church teaches that through the sacrament a person is purified, justified, and sanctified by the Holy Spirit. The following sections explain more of the history of the sacrament.

Baptism Prefigured in the Old Testament

Since the beginning of the world, water has been a source of life. In the first creation story of the Book of Genesis, the Spirit of God swept over the waters and brought forth life from them.

The liturgy of Baptism reminds us that water is a rich symbol of new life. In fact, all created life is believed to have come from the primeval waters. "In the beginning, when God created the heavens and the earth, the earth was a formless wasteland, and darkness covered the abyss, while a mighty wind swept over the waters" (Gn 1:1–2). "At the very dawn of creation [God's] Spirit breathed on the waters, making them the wellspring of all holiness" (*Roman Missal*, Easter Vigil 42: Blessing of Water). God calls each of us by name (see Isaiah 43:1) and invites us "to know, to love, and to serve him, and so to come to paradise" (*CCC* 1721). Because of God's love for us, our lives have dignity, purpose, and meaning.

Baptism also points out that God's love is constant (see Isaiah 43:2–7). Not only does God give us life; God also sustains and protects human life. The waters of Baptism remind us of the Genesis story of Noah's ark and the devastating flood that brought death to so many. "God patiently waited in the days of Noah during the building of the ark, in which a few persons, eight in all, were saved through water" (1 Pt 3:20). Just as God saved Noah and his family from the waters of death, so God saves us in the waters of Baptism. These

waters signify and make real "an end of sin and a new beginning of goodness" (*Roman Missal*, Easter Vigil 42: Blessing of Water).

In the waters of Baptism, we also recall God's saving plan to rescue Moses and the Israelites from slavery in Egypt. With God's help, the Israelites miraculously crossed the Red Sea and reached the opposite side (see Exodus 14:10–31). God gave them new life as free people, rather than slaves. He made a covenant with them and taught them to live by the Ten Commandments as his own people. They were to choose life rather than death by "loving the Lord . . . heeding his voice, and holding fast to him" (see Deuteronomy 30:19–20).

Furthermore, the waters of Baptism remind us of the promise God made to be with the Israelites always and to bring them safely to the Promised Land. Just as God led Joshua and the Israelites safely across the Jordan River into the land of Canaan (see Joshua 3:13–17), so the waters of Baptism enable us to enter the Church and live as members of the New Covenant, as God's own People.

Christ's Baptism

In the time of Jesus, a group of ascetic Jews known as Essenes preached repentance from sin by baptism of water as a way of showing one's commitment to God's covenant. While it is not known for sure if John the Baptist was a member of this sect, we do know he preached repentance from sin and urged people to become baptized as a way of showing their commitment to God's covenant. St. John the Baptist is often referred to as the "last Old Testament prophet."

In the New Testament, all four Gospels report that John the Baptist baptized people as a sign of their repentance from sin. We know that John the Baptist baptized Jesus, even though he was without sin (see Matthew 3:13–17; Mark 1:9–11; Luke 3:21–22; John 1:31–34). We also know that Jesus commissioned the Apostles to "make disciples of all nations, baptizing them in the name of the Father, and of the Son, and of the holy Spirit" (Mt 28:19). These examples at both the beginning and the end of Christ's ministry teach us the primacy of Baptism. Born without sin, Christ did not need recourse to Baptism as we do, but he submitted to it to show us the value of "self-emptying." The beautiful verse in the Letter to the Philippians describes this action of Jesus:

Who, though he was in the form of God,
did not regard equality with God
      something to be grasped.
Rather, he emptied himself,
taking the form of a slave,
coming in human likeness;
and found human in appearance,
he humbled himself,
becoming obedient to death,
      even death on a cross.
Because of this, God greatly exalted him
and bestowed on him the name
that is above every name,
that at the name of Jesus
every knee should bend,
of those in heaven and on earth and under
      the earth,
and every tongue confess that
Jesus Christ is Lord,
to the glory of God the Father. (Phil 2:6–11)

The Sacrament of Baptism also teaches us that the cross of Christ redeemed us and that Baptism is effective only because of Christ's Death. In all four Gospels, the baptism of Jesus marks the beginning of his public ministry, his preaching of the coming of God's Kingdom *and* the necessity of his own Death and Resurrection for the forgiveness of sins. His baptism with water prefigures his baptism in blood at his Death on the cross. This association becomes clear in the dialogue that occurs between Jesus and his Apostles in Mark's Gospel:

[James and John said to Jesus], "Grant that in your glory we may sit one at your right and the other at your left." Jesus said to them, "You do not know what you are asking. Can you drink the cup that I drink or be baptized with the baptism with which I am baptized?" (Mk 10:37–38)

Jesus further clarifies the connection between Baptism and the Paschal Mystery in Luke's Gospel: "There is a baptism with which I must be baptized, and how great is my anguish until it is accomplished!" (Lk 12:50). Further, in the Gospel of John's account of the Passion, it is reported that "one soldier thrust his lance into [Jesus'] side, and immediately blood and water flowed out" (Jn 19:34). The water from Christ's side alludes to Baptism. His Death is not the end, but a new beginning. Jesus will conquer death just as he conquered sin. He will rise again to new life.

In the Sacrament of Baptism, we recall the baptism of Jesus as a revelation of his true character. We express our own faith that he is the Messiah, the Son of God, who has saved us from sin and brings us to new life. We also recall the Paschal Mystery—his dying and rising from the dead. Our immersion in water signifies his Death. Our rising from the water signifies his Resurrection. As St. Paul explained to the Colossians, "You were buried with [Christ] in baptism, in which you were also raised with him through faith in the power of God, who raised him from the dead" (Col 2:12).

Christian Initiation in the Church

From the day of Pentecost, Baptism has been the way to membership in the Church. St. Peter said to the thousands who gathered in the streets of Jerusalem near the Upper Room, where Jesus had shared his Last Supper: "Repent and be baptized, every one of you, in the name of Jesus Christ for the forgiveness of your sins; and you will receive the gift of the holy Spirit" (Acts 2:38). The Apostles and other disciples offered Baptism to anyone who believed in Jesus, whether Jew or Gentile. Baptism was always connected with the gift of faith in Christ that encompassed all of Salvation History.

For example, when Philip preached about Jesus to the Ethiopian eunuch, he did not just tell him about the life and message of Jesus. He showed the man how even the ancient prophecies of Isaiah foretold Jesus' mission as Messiah (see Acts 8:27–38). Likewise today, when the Church baptizes new members at the Easter Vigil, it precedes these Baptisms with nine Scripture readings that encompass all of Salvation History. They recall for us how everything in the past either prefigured or prepared people for the coming of Jesus. Our consent to be baptized says we believe that Jesus is the center point of history. In him, everything that has happened "makes sense." He is what gives our lives meaning.

A preparation process for Baptism and the other Sacraments of Initiation evolved in the early Church. This **catechumenate** has always been accomplished by a journey and initiation in several stages. By the fourth century, these steps of our modern Christian initiation were beginning to take shape:

1. *Precatechumenate.* Basically, this period consisted of evangelization and initial conversion. From the

Soul of Christ

A traditional prayer that some Catholics pray before and after Holy Communion is also appropriate for Baptism. This prayer, called the *Anima Christi* or "Soul of Christ," dates from the fourteenth century.

> Soul of Christ, sanctify me.
> Body of Christ, heal me.
> Blood of Christ, drench me.
> Water from the side of Christ, wash me.
> Passion of Christ, strengthen me.
> Good Jesus, hear me.
> In your wounds shelter me.
> From turning away keep me.
> From the evil one protect me.
> At the hour of my death call me.
> Into your presence lead me,
> To praise you with all your saints
> For ever and ever. Amen.

catechumenate

A Greek word that means "study or instruction." In the early Church, the catechumenate was a two- to three-year period of study about Jesus and the Christian faith. Celebration of the Sacraments of Initiation did not occur until after the catechumenate.

EASTER VIGIL READINGS

The Church has chosen nine readings for the Easter Vigil—seven from the Old Testament and two from the New Testament. A list of these readings is given below. Select three of the readings and write a paragraph for each, telling how the reading prefigures or prepares people for Jesus. Also tell how you think the passage relates to Baptism. Cite at least one biblical commentary for each of the readings. Then write your own prayer responses of faith to the chosen readings.

- God creates the world (Genesis 1:1-2:2).
- God makes a covenant with Abraham (Genesis 22:1-18).
- The Israelites cross the Red Sea (Exodus 14:15-15:1).
- God loves his people (Isaiah 54:5-14).
- Come to God and you will have life (Isaiah 55:1-11).
- God's commandments bring life (Baruch 3:9-15, 32-4:4).
- God will give you a new heart (Ezekiel 36:16-28).
- We are baptized into Christ Jesus (Romans 6:3-11).
- Jesus has been raised from the dead (Matthew 28:1-10 or Mark 16:1-8 or Luke 24:1-12).

catechists

Teachers of the faith. They are ordained ministers and laypeople who help make Christian disciples.

words and actions of practicing Christians, the person heard the Good News that Jesus is the Messiah. From then on, he or she wanted to learn more. People at this stage of initiation were called "inquirers." They needed to find a good member of the Christian community to sponsor them. These sponsors got to know them and find out whether they had a true desire to follow Christ and seek Baptism. Next, the Church celebrated a rite that admitted the inquirers into the Order of Catechumens. From that moment on, these catechumens were considered part of the Church.

2. *Catechumenate.* During the time of study (often two or three years), the catechumens met to receive instruction in the Gospels and Church teaching. They were taught by **catechists** (priests, deacons, and lay teachers). Through the example of their sponsors and godparents, the catechumens gained familiarity with Christian life. They celebrated the Liturgy of the Word at Mass and attended the celebration of other liturgical rites of the Church. They became involved in the local Church's work of charity and service.

3. *Purification, Enlightenment, or Illumination.* This part of the initiation process usually coincided with Lent. On the First Sunday of Lent, the catechumens who were ready to proceed to the celebration of the sacraments took part in the Rite of Enrollment. The catechumens entered their names in the *Book of the Elect.* From then on, they were known as the *elect* or "chosen ones." During Lent, the elect intensified their prayer and preparation for the sacraments. They underwent three or more **scrutinies.** These

rites were prayer services that asked God to help them examine their lives for sins that needed Christ's healing. The prayer services also were intended to strengthen the resolve of the elect to choose good and live for Christ. By the eighth century there is evidence that the scrutinies usually took place on the Third, Fourth, and Fifth Sundays of Lent. They reminded everyone— not just the catechumens—of the need for constant repentance and conversion. At the end of Lent, the catechumens celebrated Baptism, Confirmation, and Eucharist at the Easter Vigil service. At this great Feast of the Resurrection, the catechumens joined themselves to the Paschal Mystery of Jesus and began a new life as full Church members.

4. *Mystagogia.* The fourth step, which means "mysteries," lasted just one week. Today it continues for the entire Easter season, and sometimes longer. The newly baptized, who were now called "neophytes," immersed themselves in the mysteries of Christ, the Church, and the sacraments. They took an active part in the local community—meditating on the Gospel, sharing in the entire Mass and receiving Holy Communion, and performing works of charity.

These essential elements have always played a part: proclamation of the Word, acceptance of the Gospel showing conversion, profession of faith, Baptism itself, outpouring of the Holy Spirit, and reception of the Eucharist. While infant Baptism has been the norm in the Church, by its nature it requires a post-baptismal catechumenate of instruction in faith for the child as he or she grows and an opportunity for the "flowering of baptismal grace in personal growth" (*CCC* 1231).

The Second Vatican Council restored the practice of the adult catechumenate, called the **Rite of Christian Initiation for Adults (RCIA)**. As in previous times, it includes several distinct steps. A difference between the Eastern and Western rites of the Church is that the Eastern Churches confer all three Sacraments of Initiation in infancy. There, babies who are baptized also receive Confirmation and First Eucharist at the same time. (Since the babies can't eat food, the priest puts a small spoonful of the Blood of Christ under the species of consecrated wine into their mouths.) The babies become full members of the Church at this time. In the Western Church, after infant Baptism there are years of preparation preceding reception of the Sacrament of the Eucharist (and the Sacrament of Penance) and often a few more years of preparation prior to reception of the Sacrament of Confirmation.

For Review

1. What does the plunging of the candidate into water at Baptism represent?
2. What are two other names by which the Sacrament of Baptism is known?
3. What is the lesson of the Genesis story of Noah's ark?
4. Explain the connection between Baptism and the Paschal Mystery of Jesus Christ.
5. Name and briefly explain the four steps of the catechumenate process that evolved in the early Church.
6. How do the ways the Western Church and Eastern Church confer the Sacraments of Initiation differ?

? DID YOU KNOW?

Until the liturgical reforms of the Second Vatican Council, salt was used in the Catholic liturgy of Baptism. The priest put a small amount of salt on the lips of the person to be baptized. The salt symbolized the renunciation of evil, the food of divine wisdom, and the desire for moral goodness.

For Reflection

- Share how Baptism is a sign of God's creation, love, Salvation, and constant care both for the Israelites and for people today.

- Imagine you were recounting the story of Salvation to someone who had not heard the Good News of Jesus Christ. Where would you begin? What would you say?

CELEBRATION

CELEBRATING THE SACRAMENT OF BAPTISM

Every nonbaptized person—whether an adult or a child—can be baptized. As mentioned, since the beginning of the Church, the catechumenate for adults has occupied an important place. In fact, by virtue of living a life of faith, hope, and charity, catechumens are already joined to the Church.

Also, from the Church's earliest days, infant Baptisms have taken place. In fact, when Peter spoke out the window of the Upper Room on Pentecost, he said:

> Repent and be baptized, every one of you, in the name of Jesus Christ for the forgiveness of your sins; and you will receive the gift of the holy Spirit. (Acts 2:38)

Note that Peter said, "*every* one of you." He added, "For the promise is made to you and to your children and to . . . whomever the Lord our God will call" (Acts 2:39). Several other examples in the New Testament (e.g., Acts 16:15; Acts 16:33; and 1 Corinthians 1:16) mention that entire households were offered Baptism and converted to Christianity. It is presumed that children lived in these households.

When Christianity was legalized in the fourth century and the fear of being persecuted ended, more and more families, including those with young children, sought Baptism. But this wasn't the only reason for the increase in infant Baptisms. In the fourth and fifth centuries, the doctrine of **Original Sin** became more clearly understood through the writings of St. Augustine and other theologians. The Church taught that all humans inherited Original Sin—the sin of Adam and Eve, our first parents. While it is indeed true that Baptism takes away Original Sin and all previous personal sins, people began to emphasize this aspect of the sacrament and the importance of baptizing infants because many children of this era never lived to adulthood because of disease and illness.

Entry into Christian life gives access to true freedom. The practice of infant Baptism shows that Salvation is a pure gift of Christ's grace that extends even to children and does not presuppose anything a human must do to deserve it. As more infants were baptized, the godparent assisted with the catechesis of the child. There remains in the Church a separate rite for the initiation of children. The **Rite of Baptism of Children (RBC)** is the rite in which most Catholics are initiated. The RBC calls for Christian formation and catechesis taking place gradually as the person grows, so that infants, grown up, may eventually accept for themselves the faith in which they were baptized.

The Necessity of Baptism

Jesus said Baptism is necessary for Salvation (see John 3:5), and he commanded his disciples to proclaim the Gospel to all nations and to baptize them (see Matthew 28:19–20). Baptism is necessary for those who have heard the Good News and have been able to ask for the sacrament. Jesus said upon commissioning his disciples: "Whoever believes and is baptized will be saved; whoever does not believe will be condemned" (Mk 16:16).

The Church doesn't know any other way to ensure entry to eternal life. However, while "God has bound salvation to

---

Original Sin

The fallen state of human nature into which all generations of people are born. Christ Jesus came to save us from Original Sin.

Rite of Baptism of Children (RBC)

The process by which infants are initiated into the Church and after which catechesis takes place gradually as the person grows.

the Sacrament of Baptism . . . he himself is not bound by his sacraments" (*CCC* 1257). There are three traditional examples of how this is so.

First, those who suffer death for their faith prior to being baptized with water are baptized by their death for and with Christ. This **Baptism of blood** occurred often in the first three centuries of the Church, when the catechumenate process was often three years in length and the Roman government persecuted Christians themselves. The **martyrs** received what Church Father Tertullian called "a baptism which takes the place of the baptism of water when it has not been received, and which restores it when it has been lost."

Second, catechumens who die a natural death prior to being baptized are also assured of the Salvation they were not able to receive through the sacrament because of their "desire to receive it, together with repentance for their sins, and charity" (*CCC* 1259). The Church also holds that those who never heard the Gospel, lived a life according to God's will the best they could, and would have been baptized if they had known of the necessity can also be saved through the **Baptism of desire**.

Finally is the question of children who have died without Baptism. The Church entrusts them to God's mercy, knowing that God desires all people to be saved. Jesus said, "Let the children come to me; do not prevent them, for the kingdom of God belongs to such as these" (Mk 10:14). The funeral Mass includes prayers that may be said for a child who dies without Baptism.

Rite and Symbols of the Sacrament

The meaning and the grace of the Sacrament of Baptism are revealed in the essential rite and other words, gestures, and symbols of the sacrament. The Baptism of adults normally takes place during the Easter Vigil in the presence of the assembly of the faithful; it takes place in the **baptistery**. Likewise, the Baptism of infants is typically celebrated during a Sunday Mass to highlight the connection with both the Eucharist and other members of the Church. The *Catechism of the Catholic Church* teaches:

> Baptism is the sacrament of faith. But faith needs the community of believers. It is only within the faith of the Church that each of the faithful can believe. (*CCC* 1253)

As in the early Church, the initiation process for adults includes several stages. Each of these highlights the connection with faith that is neither perfect nor mature, but developing. In a Sunday liturgy that includes the Rite of Acceptance into the Order of Catechumens, the inquirers knock on the door of the church, the priest opens the door, and a dialogue such as this one takes place:

Priest:	What do you ask of God's Church?
Inquirers:	Faith.
Priest:	What does faith offer you?
Inquirers:	Eternal life.
Priest:	Are you ready to walk by the light of Christ and to believe in him with all your heart?
Inquirers:	I am.

After the inquirers declare their resolve to turn to Christ, the priest asks their sponsors and friends a question such as this: "My brothers and sisters gathered here, and you who present these candidates: You have heard them declare their resolve. Do you testify that they have chosen Christ as Lord and that they wish to serve him alone?"

Baptism of blood
The belief that martyrs—people who die for their faith in Jesus—receive forgiveness for their sins and experience God's saving mercy if they had not yet been baptized by water.

martyrs
Literally "witnesses." A martyr is someone who has been killed because of his or her faith.

Baptism of desire
The belief that catechumens who die before receiving the Sacrament of Baptism receive forgiveness for their sins and experience God's saving mercy.

baptistery
A separately planned structure around the Baptism font.

All: We do.

Priest: Are you ready to help them come to know and follow Christ?

All: We are.

After a brief prayer, the priest then makes the Sign of the Cross on each candidate's forehead, saying, "N., receive the cross on your forehead: By this sign of his love, Christ will be your strength. Learn now to know and follow him." Then the priest may make the Sign of the Cross on each candidate's ears, eyes, lips, breast, and shoulders, ending with the words, "I sign all of you in the name of the Father, and of the Son, and of the Holy Spirit: May you live for ever and ever."

Next, the priest invites the catechumens (as they are now known) into the church for the celebration of the Liturgy of the Word. From this time onward, the catechumens are considered members of the Church.

The essential rite and symbols for the Sacrament of Baptism itself are the same for both adults and children. The sacrament consists of the following elements:

1. *Sign of the Cross.* The priest or deacon imprints a cross on the forehead of the catechumen as a sign that he or she belongs to Christ. This sign also reminds the person of the grace Christ won for us by his Death on the cross. Then the minister asks the adult to be baptized (or in the case of infant Baptism, the parents and godparents), "What do you ask of God's Church?" The response may be "faith" or some other word or phrase. Right from the beginning of the celebration, we are reminded that "Baptism is the sacrament of faith" (*CCC* 1253). Faith in Christ Jesus brings us to Baptism, and Baptism strengthens us to live as faithful members of God's people, the Church.

2. *The Word of God.* The multiple Scripture readings and Responsorial Psalms from the Easter Vigil teach that God always initiates our relationship with him. God calls us and invites us to become his sons and daughters. We, in turn, respond in faith by committing ourselves to follow his Son, Jesus.

3. *Exorcisms and Profession of Faith.* Because Baptism signifies liberation from sin and from the one who brings about sin, Satan, one or more exorcisms are said over each candidate. The priest asks publicly and authoritatively in the name of Jesus Christ that each person be protected against the power of Satan and the lure of sin. The celebrant then anoints each candidate with the Oil of Catechumens, or lays hands on him or her. Each person is thus prepared to confess the faith of the Church, which will be entrusted to the candidate by Baptism.

4. *Blessing of the water.* The celebrant calls on the Holy Spirit to bless the water that will be used for Baptism. In this blessing, "The Church asks God that through his Son the power of the Holy Spirit may be sent upon the water, so that those who will be baptized in it may be 'born of water and the Spirit' (John 3:5)" (*CCC* 1238).

5. *Essential rite of Baptism.* The essential rite of the sacrament is very simple. The celebrant immerses each candidate in the blessed water three times or pours water three times over the candidate's head. At the same time, the celebrant says, "N., I baptize you in the name of the Father, and of the Son, and of the Holy Spirit" (*Christian Initiation of Adults* 220). "Immersion in water symbolizes not only death and purification, but also regeneration and renewal" (*CCC* 1262).

6. *Anointing with Sacred Chrism.* If the celebration of Confirmation does not follow immediately (as in infant Baptism), the celebrant anoints each newly baptized (neophyte) on the crown of the head with consecrated oil known as **Sacred Chrism**.

This anointing symbolizes a special coming of the Holy Spirit to the newly baptized. It signifies that a new character, or identity, has been given to the person. He or she now officially belongs to Christ and may be called a Christian. The anointing also brings the baptized person into union with the threefold mission of Christ as priest, prophet, and king. The directives for the *Christian Initiation of Adults* state, "The anointing with chrism after Baptism is a sign of the royal priesthood of the baptized and their enrollment in the fellowship of the people of God" (33).

7. *Receiving or clothing in a white garment.* Each of the neophytes either receives or is dressed in a white robe that "is a symbol of their new dignity" (*Christian Initiation of Adults* 33). The white robe signifies that the person is now freed from the darkness of sin and has "put on Christ."

8. *Receiving of a lit candle.* Each neophyte is next given a small white candle lit from the Easter Candle, which was blessed and lit earlier in the Easter Vigil service. The small candle has two meanings. First, it symbolizes that Christ has enlightened the person. Second, it symbolizes that the neophytes also have the responsibility to bring the light of Christ to today's world. "The lighted candle shows their vocation of living as befits the children of light" (*Christian Initiation of Adults* 33).

Adults who are being initiated at the Easter Vigil usually proceed directly with the celebration of the Sacrament of Confirmation. This is then followed by the Liturgy of the Eucharist and the reception of First Communion. In the Western Church, the baptismal rite for babies concludes with a solemn blessing of the newly baptized, along with their parents and the entire assembly. This rite stems from an ancient Jewish purification, cleansing, and blessing ritual that took place after birth. One version of the blessing follows:

Celebrant: May God the almighty Father, who filled the world with joy by giving us his only Son, bless these newly baptized children. May they grow to be more fully like Jesus Christ our Lord.

All: Amen.

Celebrant: May almighty God, who gives life on earth and in heaven, bless the parents of these children. They thank him now for the gift he has given them. May they always show that gratitude in action by loving and caring for their children.

All: Amen.

Celebrant: May almighty God, who has given us a new birth by water and the Holy Spirit, generously bless all of us who are his faithful children May we always live as his people, and may he bless all here present with his peace.

All: Amen.

Celebrant: May almighty God, the Father, and the Son, and the Holy Spirit, bless you.

All: Amen.

Sacred Chrism

Blessed by a bishop, this perfumed oil is used for anointing in the Sacraments of Baptism, Confirmation, and Holy Orders. It represents the gift of the Holy Spirit.

? DID YOU KNOW?

The ordinary ministers of Baptism are bishops and priests. In the Western Church, deacons may also minister the sacrament. In emergency situations, *any* person—Catholic, Christian, or not—may baptize if he or she intends to do what the Church does when she baptizes and recites the Trinitarian baptismal formula while immersing or pouring water over the person.

The Catechumenate Today

exorcisms
Prayerful rites in preparation for Baptism that invoke God's help in overcoming the power of Satan and the spirit of evil.

Oil of Catechumens
Olive oil or another plant oil that is blessed by a bishop at the Chrism Mass on or around Holy Thursday. This blessed oil is used to anoint catechumens, giving them wisdom and strength in their journey toward Baptism.

Besides the Rite of Acceptance, the initiation process for adults includes several other rites and opportunities for prayer, reflection, and study.

Throughout the study period, the catechumens may take part in various Church rituals such as **exorcisms** and anointing with the **Oil of Catechumens**. These rites ask God to give wisdom and strength to those who prepare for Baptism, bringing them a deeper understanding of the Gospel and helping them accept the challenge of Christian living. At the end of the catechumenate, usually on the First Sunday of Lent, the Rite of Election or Enrollment of Names is held for those who will be baptized at Easter. "For a person to be enrolled among the elect, he must have enlightened faith and the deliberate intention of receiving the sacraments of the Church" (*Christian Initiation of Adults* 134).

At the Rite of Election, the catechumens sit together in church for the Liturgy of the Word. The first reading for this Sunday (Year A) recounts the sin of Adam and Eve. The Church acknowledges that simply by being human, we share in this same tendency to sin. We respond, "Wash away all my guilt; from my sin cleanse me" (Ps 51:4), a prayer that expresses our belief that our sins are forgiven through the waters of Baptism. The second reading presents Jesus the Messiah as the New Adam who obeys God perfectly and brings us the gift of overflowing grace and justice (see Romans 5:17). Finally, the Gospel tells of the temptations of Jesus (see Matthew 4:1–11), who was human like us in all things but sin.

After the homily, which calls us to overcome temptations in our own lives, the actual Rite of Election takes place. A catechist presents each elected person to the priest and gathered assembly. A dialogue like the following makes up this rite.

Priest:	I ask you godparents: Have they faithfully listened to the Word of God proclaimed by the Church?	**Priest:**	Have they sought the fellowship of their brothers and sisters and joined with them in prayer?
Godparents:	They have.	**Godparents:**	They have.
Priest:	Have they been true to the word they have received and begun to walk in God's presence?	**Priest:**	As God is your witness, do you consider these candidates worthy to be admitted to the Sacraments of Christian Initiation?
Godparents:	They have.	**Godparents:**	We do.

The elected catechumens then sign their names in the *Book of the Elect*, showing they wish to receive the Sacraments of Initiation at the Easter Vigil. After a prayer over the elect, the bishop dismisses them. The faithful remain if the Liturgy of the Eucharist follows.

During Lent, the elect will celebrate three rites known as scrutinies. Along with the catechumens, all Catholics acknowledge their sins and pray for the strength to turn away from sin and to embrace Gospel living.

COMMUNION

THE GRACE OF BAPTISM

The rite of Baptism signifies two primary graces or effects of the sacrament that are both indicated by the immersion in water of the baptized. This action symbolizes both death to the old way of sin as well as a new birth in the Holy Spirit. These and other effects of the sacrament are explained in more detail in the following sections.

The Forgiveness of Sins

In Baptism, sin is overcome. Baptism forgives both Original Sin and personal sins.

Our understanding of God's plan also helps us understand sin as "an abuse of the freedom that God gives" us (*CCC* 387). Original Sin—the sin by which the first humans disobeyed God's commands, choosing to follow their own will rather than God's will—is an essential truth of our faith. However, only through the long journey of Revelation that culminates in the Death and Resurrection of Jesus Christ can Original Sin be fully understood. As the *Catechism* teaches, "We must know Christ as the source of grace in order to know Adam as the source of sin" (*CCC* 388).

The sin of Adam was to prefer himself over God. This was the action that led to his being scorned while also leading to the proliferation of sin throughout the world and in all the generations that have followed. The harmony of **original holiness and justice** in which humans had been created was destroyed. From then on humankind was deprived of spiritual control over the body, and tensions increased

original holiness and justice
The state of man and woman before sin. "From their friendship with God flowed the happiness of their existence in paradise" (*CCC* 384).

between men and women, causing their relationship to be marked by concupiscence and self-assertion. Harmony with creation became broken. Death entered the world.

Because Adam's sin permanently wounded our human nature, it is transmitted to all generations—we are born into this condition. Adam received original holiness and justice for him and all human nature. By his *personal sin* all human nature was then affected and took on a fallen state. St. Paul wrote: "Just as through one person sin entered the world, and through sin, death, and thus death came to all, inasmuch as all sinned" (Rom 5:12).

Although we share in Original Sin, it is not a sin that each one of us committed personally. While we have lost the gift of original holiness and justice, our entire human nature has not been corrupted. While we are subject to concupiscence—the inclination to sin—and ignorance, suffering, and death, the Sacrament of Baptism grants the life of Christ's grace, erases Original Sin, and turns us back to God, albeit with a weakened nature that is inclined to evil.

Through Original Sin, Satan acquired a certain domination over us. Life, complicated and filled with the consequences of Original Sin and all the personal sins of people who have lived ever since, is a constant battle with Satan and evil. Thankfully the doctrine of Original Sin is closely connected with the Redemption of Christ.

After the Fall of humankind, God did not abandon the human race. Rather, God immediately called to us again and proclaimed his ultimate and upcoming victory and his restoration of humanity after the Fall. God spoke to Satan about his temptation of Adam and Eve and about the Lord's victory that is to come. God said to the serpent:

> I will put enmity between you and the woman,
> and between your offspring and hers;
> He will strike at your head,
> while you strike at his heel. (Gn 3:15)

This passage from Genesis is called the *Protoevangelium* ("first gospel"). It is the first announcement of the Messiah and Redeemer and of his ultimate victory over sin and death. Christian tradition understands that this passage is an announcement of the "New Adam," who, through his obedience to the will of God the Father up to Death on a cross, makes amends for the sin of Adam. We also understand from the *Protoevangelium* that the woman referred to is the "New Eve," Mary the Mother of God.

Christ's sacrifice on the cross is the source of our Salvation. Not only are we purified from Original Sin at Baptism, but our personal sins are absolved as well. Paul's Letter to the Romans also reminds us, "For just as through the disobedience of one person the many were made sinners, so through the obedience of one the many will be made righteous" (Rom 5:19).

Becoming "a New Creature"

Baptism not only offers forgiveness for our sins, but it also makes each of us "a new creature," one who can share in the divine life. In the waters of Baptism, our fundamental identity is changed. We become members of Christ and co-heirs with him. Baptism makes us children of God and temples of the Holy Spirit. The Letter to the Galatians teaches:

> But when the fullness of time had come, God sent his Son, born of a woman, born under the law, to ransom those under the law, so that we might receive adoption. As proof that you are children, God sent the spirit of his Son into our hearts, crying out, "Abba, Father!" So you are no longer a slave but a child, and

if a child then also an heir, through God. (Gal 4:4–7)

As a new creation, baptized people receive sanctifying grace, the grace of justification. This refers to not only freedom from sin but also being made holy and new through Jesus Christ. This grace

- enables us to believe in God, hope in him, and love him through the theological virtues;
- gives us the power to live and act under the Holy Spirit and through the **Gifts of the Holy Spirit**;
- allows us to grow in goodness through the **moral virtues**.

In Baptism, God claims us as his own and makes his dwelling in us. The introduction to the *Christian Initiation of Adults* defines the communion of the baptized with the Blessed Trinity. The Scripture readings from the Sacrament of Baptism reinforce the idea that Baptism forms us in the likeness of Father, Son, and Holy Spirit. For example:

Our union with God the Father. "Through faith you are all children of God in Christ Jesus" (Gal 3:26). "You received a spirit of adoption, through which we cry, 'Abba, Father!' The Spirit itself bears witness with our spirit that we are children of God, and if children, then heirs, heirs of God and joint heirs with Christ" (Rom 8:15–17). "[There is] one body and one Spirit . . . one Lord, one faith, one baptism; one God and Father of all, who is over all and through all and in all" (Eph 4:4–6).

Our union with God the Son. "All of you who were baptized into Christ have clothed yourselves with Christ" (Gal 3:27). "I live, no longer I, but Christ lives in me" (Gal 2:20). "We have the mind of Christ" (1 Cor 2:16). Your bodies are members of Christ" (1 Cor 6:15). "You are Christ's body" (1 Cor 12:27).

Our union with God the Holy Spirit. "In one Spirit we were all baptized into one body, whether Jews or Greeks, slaves or free persons, and we were all given to drink of one Spirit" (1 Cor 12:13). "The love of God has been poured out into our hearts through the holy Spirit that has been given to us" (Rom 5:5).

As a way to symbolize new life in Christ, the celebrant puts on or over the newly baptized a white garment and says:

> See in this white garment the outward sign of your Christian dignity. With your family and friends to help you by word and example, bring that dignity unstained into the everlasting life of heaven.

The white garment also reminds us of the uniqueness of each person and to live a life worthy of our Christian identity.

Incorporated into the Church

Baptism makes us members of the Church, the Body of Christ. Becoming a member of the Church, we no longer belong to ourselves but to Jesus, who died and rose for us. The baptized person is called to be subject to others, to serve others in the communion of the Church, and to obey and follow Church leaders. Among the rights that come with membership in the Catholic Church are the following:

1. *The right to receive the other sacraments.* As the Church teaches, Catholics must be baptized before they can participate in any other sacraments of the Church.
2. *The right to be nourished with the Word of God.* All baptized Catholics

Gifts of the Holy Spirit
Outpourings of God's gifts to help us live a Christian life. The traditional seven Gifts of the Holy Spirit are wisdom, understanding, counsel, fortitude, knowledge, piety, and fear of the Lord.

moral virtues
Virtues acquired through human effort and with the help of God's grace.

have the right to hear the Word of God and have it explained to them according to the Church's teaching.

3. *The right to take part in and be sustained "by the other spiritual helps of the Church"* (*CCC* 1269). Baptized Catholics have the right to take part in parish activities and to benefit spiritually from religious education classes, parish support groups, retreats, special programs, and so forth.

Through Baptism, we share in the priesthood of Christ and in his prophetic and royal mission. It is through Baptism that we become members in the common priesthood of all believers. This membership also brings with it responsibilities. Catholics are to obey and submit to Church leaders regarding faith and morals. A particular application is for the baptized to follow the **Precepts of the Church.**

Unity with Other Christians

Baptism strengthens the opportunity for unity among all Christians, including those not yet in full communion with the Catholic Church.

Precepts of the Church
Basic rules that bind Catholics who belong to Christ's Body.

Baptism acquires for them a certain, although imperfect, communion with the Catholic Church.

The Catholic Church recognizes most Christian Baptisms as valid. When a member of a mainline Christian denomination becomes Catholic, he or she is not baptized again. Baptism is to be given only once. Catholic creeds state this: "We believe in one baptism for the forgiveness of sins."

The Seal of Eternal Life

Baptism seals Christians with an indelible spiritual mark or character that cannot be repealed. Even sin cannot erase the mark, though sin can prevent a baptized person from gaining the rewards of Salvation.

The sacramental character of Baptism readies Christians for religious worship. It requires us to participate in the liturgy and to live out our baptismal priesthood through the witness of living a holy life and loving others. If we "keep the seal" and remain faithful until the end, we can be sure that God will recognize us and welcome us into his Kingdom while we are on earth and in body and spirit after our death.

For Review

1. What are the two primary graces or effects of the Sacrament of Baptism?
2. Define *original holiness and justice.*
3. What are the effects of Original Sin today?
4. What is the message of the *Protoevangelium*?
5. Name the benefits of the grace of justification.
6. Name three rights that come with membership in the Catholic Church.
7. True or false: The seal of eternal life granted at Baptism is permanent. Explain your answer.

For Reflection

- Reread the Scripture passages on page 81. Which passage speaks most to you about how you are formed in God's image?

- Explain why each of the boldfaced terms is important: **We believe** in **one baptism** for the **forgiveness of sins**.

TRANSFORMATION

LOVING GOD MORE DEEPLY

As mentioned, one of the effects of Baptism is that, through the sacrament, the Blessed Trinity offers the sanctifying grace of justification, which enables us to believe in God more deeply, to hope in him, and to love him through the theological virtues. The *Catechism of the Catholic Church* teaches that as people "incorporated into Christ by Baptism, Christians are 'dead to sin and alive to God in Christ Jesus' and so participate in the life of the Risen Lord" (*CCC* 1694, quoting Romans 6:11). Pope Benedict XVI chose the theological virtues of charity (love) and hope as the subjects of his first two encyclicals. Gaining an understanding of the virtues is helpful in living a Christian life. St. Gregory of Nyssa put it this way: "The goal of a virtuous life is to become like God." Putting virtues into practice is an effective way to avoid poor choices and sinfulness.

Virtues acquired by human efforts are known as moral or human virtues. Four of these virtues form the hinge that connects all the others. These cardinal virtues are prudence, justice, fortitude, and temperance. Human virtues are acquired "by education, by deliberate acts and by a perseverance ever-renewed in repeated efforts [and] are purified and elevated by divine grace" (*CCC* 1810). These human virtues have their roots in the theological virtues, the virtues directly related to God. The theological virtues are the foundation of a Christian's moral life. These are not gained by our efforts. They are infused into our souls to make us capable of choosing goodness over sin, of choosing right from wrong, and of meriting eternal life. More information about the theological virtues follows.

Faith

Faith is the theological virtue by which we believe in God, all that he has said, and all that the Church teaches. Faith brings us into personal relationship with Jesus Christ and helps us believe in his Gospel of Salvation. Faith begins our life in union with the Blessed Trinity. However, only professing one's faith is not enough. As the Letter of James teaches, "For just as a body without a spirit is dead, so also faith without works is dead" (Jas 2:26).

"Living the faith" often becomes more difficult with age. The teenage and young-adult years can be especially challenging as peers often put public worship (e.g., participating in Sunday Mass) on the back burner while at the same time being exposed to immoral behaviors forbidden by the Ten Commandments (e.g., stealing, lying, promiscuity).

THE CARDINAL VIRTUES

Read these descriptions of the four cardinal virtues. All other virtues come from these hinge virtues. Then write a "Prayer for Living a Virtuous Life" that incorporates each of the four virtues.

Prudence
The intelligent are not those who have studied the sayings and writings of the wise men of old, but those whose soul is intelligent, who can judge what is good and what is evil; they avoid what is evil and harms the soul and intelligently care for and practice what is good and profits the world, greatly thanking God.
　　—St. Anthony of Egypt

Justice
The bread you store up belongs to the hungry; the cloak that lies in your chest belongs to the naked; the gold that you have hidden in the ground belongs to the poor.
　　　　　　—St. Basil

Fortitude
When did it ever happen that a person had confidence in God and was lost?
　　　　　　—St. Basil

Temperance
Drunkenness is the ruin of reason. It is premature old age. It is temporary death.
　　—St. Alphonsus Liguori

But many other teens do live their faith in bold ways. Consider the "Franciscan Mystery Players," the name for several acting troupes of teenagers who perform, free of charge, biblical stories and events like the Way of the Cross, the birth of Jesus, and the healing miracles of Jesus. One performer, Samantha Chamberlain of Denver, said, "This is a chance to show that teenagers have the capacity to be faithful and to be good, you know?" Working with people of the Navajo Nation in Arizona as part of a mission trip with teens from her home diocese of Joliet, Illinois, helped sixteen-year-old Kaitlyn Hull connect faith with service as she sat alongside Navajos during a Mass. She said, "I learned you can be close to someone no matter where you live. Truly, I believe this is what God planned—for each of us to acknowledge our mission and do something to make the world a better place with the tools and resources we have been given."

Hope

In *Spe Salvi* ("Saved by Hope"), Pope Benedict XVI wrote of the dialogue that takes place between parents and the celebrant at their infant's Baptism. When they are asked what they want from the Church and respond "faith," they expect that to mean that their child will gain eternal life through the sacrament. The Pope addressed how the virtue of hope is involved here:

To imagine ourselves outside the temporality that imprisons us and in some way to sense that eternity is not an unending succession of days in the calendar, but something more like the supreme moment of satisfaction, in which totality embraces us and we embrace totality—this we can only attempt. It would be like

plunging into the ocean of infinite love, a moment in which time—the before and after—no longer exists. We can only attempt to grasp the idea that such a moment is life in the full sense, a plunging ever anew into the vastness of being, in which we are simply overwhelmed with joy. This is how Jesus expresses it in Saint John's Gospel: "I will see you again and your hearts will rejoice, and no one will take your joy from you" (16:22). We must think along these lines if we want to understand the object of Christian hope, to understand what it is that our faith, our being with Christ, leads us to expect. (*Spe Salvi* 12)

Hope is the virtue by which we desire happiness and the Kingdom of God. This is a desire written on our hearts. God calls each of us to seek him so as to find life and happiness. Hope is the virtue in which we place our trust in Christ and his promises. The foundation of our hope is the Paschal Mystery of Jesus. In every circumstance in life, we must live in hope to enjoy the joy of Heaven. No matter what despairs and sufferings we face, we must never cease in our hope. Christians from all ages knew this. St. Gemma Galgani said: "If I saw the gates of hell open and I stood on the brink of the abyss, I should not despair, I should not lose hope of mercy, because I should trust in Thee, my God."

Unfortunately many people today—including teenagers—live without hope. The number of teenagers who attempt and commit suicide is at a staggering high. Suicide is the third-leading cause of death among teens (behind auto accidents and homicides). Stressful life events are among the factors leading to suicide; for example, failure at school, breakup with a boyfriend or girlfriend, divorce, or death of a loved one. In these situations where hope is absent, Jesus calls to us. He says to us with gentleness and compassion,

> "Come to me, all you who labor and are burdened, and I will give you rest. Take my yoke upon you and learn from me, for I am meek and humble of heart; and you will find rest for your selves. For my yoke is easy, and my burden light." (Mt 11:28–30)

Charity

Jesus made charity, or love, the New Commandment. He said: "As the Father loves me, so I also love you. Remain in my love. . . . This is my commandment: love one another as I love you" (Jn 15:9, 12).

Pope Benedict, in *Deus Caritas Est* ("God Is Love"), called our belief in the love that God has for us the "fundamental decision of our life." The Christian life, begun at Baptism, is rooted completely in our love for God and neighbor. The Pope also wrote:

> No longer is it a question, then, of a "commandment" imposed from without and calling for the impossible, but rather of a freely-bestowed experience of love from within, a love which by its very nature must then be shared with others. (*Deus Caritas Est* 18)

Love is the greatest of all the virtues. Charity perfects our ability to love others and raises it to the supernatural perfection of divine love. In February 2008, a teenager was killed when his motorcycle collided with another motorcycle in Bakersfield, California. The boy, fifteen-year-old Taylor LaKamp, was remembered by an overflow crowd of his friends and classmates as someone who was happy, friendly, and well-liked by everyone. The priest presiding at his funeral reminded everyone to pray for the boy Taylor collided with, who was not seriously injured, and to not condemn him. Love in such dire situations seems impossible, except in Christ. Fr. Sam Ward described the overcast and rainy day as an expression of how everyone at the funeral was feeling. "The rain is tears from heaven, but the light of Christ will light up the world," he said.

Baptism is the essential sacrament because it "clothes" us with Christ (see Galatians 3:27). Jesus lives in us and permeates our entire selves. Another way to describe a person who has been baptized is to say he or she is "configured" to Christ. This means that through the baptized person we can recognize Jesus and grow to know him better. Others can do the same with us.

More on Living the Sacrament of Baptism

The graces or effects of Baptism remain stagnant unless we put them to use. In the Letter to the Ephesians, St. Paul implored the faithful to "be imitators of God, as beloved children, and live in love, as Christ loved us and handed himself over for us as a sacrificial offering to God for a fragrant aroma" (Eph 5:1–2). The Church offers several reminders of our Baptism both in its liturgies and in its practices. As Catholics, we are also called to prayerful reflection on the meaning of Baptism.

Some of the reminders occur in the Church's liturgy, even as a person enters the church. Churches (and some homes) have fonts near the entrances. Both on our way inside the church and on the way out, we bless ourselves with holy water while making the Sign of the

sacramental

A sacred sign (for example, objects, places, and actions) that resemble the sacraments. Through the prayers of the Church, spiritual effects are signified and obtained.

Cross. This particular **sacramental** reminds us of our unity with the Blessed Trinity. More reminders are in the liturgy itself:

- *Reading of the creation account* at the Easter Vigil. The celebration of new life in Christ begins with a reading from the creation account. Creation is the foundation of all of God's saving plans. When God saw everything he created, he found it very good.
- *Blessing of the baptismal water* at Baptism. The Church remembers the events of Salvation History that prefigure the mystery of Baptism. The celebrant prays:

  Father, you give us grace through sacramental signs,
  which tell us of the wonders of your unseen power.
  In Baptism we use your gift of water,
  which you have made a rich symbol of the grace you give us in this sacrament.
  (*Roman Missal*, Easter Vigil 42, Blessing of Water)

- *Renewal of the baptismal promises at the Easter Vigil.* "For all the baptized, children or adults, faith must grow after Baptism.

For this reason the Church celebrates each year at the Easter Vigil the renewal of the baptismal promises." (*CCC* 1254)

Besides the liturgy, we are reminded of Baptism in our personal prayer life. Contemplative prayer is a "gaze of faith" on Jesus. This form of silent prayer helps us gain real union with the prayer of Christ. In this same way, Catholics are encouraged to contemplate the mystery of Baptism, especially as it helps us follow Christ and grow closer to him. Through the power of the Holy Spirit and with our participation in the sacraments, we take part in Christ's Passion and in his Resurrection by being born to a new life.

Baptism confers sanctifying grace, the grace of justification. This grace has the power to cleanse us from our sins and to grow in holiness and goodness. Baptism is our first step on the way of the cross. This course, taken by Christ, is our way to perfection. The graces conferred on us at Baptism give us the strength to undertake this difficult yet ultimately rewarding journey that will bring us peace, joy, and eternal life. 🔵

For Review

1. Name the theological virtues.
2. How did Pope Benedict XVI say the virtues of hope and faith are related in the questioning that takes place between celebrant and candidate at Baptism?
3. What did the Pope call the "fundamental decision of our life"?
4. What are three reminders of the Sacrament of Baptism at the Easter Vigil?
5. What is the power of the grace of justification at Baptism?

For Reflection

- When we are in Heaven, which two of the theological virtues will be unnecessary? Which one will last into eternity? Explain.

- How do you and your peers "live the faith" practically?

- Contemplate on the mystery of Baptism. Write or share one or your reflections.

CHAPTER QUICK VIEW

Main Ideas

- Our "no" to sin and Satan in the Sacrament of Baptism is a statement against today's popular sinful culture. (pp. 67-68)

- Though the sacrament takes its name from a Greek word that means "to plunge" or "immerse," Baptism is also called "the washing of regeneration and renewal by the Holy Spirit" and "enlightenment." (p. 69)

- The Old Testament prefigures Baptism in several places, including the creation stories, the story of Noah's ark, and God's saving plan to rescue Moses and the Israelites. (pp. 69-70)

- Jesus was baptized himself as a way to teach his disciples the primacy of Baptism. (p. 70)

- Jesus' baptism with water prefigured his baptism in blood, which occurred at his Death on the cross. (p. 70)

- Our own Baptism is connected with the Paschal Mystery of Christ. (p. 71)

- Baptism has always been the way to membership in the Church. (p. 71)

- The catechumenate is an initiation journey of several stages including the precatechumenate; catechumenate; purification, enlightenment or illumination; and mystagogia. (pp. 71-72)

- Anyone not baptized is eligible for Baptism; Baptism is necessary for Salvation. (p. 74)

- God is not bound by this sacrament, and in fact, there are three examples of how a person could be saved without a Baptism of water: Baptism of blood, Baptism of desire, and the case of infants who die without Baptism. (p. 75)

- Baptism is a sacrament of faith and is properly celebrated with other members of the Church. (p. 75)

- The essential rite for the Sacrament of Baptism is the immersion or the pouring of water three times over the candidate while the celebrant says: "I baptize you in the name of the Father, and of the Son, and of the Holy Spirit. (pp. 76-77)

- The catechumenate today includes the Rite of Acceptance and Rite of Election. (p. 78)

- The primary graces or effects of the Sacrament of Baptism are both indicated by the immersion in water: forgiveness of sins and new birth in the Holy Spirit. (p. 79)

- Other graces of the sacrament are incorporation into the Church, unity with other Christians, and the granting of the seal of eternal life. (pp. 80-82)

- The gift of the sanctifying grace of justification infuses the baptized with the theological virtues. (p. 83)

- In the liturgy and through prayerful reflection, we are reminded of the graces of the Sacrament of Baptism. (p. 86)

Famous Catholics and the Sacraments:

THOMAS MERTON

Thomas Merton was born in France in 1915. His mother died when he was six, and his grandmother and father tried to bring a religious dimension to his life. At first, Thomas was brought up as a Protestant, but Sunday school did not particularly impress him. His father, a great spiritual influence on him, died of a brain tumor when Tom was sixteen. This was a huge loss to Tom, who grieved by overindulging in alcohol, cigarettes, and promiscuous sex.

Tom later wrote that his religious conversion began when he started reading poet William Blake. "Through Blake I would one day come, in a round-about way, to the only true Church, and to the One Living God, through His Son, Jesus Christ."

One night in Rome, Tom had a profoundly religious experience, which he described in the following way:

> I was in my room. It was night. The light was on. Suddenly it seemed to me that Father, who had now been dead more than a year, was there with me. The sense of his presence was as vivid and as real and as startling as if he had touched my arm or spoken to me. The whole thing passed in a flash, but in that flash, instantly, I was overwhelmed with a sudden and profound insight into the misery and corruption of my own soul, and I was pierced deeply with a light that made me realize something of the condition I was in, and I was filled with horror at what I saw, and my whole being rose up in revolt against what was within me, and my soul desired escape and liberation and freedom from all this with an intensity and an urgency unlike anything I had ever known before. And now I think for the first time in my whole life I really began to pray . . . praying out of the very roots of my life and of my being, and praying to the God I had never known, to reach down towards me out of His

darkness. . . . There were a lot of tears connected with this, and they did me good.

After that, Tom prayed occasionally and began to read the Bible. But his conversion did not happen instantaneously. Instead, he worked as a barker at a pornographic show at the World's Fair in Chicago. He spent the rest of the summer going to burlesque shows, drinking excessively, and smoking thirty to forty cigarettes a day.

Tom continued his wild ways while at Cambridge University in England. He "ran up bills he could not afford to pay, threw a brick through a shop window, got arrested for riding on the running-board of a car, cut lectures, and climbed in and out of his own and other colleges at night and helped various girls to do the same." Eventually, he got a girl "into trouble," and there was a lawsuit, which was settled out of court. The girl gave birth to a boy, but later both of them died during the London air raids of World War II.

In disgrace, Tom went to America, where he enrolled at Columbia University in New York. There, he demonstrated for and pursued Communism for a brief time, but soon became disenchanted with it. During his second year at Columbia, he became active in a fraternity (especially the drinking parties) and played jazz on the piano as often as possible. When two of his friends and guardians died unexpectedly, Tom suffered a severe depression, dizzy spells, and bouts of vertigo. Once again he was an orphan.

One day, Tom came across a copy of *The Spirit of Medieval Philosophy* by Etienne Gilson. In his reading, he discovered a new concept of God that made sense to him. God was the loving Father for whom he was looking. His friends at Columbia urged him to read St. Augustine's *Confessions* and *The Imitation of Christ* by Thomas à Kempis. Although the books impressed him, he did nothing about his own spiritual life. Instead, he pursued his master's degree, writing a thesis on "Nature and Art in William Blake." Merton was intrigued by Blake's belief that art helps transform people's passions into love and virtue in union with God. Little did Tom know, God was working within him.

> Suddenly, I could bear it no longer. . . . I got into my raincoat, and started down the stairs. I went out into the street. I crossed over and went along by the gray wooden fence, towards Broadway, in the light rain.
>
> And then everything inside me began to sing. . . . I had nine blocks to walk [to the brick church]. I stood in the doorway and rang the bell and waited. . . . Then I saw Father Ford coming around the corner. . . . I went to meet him and said: "Father, may I speak to you about something?"
>
> "Yes," he said, looking up, surprised. "Yes, sure, come into the house."
>
> We sat in the little parlor by the door. And I said: "Father, I want to become a Catholic."

Thomas was baptized on November 16, 1938, and received his First Communion. At last he had found his true identity as a child of God. But even this realization did not change him overnight. He still got drunk and had sexual affairs with women. Only gradually did the irresistible lure of God's love begin to change him. He became more and more drawn to spiritual reading and contemplative prayer. Three years later, he entered the Abbey of Our Lady of Gethsemani near Bardstown, Kentucky, to become a Trappist priest.

As a monk, Merton wrote many books on spirituality and contemplation, including *The Seven Storey Mountain*, the story of his conversion, which became a bestseller. For the rest of his life, he worked tirelessly to promote understanding between Catholics and Eastern religions (interreligious dialogue) and for world peace. He died suddenly in 1968 while at a conference in Bangkok, Thailand.

- Read Merton's *The Seven Storey Mountain* or another one of his books. Report on the importance Baptism had on his subsequent life.
- Find out more about Merton's love of ecumenism and desire to embrace the best in both Catholic and Eastern spirituality.
- Share three quotations of Thomas Merton on lifelong faith, religious conversion, and the importance of contemplative prayer.

THOMAS MERTON

TERMS, PEOPLE, PLACES

Provide each of the following definitions and answer the questions. Use complete sentences.

1. Define the **catechumenate**. Name and explain the primary steps for this initiation process.
2. Define the **scrutinies**. What is the purpose of the scrutinies for the elect? What effect do the scrutinies have on the rest of the faithful?
3. Define **martyr**. What is the connection between martyrs and the Baptism of blood?
4. Define the Baptism of desire. Does the Baptism of desire apply to infants who die before Baptism?
5. Define **original holiness and justice**. How is the *Protoevangelium* related to this term?

ONGOING ASSIGNMENTS

As you cover the material in this chapter, choose and complete at least three of these assignments.

1. Search for and read the homily of Pope Benedict XVI delivered on January 8, 2006, the Feast of the Baptism of the Lord, the day he baptized ten infants in the Sistine Chapel. What did the Pope say about the meaning of the Sacrament of Baptism?

2. Read the *Catholic Encyclopedia* article on exorcism: http://www.newadvent.org/cathen/05709a.htm. Report on the difference between exorcisms in the Sacrament of Baptism and other Church-sanctioned exorcisms.

3. St. Thomas Aquinas wrote: "There is nothing to prevent human nature's being raised up to something greater, even after sin; God permits evil in order to draw forth some greater good." Do you agree or disagree with St. Thomas Aquinas's opinion on why God permits evil? Explain.

4. Interview a catechist for a local parish's RCIA team about the rewards and challenges of the process. Write a summary of your interview.

5. Make a list of all the ways we use water. Write a one-page report explaining why you think the Church uses blessed water as an important sign and symbol in her liturgy of Baptism. Then make something creative (a painting, drawing, 3-D sculpture, fountain, multimedia show, etc.) showing how water is a strong symbol of life. Be prepared to share your creation at the last class session for Chapter 3.

6. Make a list of all the ways we use salt. Explain why you think the Church, for many centuries, used blessed salt in its liturgy of Baptism.

7. Who are your godparents? Interview your parents to find out why they chose these people for this role. Write a letter to your godparents telling them who you are now as an adolescent. Thank them for their role in your spiritual life. Tell them briefly about your journey of faith and what being Catholic means to you.

8. Interview your parents. Ask them to describe the day of your Baptism. Also ask why they decided to have you baptized. Find out when and where the Baptism took place, who the minister was, and who was present at your Baptism. Write a one-page report summarizing your findings.

9. Read the four accounts of the baptism of Jesus (Matthew 3:13–17; Mark 1:9–11; Luke 3:21–22; John 1:31–34). Write a short essay in which you describe the similarities among the Gospels, the differences among them, and why you think each Gospel writer included or did not include certain details.

10. Illustrate a sentence or phrase from one of the Easter Vigil readings that especially speaks to you about the meaning of Baptism. Bring your picture or painting to share with the class.

11. Attend a Baptism in your parish church. Then write a poem or a short report about your impressions of the ritual.

12. Find architectural details or photos of famous baptisteries throughout history, or visit the baptistery in your church and record its dimensions as accurately as possible. Then prepare to scale a floor plan or a 3-D model of the baptistery. Explain your floor plan or model to the class. How does the architecture reflect beliefs about Baptism?

13. Many students of genealogy find information about their ancestors from old Baptism registers found in churches. If you know the date and place of Baptism for one of your ancestors, write to the church via the Internet and ask for a duplicate baptismal certificate. (Offer to pay for postage and any other expenses.) If you do not know the date and place of Baptism for someone in your family, arrange with your parish to see the Baptism register. Alternative: Find the baptismal date and record of an important person in your town or city.

PRAYER SERVICE

Theme: Renewal of Baptismal Promises

Leader: Dear friends, through the Paschal Mystery we have been buried with Christ in Baptism, so that we may rise with him to a new life. Now let us renew the promises we made in Baptism, when we rejected Satan and his works, and promised to serve God faithfully in his holy Catholic Church.

Reader 1: Do you reject Satan?

All: I do.

Reader 2: And all his works?

All: I do.

Reader 3: And all his empty show?

All: I do.

Reader 4: Do you renounce sin, so as to live in the freedom of God's children?

All: I do.

Reader 5: Do you renounce the lure of evil, so that sin may have no mastery over you?

All: I do.

Reader 6: Do you reject Satan, the author and prince of sin?

All: I do.

Reader 7: Do you believe in God, the Father almighty, Creator of heaven and earth?

All: I do.

Reader 8: Do you believe in Jesus Christ, his only Son, our Lord, who was born of the Virgin Mary, suffered death and was buried, rose again from the dead and is seated at the right hand of the Father?

All: I do.

Reader 9: Do you believe in the Holy Spirit, the holy Catholic Church, the communion of saints, the forgiveness of sins, the resurrection of the body, and life everlasting?

All: I do.

Leader: And may almighty God, the Father of our Lord Jesus Christ, who has given us new birth by water and the Holy Spirit and bestowed on us forgiveness of our sins, keep us by his grace, in Christ Jesus our Lord, for eternal life.

All: Amen.

(From *Roman Missal*, Easter Vigil 55, Renewal of Baptismal Promises)

Leader: Let us spend several moments in silence, praying that Christ may help us remain faithful to our baptismal promises and continue to grow in the virtues.

(Students pray silently their "Prayer for Living a Virtuous Life" from The Cardinal Virtues activity, page 84.)

Leader: We are God's sons and daughters, and so we have the courage to pray,

All: Our Father . . .

The Sacrament
of Confirmation

The Gift of Speech

The grace of the Sacrament of Confirmation—especially the gift of the Holy Spirit—is witnessed over time in many visible fruits.

Understanding the Sacrament of Confirmation

Confirmation is the "sacrament of the Holy Spirit"; the Spirit's presence with the Chosen People, Jesus Christ, and the Church has been present since the beginning.

Celebrating the Sacrament of Confirmation

Other prayers and rituals that highlight the meaning of the sacrament surround the essential rite of Confirmation—the laying on of hands, an anointing with Sacred Chrism, and the words "Be sealed with the Gift of the Holy Spirit."

The Grace of Confirmation

The grace, or effect, of Confirmation is the special outpouring of the Holy Spirit; the sacrament is intimately connected with Baptism and increases and deepens baptismal grace.

Confirmation Confers a New Character

The indelible character we receive at Confirmation helps us spread and defend the faith as witnesses of Christ.

THE GIFT OF SPEECH

As a bishop begins the essential rite of the Sacrament of Confirmation—the laying on of hands, the anointing with Sacred Chrism, and the words "Be sealed with the Gift of the Holy Spirit"—he faces the candidates and the rest of the gathered faithful and prays:

My dear friends:

in Baptism God our Father gave the new birth of eternal life
to his chosen sons and daughters.
Let us pray to our Father
that he will pour out the Holy Spirit
to strengthen his sons and daughters with his gifts
and anoint them to be more like Christ the Son of God.

After a short time of silent prayer, the bishop alone asks God the Father, through his Son, Jesus Christ, to send the Holy Spirit to help and guide the candidates and to "Give them the spirit of wisdom and understanding, the spirit of right judgment and courage, the spirit of knowledge and reverence . . . fill them with the spirit of wonder and awe in your presence" (quotations are from the *Rite of Confirmation* 41, 42).

Newly given gifts are often not used on the spot. Think of gifts received on Christmas morning. They may be opened before breakfast but then shelved until the holiday festivities are over. But sure enough, any valuable gift will eventually find use. The grace of the Sacrament of Confirmation—especially the gift of the Holy Spirit—is like that. Given time, the evidence of the Spirit's power and gift can be dramatic.

Witness the story of Soeren Palumbo, a student at the University of Notre Dame. When Soeren—a Catholic who was confirmed at St. Theresa Church in Palatine, Illinois, in 2003—was a senior at Fremd High School in Palatine in 2007, he gave the speech of a lifetime to his peers at a student assembly.

Palumbo spoke out against the use of the word "retard" as teens and adults use it disrespectfully. Soeren's younger sister Olivia has an intellectual disability, and Soeren told the audience that "your mockery of them, it's

Olivia and Soeren Palumbo

nothing but another form of hatred." He also explained in his speech:

So why am I doing this? Why do I risk being misunderstood and resented by this school's student body and staff? I'm doing this because I know how much you can learn from people, from all people, even—no, not even, especially—the mentally handicapped.

I know this because every morning I wake up and I come downstairs and I sit across from my sister, quietly eating her Cheerios. And as I sit down, she sets her spoon down on the table and she looks at me. Her strawberry blonde hair hanging over her freckled face almost completely hides the question mark–shaped scar above her ear from her brain surgery two years ago.

She looks at me, and she smiles . . . it lights up her face. Her front two teeth are faintly stained from the years of intense epilepsy medication, but I don't notice that anymore. I lean over to her and say, "Good morning, Olivia." She stares at me for a moment and says quickly, "Good morning Soeren," and goes back to her Cheerios.

. . . She finishes her Cheerios and grabs her favorite blue backpack and waits for her bus driver, Miss Debbie, who like clockwork arrives at our house at exactly 7 o'clock each morning. She gives me a quick hug goodbye and runs excitedly to the bus, ecstatic for another day of school.

And I watch the bus disappear around the turn, and I can't help but remember the jokes. The short bus. The retard rocket. No matter what she does, no matter how much she loves those around her, she will always be the butt of some immature kid's joke. She will always be the butt of some mature kid's joke. She will always be the butt of some adult's joke.

By no fault of her own, she will spend her entire life being stared at and judged. Despite the fact that she will never hate, never judge, never make fun of, never hurt, she will never be accepted. That's why I'm doing this. I'm doing this because I don't think you understand how much you hurt others when you hate.

The student body and staff didn't misunderstand or resent Soeren. Instead they gave him a standing ovation. A YouTube broadcast of his speech attracted attention worldwide. The local television news and newspaper came to interview him about the speech. Months afterward, the speech was still being talked about.

His mom, Kristen Palumbo, said, "Soeren loves his sister. He's protective of her. It's been a good thing. She is a gift." Of the feeling he got from giving the speech, Soeren recalled, "It was such a rush. I was crying at the end of it. But to look out and see everyone stand up and the other people wiping their eyes . . . to see all the warm acceptance that came with it was just out of this world."

The Holy Spirit brings candidates for Confirmation into conformity with Christ and enables them to spread Christ's presence to all. The Holy Spirit is the source of holiness and love in the Church, and the bond of unity among all Christians. Confirmation has been called the "sacrament of the Holy Spirit." This chapter not only explores more of the effects of the sacrament, but also traces the origins of Confirmation, how it is celebrated, and ways the gift of the Holy Spirit and the particular seven Gifts of the Spirit transform those who receive it in ways that parallel the experience of Soeren Palumbo.

For Reflection

- How do you think you would have felt if you were Soeren Palumbo prior to giving his speech?
- When did an occasion inspire you to do something that at first you didn't think you could do?

UNDERSTANDING THE SACRAMENT OF CONFIRMATION

At Baptism, we are reborn as sons and daughters of God and called to publicly profess the faith we have received from the Church. At Confirmation we are

> more perfectly bound to the Church and are endowed with the special strength of the holy Spirit. Hence, as true witnesses of Christ, [we] are more strictly obliged to both spread and to defend the faith by word and deed. (*Lumen Gentium* 11)

The Spirit's connection with God's Chosen People and the promised Messiah has been present from the beginning. Since Old Testament times, the Spirit of the Lord has been associated with the hoped-for Messiah and his saving mission. As we are disciples of Christ and intimately united with him through Baptism, the Holy Spirit perfects our mission to share the Good News of Jesus with all.

The Book of Isaiah foretold that the Spirit would rest on the Messiah. The source of the traditional Gifts of the Holy Spirit is Isaiah 11:2. The Spirit's descent upon Jesus at his Baptism (see Luke 4:16–22) reminds us of the words of the prophet known as Third Isaiah and quoted by Christ in reference to his own mission:

> The spirit of the Lord God is upon me,
>> because the Lord has anointed me.
> He has sent me to bring glad tidings to the lowly,
>> to heal the brokenhearted,
> To proclaim liberty to the captives
>> and release to the prisoners.
> (Is 61:1)

The Spirit that Jesus received at his own baptism was not to be limited only to him, but communicated to all who heard and accepted his message. This fulfilled the words of the prophet Ezekiel: "I will give you a new heart and place a new spirit within you, taking from your bodies your stony hearts and giving you natural hearts" (Ez 36:26). Jesus promised the outpouring of the Holy Spirit several times in his ministry:

- Preaching to his disciples about their facing persecution, he said: "When they take you before synagogues and before rulers and authorities, do not worry about how or what your defense will be or about what you are to say. For the holy Spirit will teach you at that moment what you should say" (Lk 12:11–12).
- In answering the question of the Pharisee Nicodemus about how a person who is grown can be "born again," Jesus said: "The wind blows where it wills, and you can hear the sound it makes, but you do not know where it comes from or where it goes; so it is with everyone who is born of the Spirit" (Jn 3:8).
- On the last day of the **Feast of Tabernacles,** Jesus stood up and preached: "Let anyone who thirsts come to me and drink. Whoever believes in me, as scripture says: 'Rivers of living water will flow from within him'" (Jn 7:37–38). This predicted that

The Sukkot ceremony

Feast of Tabernacles

Also known as the Sukkot or Feast of Booths, the Feast of Tabernacles begins five days after Yom Kippur and lasts for eight days. It commemorates the forty years the Jews spent in the desert when they had to protect themselves by constructing huts or booths.

Advocate

A name for the Holy Spirit. The Advocate is the "Paraclete" or "helper" who will live in us and guide us to truth.

laying on of hands

A gesture that is a main rite and origin of the Sacrament of Confirmation. Acts 19:1-6 tells the story of a new group of disciples who, after being baptized, received the Holy Spirit when St. Paul laid hands on them.

the Holy Spirit that Jesus had received would also be given to his followers after his Resurrection.

- At the Last Supper, Jesus clearly promised he would send the Holy Spirit, his **Advocate**, after he returned to the Father. "If I do not go, the Advocate will not come to you. But if I go, I will send him to you" (Jn 16:7). The Spirit provides us with clarity and truth about the reality of sin, the meaning of Jesus' Death, and the defeat of Satan. "But when he comes, the Spirit of truth, he will guide you to all truth. He will not speak on his own, but he will speak what he hears, and will declare to you the things that are coming" (Jn 16:13).

The Holy Spirit came to the Apostles on Pentecost. Once the Spirit filled them, the effect was permanent. This Advocate was with them always. He "remains with you, and will be in you" (Jn 14:17). The Holy Spirit helped the Apostles bear true witness to Jesus (see John 15:26), even in times of persecution. "You will receive power when the holy Spirit comes upon you, and you will be my witnesses in Jerusalem, throughout Judea and Samaria, and to the ends of the earth" (Acts 1:8).

Origins of the Sacrament of Confirmation

From the time of Pentecost, the Apostles imparted on the newly baptized the gift of the Spirit by the laying on of hands. This completed the grace of Baptism and is "rightly recognized by the Catholic tradition as the origin of the sacrament of Confirmation, which in a certain way

perpetuates the grace of Pentecost in the Church" (*CCC* 1288, quoting Pope Paul VI).

The **laying on of hands** is an ancient ritual gesture used in Confirmation that symbolizes the giving of the Father's own Spirit to the recipient. When the bishop extends his hands over or imposes his hands on candidates for Confirmation, many similar events from Scripture are recalled. For example, Jacob blessed his grandsons Ephraim and Manasseh and gave them two portions of the Promised Land (see Genesis 48:14). Moses blessed Joshua as he commissioned him to lead the people into the Promised Land (see Numbers 27:18, 23). And, in similar fashion, Jesus offered blessings through a laying on of hands. For example:

And people were bringing children to [Jesus] that he might touch them, but the disciples rebuked them. When Jesus saw this he became indignant and said to them, "Let the children come to me; do not prevent them, for the kingdom of God belongs to such as these. Amen, I say to you, whoever does not accept the kingdom of God like a child will not enter it." Then he embraced them and blessed them, placing his hands on them. (Mk 10:13–16)

The Letter to the Hebrews (see Hebrews 6:2) describes the laying on of hands as one of the basic teachings of the Apostles. When the Apostles laid their hands on the newly baptized, they were giving a divine blessing and imparting the gift of the Holy Spirit. The same thing happens to us in Confirmation today. We receive the bishop's confirmation that the Holy Spirit resides in us and acts within us.

Very early on, an anointing with perfumed oil called chrism was added to the laying on of hands. The Old Testament often mentions the use of oil. Among the ancient Israelites (as well as peoples of other cultures), olive oil was a sign of abundance and joy. Besides being used in cooking and in providing light, oil had many other uses as well: It cleansed the body (as in anointings before and after a bath); it limbered muscles (as in anointings of wrestlers and other athletes); it helped with healing (as in anointings used to soothe bruises, wounds, and dry skin); and it beautified (as in anointings that gave radiance to the skin).

In religious uses, anointing with oil had the purpose of consecration. Among the objects anointed in the Old Testament were the Ark of the Covenant, the tent of meeting, and the furniture of the tent (see Exodus 30:22–33). Among the people anointed were priests and kings. For example, when God selected David to be king of Israel, the prophet Samuel anointed him. "Then Samuel, with the horn of oil in hand, anointed [David] in the midst of his brothers; and from that day on, the spirit of the Lord rushed upon David" (1 Sam 16:13).

To be chosen by God for a particular mission was to be God's "anointed one." The Messiah, in particular, is God's "anointed one." The name *Christ* means "anointed one" and is used to show that Jesus is the Messiah.

Sacred Chrism, the oil used in Confirmation, takes its name from Christ. Chrism is traditionally a mixture of olive oil (which by its rich and abundant nature symbolizes the Spirit's overflowing outpouring of grace) and balsam (a fragrant perfume—sometimes referred to as "the balm of Gilead"—used in healing and preservation from corruption). The balsam symbolizes the sweet "odor" of Christianity, found in virtuous living and imitating Christ (see 2 Corinthians 2:15). Those who are anointed with Sacred Chrism have a new identity—that of Christians. All anointed followers of Jesus share in his mission and have the special duty of proclaiming his Gospel to the world. **Chrismation** is the name the Eastern Church uses for the Sacrament of Confirmation (cf. *CCC* 1289).

Two Traditions of the Sacrament Emerge

In the first centuries, Confirmation was generally part of one single celebration with Baptism. St. Cyprian called it a "double sacrament." Because the original minister of the sacrament is a bishop, logistics was among several issues that led to the separate celebrations of Baptism and Confirmation. The growing number of infant

Chrismation
The name in the Eastern rites for the Sacrament of Confirmation. It comes from the chrism used as part of the sacrament.

Baptisms, the increase in rural parishes, and the growth of dioceses prevented bishops from being at each celebration of the sacrament. Because the dioceses covered vast geographic areas and transportation was primitive, it was impossible for a bishop to attend all the Baptisms in his diocese. His visits to the parishes became infrequent. It was at this time two traditions for celebrating the Sacrament of Confirmation emerged, one in the East and one in the West.

In the Roman Church (the West), there was a desire to maintain the bishop's explicit connection with the sacrament. A bishop sustains and serves the Church's unity, catholicity, and connection with the Apostles. His presence at Confirmation expresses the unity of the new Christian with the bishop and those elements.

To maintain the connection with the bishop, double anointing with Sacred Chrism was begun. The priest at Baptism gives the first anointing with Sacred Chrism. As explained in Chapter 3, it signifies that the person baptized participates in the prophetic, priestly, and kingly offices of Christ. The bishop at Confirmation confers the second anointing. However, if an adult is baptized, only one post-baptismal anointing, confirmation, is administered, and it is done by the priest.

The Eastern Churches, following their ancient practices, continue to give greater emphasis to the unity of the Sacraments of Initiation rather than separating Baptism and Confirmation by several years. In the East, Baptism and Confirmation are celebrated together, with the priest doing the anointing. To maintain connection with the bishop, the priest anoints only with *myron* (chrism) consecrated by the bishop.

Teachings about Confirmation

While the sacrament was celebrated from the beginning of the Church after being modeled and instituted by Christ's laying on of hands and sending of the Spirit, it was the Church Councils of Riez (439) and Orange (441) that first used the name *Confirmation* for post-baptismal anointings. These councils required bishops to visit rural parts of their dioceses regularly to confirm the newly baptized. The Second Council of Lyons (1274) used the name *Confirmation* on an official list of the Seven Sacraments.

In the sixteenth century, the Council of Trent defended the sacramental character of Confirmation, which had been challenged by Protestant reformers who felt that Baptism had been weakened by overemphasizing the laying on of hands and anointing. It was then common for a person to be confirmed sometime between the **age of discretion** and about age fourteen. In those years, reception of First Communion took place either before or after Confirmation, meaning the traditional order of the three Sacraments of Initiation was not consistently preserved.

age of discretion

Also called the "age of reason," it is the age (typically the end of the seventh year) at which a person becomes capable of moral reasoning.

Christ Instituted the Sacrament of Confirmation

In his famous *Summa Theologica*, St. Thomas Aquinas answered the objections to the idea that Confirmation is in fact a sacrament and that Christ instituted it:

> Concerning the institution of this sacrament there are three opinions. Some have maintained that this sacrament was instituted neither by Christ, nor by the Apostles; but later in the course of time by one of the councils. Others held that the Apostles instituted it. But this cannot be admitted; since the institution of a new sacrament belongs to the power of excellence, which belongs to Christ alone.
>
> And therefore we must say that Christ instituted this sacrament not by bestowing, but by promising it, according to John 16:7: "If I go not, the Paraclete will not come to you, but if I go, I will send Him to you." And this was because in this sacrament the fullness of the Holy Ghost is bestowed, which was not to be given before Christ's Resurrection and Ascension; according to John 7:39: "As yet the Spirit was not given, because Jesus was not yet glorified."

In 1910 Pope St. Pius X permitted children to receive First Communion at the age of seven. He desired to increase devotion to the Eucharist and encourage the faithful to receive Communion on Sundays, feast days, and even daily if possible. Before that Catholics had often felt unworthy to frequently receive Holy Communion. Because of this change, Confirmation was usually celebrated later, after First Communion, and the traditional order of the sacraments was not followed. Today this is the order for receiving the sacraments for most Catholics who are baptized as infants.

The revised *Rite of Confirmation* allows for conferences of bishops, usually from individual nations, to name the appropriate age for Confirmation. In the United States, the age of Confirmation ranges from the age of discretion to about age sixteen. The specific range varies from one diocese to another. Adults who are baptized receive all three Sacraments of Initiation at one time.

Confirmation, whether it is celebrated with Baptism or some years later, recalls a person's Baptism. The *Rite of Confirmation* approved in 1971 after the Second Vatican Council included several changes that help people see the intimate connection between Confirmation and Baptism. For example:

1. The Rite of Christian Initiation of Adults calls for all adult converts to celebrate Baptism, Confirmation, and Eucharist at the same time, usually at the Easter Vigil.
2. The *confirmandi* (plural of **confirmand**) are encouraged to use their baptismal name as their Confirmation name. This name often is that of a canonized saint or Christian hero who inspires the person to be a good Christian. In the past, the confirmandi chose a name other than their baptismal name, to show that they were being given a new identity, a new mission, in Confirmation.
3. Previously, Confirmation sponsors were usually different from the person's godparents. Today, the Church encourages baptismal godparents also to act as Confirmation sponsors (see *Code of Canon Law* 893 §2 and *CCC* 1311). It

DID YOU KNOW?

To be qualified to be a Confirmation sponsor, a person must have received all three Sacraments of Initiation, be at least sixteen years old, and lead "a life in harmony with the faith and the role to be undertaken" (*Code of Canon Law* 874; see *CCC* 1311).

confirmand
A candidate for Confirmation.

is the sponsor's duty "to see that the confirmed person acts as a true witness of Christ and faithfully fulfills the obligations connected with this sacrament" (*Code of Canon Law* 892).

4. The ritual of Confirmation, if celebrated separately from Baptism, includes a public renewal of baptismal promises by the confirmandi.

In Confirmation, we remember who we are—Christ's own possessions. We also remember how the Spirit has been working in us since Baptism to make us stronger and more committed Christians. Ⓜ

For Review
1. How is the Spirit referenced in the Book of Isaiah?
2. Name one occasion when Jesus promised the outpouring of the Holy Spirit.
3. What happened when the Apostles laid hands on the newly baptized?
4. What were some religious uses of oil?
5. Why were Baptism and Confirmation referred to as a "double sacrament"?
6. Explain how two different practices of the Sacrament of Confirmation arose in the East and West.
7. How did the traditional order of the Sacraments of Initiation fall out of practice in the twentieth century?
8. How does the Rite of Confirmation in effect today maintain the connection between Baptism and Confirmation?

For Reflection
- Describe how you imagine the Holy Spirit.
- From the age of discretion (around seven years old) to age sixteen, what do you feel is the best age for Confirmation? Explain.

CELEBRATING THE SACRAMENT OF CONFIRMATION

The celebration of Confirmation actually begins at a solemn ceremony that precedes the sacrament. This ceremony, the consecration of the Sacred Chrism, takes place once a year—either on or near Holy Thursday. Representatives from all parishes in a diocese gather for Mass in the diocesan cathedral (church of the bishop) to have the bishop bless the sacred oils that will be used in each parish throughout the year. At this Mass, the bishop blesses the Oil of Catechumens, the Oil of the Sick, and consecrates the chrism that will be used in the sacraments.

At the **Chrism Mass**, the bishop may actually make the chrism by pouring **balsam** into olive oil. (This mixing may also have occurred before Mass.) The bishop leads a prayer over the oil: "Let us pray that God our almighty Father will bless this oil so that all who are anointed with it may be inwardly transformed and come to share in eternal salvation."

Then the bishop blesses the chrism, saying a special prayer of consecration:

> God our maker, source of all growth in holiness, accept the joyful thanks and praise we offer in the name of your Church.
>
> . . . After your Son, Jesus Christ our Lord, asked John for baptism in the waters of Jordan, you sent the Spirit upon him in the form of a dove and by the witness of your own voice you declared him to be your only, well-beloved Son. In this you clearly fulfilled the prophecy of David, that Christ would be anointed with the oil of gladness beyond his fellow men.
>
> And so, Father, we ask you to bless this oil you have created. Fill it with the power of your Holy Spirit through Christ your Son. . . . Make this chrism a sign of life and salvation for those who are to be born again in the waters of baptism. . . . When they are anointed with this holy oil, make them temples of your glory, radiant with the goodness of life that has its source in you. (Consecratory Prayer of Chrism, *Sacramentary*)

Only the bishop can consecrate the Sacred Chrism. Thus, whenever it is used in a sacrament (Baptism, Confirmation, or Holy Orders), the chrism re-

minds us of the authority and approval of the bishop as the official successor of the Apostles and as the representative of the wider Church, and the connection of the bishop to the Sacrament of Confirmation.

The celebration of Confirmation itself ordinarily takes place at Mass after the Liturgy of the Word, in the presence of the Christian assembly. As the bishop is to be present, his special chair (**cathedra**) is placed in the sanctuary. This chair symbolizes the bishop's

Chrism Mass

An annual Mass celebrated in a diocesan cathedral on or near Holy Thursday in which the bishop consecrates the Sacred Chrism that will be used in the diocese throughout the year.

balsam

An oily, resinous substance that flows from certain plants, like pine, and which the Church usually mixes with olive oil for use as chrism. Another term for balsam is the "balm of Gilead."

cathedra

The chair or throne in a bishop's cathedral from which he presides over special functions. The earliest type of bishop's throne consisted of a high-backed armchair rounded at the top and made out of a single block of marble.

CONFIRMATION READINGS

Read the passages below, which are often used in the Confirmation liturgy, and select one in each group that resonates with you and relates to the other readings you have chosen about the meaning of this sacrament. Compose a "Confirmation homily" that incorporates the main theme of these readings.

First Reading
- Isaiah 11:1-4a (God's Spirit will rest on the Messiah.)
- Isaiah 61:1-3a, 6a, 8b-9 (God gives his anointed one a special mission.)
- Ezekiel 36:24-28 (God will put a new Spirit in us.)
- Joel 2:23a, 26-30a (In the messianic age, God will pour out his Spirit on all people.)

Second Reading
- Acts 1:3-8 (The Holy Spirit will empower you to be my witness.)
- Acts 8:1, 4, 14-17 (They laid hands on them, and the Holy Spirit came upon them.)
- Romans 5:1-2, 5-8 (The Spirit has poured God's love into our hearts.)
- Romans 8:14-17 (The Spirit confirms that we are children of God.)

Gospel
- Matthew 5:1-12a (Blessed are those who are poor in spirit.)
- Luke 4:16-22a (God's Spirit is upon me.)
- John 14:15-17 (God's Spirit will be with you always.)
- John 16:5b-7, 12-13a (The Spirit will lead you to all truth.)

role as leader of the diocese and presider of the local assembly gathered for Confirmation.

After the Gospel, a catechist, deacon, or priest presents the candidates for Confirmation to the bishop. If possible, each candidate's name is read aloud and the person comes forward individually to meet the bishop.

The bishop then gives a homily based on the Scripture readings. According to some local customs, he may conduct a question-and-answer dialogue with the confirmandi to make sure they understand the meaning of Confirmation.

After the homily, the candidates publicly renew their baptismal promises before the bishop.

The Rite of Confirmation

After the Profession of Faith, the bishop extends his hands over the whole group, praying for outpouring of the Spirit. He says,

> All-powerful God, Father of our Lord Jesus Christ,
> by water and the Holy Spirit
> you freed your sons and daughters
>   from sin
> and gave them new life.
> Send your Holy Spirit upon them
> to be their helper and guide.
> Give them the spirit of wisdom and
>   understanding,
> the spirit of right judgment and
>   courage,
> the spirit of knowledge and
>   reverence.
> Fill them with the spirit of wonder
> and awe in your presence.
> We ask this through Christ our
> Lord. Amen. (*The Rites*, Confirmation 42)

This extension of the bishop's hands represents the laying on of hands by the Apostles. Although the bishop is the ordinary minister of Confirmation,

he may appoint a pastor or priest to represent him if he is unable to attend. In the Eastern Church, the pastor or priest usually administers Confirmation in the bishop's name at Baptism.

The actual anointing with oil takes place next. It is often a deacon who brings the Sacred Chrism to the bishop as each candidate comes forward with his or her sponsor. The sponsor gives the candidate's name to the bishop and places his or her hand on the candidate's shoulder. The bishop dips his right thumb in the chrism. Then with his thumb, he makes the Sign of the Cross on the forehead of the person being confirmed. Simultaneously he says, "N., be sealed with the Gift of the Holy Spirit."

The person responds, "Amen."

The anointing signifies and imprints a spiritual seal (see *CCC* 1293, 1317), a grace or effect of the sacrament (see pages 21–22). This seal is a sign of identity and ownership. Before the days of government postal service, a king or an official would send a letter, decree, or document to others by way of a messenger. To show that this correspondence was authentic, the king or official sealed the paper with a wax impression of his ring. The seal was much like a notary's seal today. It guarantees that the signature really is that of the sender.

Just as God the Father set his seal on Jesus (see John 6:27), so God puts his seal on those who are confirmed through the anointing by the bishop. The anointing shows that the wider Church has accepted our Baptism. Our Christian discipleship is truly authentic; we bear the Church's official "stamp of approval." "This seal of the Holy Spirit marks our total belonging to Christ, our enrollment in his service for ever . . ." (*CCC* 1296).

After the anointing there is a Sign of Peace. The bishop says, "Peace be with you." The confirmandi answer, "And with your spirit." Everyone in the assembly then exchanges a Sign of Peace. This gesture "signifies and demonstrates ecclesial communion with the bishop and with all the faithful" (*CCC* 1301).

The rite of Confirmation ends with **General Intercessions**. These prayers are for the newly confirmed and their families. The prayers also ask God to help everyone in the Church be open to the Gifts of the Holy Spirit and give witness to the Gospel of Jesus. The intercessions may include the following examples, or something similar.

Bishop:	My dear friends: Let us be one in prayer to God our Father as we are one in the faith, hope, and love his Spirit gives.
Deacon or Lector:	For these sons and daughters of God, confirmed by the Gift of the Spirit, that they give witness to Christ by lives built on faith and love . . . For their parents and godparents who led them in faith, that by word and example they may always encourage them to follow the way of Jesus Christ . . . For the holy Church of God, in union with N. our pope, N. our bishop, and all the bishops, that God, who gathers us together by the Holy Spirit, may help us grow in unity of faith and love until his Son returns in glory . . .

For all [people] of every race and nation, that they may acknowledge the one God as Father, and in the bond of common brotherhood seek his kingdom, which is peace and joy in the Holy Spirit . . . (*Rite of Confirmation* 30)

Confirmation Blessing

The Liturgy of the Eucharist follows the rite of Confirmation. After Communion, the bishop gives all the assembled people a special blessing, reminding them of their own consecration to profess the true faith as God's children:

Bishop:	God our Father, complete the work you have begun and keep the gifts of your Holy Spirit active in the hearts of your people. Make them ready to live his Gospel and eager to do his will. May they never be ashamed to proclaim to all the world Christ crucified, living and reigning forever and ever.
All:	Amen.
Bishop:	And may the blessing of almighty God the Father, and the Son, and the Holy Spirit come upon you and remain with you forever.
All:	Amen.

DID YOU KNOW?

For many years, the rite of Confirmation called for the bishop to lightly slap each confirmand on the cheek. This gesture symbolized the sacrament's power to imbue the person with strength to fight the battle against temptation and the enemies of the faith.

Who Can Be Confirmed

Every baptized person who is not yet confirmed can and should receive the Sacrament of Confirmation. Without Confirmation and Eucharist, Baptism is certainly valid and efficacious, but nevertheless Christian initiation remains incomplete.

Sometimes, because Confirmation is called the "sacrament of Christian maturity" the reception of the sacrament is erroneously connected with achieving an adult level of faith and an adult level of growth. Preparation for the sacrament in the past has included sharing a lesson that "once confirmed, you are an adult in the Church." St. Thomas Aquinas reminds us that a person can be old in age and still not spiritually mature. In the same way, because the grace of Baptism does not need ratification to be effective, it is possible for a child to have reached spiritual maturity:

> Age of body does not determine age of soul. Even in childhood man can attain spiritual maturity: as the book of Wisdom says: "For old age is not honored for length of time, or measured by number of years." Many children, through the strength of the Holy Spirit they have received, have bravely fought for Christ even to the shedding of their blood. (*Summa Theologica* III 72, 8, quoted in *CCC* 1308)

The Church requires adequate preparation and instruction for reception of Confirmation. It should aim at leading a Christian to "a more intimate union with Christ and a more lively familiarity with the Holy Spirit" (*CCC* 1309). The preparation time should encourage a greater participation and belonging in the life of the universal Church and the parish community.

In order to receive the sacrament, one must be in a state of grace and should have received the Sacrament of Penance. The candidate should commit to more intense prayer in order to be best prepared to receive and act on the graces of the Holy Spirit. To help in the preparation, candidates seek the spiritual help of a sponsor. Recall that to be qualified to be a Confirmation sponsor, a person must have received all three Sacraments of Initiation, be at least sixteen years old, and lead "a life in harmony with the faith and the role to be undertaken" (*Code of Canon Law* 874; see *CCC* 1311). To emphasize the unity with Baptism, the sponsor should ideally be one of the baptismal godparents.

The Minister of the Sacrament

The "original minister" of the Sacrament of Confirmation is a bishop. Bishops are successors of the Apostles. They have received the fullness of the Sacrament of Holy Orders. Administering Confirmation themselves clearly demonstrates that the effect of the sacrament is to unite those who receive it more closely to the Church, to the Apostles, and to the mission of bearing witness to Christ.

There are situations when a priest may confer Confirmation. As mentioned, a priest typically is the minister of Confirmation to adults who receive all three Sacraments of Initiation at the Easter Vigil (using the Sacred Chrism consecrated by the bishop). Also, if a person is in danger of death, a priest can give him or her Confirmation.

? DID YOU KNOW?

Each diocese has a duty to keep a record of all Confirmations. According to the present *Code of Canon Law*, "The names of the confirmed with mention of the minister, the parents and the sponsors, the place and the date of the conferral of confirmation are to be noted in the confirmation register in the diocesan curia, or, where the conference of bishops or the diocesan bishop has prescribed it, in a book kept in the parish archive; the pastor must advise the pastor of the place of baptism about the conferral of confirmation, so that notation be made in the baptismal register" (*Code of Canon Law* 895).

For Review

1. What happens at the Chrism Mass?
2. Why is a special chair placed in the sanctuary during the Mass of Confirmation?
3. What is the essential rite of Confirmation?
4. What does the bishop say when he anoints a person with Sacred Chrism at Confirmation? What does this anointing symbolize?
5. For what do the General Intercessions at Confirmation usually ask?
6. Who is eligible to be confirmed?
7. Why is a bishop the original minister of Confirmation?

For Reflection

- What decision have you made about your reception of Confirmation?

- What do you think determines spiritual maturity?

THE GRACE OF CONFIRMATION

Baptism and Confirmation are intimately linked. Confirmation flows from Baptism. This is an essential teaching about these sacraments. Confirmation continues what Baptism begins. Baptism gives us new life in Christ and new identity as members of his Body, the Church. Baptism forgives sin—both Original Sin and personal sin. Confirmation, on the other hand, strengthens, intensifies, deepens, or builds on the graces we were given at Baptism. It intensifies our relationship with the Holy Spirit, who lives within us. It helps us be more receptive, more open, to his gifts that were given to us in Baptism.

Confirmation completes Baptism and perfects Baptismal grace. It helps us become more complete and perfect images of Christ and members of his Body. It strengthens us to live as Gospel witnesses in all that we do.

Just as the human body needs life and breath, a healthy endocrine system, and constant nourishment, so the Body of Christ needs Baptism, Confirmation, and Eucharist. Through Baptism, we die to sin and rise to new life with the Holy Trinity. We become God's adopted children. We become the brothers and sisters of Jesus Christ. And we become the temples of the Holy Spirit. We are united with the Trinity. We breathe in divine grace and love. We share in God's own life.

Confirmation is like our life-blood that keeps our human bodies

 **DID YOU KNOW?**

In the Eastern Church, Baptism, Confirmation, and Eucharist are celebrated together, even when it is an infant receiving the Sacraments of Initiation (see *CCC* 1318).

functioning in a healthy way. Confirmation keeps us spiritually functioning in a healthy way all throughout life. Confirmation helps us grow and mature in faith. That is why St. Thomas Aquinas once said that Confirmation is to Baptism what growth is to generation (see *Summa Theologica* III 72:6). Confirmation helps us grow as the Body of Christ and grow up spiritually.

Like Baptism, Confirmation is given only once, since it too imprints on our soul an indelible spiritual mark, the character that allows us to testify to our faith in Christ. As Jesus himself promised before he ascended to Heaven,

> And (behold) I am sending the promise of my Father upon you; but stay in the city until you are clothed with power from on high. (Lk 24:49)

Receiving the gift of the Holy Spirit is not a one-time, momentary event, though we receive the sacrament only once. Instead, Confirmation acts continually within us, providing us with the necessary spiritual gifts needed to grow closer to God. The Sacrament of the Eucharist is the daily food our bodies need in order to continue to grow in the nourishment of faith.

The grace or effect of Confirmation is the special outpouring of the Holy Spirit, much in the same way the Holy Spirit once came to the Apostles at Pentecost. Confirmation is intimately connected with Baptism and brings an increase and deepening of baptismal grace because

- it roots us more deeply in the divine filiation which makes us cry, "Abba! Father!";
- it unites us more firmly to Christ;
- it increases the Gifts of the Holy Spirit in us;
- it renders our bond with the Church more perfect; and

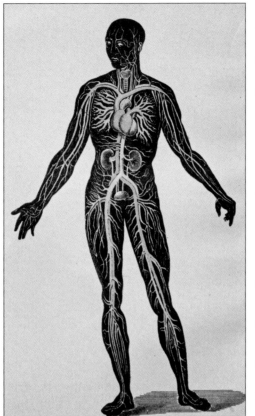

- it gives us a special strength of the Holy Spirit to spread and defend the faith by word and action as true witnesses of Christ, to confess the name of Christ boldly, and never to be ashamed of the Cross. (*CCC* 1303)

More information about these graces of the sacrament follow.

We Are Able to Live as God's Children

Our Baptism helps us experience what being a son or daughter of God means. The Letter to the Romans teaches:

> Those who are led by the Spirit of God are children of God. For you did not receive a spirit of slavery to fall back into fear, but you received a spirit of adoption, through which we cry, "Abba, Father!" The Spirit itself bears witness with our spirit that we are children of God, and if children, then heirs, heirs of God and joint heirs with Christ, if only we suffer with him so that we may also be glorified with him. (Rom 8:14–17)

Being God's children is an intimate part of our identity. When we have actually experienced God as our Father, we are more firmly established as members of his family. We have a firsthand experience, a familiarity, with the Blessed Trinity. We have felt God's grace flowing through our lives. "The love of God has been poured out into our hearts through the holy Spirit that has been given to us" (Rom 5:5).

We Are United with Christ

Confirmation "unites us more firmly to Christ" (*CCC* 1303). It helps us "more perfectly become the image" of Christ (*The Rites*, Christian Initiation 2, General Introduction). The Holy Spirit comes to us in the sacrament and helps us pray always and continually renew and deepen our relationship with Christ. St. Paul explained, "The Spirit too comes to the aid of our weakness; for we do not know how to pray as we ought, but the Spirit itself intercedes with inexpressible groanings. And the one who searches hearts knows what is the intention of the Spirit, because it intercedes for the holy ones according to God's will" (Rom 8:26–27).

The Parable of the Sower (see Matthew 13:1–9) further illustrates different ways we may or may not be united with Christ. The parable teaches that some Christians are like seeds that fall among weeds. When faced with a decision between power, money, and creaturely goods or the love of Christ, they choose to abandon Christ. Other Christians are like seeds that fall among rocks. They believe in Christ when life is going along smoothly, but when setbacks or sudden tragedies happen, they give up on their faith. Still other Christians are like seeds that fall among thorns. When they are persecuted for their faith, they choose the easy way rather than Christ. Confirmation, however, is like good soil. It nurtures faith. The grace we receive at Confirmation helps us remain faithful to Christ. As St. Paul wrote, nothing can shake our faith with God's help:

> What will separate us from the love of Christ? Will anguish, or distress, or persecution, or famine, or nakedness, or peril, or the sword? . . . I am convinced that neither death, nor life, nor angels, nor principalities, nor present things, nor future things, nor powers, nor height, nor depth, nor any other creature will be able to separate us from the love of God in Christ Jesus our Lord. (Rom 8:35, 38–39)

We Receive the Gifts of the Holy Spirit

Confirmation "increases the gifts of the Holy Spirit in us" (*CCC* 1303). The Church has traditionally defined these gifts as wisdom, understanding, counsel, fortitude, knowledge, piety, and fear of the Lord. To understand these gifts better, we need to discuss what they are, how they were perfectly present in the person of Jesus, and how they work within us and help us grow in faith.

These Gifts of the Holy Spirit help us grow in holiness and union with the Blessed Trinity. They help us listen more closely to God's Word and help us act on that Word in daily life. Here is a brief description of each gift:

- *Wisdom.* The word *wisdom* comes from a Greek word meaning "to see clearly." This gift helps us value what is most important in life and keep our priorities straight. It helps us seek God's Kingdom first (see Matthew 6:33) and make everything else less important. Wisdom helps us see ourselves, others, and God clearly—as God does. Confirmation unites us with the wisdom of God, which may seem like foolishness to most humans (see 1 Corinthians 1:25).
- *Understanding.* Have you ever heard the phrase "Things are not always as they seem"? Understanding is a spiritual gift that helps us see "the bigger picture" and not just the way things seem on the surface. It helps us see what lies underneath—the real meaning or truth. The gift of understanding helps us see "the spirit" behind laws and not just "the letter." It also helps us put ourselves "in the shoes" of others, so that we can empathize with them and show compassion.
- *Counsel.* This gift relies on the virtue of prudence. It helps us make the best decisions, based on the desire to do God's will. It

EXPRESSING THE GIFTS OF THE HOLY SPIRIT AS JESUS DID

Jesus' life embodied the Gifts of the Holy Spirit. As a child and an adolescent, he grew in wisdom; later he expressed that wisdom in his parables. Jesus understood the poor and the sick, as well as the true motives of the people who came to him. Jesus always used right judgment, even when it seemed he was breaking the law. He bravely went to Jerusalem knowing he would be arrested and crucified. As God's Son, Jesus had special knowledge of the Father. Jesus never took the world or people for granted; he loved all of nature, including the lilies of the field and the foxes in their dens.

Select one of the Gifts of the Holy Spirit. Search through the Gospels and find an example of how Jesus expressed this gift in his life and actions. Then write a paragraph, poem, or prayer about how you could express this gift in your own life and actions.

RECOGNIZING THE GIFTS OF THE SPIRIT

Write seven notes to different people (relatives, friends, peers, teachers, priests, religious) telling how each person represents one of the Gifts of the Holy Spirit. Follow these directions:

1. Write one letter for each gift of the Spirit.
2. Write the letters to seven different people.
3. Mail the letters through the U.S. mail.

Record in your journal the responses you receive from the people to whom you wrote.

---

fruits of the Spirit

Perfections that result from living in union with the Holy Spirit.

---

helps us seek advice from trusted others. Our counsel, or right judgment, also helps us give good advice to others as they try to live their Christian faith.

- *Fortitude.* A person with fortitude or courage stands up for his or her beliefs and remains true to them despite opposition, discomfort, or even persecution. Fortitude helps us overcome obstacles that arise in the practice of our religious duties, use our God-given talents bravely, and reach out to others in loving service.

- *Knowledge.* This gift helps us both know *about* God and the Church's teachings and know firsthand (really experience) him. It helps us open ourselves to be known by God in a deeper way and learn more about the religion we profess.

- *Piety.* The word *piety* means "faithful obedience and love." This gift enables us to give God true worship and praise. It helps us show proper respect for God and for everything he has made. The gift of piety, or reverence, helps us put our trust in God and not only listen to but also follow his Word.

- *Fear of the Lord.* This gift helps us be receptive to the surprising, generous, and loving presence of him in our lives. Also known as the gift of wonder and awe, it helps us never to underestimate God or think we have God completely figured out. This gift also helps us fear offending God.

We Form a Deeper Bond with the Church

The Sacrament of Confirmation strengthens our bond with the Church.

It helps us *become* the Church, the Body of Christ. The Second Vatican Council made this communion clear when it taught, "By the Sacrament of Confirmation [the baptized faithful] are more perfectly bound to the church and are endowed with the special strength of the Holy Spirit. Hence, as true witnesses of Christ, they are more strictly obliged both to spread and to defend the faith by word and deed" (*Lumen Gentium* 11). Because of the Spirit's presence and work within us, we are now *confirmed* as People of God, as Church.

> As the people of God, we become what we are when we let the Spirit come to presence in our lives, our actions, our relationships. Only when and to the extent that we let the Spirit come to presence in what we are and do, have we the right to be called "Church." To the extent that we do not let the Spirit come to presence in our lives and actions, we are "unchurched." (*The Christian Sacraments*, 131)

How can others tell we are Church? They can see in us the same Gifts of the Spirit that Jesus had. They can see we are people of wisdom, understanding, counsel, fortitude, knowledge, piety, and fear of the Lord. Furthermore, people can tell who we are by our attitudes and actions. Just as a gardener can judge a tree as good or bad by the fruit it produces, so people can judge us by the "fruit" we produce. The twelve **fruits of the Spirit** are charity, joy, peace, patience, kindness, goodness, generosity, gentleness, faithfulness, modesty, self-control, and chastity. When people see these virtues in us, they know that the Holy Spirit dwells in us. We are "the ones who hear the word and accept it and bear fruit thirty and sixty and a hundredfold" (Mk 4:20).

For Review

1. How is Confirmation intimately connected with Baptism?
2. How does the Parable of the Sower illustrate how we can be united to Christ?
3. Name the seven Gifts of the Holy Spirit.
4. What does the grace of our unity with the Church as a result of Confirmation demand us to do?

For Reflection

- How does Confirmation help you to become a more complete and perfect image of Christ?

- How is Confirmation like our lifeblood?

TRANSFORMATION

CONFIRMATION CONFERS A NEW CHARACTER

Another grace of Confirmation is related to a new, indelible character we receive in the sacrament, a different one than we received at Baptism. This character helps us spread and defend the faith as witnesses of Christ and to never be ashamed of the cross. In other words, it enables us to see ourselves as vital members of Christ's Body. We now "own" our responsibility to be "true witnesses of Christ in word and deed" (Sacred Congregation for Divine Worship, "Confirmation," *The Rites*, 289) and "to confess the name of Christ boldly, and never to be ashamed of the Cross" (*CCC* 1303). We see ourselves as God's anointed; we share more completely in the mission of Jesus to spread the Gospel message (see *CCC* 1294).

Many Catholics throughout history witnessed for Jesus despite persecution, imprisonment, and ridicule. Some even gave their lives for their faith; they died as martyrs. As times changed and the Church saw herself in a more militaristic way—as an army of God fighting heresy, infidelity, and evil—Confirmation came to be viewed in a militaristic way too. St. Bonaventure, for example, taught that

Confirmation strengthens baptized Christians so that they might become "soldiers for Christ," defending the true faith against evil.

Catholics who have received Confirmation are subsequently required to live "in God's spirit." As St. Paul told the Ephesians, "you should put away the old self of your former way of life, corrupted through deceitful desires, and be renewed in the spirit of your minds, and put on the new self, created in God's way in righteousness and holiness of truth" (Eph 4:22–24). St. Paul also wrote:

> I say, then: live by the Spirit and you will certainly not gratify the desire of the flesh. For the flesh has desires against the Spirit, and the Spirit against the flesh. . . . Now the works of the flesh are obvious: immorality, impurity, licentiousness, idolatry, sorcery, hatreds, rivalry, jealousy, outbursts of fury, acts of selfishness, dissensions, factions, occasions of envy, drinking bouts, orgies, and the like. . . . In contrast, the fruit of the Spirit is love, joy, peace, patience, kindness, generosity, faithfulness, gentleness, self-control. . . . If we live in the Spirit, let us also follow the Spirit. Let us not be conceited, provoking one another, envious of one another. (Gal 5:16–26)

The *Catechism* explains that Confirmation confers "a sacramental *character* or 'seal' by which the Christian shares in Christ's priesthood" (*CCC* 1121). "This 'character' perfects the common priesthood of the faithful, received in Baptism, and 'the confirmed person receives the power to profess faith in Christ publicly and as it were officially (*quasi ex officio*)'" (*CCC* 1305). Once we are sealed with the Holy Spirit, we are forever changed. For this reason, the Church teaches that a person may be confirmed only once (see *CCC* 1317).

While a person may celebrate the Sacrament of Confirmation only once, the *effect* of Confirmation is continual and ongoing. Recall the story of Soeren Palumbo. Not only did he give a speech as a high school senior drawing attention to the discrimination faced by people with special needs and disabilities, but he also continued to work on behalf of that cause. When Soeren enrolled at Notre Dame, he contacted the Logan Center, a local agency that serves people with special needs, and joined a service club called "Super Sibs" that provides support and friendship to children who have siblings with special needs.

Confirmation strengthens our faith. Just as the human body grows and develops, so our spiritual life must also grow and develop. Faith is not static or unchanging. It is not a "lump sum" quantity that we get once and that is it. Instead, living faith is dynamic, evolving, constantly changing. It grows as we grow emotionally, intellectually, socially, and physically. As faith evolves and matures, it becomes more sophisticated, more internalized. At the same time, it grows stronger, more unshakeable. We believe less and less in worldly "idols" such as wealth, power, popularity, or possessions. We put our faith, instead, on "what truly matters"—Father, Son, and Holy Spirit. 🅣

For Review
1. What does the indelible character we receive in Confirmation help us do?
2. Explain the militaristic view of Confirmation that developed.
3. Why can a person be confirmed only once?

For Reflection
Share an example of how the effect of Confirmation is continual and ongoing.

CHAPTER QUICK VIEW

Main Ideas

- Confirmation is often referred to as the "sacrament of the Holy Spirit." (p. 96)

- The Holy Spirit's presence with God's People has been witnessed throughout Salvation History. (p. 97)

- Jesus promised the outpouring of the Holy Spirit several times in his ministry; at the Last Supper, he clearly said he would send his Advocate after he returned to his Father. (pp. 97-98)

- The Holy Spirit came to the Apostles on Pentecost; the effect was lasting and permanent. (p. 98)

- From the time of Pentecost, the Apostles imparted on the newly baptized the gift of the Holy Spirit by laying on of hands. (pp. 98-99)

- Very early in the Church's history, the anointing with Sacred Chrism was added to the laying on of hands as part of the Sacrament of Confirmation. (p. 99)

- Baptism and Confirmation were called a "double sacrament" because in the first centuries they were generally part of one celebration. (pp. 99-100)

- To maintain unity with the bishop, a practice of double anointing with Sacred Chrism took place in the Roman Church; the bishop at Confirmation confers the second anointing. (p. 100)

- The Eastern Church celebrates Baptism and Confirmation together; the priest anoints with Sacred Chrism consecrated by the bishop. (p. 100)

- The revised *Rite of Confirmation* allows bishops from individual conferences to name the appropriate age for Confirmation; in the United States, it is celebrated any time between the age of discretion and around sixteen years old. (p. 101)

- Jesus Christ instituted the Sacrament of Confirmation through his promise of the Holy Spirit. (p. 101)

- The celebration of Confirmation begins at the Chrism Mass with the bishop's blessing of the Sacred Chrism. (p. 103)

- The rite of Confirmation usually takes place at Mass after the Liturgy of the Word. (pp. 103-104)

- The bishop, the ordinary minister of the sacrament, lays his hands on the candidates and anoints them with Sacred Chrism, saying, "N., be sealed with the Gift of the Holy Spirit." (p. 104)

- After Communion, the bishop gives all the people assembled at Confirmation a special blessing, reminding them of their own consecration to profess the true faith. (p. 105)

- Every baptized person should receive the Sacrament of Confirmation. Without Confirmation, Christian initiation remains valid and efficacious but incomplete. (p. 106)

- Though a bishop is the ordinary minister of the sacrament, a priest typically confers Confirmation on adults and children of catechetical age who receive all three Sacraments of Initiation at the Easter Vigil. (p. 106)

- Confirmation brings an increase and deepening of baptismal grace. (pp. 107-108)

- Among the graces of Confirmation are an increase of the Gifts of the Holy Spirit—wisdom, understanding, counsel, fortitude, knowledge, piety, and fear of the Lord. (pp. 109-110)

- Confirmation confers an indelible character that helps us spread and defend the faith as witnesses of Christ. (p. 111)

- Confirmation may be received only once. (p. 112)

Famous Catholics and the Sacraments:

SR. THEA BOWMAN

Bertha Bowman, an African American, was born in Canton, Mississippi, in 1937. Her father, Theon Bowman, was a doctor; her grandfather had been a slave. Bertha was raised in the Methodist faith, but at age nine she asked her parents if she could become a Catholic. She was baptized and confirmed a year later.

When she was sixteen, Bertha entered the Franciscan Sisters of Perpetual Adoration in La Crosse, Wisconsin. She was the only African American sister in the community and received the religious name Thea, which means "of God." Being a minority of one and a Catholic convert did not deter Sister Thea from keeping her family roots. As she explained later, "I bring my whole history, my traditions, my experience, my culture, my African-American song and dance and gesture and movement and teaching and preaching and healing and responsibility as a gift to the Church."

Sr. Thea was not only a talented singer and dancer; she was a good student as well. She earned a PhD in English literature and taught in Catholic schools, ranging from elementary grades through college. She became a pioneer in breaking down racial and cultural barriers in the Church, and was never afraid to speak dynamically about the need to appreciate the riches found in all cultures.

For ten years, Sr. Thea directed the Office of Intercultural Awareness for the Diocese of Jackson, Mississippi. She also founded the Institute of Black Studies at Xavier University in New Orleans. Thea undoubtedly was filled with God's Spirit as she led enthusiastic revivals at both African American and white meetings.

At age forty-six, Thea Bowman was diagnosed with breast and bone cancer. Instead of giving up, Thea prayed "to live until I die—to live, love, and serve fully until death comes." She explained her attitude this way: "I don't make sense of suffering; I try to make sense of life." She continued to exude joy, living life to the fullest—the abundant life Jesus promised his followers.

In 1989, Sister Thea was the keynote speaker at the United States Catholic Conference meeting of bishops. She reminded the bishops of the historic role of blacks in the Church, saying:

> Our history includes the services of Simon of Cyrene, the search of the Ethiopian eunuch, the contributions of black Egypt in art and mathematics and monasticism and politics, the scholarship of Timbuktu, the dignity and serenity of textile and gold and religion in Ghana, the pervasive spirituality and vitality of Nigeria, the political and social systems of Zaire.

She also recalled the slave experience of African Americans:

> Proud, strong men and women, artists, teachers, healers, warriors, and dream makers, inventors and builders, administrators like yourselves, politicians, priests: They came to these shores in the slave trade. Those who survived the indignity of the Middle Passage came to the American continents bringing treasures of African heritage, African spiritual and cultural gifts, wisdom, faith and faithfulness, art and drama. . . .

Despite the many contributions of African Americans to the United States and to the Church, Sister Thea further said: "A disproportionate number of black people are poor—poverty, deprivation, discrimination, stunted physical, intellectual, and spiritual growth. . . . More than a third of the black people that live in the United States live in poverty, the kind of poverty that lacks basic necessity."

Sister Thea proceeded to tell the bishops more about the hopes of African American Catholics:

> The Church is calling us to be participatory and to be involved. The Church is calling us to feed and to clothe and to shelter and to teach. Your job [as bishops] is to enable me, to enable God's people, black people, white people, brown people, all the people, to do the work of the Church in the modern world. . . .
>
> Today we're called to walk together in a new way toward that land of promise and to celebrate who we are and whose we are. If we as Church walk together, don't let nobody separate you. That's one thing black folk can teach you: The Church is a family . . . and families got to stay together. We know that if we do stay together, if we walk and talk and work and play and stand together in Jesus' name, we'll be who we say we are, truly Catholic; and we shall overcome the poverty, the loneliness, the alienation, and build together a holy city, a new Jerusalem . . . because we love one another.

Sister Thea died a year later, at age fifty-three. Nevertheless, her contagious spirit lives on, continuing to inspire those working to advance the cause of women, promote interracial peace and justice, and promote equality of African Americans in the United States and the Church. As she told Mike Wallace in a *60 Minutes* interview: "I think the difference between me and some people is that I'm content to do my little bit. Sometimes people think they have to do big things in order to make change. But if each one would light a candle, we'd have a tremendous light."

- Research the history, biblical references, and meaning of an African American spiritual. Share your findings in a musical presentation to the class.
- Research and share more about how Sr. Thea Bowman lived and expressed her Confirmation commitment. Give examples of how she allowed the Holy Spirit to work in her and through her to build up a multicultural Church.
- Read *Sister Thea Bowman, Shooting Star: Selected Writings and Speeches* by Celestine Cepress or *Thea Bowman: Handing on Her Legacy* by Christian Koontz. Share three quotations from Sister Thea Bowman on the importance of loving God, loving people of all cultures, or loving one's own ethnic heritage. Write your own commentary on their meanings.

THEA BOWMAN

TERMS, PEOPLE, PLACES

Choose the italicized term that best completes each sentence.

1. The age of discretion is also known as the (*age of knowledge/age of reason*).
2. The Feast of Tabernacles begins five days after (*Sukkot/Yom Kippur*).
3. Another name for the Paraclete is (*Advocate/Messiah*).
4. A novena, which is a prayer for a certain intention, lasts for (*eight/nine*) days.
5. Chrismation is the name for (*Baptism/Confirmation*) in the Eastern rite.
6. The Chrism Mass takes place annually on or near (*Holy Thursday/Pentecost*).
7. The laying on of hands, along with (*anointing with chrism/prayer of the faithful*), is part of the main rite of Confirmation.
8. Cathedra is the name for the (*church of the bishop/chair of the bishop*).
9. The Church mixes balsam with (*wine/olive oil*) to use as chrism.
10. There are (*seven/twelve*) fruits of the Spirit.
11. General Intercessions take place (*before/after*) the rite of Confirmation.

ONGOING ASSIGNMENTS

As you cover the material in this chapter, choose and complete at least three of these assignments.

1. In a poem, a drawing, or a short video, offer your own impression of the Holy Spirit.

2. No one can see a spirit; but we can see the Holy Spirit in action by the way people act and treat one another. Make a poster or collage showing your perception of the Holy Spirit as one of the following: a Spirit of holiness, a Spirit of life, a Spirit of power, a Spirit of truth, or a Spirit of forgiveness. Use magazine pictures or draw your own images. Explain why you chose the images you did. How do these images reflect your understanding of the Holy Spirit?

3. Write song lyrics that describe the Holy Spirit's role in the life of Christians. Perform your song live for others or record it on tape or a CD for the class to hear.

4. Put together a two- to three-minute audio track of what you think the Holy Spirit might sound like. Use sounds from nature, percussion rhythms, various other instruments, or CDs to make an original composition.

5. Report on the different ways we use oil in today's society. Describe what would happen if we ran out of oil completely. Finally, discuss why blessed oil is such a powerful symbol in the Sacrament of Confirmation.

6. Attend the Chrism Mass in your diocese or read about the rite of the Chrism Mass in a *Sacramentary*. Write a report about the Chrism Mass rituals and their meaning.

7. Each bishop has his own seal. Make a copy of your bishop's seal. Find out what the images, words, and shapes mean. Design your own unique seal. Choose images, words, and shapes that show who you are. Be prepared to share and explain your seal to the class.

8. Write five intercessions you would like the Church to pray for at a Confirmation ceremony.

9. Read Jesus' Parable of the Sower (Mt 13:1–9, 18–23). Work in a small group to rewrite this parable in modern terms that would speak to teenagers. Share your finished story with the class.

10. Select one gift of the Holy Spirit and prepare a report on it. List examples of people in history or modern life who exhibit this gift and how. Explain the gift to the best of your ability. Perhaps include ordinary situations in which this gift can help you today.

PRAYER SERVICE

Theme: Novena for the Seven Gifts of the Holy Spirit

Leader: O Lord Jesus Christ, who before ascending into heaven did promise to send the Holy Spirit to finish your work in the souls of your Apostles and disciples, deign to grant the same Holy Spirit to us that he may perfect in our souls the work of your grace and love.

Side 1: Grant me the Spirit of Wisdom that I may despise the perishable things of this world and aspire only after the things that are eternal.

Side 2: Grant me the Spirit of Understanding to enlighten my mind with the light of your divine truth.

Side 1: Grant me the Spirit of Right Judgment that I may ever choose the surest way of pleasing God and gaining heaven.

Side 2: Grant me the Spirit of Courage that I may bear my cross with you and that I may overcome with courage all the obstacles that oppose my Salvation.

Side 1: Grant me the Spirit of Knowledge that I may know God and know myself and grow perfect in holiness.

Side 2: Grant me the Spirit of Reverence that I may find the service of God sweet and agreeable.

Side 1: Grant me the Spirit of Wonder and Awe that I may be filled with a loving reverence toward God and may dread to in any way to displease him.

All: Mark me, dear Lord, with the sign of your true disciples and animate me in all things with your Spirit. Amen.

(Based on the *Holy Spirit Novena*)

The Sacrament *of the* Eucharist

Source and Summit
The Eucharist is the most important sacrament because in it Christ associates the Church with himself and his Paschal Mystery.

Understanding the Sacrament of the Eucharist
At the Last Supper, Jesus instituted the Sacrament of the Eucharist as a memorial of his Death and Resurrection, ensuring his presence in the Catholic Church for all ages.

Celebrating the Sacrament of the Eucharist
We come together in one place to celebrate Mass. The Mass is divided into two parts: the Liturgy of the Word and the Liturgy of the Eucharist.

The Graces of Holy Communion
Unity with Christ, forgiveness of venial sins, incorporation into the Church, and being Eucharist for others, especially the poor, are among the graces we receive from Holy Communion.

We Are Sent
There are several good reasons for participating at Mass, including the fact that the "Sunday obligation" is a requirement of the Third Commandment and a precept of the Church.

SOURCE AND SUMMIT

It is more than the cafeteria with the fresh array of lunch choices and open seating for chatting with friends. It is more than the Friday night game with the crosstown rival and the dance in the gym that follows. It is even more than the rigorous academic curriculum that prepares students well for admittance and success in the most prestigious colleges.

What truly sets Catholic high schools apart from their counterparts is the opportunity to worship God at school, particularly to celebrate the Eucharist with the school community of students, teachers, administrators, and staff and to find opportunities during a busy school day to spend time with Jesus Christ in the Blessed Sacrament.

At a recent gathering of students from Catholic high schools in the Diocese of Paterson, New Jersey, Bishop Arthur Serratelli compared the Eucharist to a family dinner table. "It is the table that ties us to the past; the table that makes the present come alive; and

the table that brings us to that table to which we are called at the end of our life."

In another part of the country, a recent high school graduate in Omaha, Nebraska, Ryan Borchers, toured the chapels at four of the city's Catholic high schools. He described the chapel at his own Skutt Catholic High School as "a little bit like being underwater. The dominant color is blue, and the stained-glass windows make the light in the room a little wavy. Lunch is going on outside in the student commons, but the sound is muffled. The muffled sound and the wavy, blue light combine to make me feel like I am in a shallow pool."

With his tour complete, Borchers reflected that visiting the sacred places was an "interesting experience" and came to understand that these once-ordinary spaces (one chapel was in the backstage of an auditorium) had been set off purposely as places where students could worship and reflect in the presence of the Lord.

Truly the opportunity to be with Jesus in the Eucharist during a school day is a unique and special opportunity afforded to students at Catholic high schools. Bishop Serratelli said the Eucharist brings a sense of connectedness. "We learn to communicate and, ultimately, we learn to love. We are nourished by the bonds of love."

This most important and special sacrament, the Eucharist, is called the "source and summit of the Christian life" (*Lumen Gentium* 11). All of the other

sacraments and works of the Church are bound with and oriented around the Eucharist because Christ himself is contained in it. The word *Eucharist* comes from a Greek word that means "to give thanks." The Sacrament of Holy Eucharist completes Christian initiation.

For Catholics, the term *Eucharist* has two principal understandings. First, it refers to the entire Mass, the Church's official form of worshiping the Father. In the Eucharist, we give God thanks and praise for all his blessings, especially for the gift of Jesus and the Salvation he won for us. Second, the word *Eucharist* refers to the consecrated species of wheat bread and grape

wine—the Body and Blood of Christ—that we receive during Communion.

Our being "sent forth" from the Eucharist reminds us that *Eucharist* can also be a verb (an action), rather than a noun (a thing). It describes what we become—the Body of Christ—when we receive the Body and Blood of Jesus in the form of the consecrated species of bread and wine. It describes our own transformation into the hands and feet of Christ in today's world as well as our actions—how we continue Jesus' work of spreading the Good News of God's love to others.

The Sacrament of Holy Eucharist has other names too, as its richness is truly inexhaustible (see *CCC* 1328–1332). For example, it is called

- the *Lord's Supper* because of its connection with the supper Jesus shared with his disciples on the night before his Passion;
- the *Breaking of Bread*, by which our communion with Christ and others is indicated;
- the *Eucharistic Assembly* because the Mass is celebrated with faithful Catholics and is a visible expression of the Church;
- the *Memorial* of the Lord's Passion and Resurrection;
- the *Holy Sacrifice* because it makes present the one sacrifice of Christ the Savior and includes the Church's offering;
- the *Holy and Divine Liturgy* because the Church's whole liturgy is centered in the celebration of this sacrament; and
- *Holy Communion* because the Eucharist unites us in one Body after receiving the Body and Blood of Christ.

Finally, Eucharist is known commonly as "Mass" because it concludes with a "sending forth" (*missio*) of the faithful so that they may fulfill God's will in their daily lives (*CCC* 1332).

Recall that because Baptism and Confirmation confer a spiritual identity or character, we may receive these sacraments only once. Eucharist, on the other hand, is like the daily food the physical body needs to maintain its strength and health. As Jesus said, "My flesh is true food, and my blood is true drink" (Jn 6:55). The Eucharist feeds our souls; it renews our commitment as Church, the Body of Christ. Just as the human body needs food each day, so we are encouraged to receive the Eucharist often.

The Eucharist is intimately connected to Jesus, the primordial Sacrament of God's love, and to the Church, the Sacrament of Jesus. It is the sacrament of the sacrifice of Jesus on the cross, which makes Jesus, in his Death and Resurrection, present to us today. This presence is called "Real Presence" because, through the consecration at Mass, the reality (substance) of the wheat bread and grape wine changes into the reality of Jesus—his risen, glorified Body and Blood. Also, the Eucharist is the sacrament of communion with the Church. It nourishes our union with one another and strengthens our identity as Church. Again, these meanings speak to its inexhaustible and mysterious meaning.

Archbishop Fulton J. Sheen, a dynamic preacher who had his own television program in the 1950s, once tried to explain the inexhaustible meaning of the Holy Eucharist:

By a beautiful paradox of Divine love, God makes his cross the very means of our salvation and our life. We have slain him; we have nailed him there and crucified him; but the love in his eternal heart could not be extinguished. He willed to give us the very life we slew; to give us the very good we destroyed; to nourish us with the very bread we buried, and the very blood we poured forth. He made our very crime into a happy fault; he turned a Crucifixion into a redemption; a consecration into a communion; a death into life everlasting.

This chapter traces the origins of the Eucharist found in Sacred Scripture, a definition of the main parts of the Mass, more on Christ's Real Presence in the Eucharist, and the grace and effects of the sacrament.

For Reflection

- How is the opportunity to participate in Mass important to you?

- Which description of the Eucharist best resonates with your understanding of the sacrament? With which description are you least familiar?

UNDERSTANDING THE SACRAMENT OF THE EUCHARIST

Bread and wine are at the heart of the Eucharist; by the words of Christ and the **invocation** of the Holy Spirit, they become for us the Body and Blood of the Lord. The signs of bread and wine signify the goodness of God's creation. In the Offertory at Mass, the priest remembers the blessing of bread and wine that God has bestowed on us:

Blessed are you, Lord God of all creation, for through your goodness we have received the bread we offer you: fruit of the earth and work of human hands, it will become for us the bread of life.

Blessed are you, Lord God of all creation, for through your goodness we have received the wine we offer you: fruit of the vine and work of human hands, it will become our spiritual drink.

When Abraham returned to Salem (a place prefiguring Jerusalem) and offered the king-priest Melchizedek gifts, Melchizedek in turn brought out bread and wine. Later, in the New Testament, Jesus is described as a priest "according to the order of Melchizedek" (see Hebrews 5:1–10). The bread and wine

invocation
A call, request, or supplication for God's help.

offered by the Church are fulfillment of Melchizedek's offering in the Old Law.

Both signs have roots in Scripture. In the Old Testament, bread and wine were offered in sacrifice among the first fruits of earth. They received new meaning in the Exodus: The manna the Israelites ate in the desert commemorated their liberation from Egypt and taught them to always rely on the Word of God for sustenance.

In the New Covenant, the "cup of blessing" at the end of the Jewish Passover added to the joy of the celebration. Jesus' public ministry had already given new meaning to the significance of bread, wine, and the common sharing of a meal. For example, Jesus' multiplication of the loaves to feed thousands is recorded in the Gospels using Eucharistic language:

> He ordered the crowd to sit down on the ground. Then he took the seven loaves and the fish, gave thanks, broke the loaves, and gave them to the disciples, who in turn gave them to the crowds. (Mt 15:36–37)

Jesus' conversion of water to wine at the Cana wedding announced his glorious Resurrection and Ascension and made present the wedding feast described for the Father's Kingdom. There, we will share in the fruits of God's love. Jesus told this news at the Last Supper:

> Amen, I say to you, I shall not drink again the fruit of the vine until the day when I drink it new in the kingdom of God. (Mk 14:25)

When Jesus first announced the Eucharist to his disciples, the explanation shocked and divided them. Jesus told them they must eat his flesh and drink his blood to gain eternal life. Many of the disciples protested: "This saying is hard; who can accept it?" (Jn 6:60). In fact, some of them left Jesus and returned to their former way of life. At the end of his discourse on the Bread of Life, Jesus clearly announced:

I am the living bread that came down from heaven; whoever eats this bread will live forever; and the bread that I will give is my flesh for the life of the world. (Jn 6:51)

He added:

Amen, amen, I say to you, unless you eat the flesh of the Son of Man and drink his blood, you do not have life within you. Whoever eats my flesh and drinks my blood has eternal life, and I will raise him on the last day. For my flesh is true food, and my blood is true drink. (Jn 6:53–55)

Jesus wondered if the Apostles were planning to leave also. Peter responded:

Master, to whom shall we go? You have the words of eternal life. We have come to believe and are convinced that you are the Holy One of God. (Jn 6:68–69)

Understanding and accepting the meaning of the Eucharist remain a challenge today. Many have left the Church not believing that Jesus' Body and Blood are truly present under the appearances of wheat bread and grape wine. Jesus' question to the Apostles, "Do you also want to leave?" is asked of us too. Just as Peter did, we discover the Good News that only Jesus has the words of eternal life and that receiving the gift of Eucharist is to receive the Lord himself.

The Institution of the Eucharist

On the night before he died, Jesus anticipated his own Passion and Death and interpreted them in terms of the Jewish Passover and its sacrifice. The history of sacrifice in the Old Covenant was well known to Jesus. Four kinds of sacrifice were common to the Jewish people. First, there were *gift offerings*. The offering (fruit, crop, or animal) was completely destroyed as an act of thanks to God for all his blessings. Examples of gift offerings were those sacrificed to God by Cain and Abel (see Genesis 4:3–5). Second, there were *shared peace offerings*. Part of the food was given to God (sacrificed); the people ate the other part. This sharing represented the people's desire for union and peace with God (see Deuteronomy 12:6–7). Third, there were *atonement offerings*. Priests offered sacrifices to God, asking for forgiveness of sins the people may have committed unwittingly (see Numbers 15:22–31). Fourth, there were *covenant offerings*. The burnt offering and the pouring of sacrificial blood of animals sealed the solemn agreement between Yahweh and the Israelites (see Exodus 24).

Though pious in themselves, none of these types of offerings were suitable for the expiation of sins. In the fullness of time, God the Father chose to send his Son as a sin offering. As first announced in the Psalms, Jesus came to the world because:

> Sacrifice and offering you did not desire,
>> but a body you prepared for me;
> holocausts and sin offerings you took no delight in.
> Then I said, "As is written of me in the scroll,
>> Behold, I come to do your will, O God." (Heb 10:5–7)

All of the Old Testament sacrifices were fulfilled and perfected in the sacrifice of Jesus on the cross. At Golgotha, Jesus, the perfect High Priest, offered the perfect victim (himself) in sacrifice to God for the forgiveness of sin. This sacrifice of Jesus transcends all history, winning justification for all the faithful who came before him and all the faithful who would come after him.

On the night before he died, Jesus instituted the Eucharist as a memorial of his Death and Resurrection. He took bread, said the blessing, broke the bread, and gave it to his disciples, saying, "This is my body, which will be given for you; do this in memory of me." He then took the cup and said, "This cup is the new covenant in my blood, which will be shed for you" (Lk 22:19–20).

By this action, Jesus gave the Jewish Passover its ultimate meaning and anticipated the final Passover of the Church in the glory of his kingdom. By giving his Apostles the power to do what he had done—change bread and wine to his Body and Blood—Jesus ensured the presence of the Eucharist in the Catholic Church for all ages.

From the beginning, the Church has been faithful to Jesus' call to celebrate the Eucharist in his memory. When the Church offers Mass, she blesses God for these great events of Salvation: from creation to the Exodus, to the Death and Resurrection of Jesus and the coming of the Holy Spirit, to the **Second Coming of Christ** and the establishment of a new Heaven and a new earth. As the Church proclaims these events, she is caught up in them. In the Eucharist, God redeems

DID YOU KNOW?

The Jewish people traditionally celebrated an annual Day of Atonement. On this day of fasting and sabbatical resting, the priest offered a blood sacrifice to "atone" for the sins of the people. The people's sins were symbolically placed on the back of a goat—called the "scapegoat"—that was taken out and left in the desert. Today the feast is known as Yom Kippur.

Second Coming of Christ
Also known as the Parousia, this is the time when the Kingdom of God will be fully established and victory over evil will be complete.

us from sin and leads us to freedom. The Holy Spirit moves in our lives. In the Eucharist, we are caught up in the new creation in which all tears are wiped away. In other words, when the Church celebrates the Eucharist, the entire Body of Christ—her head and her body—praises God for the life and Salvation that Christ has given. And we experience that life and Salvation in the present moment. In the Eucharist, the time of liberation, the time of Redemption, and the time of new creation are all *now*.

The Eucharist Through the Age of the Church

It was the first day of the week, Sunday, the day of the Lord's Resurrection, when the first Christians met to "break bread." From that time on, the Church has followed the same fundamental structure of the Eucharist. The Eucharist remains the center of Church life.

The first-century Christians continued to practice their Jewish faith as well. They met in the Temple for morning prayer. They met again at night in a member's home. First, a regular meal was shared. Then the Eucharist was commemorated (see Acts 2:42–47; 1 Corinthians 11:17–22). After the destruction of the Jewish Temple in Jerusalem by the Romans in AD 70, Christians transferred the morning Temple service of Scripture and prayer to the beginning of their evening service. The prayer service eventually became known as the **Mass of Catechumens** or the Liturgy of the Word in the Eucharistic service. Catechumens joined baptized Christians for this part of the Mass to hear readings from the Apostles and to learn about Jesus. Then they were dismissed before the second part of Mass, the Liturgy

of the Eucharist, began. Only baptized Christians participated in Communion and in the meal that followed.

Eventually, the number of Christians increased to the point that eating a regular meal together became prohibitive. St. Justin Martyr reports in his *First Apology* that by the year AD 150, the fellowship meal after the Liturgy of the Eucharist was held only on special occasions. By the beginning of the third century, the meal was dropped altogether.

By the fourth century, a Roman treatise we now call the *Apostolic Tradition* explained how Christians celebrated the Eucharist. The basic pattern consisted of readings from the Apostles, a homily that explained the readings for the catechumens in the group, a dismissal of catechumens, an offering of gifts of bread and wine, a thanksgiving prayer over these gifts, a breaking of the bread, and a reception of the Body and Blood of Christ by all present. Then the deacons took the Body of Christ to baptized members who were absent. The leader of the local Church community (a bishop or presbyter) presided at the ritual, himself representing Christ's presence.

This description of the Eucharist is one that developed in the early history of the Church. However, over time, different liturgical rites began to develop. The pattern of the Eastern liturgy (with centers in Jerusalem, Constantinople, Antioch, and Alexandria) did not change much after the sixth century. In the West (Rome), the pattern of the Eucharist reached a high point of its evolution during and after the Council of Trent.

The Council of Trent (1545–1563) established one uniform way for the celebration of Mass in the Western Church. This Mass that developed after this Council is known as the

Mass of the Catechumens

The first part of the Mass that was attended by catechumens along with baptized Catholics. The prayers, Scripture readings, and homily were meant to be a form of instruction for the catechumens. Today this part of the Mass is called the Liturgy of the Word.

Tridentine Mass and was standard for the Church until the Second Vatican Council. It was said in Latin and followed this general structure:

- Prayers at the Foot of the Altar: Sign of the Cross, Psalm 42, the Confiteor;
- Prayers at the Altar: **Introit**, Opening Prayer, Lord Have Mercy, Gloria, and **Collect**;
- Scripture Readings: Epistle reading, prayer response, Alleluia, Gospel reading, and homily or sermon;
- Profession of Faith: the **Nicene Creed**;
- Offertory: preparation of wine in the chalice and of the host on a plate called a paten, washing of priest's hands, and the **Secret**;
- The Canon: Preface, *Sanctus* (Holy Holy Holy), prayers for the living and for the universal Church, words of institution, prayers for the dead, and Amen;
- Communion Rite: Our Father, Lamb of God, Communion of the priest, Communion of the people, and post-Communion prayer; and
- Closing Rite: dismissal, final blessing, and reading from John 1:1–14.

In 1570, the *Pius V Missal* was printed and gradually put to use throughout the Roman Catholic world. This missal was in Latin and, in preference for widespread uniformity, the Church forbade translations into local languages. Not until 1897 were translations of the *Pius V Missal* finally allowed for purposes of prayer and study. In 1903, Pope Pius X encouraged laypeople to participate in Mass by singing at Mass and receiving Communion more frequently.

Sacrosanctum Concilium, the first document released from the Second Vatican Council (1962–1965), reformed the Church's liturgy and allowed for Mass to be celebrated in the vernacular, moved by a desire that "all the faithful should be led to take full, conscious, and active part in liturgical celebrations" (*Sancrosanctum Concilium* 14). These changes have done nothing to diminish the fact that the Eucharist has kept a "fundamental structure which has been preserved throughout the centuries down to our own day" (*CCC* 1346). This structure continues to be made up of the

- Liturgy of the Word (readings, homily, and General Intercessions); and the
- Liturgy of the Eucharist (presentation of the bread and wine, consecration, thanksgiving, and Communion).

Together the Liturgy of the Word and Liturgy of the Eucharist form "one single act of worship." The *Catechism* asks:

> Is this not the same movement as the Paschal meal of the risen Jesus with his disciples? Walking with them he explained the Scriptures to them; sitting with them at table "he took bread, blessed and broke it, and gave it to them." (*CCC* 1347)

In 2002, the third edition of the *Roman Missal* was published in Latin. The English translation of this editon was released in 2011. In 2007, Pope Benedict issued a *moto propio* allowing for celebration of the Tridentine Mass in extraordinary circumstances alongside the Missal of Pope Paul VI (the ordinary form of the Mass) with the desire for "interior reconciliation in the heart of the Church."

Introit
A part of a psalm that is sung when the priest enters the church and approaches the altar.

Collect
The opening prayer of the Mass. It concludes the Introductory Rites and precedes the Liturgy of the Word.

Nicene Creed
The formal Profession of Faith recited at Mass. It came from the first two Ecumenical Councils, at Nicaea in 325 and Constantinople in 381.

Secret
A prayer from the Tridentine Mass said by the celebrant in a low voice at the end of the Offertory. It is said in a low voice because it occurred at the same time the choir sang the Offertory hymn.

moto propio
Means "of his own accord." It signifies words in papal documents that were decided by the pope personally.

? DID YOU KNOW?

Only validly ordained priests (and bishops) can preside at the Eucharist and consecrate the bread and wine so that they become the Body and Blood of Christ (see *CCC* 1411).

Understanding the Eucharist as a Sacrifice

In the Eucharist, we both remember and proclaim the great works God has done for us. The events of our Salvation become present and actual. In the Eucharist, Christ is now carrying out his sacrifice of the cross. The Eucharist is a sacrifice because in it Christ gives us the very body he gave up on the cross and the very blood he "shed on behalf of many for the forgiveness of sins" (Mt 26:28). The Eucharist is a sacrifice of the Church; as a sacrifice it is offered for the sins of the living and the dead "so that they may be able to enter into the light and peace of Christ" (*CCC* 1371).

The sacrifice of Christ on the cross and the sacrifice of the Eucharist are one single sacrifice. As the Council of Trent taught: "The victim is one and the same: the same now offers through the ministry of priests, who then offered himself on the cross; only the manner of offering is different" (*CCC* 1367).

Jesus continues to offer the sacrifice of himself each time the Eucharist is offered. Each Eucharist is not a new sacrifice. Rather, each Eucharist is the presence in our midst of the *one eternal sacrifice* that Jesus made on the cross more than two thousand years ago: As the *Catechism* explains:

> In order to leave them a pledge of this love, in order never to depart from his own and to make them sharers in his Passover, he instituted the Eucharist as the memorial of his death and Resurrection, and commanded his apostles to celebrate it until his return; "thereby he constituted them priests of the New Testament." (*CCC* 1337, quoting the Council of Trent)

The Eucharist is a sacramental sacrifice in three ways: as (1) thanksgiving and praise to the Father; (2) the sacrificial memorial of Christ and his Body; and (3) the presence of Christ by the power of his Word and of his Spirit.

Thanksgiving and Praise to the Father

The Eucharist is a sacramental sacrifice to God the Father as an act of gratitude for his blessings on creation, Redemption, and sanctification. Recall that the word *Eucharist* means "thanksgiving." Above all the Eucharist thanks the Father for the gift of his Son.

At Mass, the doxology of the Eucharistic Prayer reminds us that all praise and glory are due the Father in the name of all creation so that this sacrifice is offered *through* Christ and *with* him, to be accepted *in* him (see *CCC* 1361).

Sacrificial Memorial of Christ

In 1562, the Council of Trent defined the Eucharist as "an unbloody sacrifice." What this means is that the Eucharist is really the *sacrament of the sacrifice of Jesus*. There is only one sacrifice—that of Jesus. For this reason, the *Catechism* teaches that "the sacrifice of Christ and the sacrifice of the Eucharist are *one single sacrifice*" (*CCC* 1367). The Eucharist "re-presents" and perpetuates "the sacrifice of the cross throughout the ages until [Christ] should come again" (*CCC* 1323). At every Mass, then, we are joined to Christ himself, who is present, offering his Body and Blood to God for our Salvation. The Eucharist doesn't just recall or memorialize the sacrifice of Jesus. It makes us present in the life, Death, and Resurrection of Christ. As the *Catechism* teaches,

> The Eucharist is the memorial of Christ's Passover, the making present and the sacramental offering of his unique sacrifice, in the liturgy of the Church which is his Body. (*CCC* 1362)

> The Eucharist is thus a sacrifice because it *re-presents* (makes present) the sacrifice of the cross. (*CCC* 1366)

The Eucharist is also a sacrifice of the Church. The Church offers herself with Christ by giving to the Father all praise, suffering, prayer, and work united with those of Christ. This means the sacrifice gains new value whenever we participate in the Eucharist. Also, the Church is united as one Body in communion with the whole Church—the pope and with the bishop in the place where the Mass is being offered. Again, in the Eucharistic Prayer, the priest prays:

> Remember, Lord, your Church, spread throughout the world, and bring her to the fullness of charity, together with N. our Pope and N. our Bishop and all the clergy.

The Eucharist is offered not only for those faithful on earth, but also for those who are already in heaven and the faithfully departed "who have died in Christ but are not yet wholly purified" (Council of Trent, *DS* 1743).

St. Augustine wrote of the sacrifice offered at Mass: "The Church continues to reproduce this sacrifice in the sacrament of the altar so well-known to believers wherein it is evident to them that in what she offers she herself is offered" (*De civ. Dei* 10, quoted in *CCC* 1372).

Christ's Presence in the Eucharist

Christ's presence in the Eucharist is unique to the sacrament. While he is present in many ways to the Church—in the poor, the sick, and the imprisoned, for example—in the minister of the sacraments, in the community that has gathered in his name, and in the Holy Scriptures that are read, he is most especially present in the Eucharistic species of consecrated bread and wine. In the Body and Blood of Christ, "*the whole Christ is truly, really, and substantially contained*" (Council of Trent, quoted in *CCC* 1374). This presence is "Real Presence," not because the other ways Jesus is present in the world are not real, but because it is his presence in the fullest sense.

How this presence occurs has been termed *transubstantiation* to express how the reality (substance) of bread and wine changes into the reality of Jesus—his risen, glorified Body and Blood. The Council of Trent summarized Church teaching about this belief:

> . . . by the consecration of the bread and wine there takes place a change of the whole substance of the bread into the substance of the body of Christ our Lord and of the whole substance of the wine into the substance of his blood. (Council of Trent, quoted in *CCC* 1377)

It makes perfect sense that Jesus would want to remain present in the Church in this unique way. He desired to express for us the same privileges of friendship, blessing, and love that he first afforded his disciples who walked the earth with him many years ago. (M)

For Review

1. How were the Eucharistic signs of bread and wine prefigured in the Old Testament?
2. How are Jesus' multiplication of loaves and miracle at Cana associated with Eucharist?
3. What did Jesus' disciples find difficult in his Bread of Life discourse?
4. Name the four kinds of sacrifice common to the Jewish people.
5. When did Jesus institute the Sacrament of the Eucharist?
6. How was a regular meal part of the Eucharist in the first century? When did the practice of sharing a regular meal end?
7. What is the Tridentine Mass?
8. What are the two main parts of Mass today?
9. What are three ways that the Eucharist is a sacramental sacrifice?

For Reflection

• In your own words, describe Christ's presence in the Eucharist.

• How do you understand the Eucharist to be an "unbloody sacrifice"?

CELEBRATING THE SACRAMENT OF THE EUCHARIST

We come together in one place for Mass. The gathering of people is a precondition for celebrating the Eucharist. At the head is Christ himself; he is the High Priest of the New Covenant who presides invisibly over every Eucharistic celebration. The original meaning of the term *liturgy* refers to "public work" or "service done on behalf of people." The primary meaning of the term is the participation of the Church in the "work of God" (see *CCC* 1069). This work involves people with each of these roles: The priest or bishop represents Christ, acting in the person of Christ the Head. The priest or bishop is the presider who speaks after the readings, receives the offerings, and says the Eucharistic Prayer. All in the assembly have their own active parts to play in the celebration: Some are readers, some bring up the gifts, and others give Communion. The whole people respond, "Amen"—"I agree"—to bring their participation to life.

The Mass is divided into two main parts: the Liturgy of the Word and the Liturgy of the Eucharist. Introductory and concluding rites surround them. An explanation of the order of the Mass follows.

Introductory Rites

The Mass begins with introductory rites whose purpose is "to help the assembled people to become a worshiping community and prepare them for listening to God's Word and celebrating the Eucharist" (*Sacramentary*). As the priest and ministers process to the altar, the congregation sings an entrance song. At the end of the song, the priest greets the people.

Priest:	In the name of the Father, and of the Son, and of the Holy Spirit.
People:	Amen.
Priest:	The grace of our Lord Jesus Christ and the love of God and the communion of the Holy Spirit be with you all.
People:	And with your spirit.

Next, there is either a rite of blessing and sprinkling of holy water, or there is a **penitential rite**. The priest invites the people to repent of their sins and prepare themselves "to celebrate the sacred mysteries. The actual penitential rite may consist of the **Confiteor** ("I confess") and/or the "Lord, have mercy." The Glory to God is said or sung on Sundays outside Advent and Lent. Then the priest prays an opening prayer.

Liturgy of the Word

The Liturgy of the Word is common with each sacrament. At Mass, there is a first reading, from either the Old Testament, the Acts of the Apostles, or Revelation. The cantor then leads the people in a **Responsorial Psalm**. A second reading (on Sundays and Holy Days) is proclaimed, usually from the New Testament letters. An Alleluia or Gospel Acclamation is sung by all as a reminder of the joy and hope we have because of the Good News of Jesus. The priest or deacon reads a passage from one of the four Gospels. Then he explains the Gospel reading in a homily.

If catechumens are present, they are dismissed after the homily. Then all the baptized members of the assembly say the Nicene Creed or renew their baptismal promises. General Intercessions (the Prayers of the Faithful) follow.

Liturgy of the Eucharist

The second part of Mass, the Liturgy of the Eucharist, follows this general structure:

- Presentation of the Offering;
- Eucharistic Prayer (Preface, Epiclesis, Words of Institution, Anamnesis, Intercessions for the entire Church, Doxology, and Great Amen);
- Communion Rite; and
- Concluding or Dismissal Rite.

These elements of the Liturgy of the Eucharist are discussed in the following sections.

Presentation of the Offering

The Presentation of the Offering is also called the Offertory. A monetary collection for the maintenance of the parish and the needs of the poor is taken. This practice goes back to the first days in the Church when those assembled for liturgy brought gifts of food and money for the Apostles and also gave generously to other Christians in need (see 1 Corinthians 16:1–4; Romans 15:26–29; 2 Corinthians 8–9). The congregation may sing a song as the collection takes place.

When the collection is completed, it is usually taken to the altar, along with the gifts of bread and wine. The bread and wine symbolize not only all the gifts of creation God has generously given us; they also symbolize each person assembled. With the gifts of bread and wine, we offer God the sacrifice of ourselves, in union with the sacrifice of Jesus. As the opening to *The Introduction to Christian Initiation* explains, "By offering themselves

CHRIST'S PRESENCE IN SCRIPTURE

Trace the development of and report on one of the following elements of Mass as they have been used through history:

- crucifix
- incense
- vestments (e.g., stole, alb, cincture, chasuble)
- altar
- tabernacle
- sacred vessels (e.g., chalice, paten, ciborium, cruets)

penitential rite
Part of the introductory rite at Mass when the priest invites people to repent of their sins and prepare themselves to encounter Christ in the Eucharist.

Confiteor
A term that means "I confess," it is used at the beginning of Mass and at other times to prepare to receive grace.

Responsorial Psalm
A psalm sung or said at Mass after the first Scripture reading.

Eucharistic Prayer

The Church's great prayer of praise and thanksgiving to God that takes place during the Liturgy of the Eucharist. There are four main Eucharistic Prayers in the Roman Rite.

Epiclesis

The prayer that petitions God to send the Holy Spirit to transform the bread and wine offered at the Eucharistic liturgy into the Body and Blood of Jesus Christ. This term also applies to the prayer said in every sacrament that asks for the sanctifying power of the Holy Spirit.

Words of Institution

The words said by Jesus over the bread and wine at the Last Supper. The priest repeats these words over the bread and wine at Mass as they are changed into the Body and Blood of Christ.

with Christ, [all those assembled] share in his universal sacrifice: The entire community of the redeemed is offered to God by their high priest" (*The Rites*, Christian Initiation 2, General Introduction).

At the altar, the priest—acting in the person of Jesus and in the name of the entire assembly—pours wine into the chalice. He adds a drop of water, which symbolizes the human nature of Jesus that coexists with his divinity. He also places the vessel of the hosts that are to be consecrated on a corporal (white cloth) on the altar table. When the altar has been readied, he sings or says the following prayer: "Pray, brethren, that my sacrifice and yours may be acceptable to God, the almighty Father." All respond, "May the Lord accept the sacrifice at your hands for the praise and glory of his name, for our good, and the good of all his holy Church."

Eucharistic Prayer

The **Eucharistic Prayer** is the Church's great prayer of praise and thanksgiving to God. It is the high point of the Liturgy of the Eucharist and of the Mass itself. There are four main Eucharistic Prayers in the Roman Rite. There are also Eucharistic Prayers for Masses with Children, for Mass for various Needs and Occasions, and for Masses of Reconciliation. Although each of these prayers is different in length and content, each one has the same basic structure.

The Eucharistic Prayer begins with the Preface, which is a prayer of thanksgiving to the Father. After this, everyone says or sings the Sanctus, the "Holy, Holy, Holy." The whole community thus joins in the unending praise that the Church in Heaven, the angels and all the saints, sing to the thrice-holy God.

The word *epiclesis* is a Greek word that means "calling down upon" or "invocation." This part of the Eucharistic Prayer asks the Father to send the Holy Spirit to sanctify the gifts of bread and wine. The bread and wine become the Body and Blood of Christ—not through the holiness of the priest or the assembled Church, but through the power of the Holy Spirit. The priest prays that by the Holy Spirit the gifts of bread and wine "may become the Body and Blood of your Son our Lord Jesus Christ" (Eucharistic Prayer II).

In the **Words of Institution**, the priest repeats the words of Jesus at the Last Supper. We believe that, at this time, "Christ is thus really and mysteriously made *present*" (*CCC* 1357). The bread and wine are changed into the Body and Blood of Jesus. The priest prays:

> For on the night he was betrayed he himself took bread, and giving you thanks, he said the blessing, broke the bread and gave it to his disciples saying: "Take this, all of you, and eat of it, for this is my Body, which will be given up for you." In a similar way, when the supper was ended, he took the chalice, and giving you thanks, he said this blessing and gave the

chalice to his disciples, saying: "Take this, all of you, and drink from it, for this is the chalice of my Blood, the Blood of the new and eternal covenant, which will be poured out for you and for many for the forgiveness of sins. Do this in memory of me." (Eucharistic Prayer II)

The Council of Trent clearly taught, "By the consecration of the bread and wine the whole substance of the bread is changed into the substance of the body of Christ our Lord, and the whole substance of the wine is changed into the substance of his blood" (*Eucharist* 4).

The word *anamnesis* means "memorial." Immediately after the Words of Institution, the assembled "Church calls to mind the Passion, resurrection, and glorious return of Christ Jesus" (*CCC* 1354). We say, "We proclaim your Death, O Lord, and profess your Resurrection until you come again," or another one of the memorial acclamations.

The intercessions consist of prayers for the entire Church—living and dead. Depending on which Eucharistic Prayer is selected, there are intercessions for the following:

- *All those gathered for Eucharist.* The priest prays that we may be nourished by the Eucharist, filled with the Holy Spirit, and become "one body, one spirit in Christ."
- *The pope, bishop, and all the clergy.* The priest prays for the Church's ordained leaders, reminding us we are a universal Church.
- *Catholics in need.* The priest prays that God will hear and answer the prayers of this family, whom you have summoned before you."
- *The faithful deceased.* The priest prays that God will "give kind admittance" to his Kingdom to those who died leading lives that were pleasing to him.

These intercessory prayers remind us of two important beliefs regarding the Eucharist. First, we offer this sacrificial meal in the hope that "the whole human race may be brought into the unity of God's family" (*The Rites*, Christian Initiation 2, General Introduction). Second, at each Eucharist, we join with the whole Church—all living members, those present and absent, those near and far, as well as the faithful dead—in celebrating the offering and the intercession of Christ.

The Eucharistic Prayer ends with a **doxology**, reminding us that every Eucharist strengthens our initiation into the life of the Trinity. The Church offers every Mass to praise the Trinity. It is a "sacrifice of praise to the Father ... offered *through* Christ and *with* him, to be accepted *in* him" (*CCC* 1361). So too, everything we do as Catholics aims at praising the Trinity. United with Christ, we give glory and honor to the Trinity. The priest says or sings the following prayer while holding up the Body and Blood of Christ:

> Through him, and
> with him, and
> in him, O God, almighty Father,
> in the unity of the Holy Spirit,
> all glory and honor is yours,
> for ever and ever.

The people respond by saying or singing the **Great Amen**. The word *amen* means "so be it" or "I agree." It is our "yes" to all that has been said in the Eucharistic Prayer. It professes our belief that the Risen Jesus is truly among us.

doxology
A prayer of praise to the Blessed Trinity. The Eucharistic Prayer ends in a doxology.

Great Amen
The affirmation by the faithful to the entire Eucharistic Prayer.

The Communion Rite

The Communion Rite readies the faithful to receive the Lord, the "bread of life" and the "cup of eternal salvation." The Communion Rite is made up of the Lord's Prayer, Rite of Peace, Fraction Rite, reception of Communion, and prayer after Communion.

The Lord's Prayer is another name for the Our Father. It is the prayer Jesus taught his Apostles (see Matthew 6:9–13; Luke 11:2–4). This prayer acknowledges our identity as God's adopted children, as brothers and sisters of Jesus and of one another. As the *Catechism* states, "When we pray to the Father, we are *in communion with him* and with his Son, Jesus Christ" (*CCC* 2781).

> We can adore the Father because he has caused us to be reborn to his life by *adopting* us as his children in his only Son: by Baptism, he incorporates us into the Body of his Christ; through the anointing of his Spirit who flows from the head to the members, he makes us other "Christs." (*CCC* 2782)

In the Rite of Peace, the "Church asks for peace and unity for herself and for the whole human family" (*General Instruction of the Roman Missal* 82). The gathered people exchange a Sign of Peace as an expression of their communion with one another.

During the **Fraction Rite**, the priest repeats the actions of Jesus at the Last Supper. He breaks the blessed bread. He puts a piece of the consecrated host into the chalice of wine to "signify the unity of the Body and Blood of the Lord in the work of salvation" (*GIRM* 83). Meanwhile, the people sing the Lamb of God.

The reception of Communion follows. The priest is first to receive the Body and Blood of Christ. Then he and the Eucharistic ministers distribute Holy Communion to the people. The following dialogue takes place:

Priest:	(presenting the host) The Body of Christ.
Communicant:	Amen.
Priest:	(presenting the wine) The Blood of Christ.
Communicant:	Amen.

In the Western Church, Catholics may receive the host on the tongue or in the hand, as they wish. Communion under both species (wheat bread and grape wine) is "more complete" since this is the way it was first shared at the Last Supper. However,

> since Christ is sacramentally present under each of the species, communion under the species of bread alone makes it possible to receive all the fruit of Eucharistic grace. (*CCC* 1390)

After receiving Holy Communion, people spend time in private prayer as the cantor or choir sings an appropriate Communion song or a time of silence is observed. At the end of this

Fraction Rite

The time during the Communion Rite when the priest breaks the Body of Christ. He puts a piece of the consecrated bread into the chalice containing the Blood of Christ to signify the unity of the Body and Blood of Christ.

time, the priest concludes the Communion Rite with a prayer after Communion.

Nourished by the Body and Blood of Christ, in a concluding rite, the faithful are then sent out into the world with the charge to "go and announce the Gospel of the Lord."

For Review

1. What roles do various people have at Eucharist?
2. From where are the three Scripture readings for a Sunday or Holy Day Mass usually taken?
3. What is the Scripture basis for bringing gifts of money to the altar?
4. What is the high point of the Mass?
5. Define *epiclesis*.
6. What are two important beliefs regarding the Eucharist that the intercessory prayers remind us of?
7. What elements make up the Communion Rite?

For Reflection

- What does it mean to you to say the liturgy is the "the work of God in which the Church participates"?
- Describe both the most formal and most informal Masses you have ever attended.

THE GRACES OF HOLY COMMUNION

The Eucharist helps perfect our relationship with Christ, with the Church, and with others we encounter, especially the poor. The principal effect of the sacrament is it augments our union with Christ. Consider what happened to two of Jesus' disciples shortly after the crucifixion.

The two disciples were disheartened while walking from Jerusalem to Emmaus. Along the way, a stranger joined them. He began to tell them about the meaning of the Scriptures, of Jesus' true identity as a "Suffering Servant"; that is, a Messiah who had to die for the sins of others. Later that day, when the disciples shared bread with this stranger, "their eyes were opened and they recognized him" as the Risen Jesus. This incredible experience of communion renewed the disciples and set their hearts aflame. As they said to each other, "Were not our hearts burning (within us) while he spoke to us?" They were immediately moved to go back to Jerusalem and tell everyone Jesus had risen and had appeared to them (see Luke 24:1–35). From their experience of Jesus in the figurative breaking open of God's Word and the literal breaking of the bread, they were empowered to go out and share Christ's love with others.

Likewise, our participation at Eucharist and reception of Holy Communion renew us and set us aflame

CHRISTIAN LOVE

The first encyclical of Pope Benedict XVI, *Deus Caritas Est*, was about Christian love. The Pope cited Mary, the Mother of Jesus, as an example of someone who is so united with Christ that others see Christ in her. The Pope ended his encyclical with the following prayer:

Holy Mary, Mother of God, you have given the world its true light, Jesus, your Son—the Son of God. You abandoned yourself completely to God's call and thus became a wellspring of the goodness that flows forth from him. Show us Jesus. Lead us to him. Teach us to know and love him, so that we too can become capable of true love and be fountains of living water in the midst of a thirsting world.

Write you own prayer, poem, or song to Christ in the Eucharist, asking that you may be so united with him that others may see him in you and through your actions. Pray for the increased ability to love others as Christ himself loved others.

Be prepared to share what you have written at the prayer service at the end of this chapter.

---

with Christ's compelling love (see *Sacrosanctum Concilium* 10). We become more generous, compassionate, and selfless. We are strengthened to love others because we know with certainty that God has first loved us (see 1 John 4:10). We also see the intimate connection between love of God and love of others. We know *in our hearts* the truth contained in the First Letter of John:

If anyone says, "I love God," but hates his brother, he is a liar; for whoever does not love a brother whom he has seen cannot love God whom he has not seen. This is the commandment we have from him: whoever loves God must also love his brother. (1 Jn 4:20–21)

The Eucharist not only enables us to love others *in imitation of* Christ; it also enables us to be so united with Christ that he reveals himself to others through us. The *Catechism of the Catholic Church* describes several particular fruits, or effects, of our participation in the Eucharist and reception of Holy Communion in more detail. Brief descriptions of these effects follow.

Unity with Christ

The *Catechism* states, "The celebration of the Eucharistic sacrifice is wholly directed toward the intimate union of the faithful with Christ through communion. To receive communion is to receive Christ himself who has offered himself for us" (*CCC* 1382). This communion is so intimate that Christ becomes a part of us and we become a part of him. We deepen our identity as his very body (see 1 Corinthians 12:27). That Holy Communion expands our relationship with Christ is the principal fruit of the sacrament. Holy Communion "preserves, increases, and renews the life of grace received at Baptism" (*CCC* 1392).

Separation from Sin

Holy Communion also separates us from sin. It cleanses the soul of venial sins. Also, the closer we unite ourselves with his Passion and Resurrection, "the more we share the life of Christ and progress in his friendship [and] the more difficult it is to break away from him by mortal sin" (*CCC* 1395). Though the Eucharist protects us from future mortal sins, it is not intended to forgive past mortal sins—that function is proper to the Sacrament of Penance or Reconciliation.

Becoming Church

While deepening our relationship with Christ through the Eucharist, we also become united to our brothers and sisters in the Church. Every Eucharist helps us form and build the Church. The Second Vatican Council reminded us that the Mass is "a supper of brotherly and sisterly communion" (*Gaudium et Spes* [Pastoral Constitution on the Church in the Modern World] 38). "Because the loaf of bread is one, we, though many, are one body, for we all partake of the one loaf" (1 Cor 10:17). We become "individually parts of one another" (Rom 12:5). "Really sharing in the body of the Lord in the breaking of the Eucharistic bread, we are taken up into communion with him and with one other" (*Lumen Gentium* 7). We act *as Church* whenever we participate in the Eucharist. Each Mass unites us with the whole Church through our bishop and our local community.

As a Sacrament of Initiation, the Eucharist both incorporates us more completely *into* the Church and nourishes us spiritually so that we actually *become* Church. The Second Vatican Council explained,

The liturgy daily builds up those who are in the church, making of them a holy temple of the Lord, a dwelling-place for God in the Spirit (see Ephesians 2:21–22), to the mature measure of the fullness of Christ (see Eph 4:13). At the same time it marvelously enhances their power to preach Christ and thus show the church to those who are outside. (*Sacrosanctum Concilium* 2)

Strengthened by the Eucharist, we can express in our lives and "portray to others the mystery of Christ and the real nature of the true church" (*Sacrosanctum Concilium* 2). The Eucharist helps us do this in several ways; for example:

1. We can participate actively in the entire life of the local parish.
2. We can contribute (with money, time, and goods) to the mission activity of the Church in rural areas or in other countries.
3. We can "animate" our families, workplaces, schools, and neighborhoods with "the spirit of Christianity" through our attitudes and example (see *Gaudium et Spes* 43).
4. We can engage in **evangelization**—spreading the message of Jesus to others through our daily words and actions—and we can "be witnesses to Christ in all circumstances" (*Gaudium et Spes* 43).
5. We can build community with the members of our parish.
6. We can help strengthen the unity of all Christians through prayer and dialogue.

To Be Eucharist for Others

Another fruit of the Eucharist is that it transforms us in our relationship with the poor and all those who suffer. As the *Catechism* teaches, "The

Eucharist commits us to the poor. To receive in truth the Body and Blood of Christ given up for us, we must recognize Christ in the poorest, his brethren" (*CCC* 1397). The first Christians who came together to celebrate the Eucharist also made it a point to provide for those who were needy. Christians held all things in common until there was no distinction between rich and poor (see Acts 2:44–45). The early Church continued this same practice. In the time of St. Justin Martyr (second century), Christians linked their charitable activity with the Eucharist. "Those who are able make offerings in accordance with their means, each as he or she wishes; the bishop in turn makes use of these to support orphans, widows, the sick and those who for other reasons find themselves in need, such as prisoners and foreigners" (*I Apologia* 67: PG 6, 429).

Through the Eucharist, we become the bread others need. We not only strive to provide physical food for the approximately 852 million people worldwide who are hungry; we also strive in all our relationships to provide for the emotional, psychological, and spiritual needs of others. In addition to

evangelization
The act of bringing the Good News of Jesus Christ to others.

performing the corporal works of mercy (to feed the hungry, to give drink to the thirsty, to clothe the naked, to shelter the homeless, to visit the sick, to visit the imprisoned, and to bury the dead), we also perform the spiritual works of mercy. We sacrifice our own needs, as Jesus himself did, in service to others. We counsel those who are doubtful. We advise sinners to change their ways. We instruct the ignorant. We comfort the sorrowful. We bear wrongs patiently and forgive all injuries. We pray for the living and for the dead. In union with Christ, we lose ourselves in love "to bring glad tidings to the poor"(Lk 4:18), and "to seek and to save what was lost" (Lk 19:10).

Blessed Mother Teresa of Calcutta was a modern-day Catholic whose life was transformed by the Eucharist. She spent her life "being Eucharist" to the forgotten poor in India. She nursed the dying, fed the hungry, and gave comfort to those who had been abandoned. The prayer she said daily expresses the way Christ in the Eucharist can bring us into communion with him and others, if we let him:

> Dear Jesus, help me spread your fragrance everywhere I go. Flood my soul with your spirit and love.

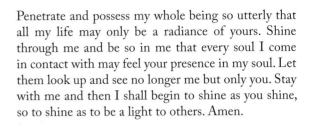

Penetrate and possess my whole being so utterly that all my life may only be a radiance of yours. Shine through me and be so in me that every soul I come in contact with may feel your presence in my soul. Let them look up and see no longer me but only you. Stay with me and then I shall begin to shine as you shine, so to shine as to be a light to others. Amen.

The Mass is both a sacrifice and a heavenly meal that facilitates our communion with the Blessed Trinity, the Church, and our neighbors. The Eucharist is also a foretaste of the heavenly banquet we will one day experience in union with the Blessed Trinity.

Requirements for Formal Reception

To prepare ourselves for such a great and holy moment as reception of Holy Communion, St. Paul called on us to examine our conscience:

> Therefore whoever eats the bread or drinks the cup of the Lord unworthily will have to answer for the body and blood of the Lord. A person should examine himself, and so eat the bread and drink the cup. For anyone who eats and drinks without discerning the body, eats and drinks judgment on himself. (1 Cor 11:27–29)

Practically, this means a person must be properly "disposed" or "in order" to receive Holy Communion. To determine proper disposition, the Church has laws regarding the reception of Communion. Foremost, because Eucharist is a sacrament of the living (people already in communion with God and the Church), we must be in the state of grace to receive Holy Communion. The Eucharist forgives venial sins; but if we have sinned mortally, we are no longer in communion with God and others in the Church. We are required to be reconciled in the Sacrament of Penance before receiving Communion.

Church law requires members to "take part in the Divine Liturgy on Sundays and feast days . . . and to receive the Eucharist at least once a year, if possible during the Easter season" *(CCC* 1389). Because the Eucharist nourishes us spiritually and strengthens our bond of friendship with God, the Church "strongly encourages the faithful to receive the holy Eucharist on Sundays and feast days, or more often still, even daily" *(CCC* 1389). A person is even able to receive Communion more than once per day, as long as he or she participates in the liturgy. For example, this occasion may arise if a persona takes part in a Saturday afternoon liturgy celebrating the Sacrament of Matrimony and then later participates in the Sunday vigil on Saturday evening.

In the past, Catholics were required to prepare spiritually for the Eucharist by fasting from midnight until receiving Communion. In the mid-1950s, the required Eucharistic fast was reduced to three hours. Today, it is defined as a one-hour fast before Communion from food and drink (excepting water).

Based on the Gospel story in which Jesus said, "Let the children come to me" (Mk 10:14), Pope St. Pius X lowered the age for First Communion to seven years in 1910. St. Pius X also approved the practice of giving Communion before Confirmation—a practice that had become popular during the nineteenth century as part of a liturgical movement that viewed Communion as an integral part of the Mass. Besides obeying the Church's rules regarding the reception of Communion, it is important to desire to be one with God in Jesus and the Holy Spirit. While human words can never adequately describe the inexhaustible richness of the Eucharist, consider how St. Thérèse of Lisieux described the oneness she felt at her First Communion:

> I knew that I was loved and I declared: "I love You, and I give myself to You for ever!" Jesus made no demand on me; He asked for no sacrifices. For a long time Jesus and little Thérèse had gazed at each other and they understood each other. On that day it was no longer a matter of gazing: it was a union. There were no longer two of us. Thérèse had disappeared like a drop of water lost in the depth of the ocean. Only Jesus remained—the Master and the King. (*Story of a Soul* 52)

We lose our separateness in the experience of Eucharistic Communion. We become more fully Christ; we become more fully the Church.

For Review

1. What happened to the two disciples on the road to Emmaus?
2. Name the fruits or effects of the Sacrament of the Eucharist. Choose one fruit of Communion and describe it in more detail.
3. What type of sin is forgiven in the Sacrament of the Eucharist?
4. Name two ways the Eucharist helps us be the Church.
5. Tell how the Eucharist can encourage charitable actions—especially to the poor.
6. What does it mean to be properly disposed to receive Holy Communion?
7. What Scripture passage did Pope St. Pius X cite when moving the age of First Communion to seven years?

For Reflection

- "The Eucharist makes us more generous, compassionate, and selfless." How is that statement true for you?

- Write a short prayer or poem to express how you can be Eucharist for others.

TRANSFORMATION

WE ARE SENT

The liturgy of the Mass contains a transformational dimension that extends beyond the liturgy. In fact, as the name *Missa* signifies, the Mass is meant to encourage outreach by those who have participated. The Dismissal Rite is when the idea of being sent forth is most clearly witnessed. The Dismissal Rite does not simply announce that the Mass is over. Instead, the priest—in the name of Jesus—sends us or commissions us to go out to the world and spread the Gospel in our daily lives. Just as Jesus commissioned his Apostles to teach the entire world about him and his message (see Matthew 28:19–20), so we are sent forth from the Eucharist to share our communion with the Blessed Trinity, the Church, and others, especially the poor.

The typical Dismissal Rite is short and simple:

Priest:	The Lord be with you.
People:	And with your spirit.
Priest:	May almighty God bless you, the Father, and the Son, and the Holy Spirit.
People:	Amen.
Priest:	Go in peace, glorifying the Lord by your Life.
People:	Thanks be to God.

The message of the Dismissal Rite, however, is not so simple. Because of the Eucharist we have just celebrated, the Lord is both with us and within us. His sanctifying grace empowers us to go forth and *to be Eucharist* for others—at home, at school, at work, in our neighborhoods, and in our country. We have an important mission—not only to spread the Good News of Jesus, but to be "other Christs" in today's world.

This is one of the reasons the Second Vatican Council clearly stated that the Eucharist is "the source and summit of the Christian life" (*Lumen Gentium* 11) and the "universal sacrament of salvation" (*Gaudium et Spes* 45). We need the Eucharist to nourish us and keep us connected more closely to Jesus, the bread of life and the true vine. At the same time, Christ, through the Eucharist, renews, strengthens, and deepens our membership in the Church that was already achieved at Baptism. We are to continue his work in today's world.

Pope John Paul II explained that incorporation into Christ is "constantly renewed and consolidated by sharing in the Eucharistic Sacrifice." He wrote that when we celebrate Eucharist, we become "a 'sacrament' for humanity . . . the light of the world and the salt of the earth . . . for the redemption of all" (*Ecclesia de Eucharistia* 22). The Eucharist sends us out into the world ready to love more completely. More, it sends us out not only as loving individuals, but also as a loving community. The Eucharist strengthens the bonds between all who receive it and makes it possible for us to demonstrate among ourselves the love we are to share with the world.

To receive the grace of Eucharist, we are obliged to attend and participate at Mass. The "Sunday obligation" is a requirement of the Third Commandment and a precept of the Church.

THE SUNDAY OBLIGATION

A precept of the Church is that "on Sunday and other holy days of obligation the faithful are bound to participate in the Mass" (*CIC* quoted in *CCC* 2180). Those who deliberately skip Mass on those days fail in the obligation and commit a grave sin.

What are reasons teens give for missing Mass? Some of the most common:

- I'd rather sleep.
- My friends are not going.
- It's boring.
- I have a lot of homework.
- I have to work.
- My parents don't go.
- I'm angry with the Church.
- I don't have a ride.
- I no longer believe in God.
- I have done some bad things and am not worthy to go.

On the other hand, it is important for us to go to Mass for several reasons, one of the foremost being that we are missed when we are absent. Our absence from Mass creates a void in the Body of Christ, just as missing any one part of the anatomy would create a void in the human body. Rather than reasons for missing Sunday Mass, we should cultivate a genuine desire to be present and be able to give reasons like the following (and those on page 4) for why we attend:

- I want to keep my baptismal vows.
- I love God and want to please God.
- Jesus asked us to do this to remember him.
- My whole family is going, so I want to go along.
- I want to praise and thank God.
- I want to be a good example to others.

- I want to go to Heaven.
- I need Jesus' presence in my life.
- It helps me live a good Christian life.
- My parish community needs my presence.
- I want to receive Communion
- I belong to the Catholic Church and want to obey her laws.

The *Catechism of the Catholic Church* teaches:

> Participation in the communal celebration of the Sunday Eucharist is a testimony of belonging and of being faithful to Christ and to his Church. The faithful give witness by this to their communion in faith and charity. Together they testify to God's holiness and their hope of salvation. They strengthen one another under the guidance of the Holy Spirit. (*CCC* 2182)

Our participation at Eucharist is paramount to being a Catholic. A recent poll conducted by a research arm at Georgetown University found that nearly one-third of U.S. Catholics surveyed said they "rarely or never" attend Sunday Mass. The number was discouraging to both those who are not availing themselves of the grace of the Sacrament and to the Church herself, who misses their presence. As Cardinal Joseph Bernardin of Chicago once explained:

> Liturgy is not an option nor merely an obligation, not a bonus, but a need—like food and drink, like sleep and work, like friends. We need to gather, listen, give praise and thanks, and share communion. Otherwise we forget who we are and whose we are; and we can have neither the strength nor the joy to be Christ's body—present in the world today.

For Review

1. What is the meaning of the term *Mass*?
2. How did Pope John Paul II compare incorporation into Christ to receiving the Eucharist?

For Reflection

- How does the Eucharist help you become a sacrament for others?

- What are your reasons for going to Sunday Mass?

CHAPTER QUICK VIEW

Main Ideas

- The term *Eucharist* refers both to the Mass and to the consecrated species of bread and wine. (p. 120)

- The Sacrament of the Eucharist has many other names because its richness is truly inexhaustible. (p. 120)

- By the invocation of the Holy Spirit, bread and wine become the Body and Blood of the Lord at Mass. (p. 121)

- The signs of wheat bread and grape wine have roots in the Old Testament and were referred to by Jesus in his ministry. (pp. 121–122)

- Though four types of sacrifice are mentioned in the Old Testament, none were suitable for the expiation of sins. (pp. 122–123)

- The Eucharist, which Jesus instituted as a memorial of his Death and Resurrection, redeems us from sin and leads us to freedom. (pp. 123–124)

- The first Christians shared a regular meal along with the Eucharist; this fellowship meal was dropped by the beginning of the third century. (p. 124)

- In the sixteenth century, the Council of Trent established one uniform way to celebrate Mass in the Western Church. (pp. 124–125)

- The Second Vatican Council approved the Mass to be celebrated in the vernacular; in 2011, a new English translation of the *Roman Missal* was published. (p. 125)

- The Eucharist is a sacrifice because Christ gives us the very body he gave up on the cross. (p. 126)

- In the Body and Blood of Christ, Jesus is "truly, really, and substantially contained." (p. 127)

- The Mass is divided into two parts: the Liturgy of the Word and the Liturgy of the Eucharist. (pp. 128–133)

- When catechumens are present, they are dismissed after the homily. (p. 129)

- The Eucharistic Prayer is the high point of the Liturgy of the Eucharist and of the Mass itself. (p. 130)

- Unity with Christ, cleansing from venial sin, unity with other Catholics, and a commitment to others, especially the poor, are graces of Holy Communion. (pp. 133–136)

- Proper disposition is required to receive Holy Communion. (pp. 136–137)

- From the Dismissal Rite, we are commissioned to go into the world and be Eucharist for others. (p. 138)

- Catholics are obliged to attend and participate at Mass on Sundays and other holy days of obligation. (pp. 138–139)

TERMS, PEOPLE, PLACES

Match the following terms with the definitions below. You will not use all the terms.

invocation

second coming of Christ

Mass of Catechumens

Introit

Collect

Nicene Creed

Secret

penitential rite

Confiteor

Responsorial Psalm

Eucharistic Prayer

Words of Institution

doxology

Great Amen

Fraction Rite

evangelization

1. a psalm sung when the priest approaches the altar
2. a supplication for God's help
3. a prayer said simultaneously with the singing of the Offertory hymn
4. a prayer of praise to the Blessed Trinity
5. a term that means "I confess"
6. a time when the priest breaks the consecrated bread and puts it into the chalice containing the Blood of Christ
7. an affirmation of faith to the entire Eucharistic Prayer
8. a name for the short prayers that occur before the reading of the Epistle

Famous Catholics and the Sacraments:

ST. JUAN DIEGO

St. Juan Diego's birth name was Cuauhtlatoatzin, which means "the talking eagle." He was born in 1474 in Cuauhtitlan, just north of present-day Mexico City. He was a poor descendant of native Aztecs, and worked hard in the fields and made mats to support himself and his wife, Maria Lucia.

When he was fifty years old, he was baptized by Franciscan missionary Fr. Peter da Gand and given the baptismal name Juan Diego. As a Catholic, Juan developed a special devotion to the Holy Eucharist. Three times a week, he walked fifteen miles barefoot to attend Mass and receive Communion—which was a very unusual practice for Catholics in those days.

On one such journey in 1531, the Blessed Mother appeared to Juan Diego on Tepeyac Hill, on the outskirts of Mexico City. He couldn't believe that Mary would talk with him, for, as he said, "I am a nobody, I am a small rope, a tiny ladder, the tail end, a leaf." Nevertheless, Mary instructed Juan to go to the local bishop and ask him to build a shrine at Tepeyac in her name. The bishop was naturally skeptical, so he told Juan to ask the lady for a "sign." On December 12, Juan returned to Tepeyac, where the Blessed Mother appeared to him again. She told him to climb the hill and pick the flowers he would find there. Although it was a very cold winter day, Juan found beautiful Castilian roses blooming. Following the Blessed Mother's directions, Juan gathered up the roses in his mantle and took them to the bishop.

The bishop was indeed surprised to see the roses, which were not native to Mexico but from Spain. But what really impressed the bishop was the beautiful image of the Blessed Mother miraculously painted on the inside of Juan's mantle. Juan had not painted it and had no idea where it had come from. The bishop was convinced by these signs; within two weeks, he built a small chapel to Mary at Tepeyac Hill.

Juan was forever changed by his encounter with the Blessed Mother. He dedicated his life to prayer. After his wife died, he lived as a hermit in a small hut on Tepeyac Hill, near the chapel the bishop had built for Mary. Juan cared for the church and the first pilgrims who came to pray.

Juan died in 1548, at the age of seventy-four. Pope John Paul II beatified him on May 6, 1990. That same day a miracle occurred in Mexico City through Juan Diego's intercession. A twenty-year-old drug-afflicted man named Juan Jose Barragan Silva stabbed himself in the presence of his mother and then jumped off a third-story balcony. As Juan Jose was falling, his mother prayed desperately to Juan Diego, asking that her son be saved. Even though Juan Jose hit the ground head first, he was completely healed three days later, with no brain damage. Doctors declared his recovery a miracle. Shortly after, on July 31, 2002, Pope John Paul II canonized Juan Diego. He was the first indigenous (native) American to become a saint. At the Eucharist that day, the Pope said,

> What was Juan Diego like? Why did God look upon him? The Book of Sirach, as we have heard, teaches us that God alone "is mighty; he is glorified by the humble" (cf. Sir 3:20).

Saint Paul's words, also proclaimed at this celebration, shed light on the divine way of bringing about Salvation: "God chose what is low and despised in the world . . . so that no human being might boast in the presence of God" (1 Cor 1:28, 29).

. . . In accepting the Christian message without forgoing his indigenous identity, Juan Diego discovered the profound truth of the new humanity, in which all are called to be children of God. Thus he facilitated the fruitful meeting of two worlds, and became a catalyst for the new Mexican identity, closely united to Our Lady of Guadalupe, whose mestizo face expresses her spiritual motherhood which embraces all Mexicans. This is why the witness of [Juan's] life must continue to be the inspiration for the building up of the Mexican nation, encouraging brotherhood among all its children and ever helping to reconcile Mexico with its origins, values, and traditions.

The feast day of St. Juan Diego is December 9. The feast day of Our Lady of Guadalupe—the vision of Mary that Juan Diego saw—is December 12. Today the image of the Blessed Virgin Mary found on Juan's mantle is preserved in the Basilica of Our Lady of Guadalupe. It shows a Mexican woman in native dress who is supported by an angel resembling the ancient gods of the region. The moon is beneath her feet, her cloak is covered with stars, and she is pregnant. The painting has come to symbolize the new birth of Christ among the peoples of the New World.

Juan Diego and Our Lady of Guadalupe have had a lasting impact on the peoples of Mexico. The Aztecs accepted the Spaniards, and more than eight million people were converted to Catholicism. A new mixed race of people—Mestizos—arose as a result. Today the Basilica of Our Lady of Guadalupe is a major place of pilgrimage for Catholics in the Americas. Our Lady of Guadalupe is the patron saint of Mexico. At the canonization Mass for Juan Diego, Pope John Paul II incorporated Aztec traditions into the ritual and urged the Church to incorporate native culture into religious ceremonies whenever possible. Because of Juan Diego's simple faith, many Catholics in Mexico today participate frequently in the Eucharist.

- Research the icon of Our Lady of Guadalupe, found in the Basilica of Our Lady of Guadalupe in Mexico City. How has this icon strengthened the faith of the Mexican people? How has it brought them closer to the Eucharist?
- Write a report on Catholics who are Mexican and Mexican American today. How have they enriched and contributed to the Body of Christ?
- Research how Hispanic Catholics in Mexico celebrate December 12. Why has this day become one of the most important dates on the Mexican calendar?

ST. JUAN DIEGO

ONGOING ASSIGNMENTS

As you cover the material in this chapter, choose and complete at least three of these assignments.

1. Find out how people can become involved in the various Eucharistic ministries in your parish or a neighboring parish. If possible, volunteer for one of these ministries throughout the semester. At the end of this course, reflect on your experience in your journal. How has this ministry strengthened your own faith in the Eucharist? How has this ministry affected your relationship with Christ? With other members of your parish?

2. Like the bread used at the Jewish Passover, the bread used at the Eucharist must not contain yeast. Experiment with several recipes for bread that have no yeast. Then conduct a "taste test" among classmates or family members to decide which recipe seems to be the best.

3. Research the menu of a typical Jewish Seder meal. Then, with a small group of classmates, assign each dish to a different student to make and bring to a "potluck" Seder meal. Reenact the Seder, using the food and the prayers/dialogue you found from your research. Perhaps perform this Seder in front of the class.

4. Make a drawing or painting, write a poem or song, or choreograph a dance to music that represents your understanding of the connection between Eucharist and Baptism. Be prepared to share (and explain if necessary) your creation with the class.

5. Read about meals Jesus shared with others in John 2:1–12; Matthew 8:14–15; and Luke 10:38–42. Then write about how these meals were a sign of oneness and of being connected to others in friendship.

6. Read about meals Jesus ate with people who did not agree with him in Luke 11:37–54; Luke 7:36–50; and Luke 19:1–10. Write about how these meals were occasions of conversion.

7. Reflect on the Lord's Prayer and then—working alone or in a small group—develop a creative way to express what this prayer is saying. Develop a slide show, dance, song, video, mobile, or sculpture that can be presented at class.

8. Find out about an organization such as Bread for the World (www.bread.org), Catholic Worker (www.catholicworker.org), the Society of St. Vincent de Paul (http://svdpusa.org), or Catholic Relief Services (http://crs.org). Write a one-page report about how this organization works to help the poor and hungry in today's world. Also report on how you and other teenagers can get involved.

PRAYER SERVICE

Theme: The Real Presence of Christ in the Eucharist

Leader: Lord, you know the various hungers we have in our hearts. Above all, you know how we yearn to see you and be with you. Help us know that you are always with us, especially in the consecrated species of bread and wine at Eucharist.

Reader 1: 1 Corinthians 10:16-17

Leader: Taste and see the goodness of the Lord. (*All repeat.*)

Side 1: I will bless the Lord at all times; His praise shall be ever in my mouth.

Side 2: Let my soul glory in the Lord; The lowly will hear me and be glad.

All: Taste and see the goodness of the Lord.

Side 1: Glorify the Lord with me, Let us together extol his name.

Side 2: I sought the Lord, and he answered me and delivered me from all my fears.

All: Taste and see the goodness of the Lord.

Reader 2: John 6:51–58

Leader: Let us spend the next few minutes in silence, aware that the Lord Jesus is truly with us. He has given us himself, not just on the cross, but each time we celebrate Eucharist. (*pause*)

I invite those of you who wish to share your prayers from the "Christian Love" activity on page 134 to do so.

Leader: Lord, you promised to give us our daily bread, everything we would need for the journey toward your Kingdom. And so, as your children, we now pray: Our Father . . .

Leader: To show our desire for communion with one another, let us give each other a Sign of Peace. (*All share a Sign of Peace.*)

The Sacraments
of Healing

STILL IN OUR "EARTHLY TENT"

Through the Sacraments of Christian Initiation, we have been given new life in Christ. We carry this life of joy in what St. Paul called the "earthen vessels" of our humanly existence. In this state, we desire to live with God fully in our "heavenly habitation" (see 2 Corinthians 5:1–5) while we remain encumbered by suffering, illness, and death that still affect our human existence.

For this reason, Jesus Christ, the Divine Physician, instituted two Sacraments of Healing: the Sacrament of Penance and the Sacrament of the Anointing of the Sick. Through the power of the Holy Spirit, Jesus commissioned that the Church continue the work of healing and Salvation even after a person has been baptized and welcomed into the Church.

These two sacraments bring forgiveness of sins and restore our spiritual, and often physical, health.

The Healing of the Paralytic

blaspheming
The act of insulting or contempt of God, holy people, or holy things.

The dual action of forgiveness of sins and physical healing occurred early in Jesus' ministry. He was at home in Capernaum, and the crowds who had come to hear him were massive. Included in the number were some of Jesus' antagonists—the scribes. At the time of his preaching, four men came to the room bringing another man who was paralyzed. There was no way for them to enter the space through the crowds. Then the familiar incident took place:

> After they had broken through [the roof], they let down the mat on which the paralytic was lying. When Jesus saw their faith, he said to the paralytic, "Child, your sins are forgiven." (Mk 2:4–5)

The scribes complained about Jesus' action. They accused him of **blaspheming**. "Who but God alone can forgive sins?" (Mk 2:7), they asked him.

Son of Man
A title Jesus frequently used in speaking of himself. It meant two things: Jesus' association with all of humanity and his identity as the righteous one who will usher in God's Kingdom at the end of time (see Daniel 7:13ff).

Then Jesus taught the scribes, the other gathered disciples, and Christians for all time that physical and spiritual healing are not exclusive of one another:

> But that you may know that the **Son of Man** has authority to forgive sins on earth . . . I say to you, rise, pick up your mat, and go home. (Mk 2:10–11)

The healing of the paralytic also teaches another important lesson for our participation in the two Sacraments of Healing: We must come to the Church with faith that their graces can be received. It was the faith of the paralytic and those who lifted him through the roof that moved Jesus to heal the man.

The Need for Sacraments of Healing

In a world without sin, we would not need Sacraments of Healing. Our conversion as sons and daughters of God through the Sacraments of Initiation would have transformed us into perfect Christians, people who from that time on live as perfect followers of Jesus Christ. Unfortunately, this type of perfection is not part of being human, nor is the world ideal.

When Jesus began his public ministry, he called people to "repent, and believe in the gospel" (Mk 1:15). He also commissioned his disciples to baptize people of all nations (see Matthew 28:19). Jesus knew that conversion is a lifelong process. We are continually tempted to sin, and sometimes we deliberately sin. Our need for God's grace is continual, as is our need for his forgiveness. This unit describes how the Sacraments of Healing are sources of his love.

From Catholic Bloggers

WE ALL NEED HEALING

I received yet another heartbreaking email from a person with a disability who tells me she went home and wept after someone in her congregation told her she is disabled because she sinned. I hear these stories and shudder because this kind of "punishment/sin" myth around disability has lingered for far too long in our society. I also want to scream to people that there are as many, if not more, miserable and unhappy people who are not disabled as there are people who are disabled.

We all need healing, but it's not about our bodies. It's about our attitudes, our outlook, our "take" on things. . . . God has healed me over and over again. As a Catholic, when I say "Just say the word and I shall be healed," I ask God to heal me spiritually, to cleanse me of my sins, to guide me toward his will, so that my own will doesn't cause me to trip over myself or others. I would be nowhere without God's healing, but I never pray those words literally for a physical cure. Why not? I have quadriplegia. I've accepted that. And that matter is entirely out of my hands. The energy I have needs to go toward being positive and using the tools I have to help others. Does it present challenges? Yes and I try to write honestly about those here. But in and of itself, being disabled is not the biggest challenge. The biggest challenge is trying to overcome the attitudes of those who only see the disability, not the person. Those who think people with disabilities are disabled because they have sinned. They are, indeed, the ones who need to be healed.

—From Ruth on the blog *Wheelie Catholic*

WE ALL NEED FORGIVENESS

When the Pope arrived in his cell, Agca was dressed in a blue crewneck sweater, jeans, and blue-and-white running shoes from which the laces had been removed. He was unshaved. Agca kissed John Paul's hand.

"Do you speak Italian?" the Pope asked. Agca nodded.

The two men seated themselves, close together, on molded-plastic chairs in a corner of the cell, out of earshot.

At times it looked almost as if the Pope were hearing the confession of Agca, a Turkish Muslim.

At those moments, John Paul leaned forward from the waist in a priestly posture, his head bowed and forehead tightly clasped in his hand as the younger man spoke.

Agca laughed briefly a few times, but the smile would then quickly fade from his face. In the first months after the assassination attempt, there had been in Agca's eyes a zealot's burning glare. But now his face wore a confused, uncertain expression, never hostile.

The Pope clasped Agca's hands in his own from time to time. At other times he grasped the man's arm, as if in a gesture of support.

John Paul's words were intended for Agca alone. "What we talked about will have to remain a secret between him and me," the Pope said as he emerged from the cell. "I spoke to him as brother whom I have pardoned, and who has my complete trust."

As John Paul rose to leave, the two men shook hands. The Pope gave Agca a small gift in a white box, a rosary in silver and mother-of-pearl. The Pope walked out.

—From a news account of Pope John Paul II's
meeting in prison with Mehmet Ali Agca,
a Turkish terrorist who attempted to kill the Pope in 1981

The Sacrament
of Penance
and Reconciliation

What's Going on with Confession?
Though practiced differently than in previous generations, the Sacrament of Penance and Reconciliation remains a necessity; it is the only ordinary way for Catholics to reconcile themselves with God and the Church.

Understanding the Sacrament of Penance and Reconciliation
The Sacrament of Penance and Reconciliation memorializes Christ's ministry of mercy, compassion, and kindness and encourages us to heartfelt conversion through the Church.

Celebrating the Sacrament of Penance and Reconciliation
The rite of the Sacrament of Penance and Reconciliation is made up of three essential actions of the penitent—contrition, confession, and satisfaction—and one of the priest, the granting of absolution.

The Grace of Penance and Reconciliation
The effects of sin lead to the graces of the sacrament and reconciliation with God, the Church, and ourselves.

We Are Changed by God's Forgiveness
The sacrament and its effects transform us into people who consider, judge, and arrange their lives according to the holiness and love of God.

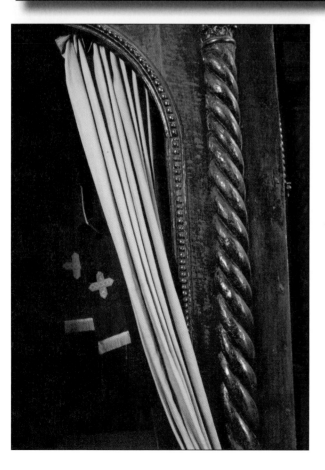

WHAT'S GOING ON WITH CONFESSION?

The second precept of the Catholic Church teaches the necessity of "confessing your sins at least once a year" by receiving the Sacrament of Reconciliation, also called Penance and several other names (see page 155). Also, the Church's new ritual for the sacrament reminds Catholics that "individual, integral confession and absolution remain the only ordinary way for the faithful to reconcile themselves with God and the Church, unless physical or moral impossibility excuses from this kind of confession" (quoted in *CCC* 1484).

Still, a recent poll commissioned by the United States Catholic Bishops through Georgetown University found that:

- 26 percent of adult Catholics say they participate in the Sacrament of Reconciliation once a year or more often;
- 30 percent say they go to confession less than once a year;
- 45 percent say they never go to confession; and
- only 2 percent say they go to confession once per month or more often.

Also, 62 percent of Catholics surveyed in the poll agreed "somewhat" or "strongly" with the statement "I can be a good Catholic without celebrating the Sacrament of Reconciliation at least once a year" (33 percent agreed "strongly").

For those who were alive prior to the Second Vatican Council, the survey results indicate a difference in how the Sacrament of Penance and Reconciliation is practiced now versus a generation ago. For example, Fr. Raymond Mann, a Franciscan priest who has spent more than fifty years as a confessor, recently offered his opinion in an article he wrote called "The Empty Box: Why Catholics Skip Confession." He noted that recently at St. Anthony Shrine in Boston, he heard just eight confessions in the course of one entire morning. He compared that with a time nearly fifty years ago when the downtown church where he ministered had nineteen confessionals, and two confessors began hearing confessions at six in the morning.

"We were often busy until 9 p.m.," he recalled. "During Advent and Lent, twelve priests were kept busy throughout the day. These days, one priest is usually sufficient."

Unlike in the former era, Catholics rarely go to confession before each time they receive Communion. Fr. Mann observed that Catholics today "focus less on isolated acts and more on attitudes and patterns of behavior."

Whether this attitude is a factor in why Catholics go to confession less or not at all today is not known. What is known is that participation in the Sacrament of Penance and Reconciliation remains, in the words of Pope Benedict XVI, "a spiritual rebirth, which transforms the penitent into a new creature."

The sacrament is necessary because it provides the grace to cleanse our souls of sin. Pope Benedict has spoken of the need to define sin and to teach about signs that show us how to live well, including the commandments. He said:

> For this reason we must also speak of sin and of the sacrament of forgiveness and reconciliation. A man who is sincere knows that he is guilty, that he must begin again, that he must be purified. And this is a marvelous reality that the Lord gives us: There is possibility of renewal, of being new. The Lord begins with us again and in this way we can begin again with others in our life.

This chapter is about the Sacrament of Penance and Reconciliation. Recall that *sacrament* is "an efficacious sign of grace, instituted by Christ and entrusted to the Church, by which divine life is dispensed to us through the work of the Holy Spirit" (see *CCC* 1131). When Jesus forgave sinners, his actions anticipated four dimensions of the sacrament:

1. *Memorial.* Sinners recalled the way God continually forgave the Israelites and called them back to the Covenant. They also recalled the many times Jesus forgave sinners.

2. *Celebration.* When sinners experienced God's forgiveness, they were filled with joy, just as in the parable about the shepherd who found his lost sheep and the woman who found her lost coin (see Luke 15:1–10).
3. *Communion.* Sinners were restored to fellowship with all those their sins had hurt.
4. *Transformation.* Sinners received God's sanctifying grace to help them grow in holiness and be people of forgiveness in their own relationships.

Today, this sacrament of healing is known by many names, depending upon which part of the sacrament is being emphasized. It is sometimes called the sacrament of **conversion**, because in it, we resolve to turn away from sin and return to God's grace. It is sometimes called **confession**, because it involves telling our sins to a priest.

It is also called **penance**, because the priest gives us a task to show that we are truly sorry for our sins and that we will try to repair any damage those sins caused. It is called **forgiveness**, because through the sacrament, God forgives our sins. And finally, the sacrament is called **reconciliation**, because through this sacrament, we are reunited with God and the Church.

Pope Benedict added, "The Sacrament of Penance gives us the occasion to renew ourselves with the power of God—which is possible because Christ took these sins, these faults upon himself. It seems that today indeed this is a great necessity. We can be healed again" (quotations from February 6, 2008, address of Pope Benedict XVI to clergy of the Diocese of Rome).

conversion
The first step of a sinner to repentance and returning in love to God the Father.

confession
Acknowledging and telling one's sins to a priest. Honest confession of sins is an essential part of the Sacrament of Penance.

penance
A sign of our true sorrow for the sins we have committed. Among other actions, penance may be a prayer, an offering, a work of mercy, an act of service to neighbor, or a voluntary act of self-denial.

forgiveness
God's merciful pardon for our sins. God forgives our sins in the Sacrament of Penance and welcomes us back into communion with him.

reconciliation
Being reunited in peace and friendship with someone we have hurt by our sins—especially God, the Church, and ourselves.

For Review
1. How does the practice of the Sacrament of Penance differ between a generation ago and now?
2. What are different names and meanings for the Sacrament of Penance?

For Reflection
- Which statistic about the Sacrament of Penance do you find most surprising? Why?
- How often do you celebrate the Sacrament of Penance? How do you determine when to go to confession?

MEMORIAL

UNDERSTANDING THE SACRAMENT OF PENANCE AND RECONCILIATION

Jesus instituted the Sacrament of Penance as a call to us for conversion—a continuing conversion that occurs after Baptism. The Sacrament of Penance makes sacramentally present Jesus' call to conversion, a sinner's first step in returning to the Father after straying through sin. The sacrament is rooted in the forgiving actions of Jesus himself, not necessarily in a specific passage or single event in the New Testament.

Only God forgives sins (see *CCC* 1441). During his public ministry, Jesus forgave sinners. For example, he forgave the sins of the paralytic who was lying on a stretcher (see Matthew 9:1–7; Mark 2:1–12; Luke 5:17–26), the woman who washed his feet with her tears (see Luke 7:36–50), the tax collector who repented of cheating people (see Luke 19:1–10), and the soldiers who nailed him to the cross (see Luke 23:34). Jesus' actions engendered the wrath of the Pharisees; they thought he was committing blasphemy in making himself God's equal. But that is exactly the point: Jesus forgives sins because he is the Son of God, the Second Person of the Trinity.

The Incarnation itself proved God's love for us. Jesus became human so that he could offer the perfect sacrifice to God that would atone, or make up, for our sins once and for all. Because of Christ, we are no longer only sinners. We are sinners *who have been forgiven.* Through Jesus we have hope; we have a way back to reconciliation with the Father (see John 14:6).

The Sacrament of Penance and Reconciliation memorializes several of Jesus' teachings and actions. First, God is infinitely merciful and kind. Second, followers of Jesus are called to continual, heartfelt conversion throughout life. And third, the reconciliation Jesus won for us is offered to us through the Church.

God's Infinite Mercy

The Sacrament of Penance and Reconciliation reminds us of God's *hesed*, a Hebrew word for God's infinite mercy. God continually calls us to have a friendship with him—not because we are God's equals or because we deserve to be God's friends, but because of God's great love for us.

Think about the friends you have. If you want to be on good terms with them, you can't just expect to reach a point of status quo and stay there forever. Relationships change all the time, because people grow and change. To maintain friendships, we have to choose to continue the relationship. And we cannot keep a friend if we hurt the other person without making amends. The same thing happens in our relationship with God. "We cannot be united with God unless we freely choose to love him" (*CCC* 1033). We cannot have a loving relationship with God if we sin against him. But our sins don't permanently doom this relationship with God. The Sacrament of Penance offers an opportunity for us to repair the relationship with the cleansing of our sins and the reception of God's mercy.

When we study the Scriptures, we realize that it is really the story of God's seeking friendship with humans, not the other way around. The Old Testament often shared a God who was compassionate, merciful, and saved his people in times of trouble (see, for example, Sirach 2:11). Jesus revealed God primarily as "Abba," a Father of love and forgiveness. The New Covenant focuses on our relationship with God along with his Law. It is the kind of relationship the prophet Jeremiah wrote about many years earlier:

> The days are coming, says the Lord, when I will make a new covenant with the house of Israel and the house of Judah. It will not be like the covenant I made with their fathers the day I took them by the hand to lead them forth from the land of Egypt; for they broke my covenant and I had to show myself their master, says the LORD. But this is the covenant which I will make with the house of Israel after those days, says the Lord. I will place my law within them, and write it upon their hearts; I will be their God, and they shall be my people. No longer will they have need to teach their friends and kinsmen how to know the Lord. All, from least to greatest, shall know me, says the Lord, for I will forgive their evildoing and remember their sin no more. (Jer 31:31–34)

According to Jesus, the Father seeks an intimate relationship with us marked by a love stronger than death. "For it is love that I desire, not sacrifice, and knowledge of God rather than holocausts" (Hos 6:6; see Matthew 9:13; 12:7). The New Covenant with God is written in our hearts. It fulfills and surpasses the Old Covenant and brings it to perfection.

Ongoing Conversion

When Jesus called people to "repent, and believe the Gospel" (Mk 1:15), his intention was not that our conversion should center around or end with the moment of Baptism. Instead, as the *Catechism* explains, "Christ's call to conversion continues to resound in the lives of Christians. . . . This endeavor of conversion is not just a human work. It is the movement of a 'contrite heart,' drawn and moved by grace to respond to the merciful love of God who loved us first" (*CCC* 1428). To Jesus, sin was equated with "hardness of heart." To sin is to harden our hearts against God's call to friendship. It cuts us off from God's invitation to love.

Conversion of heart—not just exterior acts of penance—is what God wants from us. God wants to be in a real relationship with us. Jesus explained this type of relationship when he told the Apostles they were his friends, not his servants or inferiors. "I no longer call you slaves, because a slave does not know what his master is doing. I have called you friends" (Jn 15:15). Jesus also proved what real friendship is about by dying on the cross for the sins of others. "No one has greater love than this, to lay down one's life for one's friends" (Jn 15:13).

As Jesus taught, if we truly love God, we will work throughout life to maintain a close relationship with him. We will prove our friendship by expressing our repentance for sin "in visible signs, gestures and works of penance" (*CCC* 1430). Even more important, we will try our best not to sin at all. "You are my friends if you do what I command you" (Jn 15:14). We will do our best to obey the commandments.

The Pharisees criticized Jesus because he occasionally disobeyed their strict interpretation of the Sabbath laws. These laws forbade work on the Sabbath, and yet Jesus let his disciples pick grain and prepare food on the Sabbath (see Matthew 12:1–8). He also performed miracles on the Sabbath (see Mark 3:1–6; Luke 13:10–17; Luke 14:1–6; and John 5:1–18). Why did Jesus defy these laws? He was trying to show his followers that love, generosity, and self-sacrifice for others are more important than simple obedience to laws. Our relationship with others is what is most important. Just as God is merciful toward us, so we should be merciful to others. People's needs should always be more important to us than the letter of the law.

Note, however, that Jesus did not give people license to abandon the laws of the Old Covenant. Instead, he said:

> Do not think that I have come to abolish the law or the prophets. I have come not to abolish but to fulfill. Amen, I say to you, until heaven and earth pass away, not the smallest letter or the smallest part of a letter will pass from the law, until all things have taken place. Therefore, whoever breaks one of the least of these commandments and teaches others to do so will be called least in the kingdom of heaven. But whoever obeys and teaches these commandments will be called greatest in the kingdom of heaven. I tell you, unless your **righteousness** surpasses that of the scribes and Pharisees, you will not enter into the kingdom of heaven. (Mt 5:17–20)

righteousness

The status of sinners who have been forgiven. Jesus suffered and died so that humans could be made righteous—that is, saved from sin and restored to a loving relationship with the Father.

TRACING THE HISTORY

Pope Leo the Great, ruling in the fifth century, is often credited with the foundation of confession as it is recognized today. He wrote: "It suffices that the guilt of conscience be manifested to priests alone in secret confession." Pope Leo also wrote that "the mediator between God and men, Christ Jesus, gave the rulers of the Church this power that they should impose penance on those who confess and admit them when purified by salutary satisfaction to the communion of the sacraments through the gateway of reconciliation." Research more of the teachings of Pope Leo the Great regarding the Sacrament of Penance. Summarize three other key points of his teachings.

Jesus was teaching us that our motive for obeying the commandments is just as important as keeping the commandments. If we are truly friends of God, we will want to do everything we can to maintain that relationship. Keeping the commandments nurtures God's friendship.

The Church and the Sacrament of Penance

When Jesus won the Father's forgiveness for us, he could have given us any way he wanted for us to access, or experience, that forgiveness. Jesus chose to give his Apostles the power to forgive sins in his name. There are at least three occasions in the New Testament where Jesus gave this power to his Apostles:

> "And so I say to you, you are Peter, and upon this rock I will build my church, and the gates of the netherworld shall not prevail against it. I will give you the keys to the kingdom of heaven. Whatever you bind on earth shall be bound in heaven; and whatever you loose on earth shall be loosed in heaven." (Mt 16:18–19)

> "Amen, I say to you, whatever you bind on earth shall be bound in heaven, and whatever you loose on earth shall be loosed in heaven." (Mt 18:18)

> And when he had said this, he breathed on them and said to them, "Receive the holy Spirit. Whose sins you forgive are forgiven them, and whose sins you retain are retained." (Jn 20:22–23)

The Apostles did not absolve sinners by their own authority. Rather, Christ acted through them to forgive the sins of others. We could say that Jesus delegated his authority to forgive sinners. "He entrusted the ministry of reconciliation to the Church, in the person of the Apostles" (Decree by Sacred Congregation for Divine Worship, *Rite of Penance*). In other words, future generations were to access Christ's forgiveness through the Church.

The Church's ministers of the sacrament are bishops—the Apostles' successors—and priests, the bishops' collaborators. As ministers of the sacrament, bishops and priests must primarily remain faithful to Church teaching, lead the people to moral healing and spiritual maturity, pray and do penance themselves for the penitent, and encourage everyone to confess their sins. Priests must always make themselves available for confession.

A Brief History of the Sacrament of Penance

The first clear reference to a sacramental rite of healing after Baptism occurred in the writings of the Church Fathers in the *Shepherd of Hermas* (AD 140–150). In the early years, Christians who committed serious sins after Baptism (such as idolatry, murder, or adultery) were admitted into the Order of **Penitents**. Once enrolled in this order, the sinners had to undergo very rigorous penitential discipline, sometimes for years. During this time, the sinners could not receive Communion or socialize with other Christians. Only after they successfully completed the required penance did the bishop forgive their sins and readmit them to communion with the Church. Because of the public nature and rigors of the penance, very few Christians enrolled in the Order of Penitents and received the Sacrament of Penance. If they did receive the sacrament, they did so only once in their lives.

In the seventh century, Irish missionaries changed the celebration of the sacrament out of necessity. Because no bishop was with them to absolve people completing the Order of Penitents, the missionaries began to hear private confessions. Sinners confessed their sins and expressed sorrow for them. The priest, acting in God's name and in the name of the Church, gave them a penance. When the penance was completed, the person came back to the priest to receive **absolution**. The practice of private confession eventually spread throughout the Church and became the norm. Over time, priests began to give absolution to penitents at the time of confession, with the understanding that the penitents would complete the assigned penance at a later time.

From that time on, the sacrament has been performed in secret between the penitent and the priest. During some of those years, there were misunderstandings about what is most important about the sacrament: maintaining a close relationship with God and the Church. Instead, people looked at the sacrament from the narrow viewpoint of mathematics and justice. Some believed that God keeps "score" of the times we have been good and bad and that any sin committed requires punishment. People overemphasized the justice aspect of sin and forgot about God's merciful love. Books called **penitentiaries** told confessors exactly what penance to give for each sin.

As mentioned, through most of the first half of the twentieth century, many Catholics went to confession often, sometimes weekly. Likewise, there was a common belief that for every time a person received Holy Communion, he or she should also go to confession first. Concurrently, many people avoided receiving Holy Communion, except

penitents
People who admit their sins, are truly sorry for having sinned, and wish to be restored to the good graces of God and the Church.

absolution
The prayer by which a priest, by the power given to the Church by Jesus Christ, pardons a repentant sinner in the Sacrament of Penance.

penitentiaries
Books for confessors in the past that listed all possible sins and the appropriate penance that should be given for each one.

for rare occasions. The Second Vatican Council called for a new Rite of Penance (see *Sacrosanctum Concilium* 72), which the Church approved in 1973. The new rite emphasizes the reconciliation aspect of the sacrament, our call to an ongoing covenant of love and friendship with God and the Church. Catholics are reminded that the sacrament is not only about the sinner's guilt; more important, it is also about the God of mercy who continually calls us back to union with him. God's forgiveness is truly something to celebrate.

In all eras, the Sacrament of Penance and Reconciliation not only has given us God's forgiveness; it also has given us the grace we need for lifelong conversion. The sacrament helps us maintain a good relationship with the Blessed Trinity. God's love for us balances his application of strict justice. We are forgiven sinners, not just sinners. Being God's friends is more important than superficially obeying the law. Loving God is directly expressed in loving and forgiving others. Ⓜ

For Review

1. Name one example of when Jesus forgave sinners in his public ministry.
2. How does the Sacrament of Penance remind us of God's infinite mercy?
3. What does Jesus demand of us regarding the laws of the Old Covenant?
4. Who are the ministers of the Sacrament of Penance?
5. How did private celebration of the Sacrament of Penance arise?

For Reflection

- How do you understand what is called for by "conversion of heart"?

- What is meant by "lifelong conversion"?

CELEBRATING THE SACRAMENT OF PENANCE AND RECONCILIATION

The revised Rite of Penance allows for three ways to celebrate the sacrament:

- *Private individual confession.* This is the "only ordinary way" for Catholics to be reconciled with God following the commission of a mortal sin (see *CCC* 1484). The penitent may confess his or her sins anonymously behind a screen to a priest, or the penitent may join the priest in a reconciliation room for face-to-face confession.

- *Communal celebration with individual confession and individual absolution.* This practice is common in parishes during Advent and Lent. Parishioners come together to prepare themselves for the sacrament by listening to the Liturgy of the Word with Scripture readings and a homily, by a common examination of conscience, and by a communal request for forgiveness. Then come personal confession of sins to a priest and individual absolution. Finally, the sacrament ends with the Our Father and a thanksgiving prayer (see *CCC* 1482).

- *Communal celebration with general confession and general absolution.* Because no individual confession and absolution occurs here, this form of the sacrament is reserved for cases of grave necessity. The diocesan bishop is the judge of whether or not the conditions exist for general absolution (see *CCC* 1483).

In any of its forms, Penance is a liturgical action. In the ordinary way of individual confession and absolution, the sacrament consists of several parts, including three essential acts of the penitent.

The sacrament begins with a greeting and blessing from the priest. He welcomes the penitent as Christ welcomed sinners. If we, as penitents, do not know the priest, we might introduce ourselves, explain briefly our situation in life, and give the date of our last confession. Then the following dialogue takes place:

Penitent: In the name of the Father, and of the Son, and of the Holy Spirit. Amen.

Priest: May God, who has enlightened every heart, help you to know your sins and trust in his mercy.

Penitent: Amen.

The Sign of the Cross recalls the connection of this sacrament to Baptism, the original sacrament of forgiveness.

Like the rites for all the Church's sacraments, the Rite of Penance includes one or more readings from Scripture. The purpose of this Liturgy of the Word is to help us recognize not only our sins but also God's abundant mercy. No sin is too terrible for God to forgive. The priest gives a few words relating the Scripture reading to Christian life today. Three necessary actions of the penitent and one of the confessor make up essentials parts of the sacrament.

Examination of Conscience

Before celebrating the Sacrament of Penance, it is important for both the celebrant and the penitent to prepare. As the *Rite of Penance* explains, the confessor "should call upon the Holy Spirit so that he may receive enlightenment and charity" (Intro, *Rite of Penance*, 15). We, as penitents, also have preparation to do. We should make time for an honest **examination of conscience** so that we can acknowledge any sins that have been committed since our last confession and pray for God's mercy.

When you were younger, you may have been required to memorize the **Ten Commandments**. They are certainly a good starting point for examining one's conscience. But remember, it is important to think of these commandments more in terms of relationship to God and others than in terms of simply obeying laws. Here is a sample examination of conscience (adapted from the *Rite of Penance*, 441-445) you may wish to use:

I. I, the Lord, am your God: you shall not have other gods besides me.

- Is my heart set on God, so that I really love him above all things and am faithful to his commandments, as a child loves a parent? Or am I more concerned about the things of this world? Have I a right intention in what I do? Is my faith in God firm and secure?
- Am I wholehearted in accepting the Church's teachings? Have I been careful to grow in my understanding of the faith, to hear God's Word, to listen to instructions on the faith, to avoid dangers to faith?
- Have I been always strong and fearless in professing my faith in God and the Church? Have I been willing to be known as a Christian in private and public life?
- Have I prayed morning and evening? When I pray, do I really raise my mind and heart to God, or is it a matter of words only? Do I offer God my difficulties, my joys, and my sorrows? Do I turn to God in times of temptation?

examination of conscience
An honest assessment of how well we have lived God's covenant of love. This examination leads us to accept responsibility for our sins and to realize our need of God's merciful forgiveness.

Ten Commandments
Ten rules God gave to the Israelites through Moses. These commandments told the people how they were to live in relation to God and to one another.

II. You shall not take the name of the Lord, your God, in vain.
- Have I love and reverence for God's name?
- Have I offended God in blasphemy, swearing falsely, or taking his name in vain?
- Have I shown disrespect for the Blessed Virgin Mary and the saints?

III. Remember to keep holy the sabbath day.
- Do I keep Sundays and feast days holy by taking a full part, with attention and devotion, in the liturgy, and especially in the Mass? Have I fulfilled the precept of annual confession and of Communion during the Easter season?
- Are there false gods I worship by giving them greater attention and deeper trust than I give to God: money, superstition, or occult practices?

IV. Honor your father and your mother.
- In my family life, have I contributed to the well-being and happiness of the rest of the family by patience and genuine love?
- Have I been obedient to my parents, showing them proper respect and giving them help in their spiritual and material needs?
- Have I obeyed legitimate authority and given it due respect?
- If I am given a position of responsibility or authority, do I use this for my own advantage or for the good of others, in a spirit of service?

V. You shall not kill.
- Have I done violence to others by damage to life or limb, reputation, honor, or material possessions? Have I involved them in loss?
- Have I been responsible for advising an abortion or procuring one?
- Have I kept up hatred for others? Am I estranged from others through quarrels, hatred, insults, or anger?
- If I have been injured, have I been ready to make peace for the love of Christ and to forgive, or do I harbor hatred and the desire for revenge?

fornication

Sexual intercourse between an unmarried man and an unmarried woman.

VI. You shall not commit adultery.

IX. You shall not covet your neighbor's wife.
- Have I a genuine love for my neighbors? Or do I use them for my own ends or treat them badly?
- Have I given grave scandal by my words or actions?
- Have I imposed my will on others, without respecting their freedom and rights?
- Have I kept my senses and body pure and chaste? Have I dishonored my body by **fornication**, impurity, unworthy conversation or thoughts, evil desires, or actions? Have I indulged in reading, conversation, Internet sites, and entertainment that offend against Christian and human decency?
- Have I encouraged others to sin by my own failure to maintain these standards?

VII. You shall not steal.

X. You shall not covet your neighbor's goods.

- Do I share my possessions with the less fortunate? Do I do my best to help the victims of oppression, misfortune, and poverty? Or do I look down on my neighbor, especially the poor, the sick, the elderly, strangers, and people of other races?
- Do I share in the apostolic and charitable works of the Church and in the life of my parish? Have I helped meet the needs of the Church and of the world and prayed for unity in the Church, for the spread of the Gospel among the nations, for peace and justice, etc.?
- Am I concerned for the good and prosperity of the human community in which I live, or do I spend my life caring only for myself? Do I share to the best of my ability in the work of promoting justice, morality, harmony, and love in human relations?
- In my work, am I just, hardworking, honest, and loving? Have I been faithful to my promises?
- Have I stolen the property of others? Have I desired the property of others unjustly and inordinately? Have I damaged it? Have I made **restitution** of other people's property and made good their loss?

VIII. You shall not bear false witness against your neighbor.

- Have I been truthful and fair, or have I injured others by deceit, slander, rash judgment, or the violation of a secret?
- Have I refused to testify to the innocence of another because of selfishness?

restitution
The act of repairing, restoring, or paying for any damage our sins have inflicted on others or their property.

Contrition

The most important act of the penitent is **contrition**. *Contrition* is defined as "heartfelt sorrow and aversion for the sin committed along with the intention of sinning no more" (*Rite of Penance* 6a). It is actually a movement that begins before the penitent arrives at the sacrament. The genuineness of the penance depends on an understanding of sin and then having heartfelt contrition.

Sin is an offense against God as well as a fault against reason, truth, and one's right conscience. The First Letter of John reminds us, "If we say, 'We are without sin,' we deceive ourselves, and the truth is not in us. If we acknowledge our sins, [God] is faithful and just and will forgive our sins and cleanse us from every wrongdoing" (1 Jn 1:8–9). Human nature is not perfect. Even after Baptism, we all have an inclination to sin, called **concupiscence**. Concupiscence is with us from the time of our birth to the hour of our death.

Every sin hurts our relationship with God and the Church. **Personal sins** include *mental sins* (sins of thought or attitude) and *actual sins* (hurtful actions against our covenant with God and the Church). For example, it is sinful to wish someone dead, to wish harm to others, or to plot revenge (thoughts). It is sinful to spread false rumors about others, steal from a neighbor, or commit murder (actions). It is also sinful to refuse to act or help when it would benefit another (sin of

contrition
Heartfelt sorrow and aversion for sins committed, along with the intention of sinning no more. Contrition is the most important act of penitents and is necessary for receiving absolution in the Sacrament of Penance.

concupiscence
An inclination to commit sin that can be found in human desires and appetites as a result of Original Sin.

personal sins
Any sins committed by an individual. Mental sin includes our thoughts and attitudes. Actual sin includes our words and actions.

mortal sins

Serious violations of God's law of love that result in the loss of God's life (sanctifying grace) in the soul of the sinner. To commit mortal sins, there must be grave matter, full knowledge of the evil done, and full consent of the will.

venial sins

Sins that weaken and wound our relationship with God but do not destroy divine life in our souls.

moral object

Either good moral actions or evil actions; it answers the "what" question of morality and can objectively determine if an action is right or wrong.

omission). **Mortal sins** destroy, or kill, our relationship with God and the Church. If not repented and forgiven by God, mortal sin causes a loss of God's Kingdom and the eternal death of hell. **Venial sins** weaken our relationship with God and the Church. Social sins are the expression and effect of personal sins and lead to further evil. Some examples of social sins include the failure to feed the hungry, sexism, consumerism, waging an unjust war, and discrimination against people of certain religions, ethnic groups, or sexual orientations.

The Sacrament of Penance is not an automatic or "magic" removal of sin. Just because we "go to confession" does not necessarily mean that our sins are forgiven. God's forgiveness depends on our sincere contrition for our sins, as well as our firm desire for amendment—to try our best not to sin again.

Contrition is much more than saying an Act of Contrition or saying, "I'm sorry." True contrition is heartfelt sorrow for sin. *Perfect contrition* (also known as "contrition of charity") is sorrow for sin because we love God and want to be in relationship with him. *Imperfect contrition* (or "attrition") is sorrow for sin because we fear being punished for sin. Another name for contrition is *repentance*.

Conditions for Mortal Sins

Mortal sin effectively destroys our relationship with God and kills our ability to love. Mortal sins cannot be committed by accident. For a sin to be mortal, three conditions must exist:

1. The **moral object** must be of grave or serious matter. Grave matter is specified in the Ten Commandments (e.g., do not kill, do not commit adultery, do not steal, etc.).
2. The person must have full knowledge of the gravity of the sinful action.
3. The person must completely consent to the action. It must be a personal choice.

An additional and maybe obvious condition for mortal sin is that the action must be completed. Desiring to do something evil, though reflecting a serious breach in a person's relationship with God, is not itself mortally sinful.

Confession of Sins

Confession of sins to a priest is an essential part of the Sacrament of Penance. All mortal sins committed since our last confession of which we are aware after making a serious examination of conscience (see pages 161–163) must be confessed.

Confession expresses our faith in God. Our inner examination of conscience coupled with our exterior words "I am sorry" is made in light of God's mercy. We are admitting we cannot live without God's love and generosity. Sinful behavior equates with "going it alone." Confessing our sins is a public statement in the belief that we need God.

This confession not only forms the basis of our conversion with God; it also creates a new life for ourselves in the Church. When we confess our sins to a priest, we are admitting the harm we have caused to others. We are admitting that our sin affected the entire Body of Christ. This confession also expresses our belief in the goodness of the Church that will welcome us back.

The graces we receive from a "good confession" (see pages 167–171) are many. One of the first is that it's as if a burden has literally been lifted from us through our naming our sins and declaring our sorrow. St. Mary Euphrasia Pelletier said, "It is human to fall, but angelic to rise again." St. John Neumann said of confession: "We feel what is the blessing of the removal of sin, redemption, pardon, sanctification, which are otherwise just words."

When we confess all mortal sins we remember, we place them before God's mercy for pardon. Anyone who deliberately fails to mention a sin to the priest cannot be guaranteed remission of his or her sins. The Council of Trent, quoting St. Jerome, compared the lack of gesture to a sick person's being too ashamed to show his wound to the doctor: "The medicine cannot heal what it does not know."

The Church encourages us to confess venial sins as well, as a way to come to full knowledge of ourselves and admit our need for God's grace and mercy.

Satisfaction

You may have apologized to a friend for something you did that offended him or her, only to have the friend say back to you, "Saying 'I'm sorry' is not enough!" When and why might such a response be true? Perhaps you have wronged your friend a few other times and

apologized then as well, only to repeat your same errors again. If true, it wouldn't be shocking for your latest apology to fall on deaf ears. Your friend would rather be *satisfied* that your "I'm sorry" is for real.

For example, let's say a person slandered another by gossiping or spreading untruths. Besides, saying "I am sorry" for the actions, the person must do whatever possible to repair the harm. This might involve going back to the people who were told the gossip, admitting the lies, and correcting them as much as possible with truth. A demand of justice requires an effort as simple as this. Or, if someone is guilty of stealing, an apology without the return of the stolen goods does not do much good.

The sacramental absolution does not remove penalties of satisfaction or penance for what we have done. In the sacrament, the confessor imposes a penance in line with the gravity and nature of the sins committed. It may be one of the following:

- prayer
- an offering
- works of mercy
- service of neighbor
- voluntary self-denial
- sacrifices

In whatever form, the penances help "configure us to Christ" (*CCC* 1460) and help us suffer with him. Pope St. Gregory the Great said, "It is just that the sinner, by his repentance, should inflict on himself so much the greater suffering, as he has brought greater harm on himself by his sin."

Absolution of Sin

By granting absolution, the priest completes the actions of the penitent who seeks conversion. The Church assigns such importance to this ministry and has so much respect for the penitent that every priest who hears confession is bound to keep the absolute secrecy of the sins confessed to him. This is known as the **sacramental seal**.

In celebrating the Sacrament of Penance, the priest fulfills the ministry of Jesus Christ the Good Shepherd, who seeks out those who are lost (see John 10:11–15); the Father, who awaits his prodigal son and welcomes and forgives him when he returns (see Luke 15:11–32); and the impartial judge who rules with both justice and mercy (see Luke 18:9–14).

When the priest sees that a person's conversion is genuine and hears the person make an **Act of Contrition**, he extends his hands over that person and pronounces God's forgiveness. He says:

> God, the Father of mercies, through the Death and the Resurrection of his Son has reconciled the world to himself and sent the Holy Spirit among us for the forgiveness of sins; through the ministry of the Church may God give you pardon and peace, and I absolve you from your sins in the name of the Father, and of the Son, and of the Holy Spirit. (*Rite of Penance* 46)

The priest is "not the master of God's forgiveness, but its servant" (*CCC* 1466). The priest unites himself to the intention and love of Christ. To function in his role of confessor, the priest should:

- have proven knowledge of Christian behavior;
- have experience in human affairs;
- respect and be sensitive toward the sinner;
- have a love of the truth;
- be faithful to the Magisterium of the Church; and
- lead the penitent with patience toward healing and full maturity.

The power to absolve sins is received in the Sacrament of Holy Orders. Priests receive the faculties—that is, the right or privilege—to be the minister of the sacrament from their bishop, their religious superior, or the pope. Priests must take every opportunity to encourage Catholics to confess their sins regularly in the Sacrament of Penance and must offer regularly scheduled times for the sacrament. They are also obliged to pray and do penance for the penitents, entrusting them to the Lord's mercy.

After absolution is granted, the priest leads a short dismissal rite, saying something like "The Lord has freed you from your sins. Go in peace." Like the Dismissal Rite at Mass, the dismissal in the Rite of Penance gives us a mission to complete. We are challenged to live a sinless life in communion with God the Father and the Church, to grow in holiness, and to show mercy to others as God has shown us mercy.

---

sacramental seal
The secrecy priests are bound to keep regarding any sins confessed to them.

Act of Contrition
A prayer, either formal or informal, penitents pray at the Sacrament of Penance to express sorrow for their sins.

For Review

1. What are three ways to celebrate the Sacrament of Penance?
2. In the Sacrament of Penance, what is the purpose of the Liturgy of the Word?
3. How does the Rite of Penance remind us of the sacrament's connection to Baptism?
4. How does contrition of the penitent begin prior to his or her coming to the sacrament?
5. Explain the difference between *mortal sin, venial sin,* and *social sin.*
6. Define *perfect contrition* and *imperfect contrition.*
7. Explain the three conditions required for a sin to be a mortal sin.
8. Why should we confess venial sins as well as mortal sins?
9. Name three qualities that can help a priest function in his role as confessor.

For Reflection

- What do you think would be an appropriate penance for someone who lied to a friend? Cheated on a test? Missed Mass deliberately?

- What does it mean to say that a priest is "not the master of God's forgiveness, but its servant"?

THE GRACE OF PENANCE AND RECONCILIATION

The grace of the Sacrament of Penance and Reconciliation is directly related to the effects of sin. Sin is harmful because it either weakens or severs our connection with God and others. The Sacrament of Penance repairs these rifts and brings reconciliation between the sinner and God, as well as peace of conscience, spiritual consolation, and a restoration of graces and blessings that are due to God's children.

When Jesus described himself as "the true vine" and his followers as "the branches" (Jn 15:1–5), he was saying he is the source of our life and happiness. In order to remain spiritually alive and happy, we need to stay connected to him. It's just like the human body. Every part of the physical body lives because it is connected to the heart by blood vessels. If blood vessels are severed or impaired, the body part they nourish can no longer receive oxygen and food. As a result, the part dies. Sin is like that. It cuts us apart from Jesus, the vine; consequently, we spiritually wither and die.

Sin may also be compared to the destruction caused by an earthquake; say, for example, the 1989 earthquake in the San Francisco area. During that quake, a part of the Bay Bridge—a major artery between San Francisco and the cities of the East Bay—failed. That failure brought traffic between San Francisco and Oakland to a devastating halt. In order to get home or get to work, people had to find alternate routes, many of which added hours to their daily commute.

The Nature of Reconciliation

The Sacrament of Penance does not focus just on the damage caused by sin. It also concentrates on what needs to be done to repair the damage and restore the bonds that were weakened or broken. Just as it takes time for the human body to heal from a broken bone, or just as it took time for the Bay Area to recover from the 1989 earthquake, so the process of repair and reconciliation after sin takes time. Small wounds heal quickly, but major breaks may require months or even years before healing is completed.

The word *reconciliation* comes from a Greek word that means "to restore to union, to rejoin, to put together again." That is exactly what happens as a result of the sacrament. We are restored to communion. To be reconciled with someone we have been at war with or estranged from is not the same as forgetting the sin that took place. Nor does it mean we accept the sin as now "OK." Instead, reconciliation involves our desire to be in a relationship with that person again. The relationship is so important to us that we forgive what happened, learn from that experience, and move forward together. The connection that was "dead" is now "risen." We focus on building a new life *together*, not on continually blaming one another for what went wrong.

A popular adage says, "To err is human, to forgive divine." Reconciliation is much like resurrection. It is the gift of new, restored life. It is God's gift to us, the result of our acceptance of his ongoing grace. Without the grace of the Sacrament of Penance and Reconciliation, none of us would have the ability to "go the extra mile" it takes to repair broken relationships and bring them back to life.

The Sacrament of Penance brings about forgiveness of sins, which in turn makes communion with God possible. "The whole power of the sacrament of Penance consists in restoring us to God's grace and joining us with him in an intimate friendship" (*Roman Catechism*, II, V, 18, quoted in *CCC* 1468). The sacrament also brings about reconciliation with the Church, bringing the sinner again into communion with all members of Christ's Mystical Body. Pope John Paul II also taught that the "forgiven penitent is reconciled with himself in his inmost being, where he regains his innermost truth" (quoted in *CCC* 1469). More explanation of these effects of the sacrament follows.

Reconciliation with God

"Reconciliation with God is . . . the purpose and effect of this sacrament" (*CCC* 1468). Jesus' Parable of the Prodigal Son (Lk 15:11–32) is a good description of what reconciliation with God is like. In the story, the younger son demands his inheritance and then squanders it in selfish pursuits. Only when he is penniless, jobless, and hungry does he repent of his sins.

He decides to go home, beg his father's forgiveness, and ask to work for his father as a hired servant. The father, however, rejoices the minute he sees his son returning. He embraces the boy, adorns him with new clothes and jewelry, and then orders the servants to prepare a banquet in his honor. Their relationship has been restored.

Jesus tells us that the same rejoicing occurs in Heaven when one sinner returns to God. Not only do we rejoice at being forgiven, but God rejoices to have us back! What was lost has been found. The empty chair at the table has been filled. The aching heart has been mended. Forgiving love is stronger than the hurt of sin.

The Sacrament of Penance is like a homecoming. The prophet Isaiah described this homecoming with the following images:

The Lord calls you back,
Like a wife forsaken and grieved in spirit,
A wife married in youth and then cast off, says your
    God.
For a brief moment I abandoned you,
But with great tenderness I will take you back.
In an outburst of wrath, for a moment
I hid my face from you;
But with enduring love I take pity on you,
Says the Lord, your redeemer. . . .
Though the mountains leave their place
And the hills be shaken,
My love shall never leave you
Nor my covenant of peace be shaken,
Says the Lord, who has mercy on you. (Is 54:6–8, 10)

What Are Indulgences?

As the *Catechism of the Catholic Church* teaches: "The doctrine and practice of indulgences in the Church are closely linked to the effects of the sacrament of Penance" (*CCC* 1471). *Indulgence* is defined as "a partial or total wiping away of punishment due for sins that have been forgiven."

The consequences of sin are far-reaching. Though the Sacrament of Penance brings forgiveness for our sins and communion with God, each sin causes harm far beyond what we can see. For example, consider a parent who abuses (verbally or physically) his or her child. When the child attends school, the child may repeat these same sinful behaviors in relationships with classmates. In fact, this type of sinful pattern is unfortunately perpetuated from generation to generation.

In fact, there are two consequences of sin. Mortal sin deprives a person of sanctifying grace and incurs the debt of eternal punishment if not forgiven. Both mortal and venial sins, even if forgiven, result in some degree of temporal punishment, the penalty that God, in his justice, gives for our sins. We must work off the temporal punishment in this world or the next world in the state called **Purgatory.** We do this through acts of penance (e.g., prayer, fasting, works of mercy, patient suffering).

We don't "work off" the punishment for our sins alone. We are part of the **Communion of Saints,** a unity of all the faithful: those in heaven, those expiating their sins in Purgatory, and those still on earth. In an exchange of prayers, works of mercy and charity, and various practices of penance, the "holiness of one profits others, well beyond the harm that the sin of one could cause others" (*CCC* 1475). From this infinite pool of spiritual goods of the Church's treasury that spring from the works of Christ's Redemption and also include the prayers and good works of Mary, the Mother of God, all of humankind can be set free from sin and come into communion with God the Father.

The practice of granting indulgences is part of this understanding of the Church's unity as the Body of Christ. When we have undergone a sincere conversion and have participated in the Sacraments of Penance and the Eucharist, the Church offers assistance for making up for our sins. We indicate we wish this assistance by performing certain acts. The process of asking for and receiving the Church's assistance is what is entailed in the granting of indulgences.

Purgatory
Purification after death for those who died in God's friendship but still need to be purified because of past sins before entering Heaven. It is also called "the Church suffering."

Communion of Saints
The unity of all those living on earth (the pilgrim Church), those being purified in Purgatory (the Church suffering), and those enjoying the blessings of Heaven (the Church in glory).

There are different kinds of indulgences. A *partial indulgence* frees us from *some* of the remaining responsibility we have for our sins. A *plenary indulgence* frees us from any responsibility we have for our sins. In order to receive a plenary indulgence, a person must truly love God, detest sin, place trust in the Paschal Mystery, and believe in the assistance offered by the Communion of Saints. A person must then do four things:

1. make a sacramental confession,
2. participate in the Eucharist,
3. pray for the intentions of the Holy Father (by saying an Our Father and a Hail Mary or by offering a prayer in his or her own words), and
4. perform the specific act to which the indulgence is attached; for example, by offering prayers at a specific pilgrimage site.

We can also help those in Purgatory by gaining indulgences for them. By saying prayers and performing actions approved by the Church, we can help our deceased family members and friends by removing some of the temporal punishment due to them from sins they committed while on earth.

excommunication

A serious penalty that means a baptized person is no longer "in communion" with the Catholic Church. Some excommunications are automatic, including for the sins of apostasy, heresy, and schism.

apostasy

The denial of Christ and the repudiation of the Christian faith by a baptized person.

heresy

False teaching that denies essential truths of the Catholic faith.

schism

A break in Church unity from the failure to accept the pope as the Vicar of Christ.

God calls us to return to him, to come home. No matter what we have done, he still loves us.

Reconciliation with the Church

The Sacrament of Penance also reconciles us with the Church. Only those who are in the state of grace may receive Communion at Eucharist. They can receive Communion because they are, in fact, united with other Church members. They are truly trying to live as followers of Christ.

Grave sin destroys not only our relationship with God, it also destroys our relationship with the Church. We put ourselves outside the faith community; we "excommunicate" ourselves from the group of believers. Grave sins that incur automatic **excommunication** from the Church include procuring an abortion (*Code of Canon Law* 1398); engaging in **apostasy, heresy,** or **schism** (*Canon Law* 1364); violating the seal of confession (*Canon Law* 1388); physically attacking the pope (*Canon Law* 1370); and conferring sacramental absolution by one not a priest (*Canon Law* 1378).

In most cases, receiving absolution in the Sacrament of Penance restores us to fellowship and communion with the Church. In rare cases of grave public sin, the Church has, throughout history, formally excommunicated individual sinners. In such cases, the sinner can be reconciled to the Church only by the pope or his authorized bishop or priest (see *CCC* 1463).

Reconciliation with Self

The Sacrament of Penance also brings about "peace and serenity of conscience with strong spiritual consolation" (Council of Trent, DS 1674, quoted in *CCC* 1468). You may have experienced this sense of "cleanliness" or "renewal" after you have celebrated the sacrament. Why? It is important to realize that sin also wounds our human dignity. When we choose to sin, we let ourselves down. We fail to be the people God intended us to be—his children, the brothers and sisters of Jesus.

The Sacrament of Penance can bring about a profound sense of spiritual consolation. Because we are assured of God's ongoing love and forgiveness, we can learn to forgive ourselves for our wrongdoing. We can develop inner peace of mind, true serenity of conscience. Pope John Paul II, in his 1984 apostolic exhortation, *Reconciliation and Penance*, explained this effect of Penance: "The forgiven penitent is reconciled with himself in his inmost being, where he regains his own true identity" (31.V).

Forgiving ourselves is often much harder than forgiving others. But forgiving ourselves is what God's offer of Redemption is all about. God has really saved us from sin. Jesus has truly taken away our guilt. We are now free to return to life as God's children, to once again take our place at the Eucharistic table.

Finally, with our conversion and absolution from mortal sin received in this sacrament, we also remove the one obstacle that would prevent us from entering Heaven. The sacrament restores the graces belonging to the children of God. Forgiveness of mortal sin brings not only a remission of eternal punishment but, at least in part, punishment in this world as well. By various works of charity and penance, the grace of the sacrament allows us to put away our old selves and become new. It gives us an increase of spiritual strength to live a Christian life.

PEACE BE WITH YOU

When the Risen Jesus appeared to his disciples, he wished them heartfelt peace: "Peace be with you" (Jn 20:21). True peace can happen only when we have experienced reconciliation. Think about a time in your life when you went through a process of reconciliation, either with God, the Church, someone you sinned against, or yourself. Write about this experience in your journal. Creatively express the feeling of peace you found as a song, prayer, slide show, dance, poem, mobile, painting, etc. Be prepared to share what you have created during the prayer service at the end of this chapter.

For Review

1. What did Jesus mean when he said he was the "true vine" and his followers "the branches"?
2. What does the "whole power" of the Sacrament of Penance consist of?
3. What are three ways the sacrament effects reconciliation?
4. Name and define sins that incur automatic excommunication.
5. Differentiate between a partial indulgence and a plenary indulgence.

For Reflection

• What do you find harder to do, forgiving yourself or forgiving others?

• What prayers or actions do you find of value to help you remove the consequences of sin from your life?

TRANSFORMATION

WE ARE CHANGED BY GOD'S FORGIVENESS

In the Sacrament of Penance, God's forgiving love heals us and brings us new life. Healing involves permanent change—or at least that's what it is intended to do. Whenever Jesus forgave someone, he also called the person to transform his or her life. For example, Jesus told the paralytic, "Rise, pick up your stretcher, and go home" (Mt 9:6). In other words, the man was to live in a

almsgiving

The act of giving money or material goods to anyone who is needy.

new way; he was to focus on rebuilding a loving relationship with his family. Another time Jesus said to the woman who washed his feet with her tears, "Go in peace" (Lk 7:50). He called her to a new life of peace with her husband. Likewise, Jesus told the adulterous woman, "Go, [and] from now on do not sin any more" (Jn 8:11). In short, being forgiven transforms us into new people. There is "profound change of the whole person by which one begins to consider, judge, and arrange his life according to the holiness and love of God, made manifest in his

Son in the last days and given to us in abundance" (Intro, *Rite of Penance*, 6a).

The type of life transformation described above is a final step in a true experience of conversion. The Sacrament of Penance calls us to be a new creation (see 2 Corinthians 5:17). As the *Catechism* explains, we are to "form our conscience, fight against evil tendencies, let ourselves be healed by Christ and progress in the life of the Spirit" (*CCC* 1458). In other words, each of us is to work on developing habits of thought, speech, and action "befitting a disciple of Christ" (*CCC* 1494).

The sacrament calls us to heal and to reform our lives in a number of ways, including practicing some of the forms of penance described below.

Practice Discipline

The Sacrament of Penance is not just about expressing sorrow for sin or trying to repair the damage sin has done. Penance is also about disciplining ourselves so that, in the future, we are less tempted to sin again and we refrain from sin. People who are truly transformed by the sacrament become disciplined people. They practice this discipline in three traditional ways: fasting, prayer, and **almsgiving**.

The discipline of fasting involves controlling what we eat, as well as the amount of food we eat. Some people fast from eating between meals. Others abstain from alcoholic beverages or from eating meat, sugar, or bread. Fasting represents conversion in relation to oneself. We are willing to orient ourselves toward God's love rather than to our own passions and selfishness.

Prayer represents conversion in relation to God. We realize that we need God's grace and that we can't save ourselves by our own efforts. Types of prayer include receiving the Eucharist, reading Sacred Scripture, and praying the Liturgy of the Hours and the Our Father (see *CCC* 1437).

Almsgiving equates to conversion in relation to others. We realize our connection to others as brothers and sisters of Christ, as creatures made in God's image, as people worthy of respect and right treatment. We show kindness and love to others, hoping others will assist us when we are in need.

Return Forgiveness

Our experience of God's forgiveness encourages us to become people who return forgiveness to others. Two important teachings of Jesus relate to the way we are to forgive others. First, consider the following Scripture passage:

> Then Peter approaching asked him, "Lord, if my brother sins against me, how often must I forgive him? As many as seven times?" Jesus answered, "I say to you, not seven times but seventy-seven times." (Mt 18:21–22)

In other words, we are to forgive others *always*, even if they don't apologize or admit they are wrong. Second, we are to remember that the generosity we show in forgiving others will be the measure by which God is generous with us. Thus, in the Our Father, we pray, "Forgive us our debts, as we forgive our debtors" (Mt 6:12). As Jesus said in his Sermon on the Mount, "If you forgive others their transgressions, your heavenly Father will forgive you. But if you do not forgive others, neither will your Father forgive your transgressions" (Mt 6:14).

Refrain from Anger and Revenge

True forgiveness means we stop being angry with others. Jesus told us, "If you bring your gift to the altar, and there recall that your brother has anything against you, leave your gift there at the altar, go first and be reconciled with your brother, and then come and offer your gift" (Mt 5:23–24). St. Paul concurred: "Be angry but do not sin; do not let the sun set on your anger. . . . All bitterness, fury, anger, shouting, and reviling must be removed from you, along with all malice" (Eph 4:26, 31).

True forgiveness goes beyond the requirements of justice. Jesus explained:

> "You have heard that it was said, 'An eye for an eye and a tooth for a tooth.' But I say to you, offer no resistance to one who is evil. When someone strikes you on [your] right cheek, turn the other one to him as well. If anyone wants to go to law with you over your tunic, hand him your cloak as well. Should anyone press you into service for one mile, go with him for two miles. Give to the one who asks of you, and do not turn your back on one who wants to borrow." (Mt 5:38–42)

Even if someone has hurt us or our loved ones, we do not have a right to "get even" or strike back.

In fact, Jesus' demand goes even deeper. As a result of Original Sin and our weakened human nature, we tend to hate, not love, those who wrong us and are opposed to us. That is why the following saying of Jesus is very difficult: "You have heard that it was said, 'You shall love your neighbor and hate your enemy.' But I say to you, love your enemies, and pray for those who persecute you, that you may be children of your heavenly Father" (Mt 5:43–45). When we forgive and love even our enemies, we help break the chain of violence and root out vengeance.

Pursue Justice and Peace

It takes courage to approach someone with whom we are angry. It also takes a great deal of humility to say, "I forgive you," when the other person hasn't even apologized or asked for our forgiveness. But that is the type of initiation to which Jesus called us. We are to be ambassadors of reconciliation.

> Whoever is in Christ is a new creation: the old things have passed away; behold, new things have come. And

all this is from God, who has reconciled us to himself through Christ and given us the ministry of reconciliation, namely, God was reconciling the world to himself in Christ, not counting their trespasses against them and entrusting to us the message of reconciliation. So we are ambassadors for Christ, as if God were appealing through us. We implore you on behalf of Christ, be reconciled with God. For our sake he made him to be sin who did not know sin, so that we might become the righteousness of God in him. (2 Cor 5:17–21)

Jesus calls us to work for peace and justice, no matter how difficult the challenge. Thus he said, "If your

St. Frances Cabrini

brother sins [against you], go and tell him his fault between you and him alone. If he listens to you, you have won over your brother. If he does not listen, take one or two others along with you, so that 'every fact may be established on the testimony of two or three witnesses.' If he refuses to listen to them, tell the church" (Mt 18:15–17). St. Paul echoed these sentiments: "Let us then pursue what leads to peace and to building up one another" (Rom 14:19). Just as God never gives up on us, so we are not to give up on achieving peace between others and ourselves or peace between nations.

Answer the Call to Perfection

The Gospel story of the rich young man (see Matthew 19:16–30) seems to address only earthy riches and poverty. However, the story takes on an entirely new twist when we realize that the rich young man is, like all of us, attached to sin and a sinful way of life. The young man asked Jesus what he must do to gain eternal life. Jesus told him, "If you wish to enter into life, keep the commandments" (Mt 19:17). The man proudly said, "All of these I have observed. What do I still lack?" (Mt 19:20). Basically Jesus pointed out that the young man had superficially obeyed the letter of the law but that his heart was not in it. What he really needed to do was undergo an interior conversion in which all of his actions were motivated out of sincere love for God.

The Apostles, when they heard this, shook their heads with dismay. Jesus was asking this good young man to be perfect, to go beyond what was humanly possible. No one they knew, not even themselves, could measure up to such standards. So they asked, "Who then can be saved?" (Mt 19:25). Jesus' answer is enlightening: "For human beings this is impossible, but for God all things are possible" (Mt 19:26).

Many of us, too, may feel that Christ's call to forgive others, even our enemies, is way beyond our abilities. And it is. It is impossible for fallible human beings to be perfect as God is perfect, to forgive as God forgives. But with the grace God gives us in the Sacrament of Penance and Reconciliation, all things are possible. We are not alone in our journey of conversion and repentance. God truly does give us the strength "to begin anew" (CCC 1432). "The same Spirit who brings sin to light is also the Consoler who gives the human heart grace for repentance and conversion" (CCC 1433).

When we avail ourselves of the Sacrament of Penance and Reconciliation and of the graces it brings to our lives that lead us to conversion, the fruits we bear because of this life transformation are many. St. Frances Cabrini pointed out the results of famous Christians who changed their ways:

> Did a Magdalene, a Paul, a Constantine, an Augustine become mountains of ice after their conversion? Quite the contrary. We should never had had these prodigies of conversion and marvelous holiness if they had not changed the flames of human passion into volcanoes of immense love of God.

For Review

1. What are three ways the Sacrament of Penance calls us to be spiritually disciplined people?
2. How do people transformed by the Sacrament of Penance act when it comes to restoring broken relationships, dealing with anger and the desire for retaliation, treating enemies, and working for peace?
3. How is it possible for human beings to achieve perfection?

For Reflection

- What is the relationship among true conversion, forgiveness, and transformation?

- Give a personal example of how loving an enemy helped break a chain of violence in your life.

CHAPTER QUICK VIEW

Main Ideas

- In spite of recent statistics that find that Catholics do not participate in the Sacrament of Penance as often as they did in other generations, the sacrament remains "the only ordinary way for the faithful to reconcile themselves with God and the Church." (pp. 153-154)

- The sacrament is known by many names, including Sacrament of Conversion, confession, penance, forgiveness, and reconciliation. (p. 155)

- Jesus instituted the Sacrament of Penance as a call for continuing conversion following Baptism. (p. 156)

- The sacrament reminds us that God is a loving Father ("Abba") and that he is infinitely merciful. (p. 156)

- Conversion of the heart, not just exterior penance, is a key objective of the sacrament. (p. 157)

- Jesus commissioned the Apostles to forgive sins in his name. Today the ministers of the sacrament are bishops—the Apostles' successors—and priests, the bishops' collaborators. (p. 158)

- A key development in the sacrament occurred in the seventh century, when Irish missionaries began the practice of private confessions. (p. 159)

- A new rite of the sacrament, approved in 1973, emphasizes reconciliation and an ongoing covenant of love and friendship with God and the Church. (p. 160)

- The revised rite allows for three ways to celebrate the sacrament: private individual confession, communal celebration with individual confession and individual absolution, and communal celebration with general confession and general absolution. (pp. 160-161)

- A personal private examination of conscience should precede reception of the sacrament. (pp. 161-163)

- The most important act of the penitent is contrition, that is, "heartfelt sorrow and aversion for the sin committed along with the intention of sinning no more." (p. 163)

- Mortal sins destroy our relationship with God. There are three conditions that make a sin mortal. (p. 164)

- Confession of sins to a priest is an essential part of the Sacrament of Penance. (p. 165)

continued on page 178

Famous Catholics and the Sacraments:

St. John Vianney

Born in Lyon, France, in 1786, John Vianney grew up in a poor family. It is said that even as a child he had a profound love for the Church and her teachings. At a young age, he taught other children their prayers and catechism.

John started his adult life as a farmhand and shepherd but was conscripted into Napoleon's army for a short time. After his release from the army, he pursued his dream to become a priest. However, he came to the seminary with so little education (only a little arithmetic, history, and geography) that he failed his entrance examinations the first time. He kept taking the exams until he finally passed and was granted admittance. Throughout his studies there, he was not a very good student, especially in Latin. More than once he failed the examinations required before ordination. Nevertheless, he finally became ordained in 1815 at age twenty-nine.

Three years later, Father John was assigned to the remote parish of Ars, near Lyon, which had fallen into neglect and lax attendance. He began to visit the poor and the sick in their homes and got them to return to the sacraments. He also founded an orphanage for destitute girls that was called The Providence. He instructed the girls in the catechism, and his lectures became so popular that he had to move them to the church, where large crowds gathered daily to hear him speak.

Daily, Father John taught the catechism to the people of Ars. He explained theology simply, in terms his parishioners could understand. He especially taught the importance of living one's beliefs, of translating faith into acts of "universal charity for everyone—for the good, and for the bad, for the poor and for the rich, and for all those who do us harm as much as those who do us good." Through his sermons and his own example, Father John encouraged his parishioners to pray, and to pray often. He said:

> Prayer is nothing else but union with God. In this intimate union, God and the soul are fused together like two bits of wax that no one can ever pull apart. This union of God with a tiny creature is a lovely thing. It is a happiness beyond understanding. My little children, your hearts are small, but prayer stretches them and makes them capable of loving God. Through prayer we receive a foretaste of heaven and something of paradise comes down upon us. Prayer never leaves us without sweetness. It is honey that flows into the soul and makes all things sweet. When we pray properly, sorrows disappear like snow before the sun.

Furthermore, Father John encouraged his parishioners to celebrate the Sacrament of Penance frequently:

> My children, we cannot comprehend the goodness of God towards us in instituting this great Sacrament of Penance . . . which heals the wounds of our soul. If we thought seriously about it, we should have such a lively horror of sin that we could not commit it.

> It is said that many confess, and few are converted. I believe it is so, my children, because few confess with tears of repentance.

> Put yourself on good terms with God; have recourse to the Sacrament of Penance; you will sleep as quietly as an angel. You will be glad

to waken in the night, to pray to God; you will have nothing but thanksgiving on your lips; you will rise towards Heaven with great facility, as an eagle soars through the air.

Father John sometimes spent entire days praying for his parishioners. He also practiced austere forms of penance, such as eating only potatoes and sleeping only two hours at night. Eventually he became known for his common sense, gift of prophecy, ability to discern people's hearts, and gift of making miraculous things occur in his parish. For example, he had an uncanny ability to know people's past and to predict their future, and to heal sick children.

By 1855, more than 20,000 pilgrims annually came to Ars to hear Father John preach and to celebrate the Sacrament of Penance with him. For the last ten years of his life, he spent sixteen to eighteen hours each day in the confessional. Because of his humility, gentleness, and patience, he became known affectionately as "the Curé of Ars."

Father John's devotion to the confessional was aimed at getting people to receive Holy Communion more frequently. He said in one of his sermons:

To sustain the soul in the pilgrimage of life, God looked over creation, and found nothing that was worthy of it. He then turned to Himself, and resolved to give Himself. O my soul, how great thou art, since nothing less than God can satisfy thee! The food of the soul is the Body and Blood of God! Oh, admirable Food! If we considered it, it would make us lose ourselves in that abyss of love for all eternity! How happy are the pure souls that have the happiness of being united to Our Lord by Communion! They will shine like beautiful diamonds in Heaven, because God will be seen in them.

John Vianney died of natural causes in 1859. Since then his corpse has remained incorruptible. He was beatified by Pope Pius X in 1905 and canonized by Pope Pius XI in 1925. St. John Vianney is considered the patron saint of parish priests, especially confessors. His feast day is August 4.

- Find out more about the life of St. John Vianney by reading *The Curé of Ars* by Fr. Bartholomew O'Brien or by reading an online article. What virtues did he have that attracted so many people to his confessional?
- Write a report on St. John Vianney's views toward sin, the Sacrament of Penance, or God's grace. How can we benefit from these views today?
- Interview a priest in your parish or diocese. Ask him how his ministry has drawn inspiration from St. John Vianney.

ST. JOHN VIANNEY

continued from page 175

- Satisfaction or penance includes prayer, offerings, works of mercy, service, self-denial, and sacrifices, and is an essential part of the sacrament. (p. 165)

- The priest completes the actions of the penitent by granting absolution. (p. 166)

- The graces or effects of the sacrament include reconciliation with God, the Church, and self. (pp. 167-168 and pp. 170-171)

- Indulgences are linked with the sacrament and involve a partial or total wiping away of punishment due for sins that have been forgiven. (pp. 169-170)

- The practice of granting indulgences is connected with the unity of the Church in Heaven, Purgatory, and on earth. (p. 169)

- The transformation of the sacrament extends to the way we practice penance in everyday life through discipline, forgiving others, refraining from anger and revenge, pursuing justice and peace, and answering the call to perfection. (pp. 172-174)

TERMS, PEOPLE, PLACES

Complete each of the following questions. Use complete sentences.

1. How did a priest ministering in the Sacrament of Penance use *penitentiaries*?
2. What action of *penance* may the priest administer as part of the Sacrament?
3. What results in *concupiscence*?
4. What incurs automatic *excommunication*?
5. Describe the unity of the Church named by the *Communion of Saints*.
6. Why is *contrition* the most important act of the penitent?
7. What does a person who commits a *mortal sin* lose?
8. How can you determine the *moral object* of a certain action?

ONGOING ASSIGNMENTS

As you cover the material in this chapter, choose and complete at least three of these assignments.

1. Find five examples in the New Testament where Jesus points out—through his words or his actions—that God's love and mercy are stronger than a strict sense of justice.

2. Prepare a report on the Order of Penitents in the early Church. What effect did this practice have on Church members and their participation in the sacraments?

3. Read and summarize the following Gospel passages. Explain what each teaches about the power of forgiveness:

   - John 8:1–11

   - Matthew 5:43–48

   - Matthew 18:21–22

4. Imagine you have been asked to explain to a non-Catholic friend about the necessity of confessing your sins in the Sacrament of Penance. What would you say? See the *Catechism of the Catholic Church* (1440–1449) for help in formulating your response.

5. Make a list of *Jeopardy!*-type answers for categories such as the Ten Commandments, Precepts of the Church, the Beatitudes of Jesus, types of sins, and different virtues. Make a question sheet to correspond to each of the answers. Then host a *Jeopardy!* game in the classroom. Pit three classmates against each other using the answers and questions you have developed. As in the game show, award more points as the questions get harder.

6. Watch the film *Dead Man Walking*. Write a report on the nature and importance of forgiveness in human life, using examples from the film.

7. Write an examination of confession for teens to use prior to celebrating the Sacrament of Penance. Use this examination to help you prepare for your next confession.

8. Research one of the following events: the end of apartheid in South Africa, the restoration of the Bay Bridge after the 1989 earthquake, or the assassination attempt of Pope John Paul II and the subsequent reconciliation. Or choose another topic that illustrates a real-life example of the reconciliation of a ruptured or damaged connection. Write a report based on your research.

9. Quote three passages from *The Imitation of Christ* by Thomas à Kempis that you find meaningful. Why do you think this book has been instrumental in leading people such as Thomas Merton to convert to Catholicism?

PRAYER SERVICE

Theme: God's mercy endures forever

Leader: Peace be with you.

All: And also with you.

Leader: God calls us to heartfelt conversion. He calls us home, to live again as his children. Therefore let us ask him for the grace of sincere repentance. (pause) Lord Jesus, you came to reconcile us to one another and to the Father: Lord, have mercy.

All: Lord, have mercy.

Leader: Lord Jesus, you heal the wounds of sin and division: Christ, have mercy.

All: Christ, have mercy.

Leader: Lord Jesus, you bring pardon and peace to the sinner: Lord, have mercy.

All: Lord, have mercy.

Leader: Lord, hear the prayers of those who call on you. Forgive our sins. In your merciful love, give us your pardon and your peace. We ask this through Christ our Lord.

All: Amen.

First Reading: Deuteronomy 5:1-3, 6-7, 11-12, 16-21a; 6:4-6

Second Reading: Psalm 130:1-4

All: Give thanks to the Lord, who is good, whose love endures forever (Ps 118:1).

Gospel Reading: Matthew 11:28-30

Leader: God continually calls us, not to punishment for our sins, but to a restored relationship of friendship and love. Let us reflect on the nature of this wonderful friendship by sharing our creative expressions from the "Peace Be with You" activity on page 171.

(*Allow time for sharing.*)

Leader: Let us offer one another a Sign of Peace. (*Allow time for an exchange of peace.*)

Leader: Let us pray together our closing prayer:

All: All-holy Father, you have shown us your mercy and called us to be a new creation in the likeness of your Son. Make us living signs of your love and forgiveness for the whole world to see. We ask this through Christ our Lord.

The Sacrament
of the
Anointing *of the* Sick

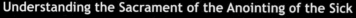

"Is Anyone Among You Suffering?"
Jesus and the Church respond to questions about suffering by uniting suffering to Christ's Passion and Death and by caring for the needs of others.

Understanding the Sacrament of the Anointing of the Sick
From the time of Jesus, the Church has offered healing for the sick through prayer, anointing with blessed oil, and laying on of hands.

Celebrating the Sacrament of the Anointing of the Sick
The Sacrament of the Anointing of the Sick is given either during sickness or immediately before death and is a true celebration of God's faithful and healing love.

The Grace of the Anointing of the Sick
The grace of the sacrament is tangible and real. The healing of the sacrament is always intended to further our Salvation.

How We Live the Effects of the Sacrament
The sacrament helps transform the lives of those who receive it by understanding their suffering as participation in the saving works of Christ.

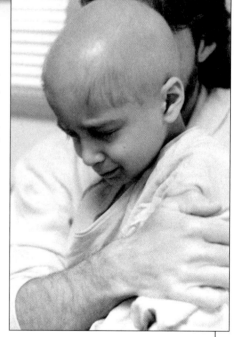

"IS ANYONE AMONG YOU SUFFERING?"

If that question posed by the Apostle James were answered in any family or community, the answer would return in the affirmative. There are people among us who are sick, even ourselves. "Illness and suffering have always been among the gravest problems confronted in human life" (*CCC* 1500).

When we face illness and suffering, we often turn inward to self-absorption, anguish, and sometimes even despair, and revolt against God. We ask the most difficult questions, which usually begin with the word *why*. We wonder:

- Why me?
- Why do I suffer?
- Why is there illness and suffering in the world?
- Why does God permit such pain?

In fact, in these questions are some answers. Very often illness can lead a person to begin a search for God and return to him. Illness can make a person more mature and lead to a discovery of what in life is really important, and what is not.

Suffering and the Old Testament

In the Old Testament, sickness was lived in the presence of God. Before God, people lamented their illness, begged him for healing, and viewed the Lord as the ultimate Master of life and death.

Part of the mindset of the Hebrew people was that sickness was part of a moral condition—a punishment for their sins. For example, the suffering and death of

theodicy

The theological question that tries to connect belief in God's justice with the reality that sometimes good people suffer unjustly and die.

apocalyptic

A genre of writing that assigns the enactment of God's justice to after death or to an end time when good people will be rewarded and evil people will be punished. In the Bible, the Books of Daniel and Revelation contain examples of apocalyptic writing.

Adam and Eve (see Genesis 3:1–19) was viewed as the consequence of their sin. The results were more than their own suffering and death; Adam and Eve transmitted to their descendants their own wounded nature and a loss of their original holiness and justice. All humans have inherited Original Sin.

As a result of Original Sin, human nature is weakened and inclined to sin. We are subject to ignorance, suffering, and death. The early Israelites believed further that all suffering directly resulted as punishment for sin, called the "Law of Retribution." They believed that people who were seriously ill or died early in life must have sinned. Or, their families must have done something to offend God. They believed that God blessed "good people" with health, many children, riches, and a long life. Jesus would eventually dismiss the legitimacy of the Law of Retribution (see pages 184–185).

Even prior to Jesus, the mentality forged by belief in the Law of Retribution was challenged in the Book of Job. It tells the story of a faithful, good man, Job, who loses everything: first his possessions, then his family, and finally his health. The issues he faces are defined by the term *theodicy*. He wants to know why God is letting this happen. For what is he being punished? Job does not so much answer the questions as he ponders the issue of suffering, lives with it, and explores it in more depth. Job rejects the conventional wisdom of his time that said he must have sinned in some way. He understands that God sends trials to those he loves, and he cries out to God for an explanation. God does not so much give a direct answer to Job for why he suffers as he reminds Job of his, God's, prerogative as Creator and Lord of all. Job's face-to-face encounter with God along with his suffering strengthens his faith. Though Job is restored to health at the end of the story, this action is somewhat anticlimactic after Job's meeting with God.

Nevertheless, the answer found in Job was not adequate for many Israelites. After all, many good people who suffer in this life are *not* restored to their riches or good health. So some Israelite writers began to adapt the Law of Retribution to a new type of thinking known as **apocalyptic**. In this genre, God's justice remains intact. If good people do not find justice in *this* life, then God will give them justice in the *next* life. At the Final Judgment, each person will be rewarded according to his or her works and according to the acceptance and refusal of grace: The Good will be rewarded with eternal life; the bad will experience everlasting punishment. Therefore, people of faith need to endure their sufferings patiently. The day will surely come, according to this belief, when God will once again make them whole in the New Jerusalem. As the prophet Isaiah predicted, "No one who dwells there will say, 'I am sick'; the people who live there will be forgiven their guilt" (Is 33:24).

Throughout the Old Testament, the Israelites lived among peoples of other religions who also looked upon sickness as a moral condition. The sick were considered "evil" people who needed to be shunned by the righteous. Anyone who was too old or too sick to

How Other Religions View Suffering

"Why do people suffer?" is a universal question that has been asked through every generation. Every major religion has attempted to answer the question. Here are some brief responses:

- *Buddhists* believe, according to the first of two Noble Truths, that all life is suffering caused by reliance on worldly possessions and attachments. It can take the form of greed, hatred, and ignorance, which, unless they are alleviated, can return to the person in the form of karma, the action that causes the entire cycle of cause and effect.
- *Hindus* understand suffering as a punishment for bad actions committed in this life or past lives.
- *Muslims* attribute some suffering to Satan or other evil spirits and believe it's allowed by Allah as a test of humility and faith.
- *Jews*, in general, hold that suffering is caused by a weakness in one's relationship with God and that God himself suffers along with the person.

keep up the pace of nomadic living was abandoned and left to die in the desert. In a society based on "survival of the fittest," the sick, the elderly, and the disabled were often considered worthless because they did not contribute to the well-being of the tribe; furthermore, since they were thought to be "evil," they might even bring God's wrath upon the entire group.

With the gift of the Law to Moses, the Israelites began to understand their moral responsibility to help weaker community members. The Fourth Commandment, "Honor your father and your mother" (Ex 20:12), told adults they needed to take care of their sick and elderly parents and not abandon them. The Books of Ruth and Tobit reinforced this message: Truly good people take care of their sick parents and other relatives, and God will reward them for doing so.

Christ the Physician

What did Jesus say about the reason people suffer? Jesus did not *say* as much about suffering as he *acted* on suffering. He is known as the Divine Physician because he treated both the physical symptoms of a person's illness as well as the person's soul by offering forgiveness for his or her sins. When Jesus observed the faith of those who carried a paralytic man to him and lifted him down through a hole in the roof, he first forgave the man's sins. When observers complained and accused him of blasphemy, Jesus said to them:

"Why are you thinking such things in your hearts? Which is easier, to say to the paralytic, 'Your sins are

forgiven,' or to say, 'Rise, pick up your mat and walk'? But that you may know that the Son of Man has authority to forgive sins on earth . . . I say to you, rise, pick up your mat, and go home." (Mk 2:8–11)

Jesus also rejected the understanding that suffering is a punishment for sin. He explicitly addressed this issue before healing the man born blind in John 9:1–41. Jesus' disciples asked him, "Rabbi, who sinned, this man or his parents, that he was born blind?" Jesus answered them clearly: "Neither he nor his parents sinned; it is so that the works of God might be made visible through him" (Jn 9:2–3).

In the days of Jesus, sick people were still treated as outcasts; they were often isolated from the life of the community—confined to their rooms or their homes. Some of them, especially lepers and those possessed with demons, had to live in the garbage dumps outside the city walls and rely on charity for their subsistence. Many of the disabled—the blind, the deaf, the crippled—were forced to beg for alms and food in public places. Under the Mosaic Laws, good Jews would become "unclean" if they touched a sick person or a corpse. Being unclean meant they could not take part in community worship and prayer unless they underwent certain purification rites to be restored to the community.

Jesus, however, defied the local customs of his day. He embraced the sick and the disabled, and he allowed them to touch him. He used human and natural signs to heal: He laid hands on them and rubbed mud on them. Through these acts of human kindness and acceptance, people experienced God's healing. They were made whole again, whether their illness was physical, mental, emotional, or spiritual. The healing miracles of Jesus proved the Father's love, echoing his words from Exodus: "I, the Lord, am your healer" (Ex 15:26).

Besides performing healing miracles, Jesus also taught about illness, death, and God's mercy. While Jesus never directly *explained* why God allows human suffering, he did make several important points:

1. *Sickness and death are not God's ways of punishing us.* Remember, before Jesus cured the man born blind, the following dialogue took place between Jesus and his disciples:

   > As he passed by he saw a man blind from birth. His disciples asked him, "Rabbi, who sinned, this man or his parents, that he was born blind?" Jesus answered, "Neither he nor his parents sinned; it is so that the works of God might be made visible through him." (Jn 9:1–3)

   In other words, people are not sick *because* they are morally evil.

2. *God loves the sick and disabled just as much as he loves healthy people.* Throughout his ministry, Jesus repeatedly stated that God welcomes the sick, blind, deaf, and disabled into the Kingdom of Heaven. In the Parable of the Great Feast, the servants are ordered to "go out quickly into the streets and alleys of the town and bring in here the poor and the crippled, the blind and the lame" (Lk 14:21). The sick and the disabled are not outcasts, but beloved children of God. They are welcome at God's table.

3. *God's love is stronger than sickness, pain, suffering, and death.* God loves us and always provides for us. He brings us healing and consolation, even though it may not be physical healing or restoration to life.

   > "Therefore I tell you, do not worry about your life . . . or about your body. . . . Look at the birds in the sky; they do not sow or reap, they gather nothing into barns, yet your heavenly Father feeds them. Are you not more important than they? Can any of you by worrying add a single moment to your life-span?" (Mt 6:25–27)

   > "Which one of you would hand his son a stone when he asks for a loaf of bread, or a snake when he asks for a fish? If you then . . . know how to give good gifts to your children, how much more will your heavenly Father give good things to those who ask him." (Mt 7:9–11)

   Suffering and death call us to have even greater faith. Jesus challenges us to trust God completely.

4. *God does not abandon us when we are sick or suffering.* Rather, he shares our suffering. By becoming man, Christ showed us that God shares our suffering. Instead of being a triumphal military general or

THE HEALING MINISTRY OF JESUS

When scribes and Pharisees noted that Jesus was eating with tax collectors and sinners, they wondered why. Jesus said: "Those who are well do not need a physician, but the sick do. I did not come to call the righteous but sinners" (Mk 2:17).

Part of Jesus' healing ministry involved forgiveness for sin. Furthermore, the healing miracles of Jesus addressed three different types of human suffering: physical illness and disability, domination by Satan or demons or psychological (mental, emotional) illness, and mourning for a loved one due to death. Here is a brief discussion of each:

- *Physical cures.* All four Gospels record examples of Jesus' ability to restore health to the sick, even those who were paralyzed or had leprosy. "People brought to him all those who were sick and begged him that they might touch only the tassel on his cloak, and as many as touched it were healed" (Mt 14:35-36). Jesus also had the ability to restore sight to the blind and hearing to the deaf.
- *Exorcisms.* Jesus freed some people from the domination of Satan, the evil one. This was also perhaps accompanied by his healing of people suffering from epilepsy, convulsions, or various types of mental illnesses who were thought to be possessed by evil spirits in Jesus' day: "When it was evening, they brought him many who were possessed by demons, and he drove out the spirits by a word and cured all the sick" (Mt 8:16).
- *Resuscitations.* According to the Gospels, Jesus raised from the dead at least three people—the daughter of Jairus (see Matthew 9:18-19, 23-26; Mark 5:21-24, 35-43; Luke 8:40-42, 49-56), the son of the widow at Nain (see Luke 7:11-17), and his friend Lazarus (see John 11:1-44). Jesus resuscitated these people, which means they were restored to life but would have to die again at some future date.

It can be understood that one of the reasons Jesus cured the physical ailments of others was to show clearly that he was the Messiah. As he told the disciples of John the Baptist, "Go and tell John what you have seen and heard: the blind regain their sight, the lame walk, lepers are cleansed, the deaf hear, the dead are raised, the poor have the good news proclaimed to them" (Lk 7:22). But it is important to realize that the healings of Jesus did much more than outwardly demonstrate his divine power. They also expressed his heartfelt love for humankind. Jesus truly cared for people who suffered. His healing miracles revealed to people his Father's love and compassion for the sick and disabled.

- Select one miracle from each type (physical healings, exorcisms, and resuscitations). Read the Scripture passage(s) and summarize what happened. Then write how this miracle can strengthen your own faith and trust in God when you or a family member is seriously sick. Finally, write a prayer asking Jesus for healing in some area of your life.

a powerful king, Jesus came as a different kind of Messiah—the Suffering Servant foretold by the prophet Isaiah:

> He was spurned and avoided by men,
> a man of suffering, accustomed to infirmity . . .
> Yet it was our infirmities that he bore,
> our sufferings that he endured,
> While we thought of him as stricken,
> as one smitten by God and afflicted.
> But he was pierced for our offenses,
> crushed for our sins,

> Upon him was the chastisement that makes us whole,
> by his stripes we were healed. (Is 53:3, 4–5)

The Gospels do not tell us whether Jesus ever got a cold or the flu, ran a fever, got a toothache, broke a bone, or was ever, in any way, sick. However, the Gospels do reveal that he got tired and hungry and that he truly suffered on the cross. Jesus redeemed us by willingly taking onto himself our sufferings and punishment for sin. He knows what we go through when we feel excruciating pain and when we fear approaching death. By his own suffering, Jesus showed us just how much God truly loves us.

resuscitation

Reviving a person who is dead or seems to be dead. Jesus performed at least three resuscitation miracles.

WHO HELPS THE SICK?

Research and report on one or more religious communities whose primary **apostolate** is to care for the sick and suffering. Also, interview a doctor, a nurse, or someone else in the medical profession. Ask his or her opinion about the role of the Spirit in healing the body. Write a report detailing the results of your interview.

apostolate

The mission, focus, or duties of a religious community.

5. *The sick should not be treated as outcasts; instead, they have an important role to play in the community.* Whenever Jesus cured lepers or other sick people who had been ostracized by society, he also told them to present themselves to their priest so that they might be declared "clean" and welcomed back to society. According to Jesus, the sick and the suffering are contributing members of the community. Their faith in the midst of suffering can serve as a strong witness to others. They can call us to greater faith, to take better care of our own health, and to value life itself.

Ultimately, Jesus answered the question about the meaning of suffering through his own Passion and Death. Through this act, "Christ took upon himself the whole weight of evil and took away the 'sin of the world,' of which illness is only a consequence" (*CCC* 1505). We can now unite our sufferings with Jesus' and thus become more like him to contribute to the Redemption of the world.

The Church Heals the Sick

During his public ministry, Jesus told his disciples to "cure the sick, raise the dead, cleanse lepers, drive out demons" (Mt 10:8). They were to continue to heal the sick while preaching the saving words of the Good News. The Church continues to respond to this command of Christ. She takes care of the sick and their needs and offers prayers for those who are ill. Christ's presence as Divine Physician is witnessed in the sacraments, especially the Eucharist, where the Body and Blood of Christ offer eternal life and are connected with bodily health (see 1 Corinthians 11:30).

When the Apostle James asked the question posed at the beginning of this section—"Is anyone among you suffering?"—he was prepared with an answer in the name of the Church. His answer is evidence of Christ's institution and desire for the Sacrament of the Anointing of the Sick, the subject of this chapter. According to the Letter of James:

> Is anyone among you suffering? He should pray. . . . Is anyone among you sick? He should summon the presbyters of the church, and they should pray over him and anoint [him] with oil in the name of the Lord, and the prayer of faith will save the sick person, and the Lord will raise him up. If he has committed any sins, he will be forgiven. (Jas 5:13–15)

The Church took up the practice of having presbyters lay hands and anoint with oil, in imitation of Jesus and the Apostles, realizing that it was sacramental—a sign of healing in which God was truly present.

MEMORIAL

UNDERSTANDING THE SACRAMENT OF THE ANOINTING OF THE SICK

St. Rose of Lima said, "Without the burden of afflictions it is impossible to reach the height of grace. The gifts of grace increase as the struggles increase." The call to suffering is significant for Catholics as it means aligning oneself with the cross of Christ.

Nevertheless, it is impossible for a person to answer that call alone. Without the help of the Holy Spirit, suffering will not free a person to love. Instead, it can break a person's spirit and weaken his or her faith. Suffering can make a person selfish, angry, irritable, demanding, and impatient. Suffering can cause unbearable loneliness that leads to despair. Jesus gave the Church the Sacrament of the Anointing of the Sick to aid those who are seriously ill and help them use their illnesses in service of Christ.

A Brief History of the Sacrament

Both during Jesus' life and after his Ascension to Heaven, his disciples anointed and laid hands on those who were sick to heal them. From the second through seventh centuries, whenever a person was seriously ill, other Christians would gather around and pray for him or her and then rub oil that had been blessed by a bishop on whatever parts of the body needed healing. It was necessary for the oil to be blessed by a bishop, but any Christian could administer it.

The first written evidence of the Rite of Anointing comes from a third to fourth century document called *The Apostolic Tradition*. At Mass, a bishop blessed the **Oil of the Sick** (olive or another plant oil), praying that the oil would bring strength to all anointed with it. Two centuries later, a letter of Pope Innocent I (416) offers further written evidence that blessed oil was used for the Sacrament of the

Oil of the Sick

Olive or another plant oil that is blessed by a bishop either at a Chrism Mass or at the time of anointing. The Oil of the Sick is an efficacious sign of healing and strength that is part of the Sacrament of the Anointing of the Sick.

---

extreme unction

A term that means "last anointing." It once referred to the time that the Sacrament of the Anointing of the Sick is received just before death. It is accompanied by a final reception of Holy Communion called *Viaticum*.

Anointing of the Sick. Christians regarded their blessed oil as an especially effective remedy and a sign of God's presence, as stated in a letter written shortly afterward in 428 by St. Cyril of Alexandria warning Christians not to turn to pagan magicians and sorcerers when they were sick. Instead, they were to turn to God's healing through the bishop and presbyters of the Church.

During the Middle Ages, concern with who actually did the anointing increased. Over time the sacrament had come to be associated with death. According to popular view, it became necessary to have a priest at the deathbed to ensure a safe departure and to carry the person into the afterlife. The Sacrament of the Anointing of the Sick came to be seen as something that accompanied a final reception of the Sacraments of Penance and Eucharist, which led to the declaration by the Council of Trent that "only priests (bishops and presbyters) are ministers of the Anointing of the Sick" (*CCC* 1516).

Over time, the Church came to view the Sacrament of the Anointing of the Sick no longer as a Sacrament of Healing but as a sacrament to prepare people for life after death. Even the name of the sacrament was changed. It became known as **extreme unction**, the final anointing. By the thirteenth century, the sacrament was given to people only when death seemed imminent, when there was no hope of physical recovery. Accompanying extreme unction was *Viaticum*, "food for the journey," the last reception of Holy Communion.

Changes after the Second Vatican Council

The Fathers of the Second Vatican Council were faced with a challenging task when it came to updating the rite of the sacrament. Should they follow the practice of the Church in the apostolic and patristic era, which celebrated Anointing as a sacrament of the sick with an emphasis on healing and faith in God's presence in suffering? Or should they follow the practice of the Church in the Middle Ages, which celebrated Anointing as a sacrament of the dying to prepare people for death?

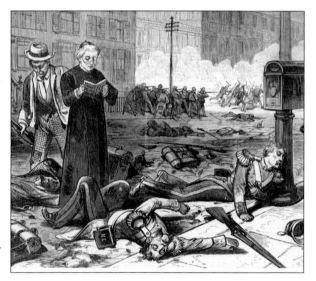

In other words, the challenge of the Second Vatican Council was to renew the sacramental practice in light of the best traditions.

In the end, the Council embraced both meanings of the sacrament. It wrote:

> "Extreme Unction," which may also and more fittingly be called "Anointing of the Sick," is not a sacrament intended only for those who are at the point of death. Hence, it is certain that as soon as any of the faithful begins to be in danger of death from sickness or old age, this

is already a suitable time for them to receive this sacrament. (*Sacrosanctum Concilium* 73)

In addition to the separate rites for anointing of the sick and for Viaticum, a continuous rite must be prepared in which sick people are anointed after they have made their confession and before they receive Viaticum. (*Sacrosanctum Concilium* 74)

The number of the anointings should be whatever suits the occasion, and the prayers which belong to the rite of anointing are to be revised so as to correspond to the varying conditions of the sick people who receive the sacrament. (*Sacrosanctum Concilium* 75)

The new Rite of the Anointing of the Sick, approved in 1974, emphasizes God's concern for the sick, Christ's healing love, and the Church's prayers for the sick person's recovery to health—both physically and spiritually. Any person of any age who has a serious or life-threatening illness or is about to undergo surgery may receive the sacrament. Several elements of how the sacrament is practiced are presented on the pages that follow. Ⓜ

For Review
1. What was St. Cyril's warning to Christians about remedies for illness?
2. What understanding about the sacrament changed during the Middle Ages?
3. How did the Second Vatican Council embrace both the emphasis on healing and the preparation for death in its revision of the Rite of Anointing?

For Reflection
How do you understand St. Rose of Lima's words about the importance of suffering in our lives?

CELEBRATING THE SACRAMENT OF THE ANOINTING OF THE SICK

Knowing some of the requirements and the rite itself for the Sacrament of the Anointing of the Sick is helpful for understanding how the sacrament can help unite a person to the Passion and Death of Jesus Christ.

As mentioned, a priest, as representative of the Church, is the minister of the sacrament. The introduction to the Church's instruction on the sacrament, the *Pastoral Care of the Sick: Rites of Anointing and Viaticum*, asks that the priest care for the sick through visits and personal acts of kindness (see page 197).

The Letter of James states that anointing should be given to a sick person to "save the sick person" and "raise him up" (see James 5:15). Determining the seriousness of the illness is up to the judgment of the person or family members in most cases. Those who are dangerously ill due to sickness or old age should be paid special attention and receive the sacrament. Also, the sacrament may be repeated if the sick person recovers only to have the illness return and become more serious. Other times the sacrament should be celebrated are as follows:

- A sick person should be anointed before surgery when a dangerous illness is the reason for the surgery.
- Old people may be anointed if they are weakened but no serious illness is present.
- Sick children may be anointed if there is sufficient reason to administer the sacrament.

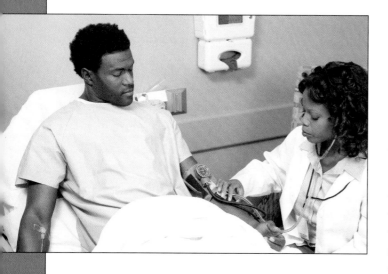

- Anointing may be conferred on sick people who have lost consciousness or the use of reason because they would have asked for it if they were in control of their faculties.

When a priest is called to administer the sacrament to someone who has already died, he prays for the person, asking God to forgive his or her sins and welcome him or her into the Kingdom. But he does not administer the sacrament. If he is unsure if the person is dead, he may administer the sacrament conditionally.

The matter for the sacrament is always the same: olive oil blessed by a bishop. (In necessary cases, other vegetable oils are allowed, and the priest may bless the oil.) A bishop usually blesses the Oil for the Sick for his diocese on or on a day close to the Mass of the Lord's Supper on Holy Thursday evening. The rite of the sacrament is explained in the following sections.

Rite of Anointing

The Sacrament of the Anointing of the Sick, given during sickness or immediately before death, is a true celebration of God's faithful and healing love. The sacrament is intended to be celebrated in a communal setting because sickness and death affect the entire Church. Family members, friends, and parishioners are strongly encouraged to surround the sick person in his or her moment of need. The sacrament may take place in the family home, a hospital, a convalescent home, a hospice, or a parish church. The sacrament may be for a single sick person or a group of sick people, depending on need (see *CCC* 1517).

In keeping with a celebration, the priest or bishop wears white vestments (see *CCC* 1516, 1530). If the Rite of Anointing takes place during Mass, it occurs after the homily. The sick person(s) and all those present are encouraged to take part in the Sacrament of Penance before Mass and to receive Communion during Mass. If the Rite of Anointing takes place outside Mass, those who are to be anointed are encouraged to celebrate the Sacrament of Penance first.

The essential rite of the Anointing of the Sick consists in the anointing of the forehead and hands of the sick person in the Roman rite, or other parts of the body in the Eastern rite, while accompanied by a prayer of the celebrant asking for the special grace of the sacrament. The new Rite of the Anointing of the Sick consists of eight parts: Introductory Rites, Liturgy of the Word, Litany or Prayer of the Faithful, Laying on of Hands, Blessing of Oil, Prayer of Thanksgiving, Anointing with Oil, and Prayer after the Anointing. A brief description of each part follows.

Introductory Rites

The priest or bishop greets the sick person(s) and gathered assembly. Then he explains what will happen. He may say words like the following:

Priest: The grace of our Lord Jesus Christ and the love of God and the fellowship of the Holy Spirit be with you all.

All: And with your spirit.

Priest: Lord God, you have told us through your Apostle James: "Is there anyone sick among you? Let him call for the elders of the Church, and let them pray over him and anoint him in the name of the Lord. This prayer, made in faith, will save the sick man. The Lord will restore his health, and if he has committed any sins, they will be forgiven." Gathered here in your name, we ask you to listen to the prayer we make in faith: In your love and kindness protect our brother (sister) N. in his (her) illness. Lead us all to the peace and joy of your kingdom where you live for ever and ever.

All: Amen.

A penitential rite is part of the Introductory Rites. Those who are sick may receive the Sacrament of Penance at this time by individual confession. If there is no sacramental confession or if it has taken place earlier, the priest invites everyone present to join in the penitential rite. Again, various options may be used. Here is one of them:

Priest:	You brought us to salvation by your paschal mystery: Lord, have mercy.
All:	Lord, have mercy.
Priest:	You renew us by the wonders of your passion: Christ, have mercy.
All:	Christ, have mercy.
Priest:	You make us sharers in your paschal sacrifice by our partaking of your body: Lord, have mercy.
All:	Lord, have mercy.

Liturgy of the Word

The Liturgy of the Word may consist of a first reading (usually from the Old Testament), a Responsorial Psalm, a second reading (usually from the New Testament), a Gospel acclamation, a Gospel reading, and a homily given by the presiding priest or bishop. In cases of necessity (such as impending death), the Liturgy of the Word may be shortened considerably. The *Catechism* explains the purpose of this part of the rite: "The Liturgy of the Word, preceded by an act of repentance, opens the celebration. The words of Christ, the witness of the apostles, awaken the faith of the sick person and of the community to ask the Lord for the strength of his Spirit" (*CCC* 1518).

The homily should call all those present to deeper faith in God's healing presence and faithful love. It should also remind everyone that the prayers of the community can have a healing effect on those who are sick.

Litany (Prayer of the Faithful)

These prayers may be adapted for the particular situation.

Priest:	My brothers and sisters, with faith let us ask the Lord to hear our prayers for our brother (sister) N. Lord, through this holy anointing, come and comfort N. with your love and mercy.
All:	Lord, hear our prayer.
Priest:	Free N. from all harm.
All:	Lord, hear our prayer.

Priest:	Relieve the sufferings of all the sick.
All:	Lord, hear our prayer.
Priest:	Assist all those dedicated to the care of the sick.
All:	Lord, hear our prayer.
Priest:	Free N. from sin and all temptation.
All:	Lord, hear our prayer.
Priest:	Give life and health to our brother (sister) N. on whom we lay our hands in your name.
All:	Lord, hear our prayer.

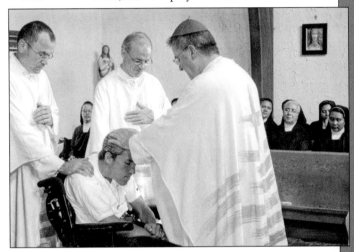

Laying on of Hands

In imitation of Jesus, who healed many sick people by touching them or laying his hands on them, the priest lays his hands on the head of the sick person(s). In silence, the priest prays over the sick in the faith of the Church. The *Catechism* explains, "This is the epiclesis proper to this sacrament" (*CCC* 1519). The priest, in the name of the whole Church, calls on God to come and fill the sick person with his healing presence.

Blessing of Oil

At the Holy Thursday Mass of the Lord's Supper, before the end of the Eucharistic Prayer or at the end of the Liturgy of the Word, representatives from each parish process to the sanctuary with the Oil of the Sick, Sacred Chrism, and Oil of Catechumens. The bishop blesses the oils, saying over the Oil of the Sick:

God of all consolation, you chose and sent your Son to heal the world. Graciously listen to our prayer of faith: Send the power of your Holy Spirit, the Consoler, into this precious oil, this soothing ointment, this rich gift, this fruit of the earth. Bless this oil and sanctify it for our use. Make this oil a remedy for all who are anointed with it; heal them in body, in soul, and in spirit, and deliver them from every affliction. We ask this through our Lord Jesus Christ, your Son, who lives and reigns with you and the Holy Spirit, one God, for ever and ever. Amen. (*Sacramentary,* 919)

In the case of necessity, any priest, who is the minister of the Anointing of the Sick, may bless the oil as part of the sacrament. He uses the same words of blessing as the bishop at the Chrism Mass.

Prayer of Thanksgiving

Using the blessed Oil of the Sick, the priest continues with the following prayer:

Priest: Praise to you, almighty God and Father. You sent your Son to live among us and bring us salvation.

All: Blessed be God.

Priest: Praise to you, Lord Jesus Christ, the Father's only Son. You humbled yourself to share in our humanity, and you desired to cure all our illnesses.

All: Blessed be God.

Priest: Praise to you, God the Holy Spirit, the Consoler. You heal our sickness with your mighty power.

All: Blessed be God.

Priest: Lord God, with faith in you, our brother (sister) will be anointed with this holy oil. Ease his (her) sufferings and strengthen him (her) in his (her) weakness. We ask this through Christ our Lord.

All: Amen.

Anointing with Oil of the Sick

In the Roman Rite, the priest (or bishop) anoints the forehead of the sick person(s), saying: "Through this holy anointing, may the Lord in his love and mercy help you with the grace of the Holy Spirit." Then he anoints the hands of the sick person, saying: "May the Lord who frees you from sin save you and raise you up." The person being anointed answers "Amen" to both prayers. This is the essential rite of the sacrament.

Prayer after Anointing

After all the anointings have taken place, the priest says a final prayer:

Priest: Lord Jesus Christ, you shared in our human nature to heal the sick and save all mankind. Mercifully listen to our prayers for the physical and spiritual health of our sick brother (sister) whom we have anointed in your name. May your protection console him (her) and your strength make him (her) well again. Help him (her) find hope in suffering, for you have given him (her) a share in your passion. You are Lord for ever and ever.

All: Amen.

No matter what setting the sacrament is celebrated in, its communal nature and the responsibility of all the faithful to care for the sick are stressed. Also, the sick person is encouraged to pray when he or she is alone or with family, friends, or those who care for him or her. The prayer should be drawn on the parts of Scripture that speak of the mystery of human suffering in Christ. Priests are encouraged to help the sick with this prayer.

Viaticum

The Sacrament of the Anointing of the Sick is for all who are seriously ill. Viaticum is a separate liturgical rite for those who are dying. Recall that the term *Viaticum* means "food for the journey." It is the person's last reception of Eucharist. The gift of the Lord's Body and Blood near the time of death strengthens the person and reminds him or her of Christ's promise of resurrection:

Amen, amen, I say to you, unless you eat the flesh of the Son of Man and drink his blood, you do not have life within you. Whoever eats my flesh and drinks my blood has eternal life, and I will raise him on the last day. (Jn 6:53–54)

All Catholics who can receive Holy Communion are bound to receive Viaticum. Those who are in danger of death are obliged to receive Communion. When possible, Viaticum should be received within Mass, under both species, to stress the meal symbolism of the Eucharist as a preparation for the heavenly banquet. If the dying person cannot receive Jesus' Body in the form of the consecrated bread, he or she may receive his Blood under the species of consecrated wine.

Outside of Mass, the ordinary minister of Viaticum is a priest. If no priest is available, Viaticum may be brought to the sick by a deacon or another member of the parish, either a man or woman who by the authority of the Church has been appointed by the local bishop to distribute the Eucharist to the faithful.

A distinctive feature of the reception of Eucharist as Viaticum is the renewal of baptismal vows by the person who is dying. Also, before a person receives Viaticum, he or she should participate in the Sacrament of Penance, if possible, and in the Sacrament of the Anointing of the Sick. Penance, Anointing, and Viaticum are the "last rites" for Catholics on their way to God. They mark the end of our earthly pilgrimage and prepare us to enter eternal life (see *CCC* 1525).

For Review

1. Name two occasions when the Sacrament of the Anointing of the Sick should be administered.
2. What should a priest do if called to administer the Sacrament of the Anointing of the Sick to someone who has already died?
3. Name the eight parts of the Sacrament of the Anointing of the Sick.
4. Who should receive Viaticum?

For Reflection

- What is your favorite Gospel story that expresses Jesus' care for the sick?

- How would you encourage someone to receive the Sacrament of the Anointing of the Sick? What if the person responded that the sacrament was "only for the dying"? How would you respond?

THE GRACE OF THE ANOINTING OF THE SICK

There are several spiritual graces or effects of the Sacrament of the Anointing of the Sick. However, prior to discussing those, it is important to remember that the sacrament is not a magic cure for physical ailments. We don't necessarily celebrate the sacrament and then find an immediate release from all our ailments. It's true that in rare cases, people are miraculously cured of their cancer or healed from their disability after celebrating the sacrament. But for most people, that's not what happens. So what are we to say? Is the Sacrament of the Anointing of the Sick just wishful thinking? The answer is an emphatic "no." Healing *always* takes place as a result of the sacrament. Those who participate in it are *always* healed in some way. The effects of the sacrament are tangible and real. The *Catechism of the Catholic Church* (1520–1523) lists four main effects of the sacrament, described in the following sections.

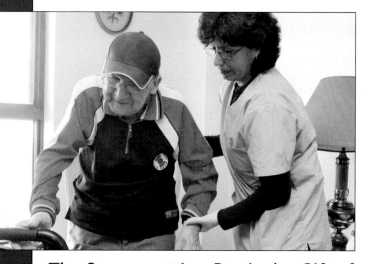

The Sacrament Is a Particular Gift of the Holy Spirit

The first grace a person experiences is to be able to accept the trials of being sick. The sacrament gives us the strength, peace, and courage to overcome the trials of a serious illness or the effects of old age. Through the assistance of Jesus, through the power of the Holy Spirit, our soul is healed, and also our body if it is God's will and helps toward our Salvation. Also, a person's sins are forgiven through the sacrament, including grave sins and eternal punishment requiring only imperfect contrition before he or she falls into unconsciousness.

The Sacrament Provides a Grace to Unite with the Passion of Christ

Suffering, a result of Original Sin, is given new meaning when we share in the saving work of Jesus. The sacrament gives us the strength and fitness of uniting to Christ more closely in illness and approaching death.

The Sacrament Is a Grace for the Church

"When the Church cares for the sick, it serves Christ himself" (*Decree on the Pastoral Care of the Sick*). By caring for a sick or dying person, the Church participates in the ministry of Christ, who did that himself. Likewise, by uniting ourselves to the Passion of Christ when we are sick, we share a witness to the truth of Christ's Redemption and provide an opportunity for the Church to live as the Body of Christ.

The Sacrament Is a Preparation for the Final Journey

We are given the supernatural strength to complete "our conformity to the death and Resurrection of Christ, just as Baptism began it" (*CCC* 1523). When the sacrament is received at the end of life, it is also called *sacramentum exeuntium* (the sacrament of those departing). In addition, near the time of death, the Church offers Viaticum, Holy Communion in the Body and Blood of Christ, as "the seed of eternal life and the power of resurrection" (*CCC* 1524).

The Sacrament of the Anointing of the Sick helps us face our illness and death with courage and dignity. We accept our situation as Jesus once accepted his same lot in the Garden of Gethsemane:

> He took along Peter and the two sons of Zebedee, and began to feel sorrow and distress. Then he said to them, "My soul is sorrowful even to death. Remain here and keep watch with me." He advanced a little and fell prostrate in prayer, saying, "My Father, if it is possible, let this cup pass from me; yet, not as I will, but as you will." . . . He prayed again, "My Father, if it is not possible that this cup pass without my drinking it, your will be done!" . . . Then he returned to his disciples and said to them, "Are you still sleeping and taking your rest? Behold, the hour is at hand when the Son of Man is to be handed over to sinners. Get up, let us go. Look, my betrayer is at hand." (Mt 26:37–39, 42, 45–46)

Another way the Sacrament of the Anointing of the Sick reminds us of our faith is through its connection with the Sacraments of Baptism and Confirmation. In both Baptism and Confirmation, we were also anointed with oil. These anointings changed our very character. The Oil of Catechumens exorcised us from the power of evil. It strengthened us in our resolve to turn away from sin and orient our lives toward God. The Sacred Chrism consecrated us as God's children. It bound us to him in a covenant relationship that sickness and death cannot destroy.

Being anointed with the Oil of the Sick has similar effects. It recalls that our lives have meaning and purpose, even when we are sick or in pain. The sacrament strengthens us and helps bring about spiritual healing, if not also physical healing.

TRANSFORMATION

HOW WE LIVE THE EFFECTS OF THE SACRAMENT

The Sacrament of the Anointing of the Sick helps transform the lives of those who receive it by helping them look at their suffering in a new way, as a participation in the saving works of Christ. Practically, this grace helps those who are sick and suffering within their own lives as they move from self-centeredness to God-centeredness. It also transforms them and the entire Church by helping them develop compassion and concern for those who suffer and reach out to them. Jesus explicitly addressed the need for Christians to care for those who are sick. Doing so, he said, is equivalent to caring for the Lord himself. In the Parable of the Sheep and the Goats, Jesus taught:

> Then the righteous will answer him and say, "Lord, when did we see you hungry and feed you, or thirsty and give you drink? When did we see you a stranger and welcome you, or naked and clothe you? When did we see you ill or in prison, and visit you?" And the king will say to them, in reply, "Amen, I say to you, whenever you did it for one of these least brothers of mine, you did for me." (Mt 25:37–40).

More information on how people who receive the Sacrament of the Anointing of the Sick are affected by its graces follows, as do practical applications for all Christians to live out the healing ministry of Jesus.

From Self-Centeredness to God-Centeredness

People struggling with sickness or pain very often get locked into their own little world. They may get angry about their situation, impatient with others, and unreasonably demanding in their expectations. They may complain a lot because no one seems to do enough for them, no one responds fast enough, and no one takes care of the problem in exactly the right way.

Job himself (see page 182) became self-absorbed with a "poor me" complex. He spent a great deal of time moaning and groaning and wondering why he was afflicted with suffering and illness. The answer to Job's problems was one of conversion. Job was challenged to put himself in God's place—to see the world and everyone in it from the Lord's perspective. Of course, Job could not do this because he was only human and not divine. Instead, Job came to accept his limitations and inability to understand the mind of God. He took up the challenge to trust in God's loving plan for all creation; he found God in the midst of his suffering. He believed that good somehow came out of his bad situation.

WORKS OF MERCY

Both the spiritual and corporal works of mercy (see page 271) help us care for the needy and identify with the suffering. One of the corporal works of mercy is to "visit the sick." This commandment comes from Jesus' command to do for the "least" as we would do for Jesus himself. As an individual, with a small group, or as a class project, identify people who are sick, either as shut-ins at home or in long-term health-care facilities. (A local parish may be able to provide information to help identify people in need.) Devise a schedule to provide regular visits and other aid to the sick. Aid may include doing errands, helping with chores, and reading the newspaper to a person, as well as sharing conversation.

Society of Jesus

A religious order established in the sixteenth century by St. Ignatius of Loyola to help with the reform of the Church. Popularly known as the Jesuits, the order is especially engaged in preaching, teaching, writing, and the ministering of schools and colleges.

The Sacrament of the Anointing of the Sick facilitates this type of conversion. Sickness is not a punishment. Instead, the sacrament helps us see sickness and suffering as opportunities for growth in holiness. We can become holy by becoming more and more like Jesus and having the same attitude he had toward suffering and death. As St. Paul wrote:

> Have among yourselves the same attitude that is also yours in Christ Jesus,
> Who, though he was in the form of God,
>> did not regard equality with God something to be grasped.
>> Rather . . . he humbled himself, becoming obedient to death, even death on a cross. (Phil 2:5–8)

Some of the Church's greatest saints knew what it meant to unite themselves with the suffering of Jesus. St. Thérèse of Lisieux, for example, longed to be a missionary—someone who did great things for God. Instead, she contracted tuberculosis as a young woman and was confined to bed. In her suffering, she slowly learned, through God's grace, to change her natural willfulness—especially her impetuous bad temper—into patient endurance. She termed this her "little way" and described her efforts like this:

> Miss no single opportunity of making some small sacrifice, here by a smiling look, there by a kindly word; always doing the small thing right and doing it all for love. . . . Remember that nothing is small in the eyes of God. Do all that you do with love. (*The Story of a Soul*, quoted in *Quotable Saints*, 117)

Thérèse died at age twenty-three, but the autobiography she left behind became a spiritual classic, encouraging many others to use their suffering as an opportunity for spiritual growth. Although she never left her sickbed, Thérèse is one of the Church's patron saints for missionaries.

Another saint whose life was impacted by his own suffering was St. Ignatius of Loyola. Ignatius came from a rich family and started his career as a brilliant soldier. But then he was seriously wounded in battle and had to spend many months in bed, convalescing. During this recuperation, Ignatius came to know the Blessed Trinity as never before. Once he was healed (although never completely), he did not return to the army. Instead, he founded the **Society of Jesus** as a spiritual type of army to bring God's love to others. As he wrote:

> Few souls understand what God would accomplish in them if they were to abandon themselves unreservedly to him and if they were to allow his grace to mold them accordingly. (*Spiritual Exercises*, quoted in *Quotable Saints*, 164–165)

Our Healing Ministry

All Catholics are called to continue the healing ministry of Jesus. We do this whenever we actively promote life, faith, hope, and love—in other words, when we follow the example of the Good Samaritan (see Luke 10:29-37). Being a minister of healing does not mean we necessarily have to become a nurse or doctor or enter the medical field. It can also mean doing a number of simple, ordinary actions of kindness. Here are a few ideas:

- When we are sick, we can sincerely thank those who care for us.
- When we are sick, we can faithfully take the medicine or treatment prescribed for us.
- We can bear our suffering with patience, knowing that it will someday (in this life or the next) end.
- If we are not sick, we can visit family members who are ill. We can brighten their day with flowers, a magazine, or cheerful conversation.
- We can hold open the door for a person on crutches or in a wheelchair.
- We can not park our cars in handicapped parking places, not sit in the handicapped chairs in movie theaters, and not use the handicapped stalls in public bathrooms.
- We can contribute money to or participate in fundraisers for research institutes trying to find cures for certain diseases.
- We can volunteer to help in hospitals, convalescent homes, retirement homes, and hospices.
- We can run errands for those who are confined to their beds or homes.
- We can pray for those who are sick, either privately or at Mass.
- We can attend the Sacrament of Anointing in our parish, to pray for and support those who are sick.
- We can offer consolation and comfort to the families of people who have recently died.

In short, we can simply *be present* to others. As Henri Nouwen also wrote:

My own desire to be useful, to do something significant, or to be part of some impressive project is so strong that soon my time is taken up by meetings, conferences, study groups, and workshops that prevent me from walking the streets. . . . But I wonder more and more if the first thing shouldn't be to know people by name, to eat and drink with them, to listen to their stories and tell your own, and to let them know in words, handshakes, and hugs that you do not simply like them but you truly love them. (*Gratias*)

These two saints, along with many others throughout the Church's history, learned to identify with Jesus through their suffering. The title *Christ* means "God's anointed one." When we are anointed with the Oil of the Sick in the Sacrament of Anointing, we are challenged to unite ourselves with Christ so completely that we also become "the anointed one." We are no longer just us, but Christ. Our suffering, his suffering, becomes truly redemptive.

From Self-Centeredness to Other-Centeredness

Transformation into "God's anointed one" means we willingly sacrifice ourselves for the good of others. Like Jesus, we bring healing to others in today's world. In Henri Nouwen's words, we allow ourselves to become "wounded healers." Nouwen was a Dutch Catholic priest who lived the last years of his life ministering with mentally disabled people at the **L'Arche community** in Toronto. We can heal others because we know what it is like to suffer and to be healed by God's love. St. Paul explained this transformation from self-centeredness to other-centeredness in his Second Letter to the Corinthians:

Blessed be the God and Father of our Lord Jesus Christ, the Father of compassion and God of all encouragement, who encourages us in our

L'Arche community
Family- and faith-based homes where people with disabilities live together. The name is French for "the Ark," as in Noah's Ark. L'Arche was founded in 1964 when Jean and Pauline Vanier welcomed two men with disabilities into their home in France.

every affliction, so that we may be able to encourage those who are in any affliction with the encouragement with which we ourselves are encouraged by God. (2 Cor 1:3–4)

The comfort we offer others comes not from pious platitudes or tired clichés. Instead, our words of faith are based on firsthand experience. We have been on the receiving end of God's compassionate love and encouragement. Thus we can profoundly encourage others to have faith too. This grace of being more Christ-like may be the most important effect of the Sacrament of the Anointing of the Sick. 🔵

For Review

1. What did Jesus say about the need to care for the sick?
2. How did suffering and illness transform Job?
3. Briefly describe the lessons St. Thérèse of Lisieux and St. Ignatius of Loyola learned about suffering.
4. What did Henri Nouwen mean by the term "wounded healer"?

For Reflection

- How is sickness an opportunity to grow in holiness?
- What acts of kindness can you perform to imitate Jesus' healing ministry?

CHAPTER QUICK VIEW

Main Ideas

- Illness and suffering have always been part of human life. (p. 181)
- When we face illness and suffering, we often turn inward to self-absorption, anguish, and sometimes even despair, and revolt against God. (p. 181)
- Sickness and evil are a result of Original Sin, when human nature was weakened and inclined to sin. (pp. 181-182)
- In the Old Testament, sickness was viewed as a moral condition—a punishment for sins. (pp. 182-183)
- The story of Job deals with a reconciliation between a good and just God and the presence of evil and suffering in the world. (p. 182 and p. 195)
- The Law of Moses helped the Israelites understand their moral responsibility to help weaker members of the community. (p. 183)
- Jesus Christ is known as the "Divine Physician." When confronted with suffering, he acted to remove it. (pp. 183-184)
- Jesus did make several points about why people suffer: (1) Sickness and death are not God's punishment; (2) God loves the sick as much as he loves the healthy; (3) God's love is stronger than sickness, pain, suffering, and death; (4) God does not abandon us when we are sick; (5) the sick have important roles to play in the community. (pp. 184-186)
- Modeled on Jesus' ministry and the example found in the Letter of James, the Church took up the practice of having presbyters lay hands on and anoint the sick with oil to bring about healing. (p. 186)

- The Sacrament of the Anointing of the Sick is to aid those who are seriously ill and to help them use their illness in service of Christ. (p. 187)
- Over time, the sacrament became a preparation for life after death and was given only as a "last anointing," called extreme unction. (p. 188)
- The Second Vatican Council embraced both the healing element and the last anointing element of the sacrament. (pp. 188-189)
- A priest, as minister of the Church, is the minister of the Sacrament of the Anointing of the Sick. (p. 189)
- The sacrament is intended for people who are dangerously ill due to sickness or old age. (pp. 189-190)
- The Rite of Anointing consists of eight main parts; the essential rites are the laying on of hands and the anointing with oil. (pp. 190-192)
- Viaticum is the separate liturgical rite for those who are dying; it is the person's last reception of the Eucharist. (pp. 192-193)
- The four main effects of the sacrament are: (1) through the power of the Holy Spirit, helping the person accept the trials of illness; (2) uniting a person with the Passion of Christ; (3) witnessing the truth of Christ's Redemption with the Church; (4) providing strength for our final journey from death to resurrection. (pp. 193-194)
- The sacrament helps transform our lives by helping us look at suffering in a new way. (pp. 195-198)

TERMS, PEOPLE, PLACES

Write a term from the following list to complete each sentence.

theodicy	apostolate	Society of Jesus
apocalyptic	Oil of the Sick	L'Arche community
resuscitation	extreme unction	Stations of the Cross

1. The _____ was founded in 1964 to provide a place for people with disabilities to live.

2. Job faced the issue of _____ as he struggled to reconcile suffering and evil with divine compassion.

3. The _____ is an efficacious sign of healing and strength that is part of the Sacrament of the Anointing of the Sick.

4. The _____ is a meditative prayer based on the Passion and Death of Jesus Christ.

5. The _____ style of writing pointed to an end time when good people will be rewarded and evil people will be punished.

6. _____ is a term that means "last anointing."

7. The _____ was established to help with the reform of the Church.

8. Many religious communities take up the _____ of caring for the sick and suffering.

9. The raising of Jairus's daughter was an example of a _____ miracle.

Famous Catholics and the Sacraments:

BL. MOTHER TERESA
OF CALCUTTA

Agnes Gonxha Bojaxhiu was born in Macedonia (then part of the Ottoman Empire, later part of Yugoslavia) in 1910. Her family was Albanian, and her father died when she was only eight. Agnes was raised Catholic and soon heard God calling her to religious life. At the age of eighteen, she entered the Sisters of Loreto, a community that taught at schools throughout India.

Agnes first arrived in India in 1929. Two years later, she took her first religious vows of poverty, chastity, and obedience and received the name Teresa. She made her final vows in 1937 while she was teaching in eastern Calcutta. Mother Teresa was greatly disturbed by the poverty she saw on the streets of that city. Many poor people were living and dying on the streets, and no one seemed to be helping or caring for them.

Mother Teresa prayed frequently for these people, until one day she heard God tell her to help these people herself. In 1948 Mother Teresa left the Sisters of Loreto to minister to the destitute and the starving on her own. She explained later, "God still loves the world and he sends you and me to be his love and his compassion to the poor."

Mother Teresa had no real plan and no money when she left the Sisters of Loreto; nevertheless, she managed to open a school in the slums to teach the children of the poor. She got an education in medicine and gradually began to visit the homes of the sick and minister to them. But even this did not seem to be what God was asking of her. Her next step was to literally go to the gutters of the city streets and minister to the dying men, women, and children she found there who had been rejected by the local hospitals.

Mother Teresa saw her work as part of her ongoing religious vocation. In 1950 she founded the Missionaries of Charity in Calcutta. The apostolate of this religious community, she explained, was to care for "the hungry, the naked, the homeless, the crippled, the blind, the lepers, all those people who feel unwanted, unloved, uncared for throughout society, people that have become a burden to the society and are shunned by everyone." There were only a few sisters at first, but they soon attracted other volunteers.

In 1952 Mother Teresa opened the first Home for the Dying in Calcutta, converting an abandoned Hindu temple for this purpose. People brought to the home received medical attention and were given the opportunity to die with dignity according to their religious faith, whether they were Muslim, Hindu, or Catholic. Mother Teresa and her sisters next opened a hospice for people suffering from leprosy; the sisters tended to the lepers' wounds, applied medication and bandages, and provided food. "The miracle is not that we do this work, but that we are happy to do it," Mother Teresa said later. "I realize that when I touch the odorous and oozing members of a leper, I am touching the Body of Christ, just as I take his Body in the Sacrament of the Eucharist."

In 1955 Mother Teresa opened her first orphanage for homeless youth. Repeatedly when she spoke in public, she talked of the need for strong family love. "The poor you may have right in your own family," she advised others. "Find them. Love them. Speak tenderly to them. Let there be kindness in your face, in your eyes, in your smile, in the warmth of your greeting. Always have a cheerful smile. Don't only give your care, but give your heart as well."

Mother Teresa was awarded the Nobel Peace Prize in 1979 for her selfless and courageous work with the destitute, the sick, and the dying. She donated her $192,000 award to the poor of India. As her work of mercy became more known, many people and organizations around the world asked for her help. She traveled worldwide to respond to the needs of the poor—ministering to the starving in Ethiopia, to radiation victims at Chernobyl, and to earthquake victims in Armenia.

At the time of her death in 1997, the Missionaries of Charity (which had grown to 4,000 sisters, 300 brothers, and more than 100,000 laypeople) were operating 610 missions in 123 countries. Primarily they ministered to people with HIV/AIDS, leprosy, and tuberculosis. The community also ran soup kitchens, orphanages, and schools throughout the world. Indeed, Mother Teresa's lifelong service was a testament to the joy of selfless love, the dignity of every person, and the value of little things done with faith. "The fruit of faith is love," she told others, "and the fruit of love is service. . . . Unless a life is lived for others, it is not worthwhile."

On October 19, 2003, only six years after her death, Pope John Paul II declared Mother Teresa "blessed." Many people hope she will soon be canonized as a saint.

In his first encyclical, *Deus Caritas Est* ("God Is Love"), Pope Benedict XVI wrote about Mother Teresa's generous service. "In the example of Blessed Teresa of Calcutta we have a clear illustration of the fact that time devoted to God in prayer not only does not detract from effective and loving service to our neighbor but is in fact the inexhaustible source of that service" (*Deus Caritas Est* 36). Mother Teresa herself would have explained it much more simply. As she once said, "To keep a lamp burning we have to keep putting oil in it."

- Research the work of the Missionaries of Charity in the United States. What is the closest ministry to you? Find out how teens can get involved in this ministry.
- Find out more about the life and words of Blessed Teresa of Calcutta. Report on the progress of her canonization process.
- Find three quotes from Mother Teresa that attest to the importance of selfless service, to the dignity of all people, or to the need to pray often. Create an art poster or project that displays these words. Share them with your classmates.

BL. MOTHER TERESA OF CALCUTTA

ONGOING ASSIGNMENTS

As you cover the material in this chapter, choose and complete at least three of these assignments.

1. Explain the different uses of oil in the Sacraments of Baptism, Confirmation, and the Anointing of the Sick.

2. Read the Book of Ruth and summarize it. How is Ruth a role model to other Jews? To us? How does God reward her?

3. Watch the film *Lorenzo's Oil*. Then write a report answering the following questions:
   - What types of healing took place in the movie? Was Lorenzo the only one who benefited from the oil?
   - If you could discover a cure for a certain disease, what disease would it be? Why?
   - What are similarities between the actions in the film and what occurs in the Sacrament of the Anointing of the Sick?

4. Read one of the following Scripture passages and answer the corresponding questions in a one-page essay.
   - John 9:1–41 (the man born blind). How does this passage show that sickness and death are not God's way of punishing us?
   - Luke 14:15–24 (Parable of the Great Feast). How does this parable show that God loves the sick and disabled just as much as healthy people?
   - Matthew 6:25–34 (dependence on God). How does this passage show that God's love is stronger than sickness, pain, and death?

5. Read one of the following Scripture passages and answer the corresponding questions in a one-page essay.
   - Matthew 8:14–15 (Jesus cures Peter's mother-in-law). How does this passage show that the sick have an important role to play in the community?
   - Matthew 25:35–46 (the Last Judgment). How does this passage show that Catholics have a moral responsibility toward the sick, disabled, and dying?

6. Attend a communal celebration of the Sacrament of the Anointing of the Sick at Mass. Write a poem or short story about the experience that reflects how you believe that the people who received the sacrament felt about its effects.

7. Write a short prayer for a sick person you know. Pray the prayer each day for one week.

8. Cemeteries of baptized people are sacred ground. With a group of classmates, visit a local Catholic cemetery. With permission of the caretaker, spend several hours cleaning up the graves—raking leaves, trimming the grass, cleaning the gravestones. Pray for the people who are buried there.

PRAYER SERVICE

Theme: Stations of the Cross

Leader: Jesus told his disciples, "Whoever wishes to come after me must . . . take up his cross, and follow me" (Mt 16:24). As we reflect now on the Passion, Death, and Resurrection of Jesus, let us begin with the Sign of the Cross.

Leader: We adore you, Christ.

All: Because by your holy cross you have redeemed the world.

(*Throughout the prayer service, students stand before each of the Stations of the*

Cross located in a chapel or church. Another option is for the students to create their own artistic renderings of the Stations that can be used for this Prayer Service.)

Reader 1: The First Station: Pilate condemns Jesus to death.

Reader 2: The Second Station: Jesus takes up his cross.

Reader 3: The Third Station: Jesus falls the first time.

Reader 4: The Fourth Station: Jesus meets his Mother Mary.

Reader 5: The Fifth Station: Simon of Cyrene helps Jesus carry his cross.

Reader 6: The Sixth Station: Veronica wipes the face of Jesus.

Reader 7: The Seventh Station: Jesus falls a second time.

Reader 8: The Eighth Station: Jesus meets the women of Jerusalem.

Reader 9: The Ninth Station: Jesus falls a third time.

Reader 10: The Tenth Station: The soldiers take away Jesus' garments.

Reader 11: The Eleventh Station: The soldiers nail Jesus to the cross.

Reader 12: The Twelfth Station: Jesus dies on the cross.

Reader 13: The Thirteenth Station: The soldiers take Jesus down from the cross.

Reader 14: The Fourteenth Station: Joseph of Arimathea places Jesus in his own tomb.

Reader 15: The Fifteenth Station: Jesus rises from the dead.

Leader: Let us pray:

All: God of all mercies and consolation, comfort us in our afflictions that we in turn might comfort those who are in trouble with the same consolation we have received. Grant this through Christ our Lord. Amen.

(*Catholic Household Blessings and Prayers*, 313)

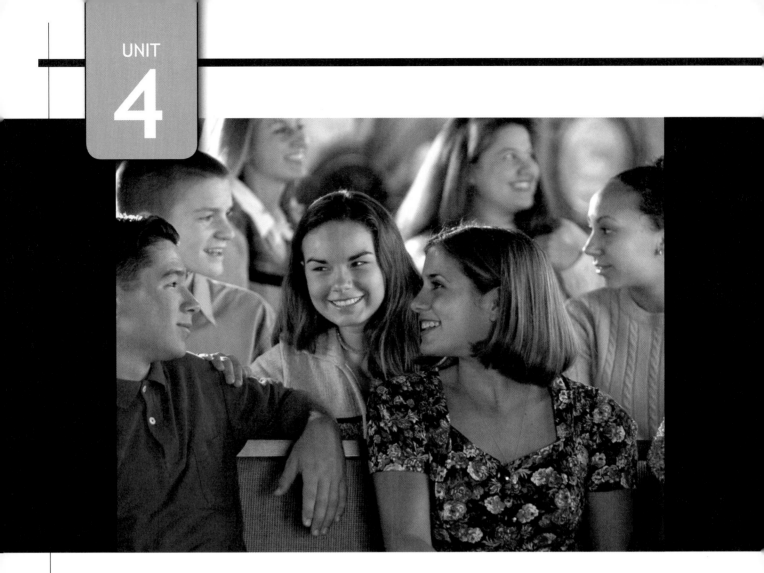

The Sacraments *at the* Service *of* Communion

ORDERED FOR SERVICE

Holy Orders and Matrimony are two sacraments whose primary purpose is to create, build, and maintain the Church community. That is why they are called Sacraments at the Service of Communion. Through each of these sacraments, baptized Church members serve the Church in different ways. Holy Orders, the focus of Chapter 8, concerns the actual structure and governing of the Church. It provides *ordained* ministers who "nourish the church with the word and grace of God" (*Lumen Gentium* 11§ 2). The sacrament includes three degrees: episcopacy, presbyterate, and diaconate. The word *order* is from the Latin word *ordanatio*, which means "incorporation into an order." (Other groups like catechumens, virgins, sponsors, and widows were also incorporated into orders in the history of the Church.) Deacons do not share the priestly ministry; they are ordained for other kinds of service.

Matrimony, the subject of Chapter 9, emphasizes the *common* priesthood of all the faithful, which we share through Baptism. Married couples serve the Church by producing new generations of Catholics, by educating these new members in faith and morals, and by working to bring Christ to all aspects of modern society.

Both Holy Orders and Matrimony have their roots in Baptism. Both types of priesthood are directed toward loving service and Salvation of others; both are needed for the Church's existence. Basically, we may say that the common priesthood (given at Baptism) concerns itself primarily with serving the needs of today's world. The ordained priesthood (clergy) concerns it-self primarily with "service of the common priesthood" (*CCC* 1547).

Similarly, the Sacrament of Matrimony is rooted in the service of others. The real pleasure of marriage and family life comes when each member of the family is at the service of others. The *Catechism of the Catholic Church* summarizes well the purpose of these sacraments:

> Those who receive the sacrament of Holy Orders are *consecrated* in Christ's name "to feed the Church by the word and grace of God." On their part, "Christian spouses are fortified and, as it were, *consecrated* for the duties and dignity of their state by a special sacrament." (*CCC* 1535, quoting *Lumen Gentium* and *Gaudium et Spes*)

On Becoming a Disciple

Study of the two Sacraments at the Service of Communion is important for you, as a high school student, as you begin the ever-nearing task of answering the call to vocation and discipleship. *Vocation* comes from a Latin word that means "call." For Christians, the primary call is to become disciples of Christ. This path may include a more specific call by God to life choices that involve being married, discerning priesthood (if you are a male) or the consecrated life of a religious sister or brother, or choosing to live as a dedicated single person (see *CCC*, 2231). Whatever specific road you choose, your journey will be that of a disciple of Jesus Christ.

The word *disciple* means "learner." Discipleship takes a conscious decision on your behalf. As you near adulthood, discipleship can no longer be a rote decision, one based on the practice or lack of practice of faith by your parents. Discipleship cannot be based only on what you learn in religion class. It cannot be about following commandments and rules without deeper reflection on their meaning and significance. Discipleship means asking these questions over and over: "What is it that I believe? Why do I believe? How does this belief impact my life and the lives of others?"

Baptism, Confirmation, and Eucharist are Sacraments of Christian Initiation. They form the common vocation of all Catholics—a vocation to holiness and to the mission of evangelizing the world. The Sacraments at the Service of Communion provide the graces for specific ways our common Christian vocation is lived out today.

From Catholic Bloggers

WHY NOT YOU?

Three years ago this morning I was ordained a priest of Jesus Christ. Not a day goes by that I am not grateful to the Lord for calling me to his service, frail and weak as I am. When I hold his Body in my hands, I am fully aware of how unworthy I am for such service. Yet, nonetheless, he has chosen me.

Why did the Lord choose me to serve him in this way? I do not know. There is nothing extraordinary about me, nothing so unique. I am a man who prefers the quiet of a library to the bustle of large groups of people. Being an introvert I seem a strange choice for such an extroverted ministry. Yet the Lord chose me.

My life differs from that of others only in that it has been marked with much suffering. Yet even in this I am not alone. Who of us does not suffer in some way? A suffering that is bearable for one is completely unbearable for another. There is nothing too different about me; I am a man like all others. Why should the Lord choose me?

I remember very clearly a conversation I had with a Sister while I was in college. We were discussing my vocation; I had already discerned a call to the priesthood and I accepted it, but still I wondered why the Lord chose me. She simply responded, "Why not you?" And I had no answer.

And so I ask you young men who may be reading this post: Why not you? Why should the Lord not want to use you as his humble instrument? The Lord has great skill at making use of fragile instruments. Won't you let him use you?

—A post from the blog *Servant and Steward*
by Fr. Daren Zehnie of Effingham, Illinois

What is a vocation? It is a gift from God—it comes from God himself! Our concern, then, should be to know the will of God. We should enter onto the path that God wills for us, not by "forcing the door," but when God wills and as God wills.

—St. Gianna Beretta Molla

The Sacrament
of Holy Orders

Why Men Become Priests
A variety of talented men continue to answer God's call to the priesthood while being formed to be a pastoral presence in service of the Church.

Understanding the Sacrament of Holy Orders
The ministerial priesthood shares in the unique priesthood of Christ. Bishops, priests, and deacons share in the ministry of Christ's priesthood based on the degree of the Holy Orders they receive.

Celebrating the Sacrament of Holy Orders
Although Holy Orders is a single sacrament, it is celebrated in three degrees: bishop, priest, and deacon. The fullness of the Sacrament of Holy Orders is conferred at the ordination of bishops.

The Grace of the Sacrament of Holy Orders
The sacrament confers an indelible spiritual character on bishops, priests, and deacons and allows them to act as representatives of Christ in his offices of priest, prophet, and king.

Ordination Leads to a Ministry of Service
The Sacrament of Holy Orders provides the means and opportunities for men to deepen their own holiness and oneness with God while being at the service of others.

WHY MEN BECOME PRIESTS

Recently, the United States Catholic bishops sent a survey to men who were about to be ordained to the priesthood. One item on the survey asked the men to complete the phrase "People would be surprised to know that I . . ." There were several different responses, including the ones shared below:

- played guitar in a rock-and-roll band.
- flew fighter jets.
- was called "Killer" on the football field.
- was a successful lawyer.
- was an atheist.
- built my own home and was once engaged to be married.
- rode a bike from St. Louis to Toronto with twenty other seminarians for World Youth Day.
- owned a townhouse, a BMW, and a Rolex watch before entering the seminary.
- was so afraid of public speaking that I ran from my vocation.

discern

To perceive differences between more than one option.

The unique lives that men leave behind to become priests today parallel the response of the first disciples to Jesus' call to "Come after me, and I will make you fishers of men" (Mt 4:19; Mk 1:17). Simon (later called Peter) and his brother Andrew were fishermen. They left their fishing nets to follow Jesus. Likewise, James and his brother John, sons of Zebedee, were also on their fishing boat when Jesus approached them. They not only left their nets and boat to follow Jesus, they left their father behind too. Even today, some people are willing to give up everything to follow Jesus as he demanded. Once, a would-be disciple said he would follow the Lord after he had a chance to first bury his deceased father. Jesus responded in a way that teaches us the radical nature of discipleship: "Follow me, and let the dead bury the dead" (Mt 8:22). This type of commitment is a strong element of the priesthood.

In many parts of the world, the Church has had some difficulty in recent years filling her seminaries and ordaining larger numbers of men to the priesthood. However, good men are still listening to and accepting God's call to a radical commitment of discipleship that is vitally necessary for the Church. Several people can't help but wonder why men want to become priests today. Several common answers emerge to help answer that question.

First, many men are attracted to the priesthood because of the essential sacramental role the priest has for the Church. The priest has the unique tasks of consecrating the Eucharist into the Body and Blood of Jesus Christ, offering absolution for sins in God's name, and bringing healing in the Sacrament of the Anointing of the Sick. This central role of being Christ for the world appeals to many men considering the priesthood.

Second, the examples of men who are already ordained inspire those considering the priesthood. Almost all candidates for the priesthood can point out a day and time when a priest they know invited them to consider the priesthood. Fr. John Regan of Joliet Diocese in Illinois recalls that one Saturday afternoon when he was in high school, his pastor said to him, "John, if you ever think about being a priest, I think you would be good." These simple words of invitation were the impetus for the high school senior to begin to **discern** more seriously the call to priesthood.

There are several other reasons men continue to want to be priests. An experience with the pope and World Youth Day may have inspired them. Typically a candidate has a great devotion to Jesus in the Blessed Sacrament and feels great comfort from participating at Mass.

The reasons men today continue to accept the call to priesthood are different than they were in previous generations. However, a constant remains. It is still the Lord who calls men to receive Holy Orders, as he once called Peter, Andrew, James, John, and the other leaders of the early Church. A prayer for the Church today is that more men will hear Christ's call and respond affirmatively in accepting this life of ministry and service.

Who Can Be Ordained

The subject of this chapter is the Sacrament of Holy Orders. It is the sacrament of apostolic ministry. Jesus entrusted his mission to the Apostles. This sacrament is the means for perpetuating that mission to the end of time. It includes three degrees: episcopate (bishop), presbyterate (priest), and diaconate (deacon).

Not everyone can receive the Sacrament of Holy Orders. The *Catechism of the Catholic Church* teaches, "No one has a *right* to receive the sacrament of Holy Orders. Indeed no one claims this office for himself; he is called to it by God" (*CCC* 1578).

What is this call like? Actually the "call" to priesthood may be present from early in life. Even at a very young age, a boy may recognize that God is calling him to a different kind of life. He may think of himself as a leader. He may recognize in himself the gift of compassion for others and empathy for the larger problems of the world. Primarily, he may feel a deep connection with God and an attraction to the Gospel of Jesus Christ. Someone who feels this call of God to the priesthood is wise to discern the calling by doing things like praying more, attending Eucharist often, speaking with a spiritual director, doing research on the priesthood, participating in a discernment program sponsored by a diocese or religious community, and living the Christian virtues.

Reception of the Sacrament of Holy Orders is also reserved only for baptized males. Some have cited this issue as being unjust, usually using the argument of the fundamental equality of men and women and the proven ability of women to work as or more capably in many of the same careers chosen by men. However, the Church teaching that only men can be priests is not rooted in injustice. Rather, it focuses on the belief that although men and women are fundamentally equal, they are not the same. Our gender is not incidental. It is an essential part of who we are. It has an impact on how we relate to others, including our relationship with God and the Church.

Primarily, the reason ordination of women is not possible is that the Church is bound to the choice made by the Lord himself. Jesus chose twelve men to be his Apostles. The

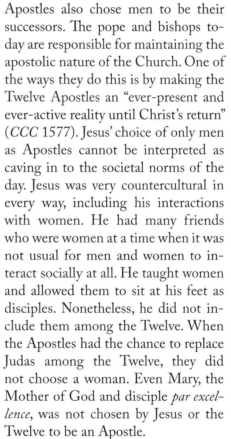

Apostles also chose men to be their successors. The pope and bishops today are responsible for maintaining the apostolic nature of the Church. One of the ways they do this is by making the Twelve Apostles an "ever-present and ever-active reality until Christ's return" (*CCC* 1577). Jesus' choice of only men as Apostles cannot be interpreted as caving in to the societal norms of the day. Jesus was very countercultural in every way, including his interactions with women. He had many friends who were women at a time when it was not usual for men and women to interact socially at all. He taught women and allowed them to sit at his feet as disciples. Nonetheless, he did not include them among the Twelve. When the Apostles had the chance to replace Judas among the Twelve, they did not choose a woman. Even Mary, the Mother of God and disciple *par excellence*, was not chosen by Jesus or the Twelve to be an Apostle.

In 1995 Pope John Paul II stated that the Catholic practice of ordaining only men to the priesthood could not be changed. He said the practice of ordaining only males to the priesthood is part of the Church's **Deposit of Faith**, and as such, it must be accepted in faith. In official pronouncements about this issue, the Church stresses the equality of women and the

Deposit of Faith
The body of saving truth entrusted by Christ to the Apostles and handed on by them to be preserved and proclaimed by the Church's Magisterium.

DID YOU KNOW?

A psychological assessment is an integral part of the admission process for candidates to the priesthood. The assessments are intended to look at the emotional health of the candidate. Special attention is given to candidates who come from dysfunctional family backgrounds and who manifest symptoms of dysfunction. Sometimes therapy is suggested and admission to the seminary is postponed or denied due to these issues.

---

celibacy

The renunciation of marriage made by those who receive the Sacrament of Holy Orders for more perfect observance of chastity. Celibacy also extends to consecrated life and to those who forego marriage for some honorable end.

---

seminary

The place where the training of candidates for the priesthood takes place. The Council of Trent instructed the bishops in each diocese to set up a seminary college to train men for the priesthood.

significance of motherhood. Like ordination, motherhood can be received only as an unmerited gift. Also, motherhood is ordered not primarily for the good of the mother, but for the good of the child. Likewise, priesthood is ordered primarily for the service of others.

More Requirements for Reception of Holy Orders

With the exception of permanent deacons, men who are normally chosen for ordination in the Latin Church live a celibate life and intend to remain celibate for the sake of God's Kingdom. In the Eastern Church, bishops are chosen solely among celibate men, while married men can be ordained as priests and deacons.

Celibacy is a sign of new life and service to which the Church's minister is made holy. Celibacy for the ordained in the Church is a discipline, not a doctrine. There are several reasons celibacy is a gift to the ordained and an enhancement of his ministry. For example:

- The commitment to celibacy is in imitation of Christ, who himself was celibate.
- Remaining celibate allows a priest to dedicate himself more to Christ and the service of the Church.
- By not marrying, the priest is a sign of the future Kingdom, in which there will be no marriage and Christ will be the Church's only spouse.
- The priest answers Jesus' charge to give up one's life for his sake and the Gospel. Jesus said, "And everyone who has given up houses or brothers or sisters or father or mother or children or

lands for the sake of my name will receive a hundred times more, and will inherit eternal life" (Mt 19:29).

Related to this promise, a priest also pledges to follow the spiritual gifts of humility and obedience and, particularly in the case of religious-order priests, voluntary poverty of worldly goods.

There is a long period of candidacy for men whom the Church calls to ordination. Four important areas of formation aid in this preparation:

- *Human formation* aids the formation of the candidate's personality so that he will relate well to others.
- *Spiritual formation* allows the candidate to cultivate an intimate friendship with Jesus Christ. Attention to this area leads to a lifelong commitment to personal prayer and devotion.
- *Intellectual formation* involves taking a course of study in theology, primarily, but also in philosophy, which leads to a deeper understanding of what it means to be human.
- *Pastoral formation* is the goal of the whole formation of the candidate. Priests are to be formed in pastoral ministry to make them shepherds of souls in imitation of Jesus Christ, the Good Shepherd.

All of these areas of priestly formation—human, spiritual, intellectual, and pastoral—take place in a **seminary**, which fosters another important quality of priests: fraternal love and communion among seminarians and eventual brother priests.

MEMORIAL

UNDERSTANDING THE SACRAMENT OF HOLY ORDERS

Since the beginning of the Church, the Sacrament of Holy Orders has been conferred in three degrees: the episcopate, presbyterate, and diaconate. These ordinations lead to the ministries of bishop, priest, and deacon. The *orders* of bishop and priest enable the one who is ordained to act in the person of Christ, the Head of the Body, in celebration of the sacraments. Deacons are ordained to help and serve the priests and bishops in their work. Priests and bishops are configured to Christ that they might act as the head of Christ's Body, the Church. Deacons are configured to Christ that they might serve as he served. Bishops, priests, and deacons are irreplaceable for the structure of the Church; in fact, without them one cannot speak of the Church.

Tracing the priesthood in both the Old Testament and New Testament can provide an understanding of how the modern orders of bishop, priest, and deacon are related to the duties of the priests of Israel and especially the High Priesthood of Christ.

Priesthood in the Old Testament

There was no ordained priesthood in early Israel. The father of a family or the head of a clan acted as

the group's priest. He performed spiritual duties and was responsible for teaching his children about God and Israelite beliefs. Around the time of the Exodus, the clan of Aaron and the tribe of Levi were set aside as priests (see Exodus 28–29; 32:25–29). Sometimes the men were anointed with oil before they assumed their sacred duties (see Leviticus 8–9). For the most part, these priests were married, and the priesthood was passed on to their sons.

During the Exodus from Egypt, Moses selected seventy elders to aid him in discerning God's will and leading the twelve tribes (see Numbers 11:24–25). These elders were typically mature men known for their administrative skills, moral character, and loyalty to the Law. They were called priests.

After the construction of the first Jerusalem Temple, the main role of the priests was Temple duty—offering sacrifices to God on behalf of the people. When the third Temple was destroyed in AD 70, the Jewish priesthood effectively ended. However, the priesthood of the Old Testament has much deeper significance as it prefigures the priesthood of Christ and the Church he founded.

The Church views the priesthood of Aaron and the seventy elders and the service of the Levites as a prefiguring of the ordained ministry of the New Testament. At the ordination of priests, the Church prays:

> Lord, holy Father . . .
> when you had appointed high priests to your people,
> you chose other men to help them in their task. . . .
> You extended the spirit of Moses to seventy wise men. . . .
> You shared among the sons of Aaron
> The fullness of their father's power. (*Roman Pontifical*, Ordination of Priests, 22, Prayers of Consecration)

The Priesthood of Christ

Jesus was not a Temple priest, nor did he "ordain" his Apostles as priests in a special ritual. Rather, Jesus is the High Priest of the New Covenant, acting both as Priest and Victim in his sacrifice on the cross to the Father. The ministerial priesthood shares in the unique priesthood of Christ. As St. Thomas Aquinas wrote, "Only Christ is the true priest, the others being only his ministers." The Letter to the Hebrews explains further:

> But when Christ came as high priest of the good things that have come to be, passing through the greater and more perfect tabernacle not made by hands, that is, not belonging to this creation, he entered once for all into the sanctuary, not with the blood of goats and calves but with his own blood, thus obtaining eternal redemption. (Heb 9:11–12)

Recall from the study of Baptism that the entire community of believers is priestly. Through Baptism and Confirmation, we share in the common priesthood. The ministerial or hierarchical priesthood of bishops and priests differs from the common priesthood because

the ministerial priesthood "confers a sacred power for the service of the faithful" (*CCC* 1592). Though "ordered to one another," the common priesthood functions by the unfolding of baptismal grace—living a life of faith, hope, and love, according to the graces of the Holy Spirit. The ministerial priesthood is at the service of the common priesthood. It is the means by which Christ builds up the Church.

Because Jesus himself is present to the Church in the ordained minister as "Head of his Body, Shepherd of his flock, high priest of the redemptive sacrifice" (*CCC* 1548), Jesus is the perfect Mediator between God and humanity, and he called Twelve Apostles to continue his work (see Mark 1:17, 3:13–19; Matthew 10:1–42). He made of these Apostles a Church, a permanent assembly or college, with Peter as their head (see John 21:15–17; Matthew 16:18–19). Their mission was to be his witnesses to the ends of the earth, through the power of the Holy Spirit. They were to make all people his disciples (see Acts 1:8, 2:1–36; Matthew 28:16–20; Mark 16:15; Luke 24:45–48).

The priesthood is ministerial. It has been instituted for the good of all people and the Church. The Twelve Apostles soon realized they needed others to help them in their rapidly expanding ministry. The Apostles began to organize the Church, following the

structure of the Greek society in which they lived. They chose seven men—Stephen, Philip, Prochorus, Nicanor, Timon, Parmenas, and Nicholas of Antioch—to serve as deacons, or ministers (see Acts 6:6). Deacons attended to the internal needs of the community—both at the Eucharistic table and outside the Eucharist. They read aloud the Scriptures, administered Communion during Eucharist, taught catechumens, ministered to the sick, and distributed food and clothing to the poor, especially widows and orphans.

The Apostles also chose men, such as James "the brother of Jesus," to be **presbyters**, or elders, of each local Church (see Acts 1:15–26, 15:13–21), and others, such as Barnabas and Saul, to serve like a Greek *episcopos* (overseer) over a larger area of the Church (see Acts 13:2–3). The Apostles invested these men through some type of ritual that involved prayer and the laying on of hands. The Apostles selected the *episcopoi* to be their successors, to continue their work after their deaths. Decisions affecting the entire Church were made at general councils by the *episcopoi* acting together (see Acts 15). Eventually, the *episcopoi* were called **bishops**.

Brief History of the Sacrament to the Present

By the early second century, Ignatius of Antioch had decreed that only a bishop or his appointee could preside at Eucharist or baptize. In the early Church, the community as a whole chose bishops and other Church leaders. A man was chosen as bishop because of the apparent presence of the Holy Spirit within him. After his election, a bishop received imposition of hands from another bishop. He was ordained to proclaim the Word, forgive sins, preside at Eucharist, and supervise the work of presbyters and deacons. The bishop ordained presbyters, and other presbyters joined in

the laying on of hands at the rite of ordination. Deacons were ordained by the bishop alone and were ordained specifically to assist the bishop in his ministry.

In the fourth century, after Christianity became the official state religion of the Roman Empire, the **clergy** gained a more privileged status. Increasingly the Church expected them to live a higher spiritual life and a more perfect moral life. A view took hold that the clergy were people devoted to "higher things of the spirit," while laypeople were obliged to the "lower things of the flesh." The desire of the people to elect a particular person as bishop was no longer enough to guarantee he would become bishop; state approval was also necessary. Still, the Council of Chalcedon (451) stated that priests were to be called by the people of a particular **parish** and ordained for work within that parish. Any other ordination was considered null and void. Bishops and priests were paid salaries by the state.

There were different influences on the Holy Orders between the Middle Ages and the Council of Trent. Because bishops increasingly needed priests who could celebrate Mass (deacons did not have that power), the diaconate as an active ministry declined. Gradually the diaconate became a step on the way to priesthood. A series of minor orders took hold. For example:

- Porters gathered the community to worship.
- Lectors read the Word of God at liturgy.
- Exorcists assisted bishops and priests in caring for catechumens.
- Acolytes served the deacon and priest at Mass.

These minor orders have since been abolished, though the Church

presbyters
Priests or members of the order of priesthood who are coworkers with the bishops and are servants to God's People, especially in celebrating the Eucharist.

bishops
Successors to the Apostles. A bishop governs the local Church in a given diocese and governs the universal Church with the pope and college of bishops. A bishop receives the fullness of the Sacrament of Holy Orders.

clergy
A term for ordained men; it comes from a Greek word for "lot."

parish
A diocesan subdivision headed by a pastor. A parish is a local Church community.

WHAT IT TAKES TO SERVE

Interview the vocation director for priestly vocations in your diocese. Ask him what one must do to be ordained. Ask about the type of seminary training. Research statistics about the number of seminarians, the number of ordinations, the demographics of seminarians, and other important information you can find. Summarize your findings in a written report.

has kept the ministries of lector and acolyte, which are open to laypeople.

Also during this time, an increase in monastic life influenced the priesthood. Though most monks were not priests, many priests did adopt the religious habits, prayers, study, and strict discipline of monasticism, including celibacy. This movement helped lead to the requirement of celibacy for the ordained in 1215. Prior to that time, priests were permitted to be married, though many priests already lived a single, celibate life.

The Protestant reformers of the sixteenth century pointed to some abuses in the clergy of that time, including a lack of education. The Council of Trent required the seminary training of priests. The council also reaffirmed Holy Orders as a sacrament and emphasized the teaching that Holy Orders gave priests the power to celebrate Eucharist and forgive sins in Christ's name.

There were no major changes in the Church's ordination rite until the twentieth century. The Second Vatican Council called for restoring the permanent diaconate in the West (which happened in 1967). The Council also called for a new Rite of Ordination (approved in 1968) that recalled the original meaning of ordained ministry. It also reminded the Church of the differences between the ministerial or hierarchical priesthood and the common priesthood, and also pointed out their interrelation.

The Second Vatican Council acknowledged the authority Jesus gave to his Apostles and their successors to govern the Church. Bishops and priests are entrusted with the sacred power of ministry and service; they are to act as Christ, Head of the Body. They are "to serve in the name and in the person of Christ the Head in the midst of the community" (*CCC* 1591). In *Lumen Gentium*, the Council further reminded people of the real nature of ordination: its service of communion. Bishops and priests are primarily to be visible signs of Christ in today's Church. They are to work for the Salvation of others. "Bishops, eminently and visibly, take the place of Christ himself, teacher, shepherd and priest, and act in his person" (*Lumen Gentium* 21). Thus, the revised Rite of Ordination emphasizes the way Jesus ministered to others and how he wanted his disciples to minister to others.

For Review

1. Cite the sacred duties of the Old Testament priesthood as described in Leviticus 8-9.
2. What is the main significance of the Old Testament priesthood for Christians?
3. How is the ministerial priesthood different from the common priesthood?
4. What were Jesus' words to Peter when he chose him to lead the Church?
5. Explain the ministry of deacons in the early Church.
6. How did the Apostles appoint the first bishops?
7. Explain the differing views of the clergy and laity in the fourth century.
8. Why did the permanent diaconate decline in the Middle Ages?
9. What influences did monasticism have on the priesthood?
10. What did the Council of Trent teach about Holy Orders?
11. Name two changes regarding Holy Orders effected by the Second Vatican Council.

CELEBRATION

CELEBRATING THE SACRAMENT OF HOLY ORDERS

Although Holy Orders is a single sacrament, it is celebrated and exercised in three degrees. The two degrees of the ministerial priesthood are the episcopacy and presbyterate. The diaconate is the third degree and is intended to help and serve the other two orders. All three degrees of Holy Orders are confirmed by a sacramental act called ordination. Only bishops can confer the Sacrament of Holy Orders on deacons, priests, and other bishops (see *CCC* 1600).

> The *essential rite* [matter and form] of the sacrament of Holy Orders for all three degrees consists in the bishop's imposition of hands on the head of the **ordinand** and in the bishop's specific consecratory prayer asking God for the outpouring of the Holy Spirit and his gifts proper to the ministry to which the candidate is being ordained. (*CCC* 1573)

The ordination of a bishop, priest, or deacon is very important to the life of the Church. It normally takes place within the celebration of Eucharist on either a Saturday or a Sunday in the diocesan cathedral so as many people as possible may attend. As explained on pages 211–212, the Church confers the Sacrament of Holy Orders only on baptized males "whose suitability for the exercise of the ministry has been duly recognized" (*CCC* 1598). In the Latin Church, before the candidate is ordained, he is presented to the bishop, and the bishop and the community are assured he has received the necessary training and was chosen for ordination in accordance with the teaching and practice of the Church. The bishop, who has been validly ordained himself, ordains the candidate. The congregation gives assent to the election. The basic structure of the Rite of Ordination in the three degrees is listed in the following chart:

ordinand

A person receiving the Sacrament of Holy Orders at any level: episcopate, presbyterate, or diaconate.

RITE OF ORDINATION		
BISHOP	**PRIEST**	**DEACON**
After Gospel: Presentation of Bishop-Elect Reading of **mandate** from the Holy See Consent of the People	After Gospel: Calling of the Candidate, Presentation of Candidate Election by the Bishop Consent of the People	After Gospel: Calling of the Candidate, Presentation of Candidate Election by the Bishop Consent of the People
Homily by principal bishop	Homily by bishop	Homily by bishop
		Commitment to Celibacy (if candidate is not married)
Examination of the Candidate	Examination of the Candidate	Examination of the Candidate
	Promise of Obedience to the bishop and his successors	Promise of Obedience to the bishop and his successors
Litany of Saints	Litany of Saints	Litany of Saints
Laying on of Hands	Laying on of Hands	Laying on of Hands
Prayer of Consecration	Prayer of Consecration	Prayer of Consecration
Anointing of the Bishop's Head with Sacred Chrism		
Presentation of Book of the Gospels	Investiture with stole and chasuble	Investiture with stole and dalmatic
Investiture with Ring, Mitre, and Crosier	Anointing of Hands with Sacred Chrism	Presentation of Book of the Gospels
Seating of the new bishop		
Liturgy of the Eucharist (new bishop concelebrates with other bishops)	Liturgy of the Eucharist (new priest concelebrates with bishop and other priests)	Liturgy of the Eucharist

mandate

An official appointment from the pope that says a certain priest has been chosen to be a bishop.

nuncio

An archbishop who acts as the official Vatican delegate for a nation. He is also called the Apostolic Delegate.

The Ordination of Bishops

The fullness of the Sacrament of Holy Orders is conferred with the bishop's consecration. This consecration ordains the bishop for the high priesthood, the summit of sacred ministry. The pope chooses bishops. Suitable candidates are identified in local dioceses and recommended by a **nuncio** to the Vatican. The appointment of a bishop is formally made in a mandate, an apostolic letter from the Holy See. During the Rite of Ordination of a bishop, this mandate is read aloud to the assembly. Upon ordination, a bishop becomes part of an unbroken succession of leadership that can be traced to the Apostles.

The **ordinary bishop** confers the Sacrament of Holy Orders on the bishop-elect through the laying on of hands and the following consecratory prayer:

God the Father of our Lord Jesus Christ, Father of mercies and God of all consolation, you dwell in heaven, yet look with compassion on all that is humble. You know all things before they come to be; by your gracious word you have established the plan of your Church.

From the beginning you chose the descendants of Abraham to be your holy nation. You established rulers and priests, and did not leave your sanctuary without ministers to serve you. From the creation of the world you have been pleased to be glorified by those whom you have chosen.

So now pour out upon this chosen one that power which is from you, the governing Spirit whom you gave to your beloved Son, Jesus Christ, the Spirit given by him to the holy Apostles, who founded the Church in every place to be your temple for the unceasing glory and praise of your name.

Father, you know all hearts. You have chosen your servant for the office of bishop. May he be a shepherd to your holy flock, and a high priest blameless in your sight, ministering to you night and day; may he always gain the blessing of your favor and offer the gifts of your holy Church. Through the Spirit who gives the grace of high priesthood grant him the power to forgive sins as you have commanded, to assign ministries as you have decreed, and to loose every bond by the authority which you gave to your Apostles. May he be pleasing to you by his gentleness and purity of heart, presenting a fragrant offering to you, through Jesus Christ, your Son, through whom glory and power and honor are yours with the Holy Spirit in your holy Church, now and for ever. Amen. (*Ordination of a Bishop* 26)

After the prayer of consecration, the ordaining bishop anoints the new bishop's head with Sacred Chrism. This is the fourth anointing the bishop has received in his lifetime (the first at Baptism, the second at Confirmation, and the third at ordination to the priesthood), which signifies the bishop's role as the Head of Christ's Body in his diocese. Next, the new bishop is given a Book of the Gospels as a sign of his ministry to proclaim the Word and to witness to the truth. Finally, the new bishop is invested with the ring, the mitre, and the crosier. The bishop's *ring* is a sign of his lifelong commitment and fidelity to the Church, the Bride of Christ. The *mitre*, a hat that consists of two triangular pieces of stiffened material sewn together on the sides with an opening for the head at the base, is a sign of the bishop's authority. The *crosier* is a sign of the bishop's role as shepherd of the Lord's flock.

ordinary bishop

The name for the diocesan bishop. He is the pastoral and legal representative of his diocese.

DID YOU KNOW?

Usually several bishops participate in the ordination of a new bishop as a sign of the collegial nature of the episcopacy.

stole

A long, narrow band of fabric, like a scarf. A deacon's stole is worn diagonally from one shoulder. A priest's stole is worn straight from the shoulders.

chasuble

The outer vestment worn by a priest at liturgy. Its color follows the liturgical seasons—purple for Advent or Lent; white for Christmas, Easter, and other feasts of Christ; red for Good Friday and Pentecost; and green for Ordinary Time.

dalmatic

The outer liturgical vestment of a deacon. It may also be worn by bishops under the chasuble and certain solemn liturgies.

The Ordination of Priests

After a candidate for priesthood has been presented to the bishop and the community has given its assent, the candidate is instructed in the nature of the duties he is about to assume, and his willingness to accept those duties is examined. This is followed by a recitation of the litany of the saints. The local Church calls on the entire Church in Heaven and on earth to pray for the ordinand. He then kneels before the bishop for the essential rite of the sacrament. The bishop confers the Sacrament of Holy Orders on the ordinand through the laying on of hands and the following consecratory prayer:

Come to our help, Lord, holy Father, almighty and eternal God; you are the source of every honor and dignity, of all progress and stability. You watch over the growing family of man by your gift of wisdom and your pattern of order. When you had appointed high priests to rule your people, you chose other men next to them in rank and dignity to be with them and to help them in their task; and so there grew up the ranks of priests and the offices of Levites, established by sacred rites.

In the desert you extended the spirit of Moses to seventy wise men who helped him to rule the great company of his people. You shared among the sons of Aaron the fullness of their father's power, to provide worthy priests in sufficient number for the increasing rites of sacrifice and worship. With the same loving care you gave companions to your Son's Apostles to help in teaching the faith: they preached the Gospel to the whole world.

Lord, grant also to us such fellow workers, for we are weak and our need is greater.

Almighty Father, grant to this servant of yours the dignity of the priesthood. Renew within him the Spirit of holiness. As a co-worker with the order of bishops may he be faithful to the ministry that he receives from you, Lord God, and be to others a model of right conduct. May he be faithful in working with the order of bishops, so that the words of the Gospel may reach the ends of the earth, and the family of nations, made one in Christ, may become God's one, holy people.

We ask this through our Lord Jesus Christ, your Son, who lives and reigns with you and the Holy Spirit, one God, for ever and ever. Amen. (*Ordination of a Priest* 22)

The new priest is invested with a **stole** and a **chasuble**, the liturgical vestments of priesthood. The priest's stole is worn over both shoulders and hangs down in front. It is a sign of the priest's authority. The chasuble is the outer vestment worn at liturgy. Its color follows the liturgical seasons—purple for Advent or Lent; white for Christmas, Easter, and other feasts of Christ; red for Good Friday and Pentecost; green for Ordinary Time.

Then the bishop anoints the new priest's hands with chrism. An anointing with Sacred Chrism at ordination offers the priest the grace of the Holy Spirit to make his future ministry fruitful. According to the *Code of Canon Law*, only ordained priests (and bishops) may validly consecrate the bread and wine at Mass. Also, only ordained priests (and bishops) may absolve penitents from their sins in the Sacrament of Penance.

The Ordination of Deacons

This order is given both to transitional deacons (those going on to priesthood) and to permanent deacons. In the West, transitional deacons must be celibate and promise to remain celibate throughout life. By this promise, the transitional deacons are "called to consecrate themselves with undivided heart to the Lord" (*CCC* 1579).

The bishop confers the Sacrament of Holy Orders on the ordinands through the laying on of hands and the following consecratory prayer:

Almighty God, be present with us by your power. You are the source of all honor, you assign to each his rank, you give to each his ministry. You remain unchanged, but you watch over all creation and make it new through your Son, Jesus Christ, our Lord: he is your Word, your power, and your wisdom. You foresee all things in your eternal providence and make due provision for every age. You make the Church, Christ's body, grow to its full stature as a new and greater temple. You enrich it with every kind of grace and perfect it with a diversity of members to serve the whole body in a wonderful pattern of unity.

You established a threefold ministry of worship and service for the glory of your name. As ministers of your tabernacle you chose the sons of Levi and gave them your blessing as their everlasting inheritance. In the first days of your Church under the inspiration of the Holy Spirit, the Apostles of your Son appointed seven men of good repute to assist them in the daily ministry, so that they themselves might be more free for prayer and preaching. By prayer and the laying on of the hands the Apostles entrusted to those chosen men the ministry of serving at tables.

Lord, look with favor on this servant of yours, whom we now dedicate to the office of deacon, to minister at your holy altar.

Lord, send forth upon him the Holy Spirit, that he may be strengthened by the gift of your sevenfold grace to carry out faithfully the work of the ministry.

May he excel in every virtue: in love that is sincere, in concern for the sick and the poor, in unassuming authority, in self-discipline, and in holiness of life. May his conduct exemplify your commandments and lead your people to imitate his purity of life. May he remain strong and steadfast in Christ, giving to the world the witness of a pure conscience. May he in this life imitate your Son, who came, not to be served but to serve, and one day reign with him in heaven.

We ask this through our Lord Jesus Christ, your Son, who lives and reigns with you and the Holy Spirit, one God, for ever and ever. Amen. (*Ordination of a Deacon* 21)

The new deacon is invested with a stole and a **dalmatic**. He also receives a Book of the Gospels, a sign of his mission to proclaim the Gospel of Christ.

For Review

1. What is the essential rite of the Sacrament of Holy Orders?
2. What does a "mandate" have to do with the appointment of a bishop?
3. What does the anointing of chrism received by a bishop at his ordination signify?
4. Explain the symbolic meanings of the bishop's ring, mitre, and crosier.
5. What does the priest's stole signify?
6. What is the difference between a transitional deacon and a permanent deacon?

For Reflection

- Your anointing at Baptism (and Confirmation) has made you holy. How so?

- Share a story of personal contact you have had with a priest or bishop when you experienced his shepherding of you or others.

COMMUNION

THE GRACE OF THE SACRAMENT OF HOLY ORDERS

Holy Orders conforms the ordained minister even more closely to Christ, giving him an indelible character—something that can never be taken away. Also, through the gift of sanctifying grace, Holy Orders joins the recipient even more intimately to the Blessed Trinity than he had been after being baptized and confirmed. As the *Catechism* explains, the grace of the Holy Spirit in this sacrament configures the ordained minister to Christ as "Priest, Teacher, and Pastor" (*CCC* 1585). Like Baptism and Confirmation, this share in Christ's office is given once and for all and cannot be repeated or conferred temporarily.

The vocation of bishops, priests, and deacons involves full-time, wholehearted service of the Church. Bishops receive special graces to guide and defend the Church, to proclaim the Gospel, and to be a model for others. Priests receive special graces to proclaim the Gospel, to offer the Eucharistic sacrifice, and to absolve sins. Deacons are given special graces through Holy Orders to proclaim the Gospel, to assist in the liturgy, and to perform works of charity (see *CCC* 1588). Also, among other graces of the sacrament is the conversion of the man who receives Holy Orders from:

1. *Self-centeredness to God-centeredness.* A priest's motive for living and working is no longer to get rich, to wield power, or to gain personal fame. Priests put aside their own wants, dreams, and desires so that they may serve the will of God. The Jesuits call this selflessness **indifference**. It is also related to the promise of obedience made to the priest's bishop or religious superior.

2. *Duty ("I should do this") to genuine love ("I want to go the extra mile because I truly love God and love others").* Priesthood is not drudgery. St. John Vianney (1786–1859), a small-town priest in France, described priesthood as "the love of the heart of Jesus." Priests are called to be genuine and loving people because they have a loving, personal relationship with Jesus. As Father Pedro Arrupe, S.J., former Superior General of the worldwide Jesuits, wrote:

> Nothing is more practical than finding God, that is, than falling in love in a quite absolute, final way. What you are in love with, what seizes your imagination, will affect everything. It will decide what will get you out of bed in the morning, what you will do with your evenings, how you will spend your weekends, what you read, who you know, what breaks your heart, and what amazes you with joy and gratitude. Fall in love, stay in love, and it will decide everything. (Quoted in *My Life with Saints*, 119)

3. *Pleasure-driven to Kingdom-driven.* Certainly the promise to a life of celibacy in imitation of Christ and to model God's Kingdom on earth involves a certain movement from pleasure to discipline. The end purpose of celibacy, however, is not greater self-mastery or discipline, but rather developing a greater capacity to love.

---

indifference

Selflessness that is open to going wherever one is most needed and to doing whatever seems best. God's will takes precedence over an individual's will.

DID YOU KNOW?

Archbishop is an honorary title for a bishop who heads a larger diocese or a diocese of special importance. *Titular bishop* is the title given to auxiliary bishops or other bishops in administrative posts who are not ordinaries of their own dioceses, so that they can head dioceses that once existed in countries surrounding the Mediterranean or in other areas of the world where there are not great numbers of Christians. *Cardinal* is the title given to certain bishops and archbishops, though to be named a cardinal does not require being either. Cardinals have been called "Princes of the Church" and have the exclusive role of electing a new pope.

Also, some ordained men face harsh lives of persecution and suffering following the public commitment made at the Sacrament of Holy Orders. Some bishops, priests, and deacons are even called to take this gift another step, to give up their lives and be martyrs for their faith, for their love of Jesus, and for their service of others. An example of a recent bishop who "gave his life for his sheep" (see *CCC* 1586) is Oscar Romero of San Salvador in El Salvador. This bishop, during his ministry, had a conversion that led him to side with the poor in his country and to speak up courageously for their rights before the government. Because of his stance on justice, Archbishop Romero was assassinated in 1980 while saying Mass in San Salvador.

Archbishop Oscar Romero

Other examples of ordained ministers who gave their lives for others include St. Stephen, one of the first deacons of the first-century Church; St. Lawrence (d. 258); Fr. Andrew Kim Taegon (1821–1846); and Fr. Damien (Joseph de Veuster) (1840–1889).

- St. Stephen was not afraid to preach the Gospel, even to people who did not want to hear the truth. He was stoned to death by enemies of Jesus (including Saul, who later converted and became St. Paul) who accused him of blasphemy. Today Stephen is remembered as the first Christian martyr.
- St. Lawrence served as deacon in the Church of Rome. Instead of giving his money to the government, Lawrence gave all his possessions to the Church for the poor. For this act of generosity, he was ultimately scourged and burned to death.
- Andrew Kim Taegon was the first native of Korea to be ordained to the priesthood. During the persecution of Catholics that began in 1839, Taegon was arrested, tortured, and beheaded near Seoul. He was only twenty-five years old.
- Born in Belgium, Father Damien devoted his life to serving people whom no one else wanted to be around. He served the exiled lepers of Molokai, Hawaii, until his own death from leprosy in 1889.

In all cases, the sacred power and character conferred by the Sacrament of Holy Orders allow bishops, priests, and deacons to serve the Church as Christ the High Priest, Christ the Teacher, and Christ the Good Shepherd:

Christ the Lord set up in his church a variety of offices whose aim is the good of the whole body. Ministers, invested with a sacred power, are at the service of their brothers and sisters, so that all who belong to the people of God and therefore enjoy true Christian dignity may attain to salvation through their free, combined and well-ordered efforts in pursuit of a common goal. (*Lumen Gentium* 18)

These special functions as they apply especially to the ministries of bishops and priests are explored in more depth in the sections that follow.

Acting as Christ the High Priest

In the New Covenant, there is only one sacrifice and only one priest. The sacrifice of Jesus replaces the Temple sacrifice of the Old Testament. Because Jesus offered the perfect sacrifice of himself on the cross, he is the one and only Mediator we will ever need between God and the human race (see 1 Timothy 2:5). There is no longer any need for a priest "to offer sacrifice day after day, first for his own sins and then for those of the people; [Christ] did that once for all when he offered himself" (Heb 7:27).

Today's priests do not offer a new sacrifice when they preside at the Eucharist. It is Christ, the eternal High Priest, who acts through the ministry of the priests to offer the Eucharistic sacrifice. In the name of the Church, priests ask the Father to send the Holy Spirit to make Christ's sacrifice present to us so that we can share in it and receive its redeeming graces. Bishops and priests also act as Christ the High Priest whenever they bring the Mass and sacraments to the community. By the power of the Holy Spirit, through their actions, they help make the entire Church, the Body of Christ, holy.

The Church Acts through the Priest

Because Christ acts through a priest in the sacraments, the Church also acts through a priest in the sacraments. The Church is the Body of Christ; therefore whatever is done in the name of Christ is done in the name of the Church as well. When a priest gives voice to Christ, his voice becomes the voice of Christ's Body, the Church. When a priest baptizes, it is Christ who baptizes. Because it is Christ who baptizes, it is the whole Church—the Body of Christ—that baptizes. When a priest forgives in the Sacrament of Penance, it is Christ who forgives. Because it is Christ who forgives, it is also the Church that forgives. When a priest offers the Body of Christ to the Father during the Eucharist, it is Christ who is offering himself. Because Christ is offering himself, the whole Church—the whole Body of Christ—also offers herself "'through him, with him, in him,' in the unity of the Holy Spirit" (*CCC* 1553).

The presence of Christ within a man who has been ordained does not preserve him from human weaknesses, errors, or sins. The Sacrament of Holy Orders does not guarantee that the minister will always act in the person of Christ, nor that he will not harm the Church. Unfortunately, bishops, priests, and deacons sometimes make bad mistakes and commit sin, just as every human does.

Nevertheless, any sinfulness of the priest does not affect the validity of the sacrament he has received or offers. The Sacrament of Holy Orders ensures that God always "acts and effects salvation through the ordained minister" (*CCC* 1584). Recall again that when the Church celebrates Baptism, Confirmation, Eucharist, Penance, and the other sacraments, it is really Christ who is baptizing, confirming, consecrating the bread and wine, and absolving sins. The unworthiness of the ordained minister "does not prevent Christ from acting" (*CCC* 1584). The spiritual powers given by the Holy Spirit in Holy Orders apply to the *sacraments* that the deacon, priest, or bishop administers, not to the *personal or moral character* of the ordained minister himself. Thus, even if the priest is sinful, the Holy Spirit continues to work through him to bring the real, full grace of the sacraments to all Catholics.

Acting as Christ the Teacher

Throughout his public ministry, Jesus used every opportunity in life—a dinner conversation with Pharisees, a prayer service in the synagogue, time with his Apostles on a boat, a hillside gathering of people, a chance encounter at the local well—to teach people about God's saving love. Jesus said, "I am the way and the truth and the life. No one comes to the Father except through me" (Jn 14:6). "For this I came into the world, to testify to the truth. Everyone who belongs to the truth listens to my voice" (Jn 18:37–38).

Jesus commissioned his Apostles to teach the truth to others. "Go, therefore, and make disciples of all nations, baptizing them in the name of the Father, and of the Son, and of the holy Spirit, teaching them to observe all that I have commanded you" (Mt 28:19–20). Jesus sent his Spirit of Truth to the Apostles at Pentecost so that they could fearlessly preach the Gospel and give spiritual nourishment to others. "If you remain in my word, you will truly be my disciples, and you will know the truth, and the truth will set you free" (Jn 8:31–32). Likewise, a task for the contemporary priest is to act as Christ the Teacher by sharing the Gospel of Truth.

The Sacrament of Holy Orders reminds us that bishops and priests are witnesses of the truth, especially in matters of faith and morals. The Second Vatican Council taught specifically about the ministry of bishops: "By virtue, therefore, of the holy Spirit who has been given to them, bishops have been constituted true and authentic teachers of the faith, pontiffs and pastors" (*Christus Dominus* [Decree on the Pastoral Office of Bishops in the Church] 2). Further:

> Bishops should present Christ's teaching in a manner relevant to the needs of the times, providing a response to those difficulties and problems which people find especially distressing and burdensome. They should also safeguard this doctrine, teaching the faithful themselves to defend and spread it. (*Christus Dominus* 13)

Regarding the ministry of priests: "It is the first task of priests as co-workers of the bishops to preach the Gospel of God to all. . . . Priests owe it to everybody to share with them the truth of the Gospel in which they rejoice in the Lord" (*Presbyterorum Ordinis* 4). Among their other tasks, deacons also are to be teachers. They are "to read the sacred scripture to the faithful" and "to instruct and exhort the people" (*Lumen Gentium* 29).

In short, bishops, priests, and deacons preach the Gospel message by word and behavior. They are to proclaim the mystery of Christ, explain the Church's faith, and treat contemporary problems in the light of Christ's teaching. "In every case their role is to teach not their own wisdom but the word of God and to issue a pressing invitation to all men and women to conversion and to holiness" (*Presbyterorum Ordinis* 4).

Acting as Christ the Good Shepherd

Jesus is the Good Shepherd who serves the needs of his sheep:

I am the good shepherd. A good shepherd lays down his life for the sheep. A hired man, who is not a shepherd and whose sheep are not his own, sees a wolf coming and leaves the sheep and runs away, and the wolf catches and scatters them. This is because he works for pay and has no concern for the sheep. I am the good shepherd, and I know mine and mine know me, just as the Father knows me and I know the Father; and I will lay down my life for the sheep. (Jn 10:11–15)

Bishops, priests, and deacons are to engage in a ministry of service. Bishops, especially, are to act as Christ the Good Shepherd. As leaders of their **diocese**, they are to give their lives in service to the spiritual needs of Catholics.

The bishops also have been designated by the Holy Spirit to take the place of the Apostles as pastors of souls and, together with the supreme pontiff and subject to his authority, they are commissioned to perpetuate the work of Christ, the eternal Pastor. (*Christus Dominus* 2)

Chosen to shepherd the Lord's flock, these pastors [bishops] are servants of Christ and dispensers of the mysteries of God (see 1 Cor 4:1), to whom is entrusted the duty of affirming the Gospel of the grace of God (see Rom 15:16; Acts 20:24), and the glorious service of the Spirit and of justice (see 2 Cor 3:8–9). (*Lumen Gentium* 21)

That is why that, as a sign of their shepherding role in the Church, bishops are given a crosier at the episcopal rite of Holy Orders. This pole with a hook at the top is a reminder of the staff shepherds once carried to herd their sheep.

USING YOUR GIFTS

Consult with a priest you know and come up with a plan for serving at a parish or in the local community. Ideas include volunteering to baby-sit during Mass, serving food at parish gatherings, cleaning up after a parish gathering, helping plan a youth retreat, beautifying the church grounds, raising money to help the homeless or a specific family who is in need, etc.

Make a plan of service you can carry out for the next month. Know exactly when you are needed and what you are to do. After the month is finished, reflect on your experience. How did your actions help build community in the parish? How did your actions help others grow closer to Christ? How did your actions help you grow closer to Christ? Share your reflections in an oral or written presentation.

diocese

A geographic section of the Church, made up of parishes, that is headed by a bishop.

For Review

1. Define "indelible spiritual character" in relation to ordination.
2. What are special graces of bishops, priests, and deacons?
3. What is the priest's role in the Eucharistic sacrifice?
4. What did the Second Vatican Council teach about the role of bishops as teachers?
5. How are bishops to act as Christ the Good Shepherd?
6. Explain why the validity and effectiveness of sacraments are not dependent on the worthiness of the minister.

For Reflection

Tell how you might move from being pleasure-driven to Kingdom-driven.

TRANSFORMATION

ORDINATION LEADS TO A MINISTRY OF SERVICE

vicar

One who serves as a substitute, an agent, or a representative of another. Bishops are vicars of Christ; they take his place in the Church. The pope is the Supreme Vicar of Christ.

Like marriage, priesthood is a lifelong vocation. Just as the Sacrament of Matrimony gives the husband and wife special graces to live out their vocation, so the Sacrament of Holy Orders gives priests special graces to be faithful to their vocation.

Essentially, the Sacraments of Matrimony and Holy Orders *consecrate* the people celebrating them for their vocations. Through these sacraments, the Church officially "sets people apart" to serve God according to their respective vocations. However, the Second Vatican Council also emphasized that:

The priests of the New Testament are, it is true, by their vocation and ordination, set apart in some way within the people of God, but this is not in order that they should be separated from that people or from any person, but that they should be completely consecrated to the task for which God chooses them. (*Presbyterorum Ordinis* 3)

The ministries of bishops, priests, and deacons are varied. Some priests are *secular* or *diocesan priests* who are ordained for a diocese and serve where the bishop places them. Other priests are *religious priests*, meaning they are part of a religious order or community and follow the rule of that community under the leadership of a religious superior.

Furthermore, bishops especially take the place of Christ himself in today's Church. Each bishop is the **vicar** of Christ, his representative. "The bishops have by divine institution taken the place of the apostles as pastors of the church in such wise that whoever hears them hears Christ and whoever rejects them rejects Christ and him who sent Christ" (*Lumen Gentium* 20).

Bishops and priests serve the People of God by providing them with means and opportunities to deepen their own holiness and oneness with God. In general, the three main ways this is accomplished is "by teaching (*munus docendi*), divine worship (*munus liturgicum*) and pastoral governance (*munus regendi*)" (*CCC* 1592). These tasks are carried out by bishops while being assisted by priests and deacons on two simultaneous levels: in the universal Church and the local Church. More information about each of those tasks follows.

Service to the Universal Church

Within his diocese, the bishop is the highest Church authority. Bishops have "a power which they possess in their own right and are most truly said to be at the head of the people whom they govern" (*Lumen Gentium* 27). Each bishop, however, is not autonomous or totally independent. He cannot make his own rules or interpret Church doctrine in a way that differs from the universal Church. Ordination to the Office of Bishop makes each bishop a member of the **episcopal college**. This assembly of bishops functions as a governing body in union with the pope, the Bishop of Rome. "Bishops installed throughout the whole world [live] in communion with one another and with the Roman Pontiff in a bond of unity, charity, and peace" (*Lumen Gentium* 22).

Individual bishops have a duty to build and maintain communion with the universal Church. The Bishop of Rome has supreme authority because of the primacy of Rome as the place where St. Peter founded the Church, ministered, died, and was buried. From that time on, the Bishop of Rome, or pope, was in a position of primacy. The pope is part of an unbroken succession of leadership that can be traced to the Apostles. The Apostles were given a special outpouring of the Holy Spirit by Christ, and by the laying on of hands, passed on this gift of the Holy Spirit to bishops at ordination.

Regional assemblies of the episcopal college, such as the United States Conference of Catholic Bishops, meet regularly to discuss the needs of the Church in a certain geographical area. Two other expressions of the episcopal college are **synods of bishops** and **Ecumenical Councils**. Pope Paul VI established the Synod of Bishops in 1965. A synod is a representative group of bishops, usually chosen from throughout the world, that comes together to advise the pope on certain Church matters. An Ecumenical Council is an assembly of all (or most) bishops from throughout the world in union with the pope. (The Second Vatican Council was an Ecumenical Council.) Such a council is the highest authority in the universal Church when it comes to deciding matters of faith and morals if it is united with the Roman Pontiff, the pope.

The Sacrament of Holy Orders ensures the influence of the Holy Spirit in all decisions made by the Church's Magisterium (pope and bishops acting together), so that what it teaches is the truth handed down faithfully from Christ and the Apostles. The pope, as head of the college of bishops, has the added charism of **infallibility** from the Holy Spirit when he proclaims a doctrine of faith *ex cathedra*, that is, from the chair of St. Peter. The pope rarely makes infallible statements. The last one was in 1954 by Pope Pius XII, regarding the doctrine of the Assumption of Mary into Heaven after her death.

One way individual bishops exercise their teaching role in the Church is by establishing catechetical guidelines for their dioceses, including the review of catechetical books used in Catholic schools and parish religious education programs. The local bishop must give his **imprimatur**, or consent to publish, which says that all contents in the book are free of doctrinal and moral error. Religion textbooks used in Catholic schools and parish religious education programs must have a bishop's imprimatur.

episcopal college
The unity of all ordained bishops in the worldwide Church, in both the East and the West. The pope heads the episcopal college.

synod of bishops
A group of bishops, usually chosen from throughout the world, who come together to advise the pope on certain issues.

Ecumenical Council
An assembly of all (or most) bishops from throughout the world in union with the pope. Such a council is the highest authority in the universal Church.

infallibility
The charism or gift of the Church offered by Christ whereby she is protected from error in matters of faith and morals. The pope or an Ecumenical Council most exclusively exercises the gift.

imprimatur
A bishop's approval to print a religion textbook because its contents agree with Church teaching.

Service to the Local Church

Bishops also have the task of building and maintaining communion with the local Church or parishes. "Individual bishops are the visible source and foundation of unity in their own particular churches" (*Lumen Gentium* 23). And, "As to the faithful, they should be closely attached to the bishop as the church is to Jesus Christ, and as Jesus Christ is to the Father, so that all things may conspire towards harmonious unity, and bring forth abundant fruit to the glory of God (see 2 Cor 4:15)" (*Lumen Gentium* 27).

The Second Vatican Council also strongly recommended that each bishop receive help in his task of teaching, sanctifying, and governing the diocese from synods of priests (sometimes called the priests' senate) and a diocesan council (made up of religious, clergy, and laypeople). To help maintain communion within the diocese, the bishop "should not refuse to listen to his subjects whose welfare he promotes as of his very own children and whom he urges to collaborate readily with him" (*Lumen Gentium* 27).

As mentioned, most dioceses have two types of priests: diocesan and religious. Diocesan priests usually live and serve at a parish; they have made a promise of lifelong celibacy and obedience to the bishop. Religious priests usually live in community groups devoted to a particular charism or spiritual founder; in addition to making a promise of lifelong celibacy and obedience to the bishop, they also take vows of poverty, chastity, and obedience.

Within each diocese, the priests assist the bishop in his tasks of preaching the Gospel, sanctifying the faithful, and governing. In each parish, the priests represent the bishop. In all parish functions, especially the liturgy, priests "make the bishop present" (*Lumen Gentium* 28). The authority of priests is not autonomous; it comes from their communion with the bishop.

> Priests can exercise their ministry only in dependence on the bishop and in communion with him. The promise of obedience they make to the bishop at the moment of ordination and the kiss of peace from him at the end of the ordination liturgy mean that the bishop considers them his co-workers, his sons, his brothers and his friends, and that they in return owe him love and obedience. (*CCC* 1567)

A basic statement of a priest's "job description" is to build and maintain communion in the local Church. They do this in three main ways: through preaching the Gospel of Christ to all, through the Eucharist and other sacraments, and through pastoral ministry. Here is a brief explanation of each task:

1. *To preach the Gospel to all.* A priest's homily is a teaching vehicle for breaking open the Word of God. The Second Vatican Council taught that the priest's "role is to teach not [his] own wisdom but the Word of God and to issue a pressing invitation to all men and women to conversion and to holiness" (*Presbyterorum Ordinis* 4). This also explicitly takes place when priests engage in teaching in religious education classes at the parish and through their writings, often published in a Sunday bulletin or newsletter. Deacons also share in this ministry of preaching and teaching at the parish level. Their official duties include reading the Sacred Scripture to the faithful and instructing and exhorting the people (see *Lumen Gentium* 29).

2. *To sanctify the People of God by providing the Eucharist and other sacraments.* Through the Sacrament of Holy Orders, priests have the authority to preside at Mass and the sacraments, except conferring Holy Orders. Bishops have the authority to preside at all the sacraments. While bishops are the original ministers of Confirmation, they can delegate this role to priests. Both validly ordained bishops and priests may baptize, reconcile sinners with God and the Church, anoint the sick, consecrate the bread and wine at Mass, and preside at the wedding of a Catholic man and woman (see *Presbyterorum Ordinis* 5). Furthermore, priests are obligated every day to pray for the holiness of the people they serve by praying the Liturgy of the Hours from a liturgical book formerly called the **breviary** (see *Presbyterorum Ordinis* 5).

Deacons also assist priests in their task of sanctifying the Church. As the Second Vatican Council's *Lumen Gentium* states:

> It is a deacon's task, as authorized by the competent authority, to administer Baptism solemnly, to reserve and distribute the Eucharist, to assist at and to bless marriages in the name of the church, to take Viaticum to the dying . . . to preside over the worship and the prayer of the faithful, to administer sacramentals, and to officiate at funeral and burial services. (*Lumen Gentium* 29)

3. *To govern the parish through pastoral ministry.* Priests represent the bishop and are charged with governing the parish Church. This type of governance is also in collaboration with all members

of the parish for the good of the parish. As Canon Law 536 states, "A pastoral council is to be established in each parish; the pastor presides over it and through it the Christian faithful along with those who share in the pastoral care of the parish in virtue of their office give their help in fostering pastoral activity." While a parish council does not have the power to make decisions without the consent of the pastor, it serves in an important advisory capacity in promoting communion in the local Church.

Facilitating a Call to Serve

In general, to be accepted as a candidate for ordination, a person must be a mature male at least eighteen years old, who has completed Christian initiation, who willingly and knowingly wishes to be ordained, and who has been accepted as a candidate by Church authorities. More important, the candidate must be called by God to this vocation, recognize the call, and respond to it. Pope John Paul II wrote:

> The history of every priestly vocation, indeed of every Christian vocation, is the history of an inexpressible dialogue between God and human beings, between the love of God who calls and the freedom of individuals who lovingly respond to him. (*Pastores Dabo Vobis* 36)

While it is the responsibility of the man called by God to priesthood to answer affirmatively, other Catholics have the responsibility to encourage and facilitate the call to serve. No one should have to determine his or her life's vocation in isolation. We all need to rely on the support, prayers, and discernment of other people of

breviary
A common name for a liturgical book from which priests pray the Liturgy of the Hours each day.

faith to help us along the way. If we think God is calling a young man we know to the priesthood, we have a responsibility to tell that person.

As St. Paul reminded us, all Catholics (including bishops, priests, and deacons) "hold this treasure in earthen vessels, that the surpassing power may be of God and not from us" (2 Cor 4:7). Just as all people in the Church need the support of the community to be faithful to their Christian vocation, so do bishops, priests, and deacons need our prayers and support to answer, persevere, and remain faithful in their service of the Church.

For Review

1. What are the three main ways that bishops and priests serve the People of God?
2. Explain why a bishop is not totally independent in decision-making within his diocese.
3. Define *infallibility* as it pertains to the pope.
4. Differentiate between diocesan and religious priests.
5. Name three ways a priest builds and maintains communion in the local Church.

For Reflection

- In what ways are priests both set apart from and within the People of God?

- Who do you know who you believe would make a good priest? Why?

CHAPTER QUICK VIEW

Main Ideas

- Even today people are willing to give up everything to follow Jesus. (p. 210)
- Men are attracted to the priesthood because of the sacramental role of the priest and by the examples of men who are already ordained. (p. 210)
- No one has the right to ordination; God must call him to ordination. (pp. 210-211)
- Reception of the Sacrament of Holy Orders is reserved only for baptized males. (p. 211)
- In the Latin Church, with the exception of some permanent deacons, men who are chosen for ordination live a celibate life and promise celibacy for the sake of God's Kingdom. (p. 212)
- Those preparing for ordination receive human, spiritual, intellectual, and pastoral formation. (p. 212)
- There are three degrees of the Sacrament of Holy Orders: the episcopate, presbyterate, and diaconate. (p. 213)
- The priesthood of the Old Testament prefigured the High Priesthood of Christ and the ordained ministry he instituted. (pp. 213-214)
- Christ is the only "true priest, the others being only his ministers." (pp. 214-215)
- Christ's choice of the Apostles is the origin of the Sacrament of Holy Orders. (p. 211 and pp. 214-215)
- The Council of Trent reaffirmed Holy Orders as a sacrament and emphasized the teaching that Holy Orders gave priests the power to celebrate Eucharist and forgive sins in Christ's name. (p. 216)
- All three degrees of Holy Orders are confirmed by a sacramental act called ordination. (p. 217)
- The fullness of the sacrament is conferred with the bishop's consecration. (p. 217)

- The essential rite of ordination includes laying on of hands, a prayer of consecration, and anointing with chrism. (pp. 217-218)
- The bishop is the minister of the Sacrament of Holy Orders. (pp. 217-221)
- Holy Orders conforms the ordained minister more closely with Christ, giving him an indelible spiritual character that can never be taken away. (p. 222)
- The vocation of bishops, priests, and deacons involves full-time, wholehearted service of the Church. (p. 222)
- The grace of the sacrament allows bishops, priests, and deacons to serve the Church as High Priest, Teacher, and Good Shepherd. (pp. 223-225)
- The sinfulness of the priest does not affect the validity of the sacrament he has received. (p. 224)
- The Sacrament of Holy Orders consecrates men for the lifetime service of others in both the local and universal Church. (pp. 226-229)
- We should pray for and encourage men who are called to ordination to explore and accept this call. (pp. 229-230)

TERMS, PEOPLE, PLACES

Complete each sentence by choosing the correct answer from the list of terms below. You will not use all of the terms.

discern	clergy	indifference	infallibility
Deposit of Faith	ordinand	diocese	imprimatur
celibacy	mandate	vicar	parishes
seminary	nuncio	episcopal college	breviary
presbyters	stole	synod of bishops	
bishops	chasuble	Ecumenical Council	

1. The Council of Trent required each diocese to sponsor a _____ for the training of priests.
2. _____ is a Greek word that meant "elders of the Church."
3. The _____ are direct successors of the Apostles.
4. At a bishop's ordination, a _____ is read that verifies his appointment from the pope.
5. A _____ is a sign of a priest's authority.
6. A _____ is the outer vestment worn by the priest with colors that follow the liturgical season.
7. The _____ often come together to advise the pope on certain issues.
8. The gift of _____ is most exclusively exercised by the pope or an Ecumenical Council.
9. _____ are subdivisions within a diocese, headed by pastors.
10. The archbishop who acts as the official Vatican delegate for a nation is called the _____.

Famous Catholics and the Sacraments:

ST. MAXIMILIAN KOLBE

R aymond Kolbe was born in Poland in 1894. His father was a poor weaver. He was always a devout child, and near the time of his First Communion, twelve-year-old Raymond received a vision of the Blessed Virgin Mary. Later, he wrote about the experience:

> I asked the Mother of God what was to become of me. Then she came to me holding two crowns, one white, the other red. She asked if I was willing to accept either of these crowns. The white one meant that I should persevere in purity, and the red that I should become a martyr. I said that I would accept them both.

Raymond joined the Conventual Franciscan Order in 1910 and received the religious name Maximilian. He made his first vows in 1911 and his final vows in 1914. Being a very bright student, he studied theology and philosophy at the Pontifical Gregorian University in Rome and eventually received two doctoral degrees.

Throughout his life, Maximilian Kolbe had a profound love for the Blessed Virgin Mary. In 1917 he founded the Knights of the Immaculata, a sodality devoted to the Immaculate Conception. He later wrote of Mary, "She must be the Queen of Poland in every Polish heart. We must labor to win each and every heart for her. . . . Let us give ourselves to the Immaculata [Mary]. Let her prepare us to receive [Jesus] in Holy Communion. This is the manner most perfect and pleasing to the Lord Jesus and brings great fruit to us."

Maximilian was ordained a priest in 1918, despite suffering from tuberculosis and having only one functioning lung. As a priest, Maximilian never used his illness as an excuse to get out of hard work or to not serve others in the Church. He also spent a great deal of time daily in front of the Blessed Sacrament, saying, "God dwells in our midst in the Blessed Sacrament of the altar."

In addition to being a good writer, Father Maximilian had a gift for organization and leadership. Among his other accomplishments, he built a self-supporting friary called The City of Mary Immaculate. This friary, located west of Warsaw, soon became the site of Poland's largest Catholic publishing house. The monks printed eleven different Catholic magazines and a daily newspaper called *The Little Daily*. As superior of the friary and director of the publishing company, Kolbe worked tirelessly. He added a radio station and even had plans to build a movie studio. He wrote more than 10,000 letters and 396 other writings, including newspaper articles, magazine articles, homilies, and catechetical texts. In addition to writing about religious matters, Kolbe used the press to write about national political and cultural problems.

For several years, Fr. Kolbe served as a missionary in Japan. He founded another friary in Nagasaki, which is still standing today. Then, in the prewar era of 1936, his superiors recalled him to the friary he had founded near Warsaw.

Once back in Poland, Maximilian continued writing with zeal. He not only wrote about Mary and his devotion to her; on more than one occasion, he also criticized the Nazis and presented them as enemies of Jesus. After the Nazis invaded Poland in 1939, they briefly arrested Kolbe. When he was released, he returned to the Warsaw friary.

Maximilian Kolbe is sometimes criticized for being anti-Semitic because he asked his readers to pray for the "straying children of Israel," that God would "lead them to the knowledge of the truth and the achievement of true peace and happiness." The truth, however, was far different; Kolbe had great love and respect for the Jewish people. This became evident during the growing Nazi persecution of the Jews in Poland. Kolbe organized a shelter for 3,000 Polish refugees, 2,000 of whom were Jews. He wrote, "We must do everything in our power to help these unfortunate people who have been driven from their homes and deprived of even the most basic necessities. Our mission is among them in the days that lie ahead."

Despite the growing violence leading up to World War II, Maximilian continued to publish. In early 1941, he wrote the following:

> No one in the world can change Truth. What we can do and should do is to seek Truth and to serve it when we have found it. The real conflict is inner conflict. Beyond armies of occupation and the catacombs of extermination camps, there are two irreconcilable enemies in the depth of every soul: good and evil, sin and love. And what use are victories on the battlefield if we ourselves are defeated in our innermost personal selves?

In February 1941, the Nazis rearrested Kolbe for helping the Jews and for criticizing the Nazis. In May, they sent him to Auschwitz, a notoriously cruel concentration camp of extermination. There he was branded as prisoner number 16670 and forced to do hard labor despite his one collapsed lung and failing health. "Mary gives me strength," he is reported to have said. "All will be well."

Although the Nazis deprived Kolbe of vestments, he continued to serve others as a priest. Whenever he could, he ministered to the other prisoners, teaching them about Jesus, explaining the Bible, and hearing their confessions. He even celebrated Mass with them with smuggled bread and wine.

One day at Auschwitz, a prisoner in Kolbe's barracks escaped. The resulting punishment was that ten other prisoners in the same barracks would be put to death by starvation. Randomly and mercilessly, the Nazis chose ten men to die. Among them was Franciszek Gajowniczek, a young Jewish man with a wife and children, who pleaded for his life. His pleas fell on deaf ears, but then, to everyone's surprise, Father Kolbe stepped forward and said,

"I am a Catholic priest. Let me take his place. I am old. He has a wife and children."

The Nazis agreed to let Kolbe die in place of the younger man. He and the other nine condemned men were locked in a bunker with no food, drink, or sanitation. While slowly being starved to death, Father Kolbe continued to pray the Rosary, sing hymns to Mary, and tell his fellow death mates about Jesus. After two weeks, Father Kolbe was the only one of the ten prisoners still alive. Because the Nazis needed the starvation bunker for new prisoners, they killed him with a lethal injection of carbolic acid.

Franciszek Gajowniczek, the man Father Kolbe had saved, survived Auschwitz. Until his own death on March 13, 1995, he continuously told people about Kolbe's heroic sacrifice for him.

After the war, Polish bishops told the Vatican that Father Kolbe's writing had been instrumental in preparing the Polish people to survive the horrors of the Holocaust. The bishops also attested, "The life and death of this one man alone can be proof and witness of the fact that the love of God can overcome the greatest hatred, the greatest injustice, even death itself."

Maximilian Kolbe was beatified by Pope Paul VI in 1971 and canonized by Pope John Paul II in 1982. His feast day is August 14. Today, he is the patron saint of journalists and prisoners. The cell where he died is now a shrine.

- Research the death camp Auschwitz-Birkenau and what happened there during World War II. In addition to the millions of Jews who were killed there, find out how many others, including Catholics, were also put to death.
- Share three quotations of Father Maximilian Kolbe on the importance of prayer to Mary and receiving Holy Communion in Christian life.
- Maximilian Kolbe encouraged Catholics to wear the Miraculous Medal of Mary. Find out the history of this sacramental and how it continues to be an aid to Marian devotion today.

ONGOING ASSIGNMENTS

As you cover the material in this chapter, choose and complete at least three of these assignments.

1. Using the library or the Internet, research one of the following orders in the Church: subdeacon, acolyte, exorcist, lector, porter. Explain what each order did historically and who could join it.

2. Make a list of the various ways priests in your diocese serve the Church as teachers.

3. Research the background of your bishop. Where did he grow up? Where did he attend the seminary? When was he ordained? What service has he given to the Church since ordination?

4. Research one of the titles of the pope. Explain what the title means and what ministry it entails.

5. Report on the life of Pope Benedict XVI. How did he serve the Church before becoming pope?

6. For a week, keep a diary of the times and situations that have called you to serve others according to your common baptismal priesthood. How did you respond in each situation? How could you have been more Christ-like?

7. Consulting the library or the Internet, find out more about the life of Fr. Damien (Joseph de Veuster) of Molokai or Fr. Andrew Kim Taegon. Write a 500-word essay summarizing your findings.

8. Read about the martyrdom of St. Stephen in Acts 6:8–7:60 or consult the Internet to find out about the life and death of St. Lawrence. In your journal, reflect on ways that you as a Catholic teenager can imitate the saint in situations that conflict with Christian values in modern life.

9. In recent times, a number of priests, deacons, bishops, and laypeople have sacrificed their lives in serving the Church. Find out about and report on one contemporary Catholic. Why was this person willing to give everything to his or her priesthood (either ordained or baptismal)?

10. Martyrdom continues to be very real and the fullest way for a person to configure his or her life to Christ. Explore its enduring value by researching the life of a contemporary martyr. Write a short report that details how the person lived and died for Christ.

PRAYER SERVICE

Theme: Litany of Saintly Ordained Ministers

Leader: Heavenly Father, you have blessed your Church with faithful servants in the Sacrament of Holy Orders. Let us remember them now in prayer, and ask them to pray for us.

Reader 1: For each of these popes, please respond, "Lead us to Christ."

St. Martin I . . . St. Pius V . . . St. John I . . . St. Gregory VII . . . St. Sixtus II . . . St. Pontian . . . St. Pius X . . . St. Gregory the Great . . . St. Cornelius . . . St. Callistus I . . . St. Leo the Great . . . St. Clement I . . . All holy popes. . . .

Reader 2: For each of these bishops, please respond, "Strengthen our faith."

St. Basil the Great . . . St. Gregory Nazianzen . . . St. John Neumann . . . St. Francis de Sales . . . Sts. Timothy and Titus . . . Sts. Cyril and Methodius . . . St. Peter Damien . . . St. Patrick . . . St. Cyril of Jerusalem . . . St. Anselm . . . St. Athanasius . . . St. Augustine . . . St. Boniface . . . St. Bonaventure . . . St. John Chrysostom . . . St. Charles Borromeo . . . St. Martin of Tours . . . St. Albert the Great . . . St. Ambrose . . . St. Thomas Becket . . . All holy bishops. . . .

Reader 3: For each of these priests, please respond, "Increase our love."

St. John Bosco . . . St. Thomas Aquinas . . . St. Vincent Ferrer . . . St. John Baptist de la Salle . . . St. Philip Neri . . . St. Ignatius of Loyola . . . St. John Vianney . . . St. Dominic . . . St. Maximilian Kolbe . . . St. Peter Claver . . . St. Andrew Kim Taegon . . . St. Vincent de Paul . . . St. Jerome . . . St. Isaac Jogues . . . St. Francis Xavier . . . St. John Damascene . . . St. John of the Cross . . . St. Peter Canisius . . . All holy priests. . . .

Reader 4: For each of these deacons, please respond, "Teach us to serve."

St. Vincent . . . St. Stephen . . . St. Ephrem . . . St. Anthony of Padua . . . St. Lawrence . . . All holy deacons . . . .

Leader: Let us pray now for the bishops, priests, and deacons we know, that they may always serve the Church faithfully. (*Pray for these people by name.*)

Leader: Let us pray:

All: God our Father, in these saintly ordained ministers you gave a light to your faithful people. You made them pastors of the Church to feed your sheep with their word and to teach by their example. Help us by their prayers to keep the faith they taught and follow the way of life they showed us. Grant this through Christ our Lord. Amen.

(Adapted from *Mass for Common of Pastors* #5)

The Sacrament
of
Matrimony

Helping Each Other Grow in Love

Like the effects of the Sacrament of Holy Orders, the effects of the Sacrament of Matrimony are directed at others, not at oneself.

Understanding the Sacrament of Matrimony

From the beginning of time, God intended for man and woman to be married. Jesus reiterated the indissoluble nature of marriage and raised it to a sacrament between baptized Christians.

Celebrating the Sacrament of Matrimony

The essential rite of the Sacrament of Matrimony is the free consent and exchange of vows of the husband and wife.

The Graces of the Sacrament of Matrimony

The effects of the sacrament are long ranging and add to the communion of the married couple not only with each other but with God, children, Church, and society.

Christian Marriage: A Sign of God's Eternal Covenant with Humanity

The indissolubility and fruitful love of Christian marriage help spouses model the unending love Christ has for his Church.

HELPING EACH OTHER GROW IN LOVE

God established marriage for two purposes: for the good of the husband and wife and for the procreation and education of children. Marriage offers a way for men and women to support each other and help each other grow in love. The deeper a person's understanding and experience of love, the closer that person will be to God.

As with Holy Orders, the other Sacrament at the Service of Communion, the focus of Matrimony for those who receive this sacrament is on others, not themselves. In fact, the effects of the sacrament are directed to the Salvation of the spouse primarily, and children as well. If the effects of the sacrament do contribute to the person's own Salvation, "it is through service to others that they do so" (*CCC* 1534).

There are many examples of faithful and loving marriages in which the graces of the sacrament are witnessed.

Consider the story of Joe and Mary Clare Pajakowski. Shortly after their fifty-first wedding anniversary, Mary Clare suffered a debilitating stroke. Though she survived, she needed indefinite physical therapy and speech therapy, along with someone to manage intake of a bevy of new medications.

Joe, a retired machine operator, became Mary Clare's primary caretaker. He drove her to therapy, communicated and deciphered messages from doctors, cooked meals, and even helped Mary Clare get dressed. All of these actions were uncharacteristic of much of Joe's behavior through the previous years of their married life. While he had focused on his job, working long hours on the second shift, Mary Clare had taken care of the home, consoled him over difficulties he faced at work, and handled most of the responsibilities that came with raising their four children.

With her own challenging medical condition, Mary Clare provided an opportunity for Joe to do things he hadn't done before. Because of her illness, Joe learned patience. He learned to put the needs of his wife before his own. He prayed and went to Church more often.

These things in effect would help facilitate Joe's own Salvation. He wouldn't have had these same opportunities without his wife.

Joe was also providing Mary Clare an avenue to love in a new way and to grow closer to God. In depending on Joe for her care, Mary Clare grew in her dependence on God and her trust in divine providence. With someone to share in her suffering, she was able to "let go" and better "lose her life" for the sake of Jesus Christ and the Gospel. She wouldn't have had these same opportunities without her husband.

Mary Clare lived five years after her stroke. Her last four nights were spent in a hospital intensive care unit as her heart and kidneys failed. Joe slept in her room in a chair, leaving only to shower. He was with her when she died at 3:15 on the morning of their fifty-sixth wedding anniversary.

An Intimate Communion

God established the intimate communion of life and love that is the essence of married life. From the beginning, one of the primary ways God has shared his love with men and women has been by giving them a way of sharing a deep and unifying love with each other. Men and women have been created as one, to be one. The consequence of Original Sin was the rupture of the original communion between man and woman.

The Sacrament of Matrimony gives men and women the grace they need to overcome divisions between the sexes (which is a result of sin) so that they may be one again, as God intended them to be. When a husband and wife embrace the grace of the sacrament and truly become one, they are given a glimpse of the love and unity that are shared in the Blessed Trinity. They are given a glimpse of the God who is love.

The Sacrament of Matrimony adds a whole new dimension to natural marriage. Because marriage is a sacrament, the man and woman not only pledge to love each other physically and emotionally; they love each other *in Christ*. They are one in faith. They find God's presence in their love for one another and in their love for their children. Furthermore, they become a sign to one another and to society of God's faithful love through their daily fidelity to their marriage vows.

Matrimony, in many ways, intensifies Baptism. God calls the bride and groom in a special way to share in Christ's mission as priest, prophet, and king. They exercise their common priesthood by offering the daily sacrifices needed in loving one another exclusively and in raising a family. They help each other and their children grow in holiness and friendship with God. Just as Baptism consecrates all Christians "to be . . . a holy priesthood" (*CCC* 1546, quoting *Lumen Gentium*), so the Sacrament of Matrimony consecrates Christian spouses "for the duties and dignity of their state" (*CCC* 1535, quoting *Gaudium et Spes*).

Sacred Scripture begins in the Book of Genesis with the creation of man and woman as partners in the image of God, and concludes with the wedding feast of the Lamb in the Book of Revelation (see Revelation 19:5–8). It is in the marriage of man and woman that Christ's love for the Church is glimpsed and where we have a foretaste of the intimate communion and tremendous joy that await us in Heaven (see *CCC* 1642).

For Review
1. How does Matrimony fit the definition of a Sacrament at the Service of Communion?
2. How does the Sacrament of Matrimony add a new dimension to natural marriage?

For Reflection
Describe a Catholic married couple you know. How does each spouse work toward the Salvation of the other?

UNDERSTANDING THE SACRAMENT OF MATRIMONY

From the beginning of creation, marriage, in one form or another, has existed in human society. "The vocation to marriage is written in the very nature of man and woman as they came from the hand of the Creator" (*CCC* 1603). Genesis 2:4–25 describes Adam's creation, along with his loneliness at not having a suitable partner with whom to share his life.

The Lord agreed: "It is not good for the man to be alone. I will make a suitable partner for him." When Adam finally saw the woman, he said, "This one, at last, is bone of my bones and flesh of my flesh." The *Catechism* teaches further:

> The woman, "flesh of his flesh," his equal, his nearest in all things, is given to him by God as a "helpmate"; she thus represents God from whom comes our help. (*CCC* 1605)

Without a doubt, God's Chosen People longed for the unity and indissolubility of marriage, which God intended from the beginning and which they learned from the Mosaic Law. "Seeing God's covenant with Israel in the image of exclusive and faithful married love, the prophets prepared the Chosen People's conscience for a deepened understanding of the unity and indissolubility of marriage" (*CCC* 1611). In fact, it is important to remember that marriage is not purely a human institution that must face, adapt, and deal with the corruption of sin. The Scriptures teach that God created man and woman for one another: "That is why a man leaves his father and mother and clings to his wife, and the two of them become one body" (Gn 2:24). From the beginning, God showed that marriage entails an unbreakable union between a man and a woman so "they are no longer two, but one flesh" (Mt 19:6).

The most elevated status of marriage in the Old Testament is presented in the Books of Ruth and Tobit, especially regarding the fidelity of marriage and the tenderness of spouses to one another. Church Tradition has always held the Song of Songs to be a unique expression of marital love as a reflection of God's love:

> Set me as a seal on your heart,
> as a seal on your arm;
> For stern as death is love,
> relentless as the nether world is devotion;
> its flames are a blazing fire.
> Deep waters cannot quench love,
> nor floods sweep it away.
> Were one to offer all he owns to purchase love,
> he would be roundly mocked. (Sg 8:6–7)

The history of marriage, even through the Old Testament, is affected by the sinfulness of humankind. Marriage during the time of the Old Testament was primarily a private contract between two male heads of families, and the contract was regarded as a type of purchase, much like the buying and selling of property. A father "owned" his daughters and was entitled to any profit they made from working in the fields, sewing, spinning, or cooking. A young man who wanted to marry a girl had to pay her father a "bride price" to compensate him for losing a valuable worker and

divorce

The ending of a civil marriage contract. Church law forbids divorced Catholics from remarrying unless their first marriage has been declared null. It also forbids a Catholic from marrying a divorced person of any faith unless that marriage has been declared null.

polygamy

Being married to two or more people at the same time. It is contrary to conjugal love, which is undivided and exclusive.

adultery

Infidelity in marriage whereby a married person has sexual intercourse with someone who is not the person's spouse.

 DID YOU KNOW?

Some traditional wedding customs today are based on ancient practices. An engagement ring, for example, now takes the place of the bride price. The father who accompanies the bride down the aisle to the altar is reminiscent of the father who had property rights over his daughter. He gives her to her new husband.

income producer. Once the bride price was paid, the father escorted the girl to the man's home.

The Law of Moses was clear in protecting the wife from cruelty and domination by her husband. Mosaic Law did permit a decree of **divorce**. Jesus later explained that "hardness of heart," a residue of sin, had allowed this decree because "from the beginning it was not so" (Mt 19:8). **Polygamy** was practiced among the Israelites, but even more by neighboring peoples. Polygamy was understood as a sign of privilege and wealth; it was a means of establishing political alliances with other countries and clans; it also assured that a man would have male heirs. In the Old Testament, polygamy was allowed in certain cases among patriarchs and kings, but the understanding and practice of marriage under Mosaic Law and the teachings of the prophets evolved to examples of exclusive and faithful married love far beyond what was being practiced by the Canaanites and other pagan religions. Mosaic Law also forbade **adultery** because, like divorce and polygamy, it is a grave offense against the dignity of marriage.

Since the Fall of man and the first sin, marriage has helped couples overcome selfishness and greed while choosing to be open to others, to care for one another, and to be self-giving.

Marriage in the New Covenant

The covenant between God and his people in the Old Testament prepared the way for the New Covenant, in which Jesus not only restored marriage to its original state before the Fall of Adam and Eve, but raised it to a sacrament among the baptized.

In his preaching, Christ clearly taught the original meaning that marriage is indissoluble. He said: "What God has joined together, no human being must separate" (Mt 19:6). While that's a difficult command, Jesus comes into the life of the married couple in the Sacrament of Matrimony to help them keep it. Some effects of the sacrament remain present to the couple through all their days of marriage. Husbands and wives love each other with faithfulness that does not end until death, just as Christ was faithful to his mission until his Death on a cross.

St. Paul explained that the relationship between a husband and wife takes on the same intimate relationship that Christ has with the Church. The husband should love his wife with the same depth of love that Christ has for the Church (see Ephesians 5:25–26, 31–32). The Sacrament of Matrimony signifies the union of Christ and the Church. "This grace of Christian marriage is a fruit of Christ's cross, the source of all Christian life" (*CCC* 1615).

As the Sacrament of Matrimony developed in the Church, civil marriages were blessed later by priests. Eventually, weddings were held on the church steps and a clergyman was present to offer a blessing. From the beginning, the essential rite of the sacrament was understood to be the consent that each couple extended to the other. This consent is the "form" of the sacrament and was defended by St. Thomas Aquinas in the thirteenth century. He wrote that marriage is a sacrament that gives grace to the couple on their journey toward holiness. Franciscan theologian John Duns Scotus (1266–1308) agreed with Aquinas and taught that the bride and groom are the ministers of the sacrament. The priest serves as the official Church witness. This remains the understanding in the Latin Rite today.

The Council of Trent (1545–1563) upheld the Church teaching that Matrimony is a sacrament that confers grace. Furthermore, the council stated that Matrimony is a public commitment—not only for the good of the couple but also for the good of society and the Church. Thus, baptized Catholics should celebrate Matrimony in church during Mass. This continues to be the teaching and practice today:

> It is therefore fitting that the spouses should seal their consent to give themselves to each other through the offering of their own lives by uniting it to the offering of Christ for his Church made present in the Eucharistic sacrifice, and by receiving the Eucharist so that, communicating in the same Body and the same Blood of Christ, they may form but "one body" in Christ. (*CCC* 1621)

Martin Luther and John Calvin, Protestant reformers of the sixteenth century, did not accept marriage as a sacrament. They believed it belonged under the sole jurisdiction of civil authority, and therefore, divorce was possible. Technically, divorce ends a civil marriage—a contract before the law. A **declaration of nullity**, which the Church does permit, says a particular marriage was never a *valid* marriage, according to prescribed Church standards.

The Sacrament of Marriage Today

The Second Vatican Council reiterated that only marriage between baptized Christians can be a sacrament. Furthermore, it taught that no Christian marriage is sacramental unless it is contracted in the presence of a priest or deacon and two witnesses. The Council also taught that remarriage of persons divorced from a living, lawful spouse contravenes the plan and law of God as taught by Christ. They are not separated from the Church, but they cannot receive Holy Communion. They are to lead Christian lives especially by educating their children in the faith.

The Second Vatican Council delineated more about the Church's understanding of the purpose of marriage. In addition to the procreation and education of children, Christian marriage is to help both spouses grow in spiritual perfection (*Code of Canon Law* 1055, 1). Marriage is also the means through which the couple serves the common good of the Church and society (see *Apostolicam Actuositatem* [Decree on the Apostolate of Lay People] 11). As the *Catechism* says, "The well-being of . . . both human and Christian society is closely bound up with the healthy

declaration of nullity
The Church's declaration that a particular marriage—whether presumed as a sacramental bond or simply a natural bond—was never valid.

? DID YOU KNOW?

The Church is also opposed to the so-called *free union* where a man and woman live together but without marriage. Those who choose this course offer different reasons; for example, they "reject traditional marriage" or "do not want a long-term commitment." All of these situations are against the dignity of marriage. They weaken the sense of fidelity and destroy the very idea of family. The sexual act must always take place within marriage. "Outside of marriage it always constitutes a grave sin and excludes one from sacramental communion" (*CCC* 2390).

state of conjugal and family life" (*CCC* 1603, quoting *Gaudium et Spes*).

Also, the Council called for a revision of the Rite of Marriage to symbolize more clearly the grace of the sacrament to emphasize the spouses' duties to one another.

The revised Rite of Matrimony, approved in 1969, now points out the sacramental aspects of Christian marriage, explained in more detail in the next sections. Ⓜ

For Review

1. When did marriage begin?
2. How did Mosaic Law respond to offenses against marriage (i.e., divorce, polygamy, adultery)?
3. What did Jesus teach about the indissolubility of marriage?
4. To what did St. Paul compare the relationship between a husband and wife?
5. What has always been the essential rite of the Sacrament of Matrimony?
6. Who are the ministers of the Sacrament of Matrimony?
7. When and where does the Church say Catholics should celebrate Matrimony?
8. What did the Second Vatican Council teach about the purpose of marriage?

For Reflection

• What do you find positive about the Church's teaching of the indissolubility of marriage?

• Write a motto or saying that expresses the meaning of Christian marriage.

CELEBRATING THE SACRAMENT OF MATRIMONY

There are three rites in the revised Rite of Marriage; two of these rites celebrate the Sacrament of Matrimony. The first option is the Rite for Celebrating Marriage During Mass. This is the preferred option for two baptized Catholics. There is also a Rite for Celebrating Marriage Outside Mass, which typically occurs in a wedding between a Catholic and a baptized person who is not Catholic. Finally, the Church offers a Rite for Celebrating Marriage Between a Catholic and an Unbaptized Person. In this case, the marriage is not sacramental. Each option highlights the couple's free consent and exchange of vows.

Recall that according to the *Roman Ritual*, the bride and groom are the ministers of Matrimony. They "mutually confer upon each other the sacrament of Matrimony by expressing their consent before the Church" (*CCC* 1623). The Church strongly recommends and often requires engaged couples to enter a marriage preparation program before getting married. Such programs help the couple discuss issues that will be important in their married life: finances, in-laws, number of children and their education, values, likes and dislikes, sexuality, how to handle disagreements, and so forth. Such preparation programs can also help the couple plan their wedding ceremony so that it reflects the uniqueness of their personalities.

The priest or deacon, who acts as the Church's witness, wears white vestments. The Rite of Marriage consists of the consent of the bride and groom and their exchange of vows. This is the essential element that "makes the marriage" (*Code of Canon Law* 1057). A blessing and an exchange of rings may also take place. If the wedding takes place during Mass, a **nuptial blessing** after the Lord's Prayer and a special blessing of the couple at the end of Mass occur.

More information on these elements of the Sacrament of Matrimony follows.

Free Consent and Exchange of Vows

During the wedding ceremony, the bride and groom must express their consent to enter into marriage. This consent must be freely given. It is the indispensable element of the sacrament. Furthermore, each spouse should have a sincere desire to be faithful to the other person and be open to new life, especially the procreation and upbringing of children.

The priest (or deacon) who assists at the wedding receives the consent of the spouses in the name of the Church. The presence of the priest and two other witnesses visibly expresses that the marriage is a Church reality with certain rights and responsibilities and requires certification. The priest first questions the bride and groom separately on their freedom of choice, faithfulness to each other, and acceptance and upbringing of children:

Priest:	N. and N., have you come here freely and without reservation to give yourselves to each other in marriage?
Bride:	Yes.
Groom:	Yes.
Priest:	Will you honor each other as man and wife for the rest of your lives?
Bride:	Yes.
Groom:	Yes.
Priest:	Will you accept children lovingly from God, and bring them up according to the law of Christ and his Church?
Bride:	Yes.
Groom:	Yes.

The priest then invites the couple to give their consent. The bride and groom do this by exchanging their **marriage consent**. They typically recite an option like the one shown below:

nuptial blessing
Nuptial is a Latin-derived word that means "wedding." The nuptial blessing sanctifies the marriage covenant of the bride and groom. It takes place after the couple gives their consent to be married.

ENHANCING CHRISTIAN FAMILY LIFE

The Christian Family Movement has done a great deal to support family life. Research and report on the mission and functions of this organization. View its website at www.cfm.org for more information.

marriage consent
The promises made by the bride and groom to honor one another and to be faithful in good times and in bad, in sickness and in health throughout their lives. By their consent to one another, the couple establish a permanent covenant in love.

Priest: Since it is your intention to enter into marriage, join your right hands, and declare your consent before God and his Church.

Groom: I, N., take you, N., to be my wife. I promise to be true to you in good times and in bad, in sickness and in health. I will love you and honor you all the days of my life.

Bride: I, N., take you, N., to be my husband. I promise to be true to you in good times and in bad, in sickness and in health. I will love you and honor you all the days of my life.

The priest, on receiving the consent of the bride and groom, says:

You have declared your consent before the Church. May the Lord in his goodness strengthen your consent and fill you both with his blessings. What God has joined, men must not divide.

Blessing and Exchange of Rings

The Rite of Marriage includes the blessing and exchange of rings. These rings, which have no beginning or end, symbolize the eternal love God has for humans, the eternal commitment of Christ to the Church, and the promise by the bride and groom to be faithful to one another until death. One option for this part of the wedding rite is as follows:

Priest: Lord, bless and consecrate N. and N. in their love for each other. May these rings be a symbol of true faith in each other, and always remind them of their love. We ask this through Christ our Lord.

Bride and Groom: Amen.

Groom: N., take this ring as a sign of my love and fidelity. In the name of the Father, and of the Son, and of the Holy Spirit.

Bride: N., take this ring as a sign of my love and fidelity. In the name of the Father, and of the Son, and of the Holy Spirit.

Another symbol is the bride's traditional white gown. It reminds everyone of the white garment given to the newly baptized. Just as the baptismal garment symbolizes the person's desire to leave behind sin and put on Christ, so the white gown symbolizes the bride's desire to leave behind her former life and become one with her husband in Christ. In addition, the wedding gown is also a reminder of the First Communion dress worn by most girls, emphasizing the intimate connection between the Eucharist and the Sacrament of Matrimony.

Nuptial Blessing

After the Our Father, the priest faces the couple and gives them a nuptial or wedding blessing. The blessing is intended to bring the love of God and his graces on the couple throughout all the days of their married life. One option for a nuptial blessing begins as follows:

Let us pray to the Lord for this bride and groom, who come to the altar as they begin their married life, that (partaking of the Body and Blood of Christ) they may always be bound together by love for one another.

Holy Communion

Prior to the wedding, the bride and groom celebrate the Sacrament of Penance in order to be properly disposed to receive Holy Communion. During the wedding liturgy, they are the first to receive Holy Communion under both species, bread and wine. It is appropriate for the man and woman, who have just been joined as one, to drink from the common cup. It is the Holy Eucharist that will strengthen and nourish their married life.

Blessing at the End of Mass

Before dismissing the people at the end of Mass, the priest blesses the bride and groom. A series of petitions may include intentions for never-ending love, children, peace, friends, happiness and satisfaction in work, and the absence of undue anxiety. Ultimately, the blessing is offered that, after many happy years together, the couple may be welcomed into the eternal Kingdom of Heaven.

For Review

1. What is the preferred Rite of Marriage for the wedding of two baptized Catholics?
2. What is the essential element of the Sacrament of Matrimony?
3. Why are a priest and two witnesses necessary for the validity of the sacrament?
4. What do the wedding rings symbolize?

For Reflection

Write a prayer of blessing for a newly married couple. Pray the prayer for the couple.

THE GRACES OF THE SACRAMENT OF MATRIMONY

Jesus made every sacramental marriage a sign of God's faithfulness. The loving and faithful relationship between a husband and wife is now the visible sign of the loving and faithful relationship between Christ and his Church. The love that sustains the Church and makes her one is the love that allows a man and woman to truly become one—one body, one heart, one mind, and one soul. The commitment of the spouses to one another becomes part of God's commitment to his people.

The self-giving of the husband and wife takes the form of a covenant. A covenant is different from a contract in that it is personal; that is, between both the man and woman and between them together and God. A covenant has no time limit. It lasts forever.

The Sacrament of Matrimony is not contained within the time limits of the wedding ceremony. In other words, the sacrament does not end when the bride and groom leave the church building. Instead, the graces and effects of the sacrament continue to accompany the couple throughout their marriage. The graces of the sacrament help the spouses grow in love and holiness as they meet the challenges of daily life together. The fullness of the sacrament is realized only over time—after years of fidelity and affection.

Sacramental marriage is essentially about communion. The husband and wife share a unity—their mental, emotional, spiritual, and physical unity. The husband and wife are also in relationship with Christ, and they perfect the practice of loving one another as God loves them. There is also a communion between husband and wife and their children—the oneness

fidelity

An attribute of God that describes his eternal faithfulness to his promises.

of family life. As a Sacrament at the Service of Communion, Matrimony also calls husbands, wives, and children to serve others outside the family. This involves communion with both the Church and all of society. Each of these types of communion, or unity, is explained further in the next sections.

Communion between Spouses

The communion between spouses found in marriage "helps to overcome self-absorption, egoism, pursuit of one's own pleasure, and to open oneself to the other, to mutual aid and to self-giving" (*CCC* 1609). The man and woman become one. They enter into a covenant so that they "might no longer live for themselves" (2 Cor 5:15).

Such absolute self-giving to one's spouse can seem both awesomely good yet scary. How can someone really say, "I'll love you forever," if we don't know any of the details of that forever? Will we still love the other person if he becomes bald, wrinkled, or loses a limb? Will we still love our spouse if she becomes fat, gray, or confined to

a wheelchair? Having such unconditional love is very difficult for humans to achieve and sustain. Thus, Christian spouses acknowledge their need for God's continual presence in their marriage, helping them continue loving one another even when the romantic feeling of being "in love" is gone. The Sacrament of Matrimony helps spouses continue choosing to love one another, whether or not they "feel" like it.

True communion between spouses is always fruitful. Fruitful love means more than openness to having children. It also means supporting one another and helping the other become his or her best self. Fruitful love, for example, may involve the choice to support a spouse while he or she goes back to school. It may also involve moving to a new location so that a spouse can take a better job or get needed health care. This is why Matrimony is a Sacrament at the Service of Communion.

Mutually consenting sexual expression is important in furthering conjugal communion and communication. Healthy sexual intimacy involves exclusivity. One of the ongoing graces of Matrimony is **fidelity**. Fidelity is one of the characteristics of God. The more spouses grow in holiness, the more they become like God—more faithful to their promises. Day-to-day fidelity helps the couple "grow continually in their communion . . . to their marriage promise of total mutual self-giving" (*CCC* 1644, quoting *Familiaris Consortio*).

In addition to exclusivity and fidelity, a healthy sexual relationship in marriage involves honor and respect between spouses. The Second Vatican Council taught that "the unity of marriage, confirmed by our Lord, is clearly apparent in the equal personal dignity which is accorded to man and wife in mutual and unreserved affection" (*Gaudium et Spes* 49). St. Paul expressed the

same truth more simply: "Each one of you should love his wife as himself, and the wife should respect her husband" (Eph 5:33).

Communion in Christ

Like every sacrament, Matrimony brings people into union with the Blessed Trinity. "The spouses receive the Holy Spirit as the communion of love of Christ and the Church. The Holy Spirit is the seal of their covenant, the ever-available source of their love and the strength to renew their fidelity" (*CCC* 1624). Christian spouses share in the life of the Blessed Trinity so that they may be transformed by holiness and made more divine. Through Matrimony, Christian spouses encounter Christ in one another. They act as Christ to one another by loving one another as they know Christ loves them.

The Sacrament of Matrimony helps husbands and wives enter into the Paschal Mystery of Christ in a special way. Marriage becomes, for them, a way of discipleship, a way of dying to sin and rising to holiness:

> [Christ] himself gives the strength and grace to live marriage in the new dimension of the Reign of God. It is by following Christ, renouncing themselves, and taking up their crosses that spouses will be able to "receive" the original meaning of marriage and live it with the help of Christ. This grace of Christian marriage is a fruit of Christ's cross, the source of all Christian life. (*CCC* 1615)

Through their faithfulness to their marriage commitment, Christian spouses are able to love each other with the love that Christ has loved his Church. "[Christ] abides with them in order that by their mutual self-giving spouses will love each other with enduring fidelity, as he loved the church and delivered himself for it" (*Gaudium et Spes* 48).

Communion with Christ's Paschal Mystery gives spouses the strength to make loving sacrifices for one another. It also enables them to forgive one another for mistakes, failings, and sins. Just as God is gracious, merciful, and "slow to anger, abounding in kindness" (Ps 103:8), so Christian spouses are challenged by the Sacrament of Matrimony to seek peace and reconciliation despite times of disagreement and conflict. What St. Paul said about the life of all disciples applies in a special way to Christian spouses:

> Put on then, as God's chosen ones, holy and beloved, heartfelt compassion, kindness, humility, gentleness, and patience, bearing with one another and forgiving one another, if one has a grievance against another; as the Lord has forgiven you, so must you also do. And over all these put on love, that is, the bond of perfection. And let the peace of Christ control your hearts, the peace into which you were also called in one body. (Col 3:12–15)

Only genuine communion in Christ can enable Christian spouses to love each other in such a way. That is why, in the Rite of Marriage, the Church prays for all married couples and especially asks God's continued blessing on their love—that it may be unconditional, complete, and unselfish.

> Lord, hear our prayers and accept the gifts we offer for N. and N. Today you have made them one in the sacrament of marriage. May the mystery of Christ's unselfish love, which we celebrate in this Eucharist, increase their love for you and for each other. (Prayer over the Gifts, *Mass of Marriage*, 114)

THE IMPORTANCE OF FRIENDSHIP

At your age, cultivating trusting and true friendships is important preparation for your possible future marriage. Review and rate yourself in the following skills of friendship:

- I am good at sharing ideas with others.
- I have many interests.
- I am patient with myself and others.
- I can forgive and ask for forgiveness.
- I am growing in self-understanding.
- Jesus is an important part in my life.

Together with a classmate, develop a short presentation on the importance of friendship that is geared to students in the elementary grades. Arrange to share the presentation, along with helpful tips for making and keeping friends, at a school, religious education class, or after-school program in your area.

domestic church

A term for the family, the Church in miniature.

parochial school

A private school sponsored by a parish. Catholics and other Christian denominations run parochial schools to educate children in the Faith.

DID YOU KNOW?

St. Elizabeth Ann Seton is the first American-born saint of the Catholic Church. Her feast day is January 4.

Family Communion

The Sacrament of Matrimony helps not only the bride and groom throughout life. It also helps them form a family, an intergenerational community of faith, hope, and love. Furthermore, the ongoing graces of Matrimony help all family members act as Christ to one another. Just as the Blessed Virgin Mary said "yes" to God in becoming the Mother of Jesus, and just as St. Joseph said "yes" to being Mary's faithful partner in raising Jesus, so Christian spouses are called to affirm Jesus in today's world. Many married couples do this by becoming parents and raising their children. They find Christ in their children, and they act as educators in faith, helping their children grow more and more into the image of Christ.

"To be Christ to one another" means that all family members do their best to build relationships animated by love. It means showing honor and respect for the dignity and unique needs of each family member. It means promoting each person's sense of self-esteem, worth, and lovability. In short, to act as Christ means to build true Christian community. As Pope John Paul II explained in *Familiaris Consortio*, his 1981 Apostolic Exhortation on the family, "The Christian family . . . is the first community called to announce the Gospel to the human person during growth and to bring him or her, through a progressive education and catechesis, to full human and Christian maturity" (*Familiaris Consortio* 2).

Matrimony helps Christian families mirror the love between Christ and his Church so completely that the family actually becomes a **domestic church**. This term was first used in the Second Vatican Council's *Lumen Gentium* and has since been echoed and described by many other Church documents. The family, in a very real way, is the most basic unit of the Church. As the *Catechism* explains, "the father of the family, the mother, children, and all members of the family exercise the *priesthood of the baptized* in a privileged way 'by the reception of the sacraments, prayer and thanksgiving, the witness of a holy life, and self-denial and active charity'" (*CCC* 1657, quoting *Lumen Gentium*). In addition, "The Christian home is the place where children receive the first proclamation of the faith. For this reason the family home is rightly called 'the domestic church,' a community of grace and prayer, a school of human virtues and of Christian charity" (*CCC* 1666).

Communion with the Church

Husbands and wives and their children are, as God's children, the basic unit of the Church, but they are not self-contained, self-serving units. Instead, God calls Christian families to transform their love into outward action; they are to share in the life and mission of the Church. The *Catechism* explains further that Christian families "proclaim the Good News that God loves us with a definitive and irrevocable love, that married couples share in this love, that it supports and sustains them, and that by their own faithfulness they can be witnesses to God's faithful love" (*CCC* 1648).

How are Christian families to join in the Church's mission? Two ways are shared below:

1. *Christian families can promote faith and evangelization, both at home and with others.* One of the aims of the domestic church is the sanctification and religious education of all family members. Every Christian family is to be a believing and evangelizing community in dialogue with God. Christian families do this by worshiping together at Sunday Mass and by frequent participation in the Sacrament of Penance and the other sacraments. Christian families also schedule time for family prayer and Scripture reflection. Parents lead their children by example by participating in activities and events like parish religious education classes, retreats, and special programs. Families also meet on a regular basis with other families to form small Christian communities and to support one another in the faith.

2. *Christian families can help serve the needs of the parish.* Most parishes always need volunteers of all ages and talents. Christian families help during liturgy by bringing up the gifts of bread and wine at Mass or acting as ushers, lectors, altar servers, extraordinary ministers of Holy Communion, and choir members. They can also help with special parish projects, such as cleaning up after Mass, decorating for Christmas, serving at a fish fry, and helping with bingo or an annual bazaar. Some Christian families act as Church by visiting the sick and elderly in Catholic hospitals and retirement homes. They help collect clothes, food, and furniture for the St. Vincent de Paul Society. They give rides to the poor, work with the deaf and the blind, catechize adolescents, console single and divorced Catholics, and serve on parish councils and diocesan committees.

One example of a family who acted as Church is the thirteenth-century Hungarian family of St. Elizabeth. Elizabeth was queen of Thuringia; her children were royal heirs who lived in a luxurious castle. Instead of relishing their riches, Elizabeth and her children worked daily to help the poor in their kingdom. They distributed food and clothing. They helped nurse the sick. They even housed the homeless in their own rooms.

Another example of a family who served the Church is the nineteenth-century American family of St. Elizabeth Seton. Widowed with five children, Elizabeth became involved in social work in New York City. She not only educated her own children in the faith, she began the first **parochial school** in the United States to help educate other children in the Catholic faith.

Communion with Society

The Sacrament of Matrimony calls Catholic spouses and their children to become involved in all aspects of society—workplace, marketplace, entertainment, athletics, politics—to help build a world of justice, peace, and love.

Christian families can serve society in a number of ways. Here are three examples:

1. *Husbands and wives participate in the development of society by socializing their own children.* The Church recognizes the family as "the primary vital cell of society" (*Apostolicam Actuositatem* 11). The family is the first place where children learn how to communicate and socialize, to become aware of the rights and needs of others, and to realize their own responsibility to contribute to the common good. "The family is the place where different generations come together and to help one another to grow in wisdom and harmonize the rights of individuals with other demands of social life; as such it constitutes the basis of society" (*Gaudium et Spes* 52). The family is the first place where children learn social values such as respect for life, love of the poor, obeying rules, and good citizenship. As Pope John Paul II wrote, "The fostering of authentic and mature communion between persons within the family is the first and irreplaceable school of social life, an example and stimulus for the broader community of relationships marked by respect, justice, dialogue, and love" (*Familiaris Consortio* 43).

2. *Christian families participate in politics, especially with a view to promoting and safeguarding family values in society.* The Church encourages laypeople to become involved in politics—as candidates, as voters, as lobbyists—to ensure the rights of every family in society. Among the rights all families should have are the following:

CHURCH OF THE HOME, CHURCH OF THE PARISH

The rhythm of life in a family—the domestic church or "church of the home"—is parallel to the rhythm of life we celebrate as a faith community in the parish Church. Write or discuss how the Church of the home and the Church of the parish fulfill each of these human needs in a loving way:

- Welcomes and initiates new members
- Shares meals of unity
- Fights and forgives
- Heals and comforts one another
- Encourages her members to positions of service leadership
- Nurtures life-giving relationships

Compose a prayer, song lyrics, or a poem that expresses the love in the Church, domestic or parish.

- The right to marry, to establish a family, and to have adequate means to support it.
- The right to act responsibly regarding the transmission of life and the education of children.
- The right to the intimacy of conjugal love and family life.
- The right to the permanent stability of the marriage bond.
- The right to believe in and profess one's faith and to teach it.
- The right to bring up children according to one's own values.
- The right to obtain physical, social, political, and economic security, especially when poor and sick.
- The right to suitable housing.
- The right to political expression and representation.
- The right to form associations with other families.
- The right to protect minors from drugs, pornography, alcohol, etc.
- The right to wholesome family recreation.
- The right of the elderly to a worthy life and a worthy death.
- The right to emigrate as a family in search of a better life. (*Familiaris Consortio* 46)

3. *Christian families work to build a more just and peaceful society.* Christian families serve the needs of the poor, offer hospitality to those who suffer from want, and see that no one is neglected or unwanted. Christian families take a strong stand against situations of injustice that violate basic human dignity: racism, sexism, nationalism, and consumerism.

Among the various works of the family apostolate the following may be listed: adopting abandoned children, showing a loving welcome to strangers, helping with the running of schools, supporting adolescents with advice and help, assisting engaged couples to make a better preparation for marriage, taking part in catechism-teaching, supporting married people and families in a material or moral crisis, and, in the case of the aged, providing them not only with what is indispensable but also procuring for them a fair share of the fruits of economic progress. (*Apostolicam Actuositatem* 11)

Families promote peace by teaching their children conflict-resolution techniques at home and by emphasizing the Christian belief that all humans are created in God's image and thus have both dignity and rights.

Note that it is never easy to balance family life with service of others. That is one reason the graces of Matrimony are needed. Only by being grounded and rooted in Christ can Christian families transform their love for one another into a love that encompasses the needs of both the Church and modern society.

For Review

1. What are some ways spouses find true communion with one another?
2. How does marriage facilitate a way of Christian discipleship for husbands and wives?
3. Define *domestic church*.
4. Name two ways Christian families join in the Church's mission.
5. Name three ways Christian families can serve society.

For Reflection

- Why do you think both fidelity and affection are essential for a successful marriage?

- How would you describe the difference between "loving someone" and being "in love"?

- Choose three rights for families named in *Familiaris Consortio* and explain why you feel they are most essential.

TRANSFORMATION

CHRISTIAN MARRIAGE: A SIGN OF GOD'S ETERNAL COVENANT WITH HUMANITY

As a sacrament, Matrimony is "a covenant by which a man and a woman establish between themselves a partnership of their whole life" (*Code of Canon Law* 1055; see *CCC* 1601). The Sacrament of Matrimony recalls and signifies God's eternal covenant with humanity. God established a covenant with Abraham and his descendants. This covenant brought the Israelites to the Promised Land; even more important, it established a lasting relationship between God and the people. Recall that a covenant differs from a contract in that it has no time limit. A covenant lasts forever. Unlike a contract, it cannot be dissolved.

The Old Testament is filled with stories about how, time and time again, the Israelites turned away from this covenant and pursued false gods. Despite their sinfulness, God remained steadfast, faithful, and loving. His love lasts forever.

Hosea was one of the first prophets in the Old Testament to compare God's relationship with the Israelites to a marriage. Hosea likened God to a bridegroom who chooses to marry the woman he loves:

> I will espouse you to me forever:
> I will espouse you in right and in justice,
> in love and in mercy;
> I will espouse you in fidelity,
> and you shall know the Lord. (Hos 2:21–22)

Another prophet, recorded in the Book of Isaiah, echoed this same imagery:

> As a young man marries a virgin,
> your Builder shall marry you;
> And as a bridegroom rejoices in his bride
> so shall your God rejoice in you. (Is 62:5)

Even though Israel turned out to be unfaithful to God, God continued to love her and forgave her:

> The Lord calls you back,
> Like a wife forsaken and grieved in spirit . . .
> With great tenderness I will take you back. (Is 54:6, 7)

Like God's eternal covenant with humans, the marriage covenant cannot be retracted. Sacramental

abortion

The direct and deliberate ending of a pregnancy by killing the unborn child. Direct abortion, willed either as a means or an end, gravely contradicts moral law.

contraception

Any artificial means (e.g., pills, condoms, diaphragms, surgeries) that deliberately and directly has as an outcome closing off one of the aims of sexual intercourse—the sharing of life. Contraception also opposes the unitive aspect of the conjugal act by not allowing for the total self-giving of the couple to one another.

sterilization

Any surgical procedure that prevents conception. Some sterilization procedures in women include tied or cut fallopian tubes, removal of ovaries, and/or removal of the uterus. Sterilization procedures in men include vasectomy (cutting tubes carrying sperm from the testicles) or castration (removing the testicles). Deliberate sterilization is contrary to one of the characteristics of sacramental marriage: the openness to children.

<u>Natural Family Planning</u>

A Church-approved method for regulating births in a marriage that is in accord with God's will because it is pursued by spouses without external pressure nor motives of selfishness and is practiced through natural means of periodic continence and use of infertile periods.

marriage is indissoluble (*Code of Canon Law* 1056); it lasts for as long as both spouses live. Thus, Jesus took a strong stand against divorce. "What God has joined together, no human being must separate" (Mt 19:6; see *CCC* 1664). The eternal nature of the Sacrament of Matrimony is also witnessed explicitly in two other ways: in the fruitful love that is open to having children and in the model of unity between husbands and wives that bears a striking similarity to the relationship between Christ and the Church. These ways are discussed in the next sections.

Openness to New Life

"Fruitful love" describes a mutual love between husband and wife that is productive and open to the creation of children. The sacrament recalls God's command to Adam and Eve, "Be fertile and multiply" (Gn 1:28). In a sacramental marriage, both husband and wife are open to the fertility that can result from their sexual union (see *CCC* 1664). They recognize their call to become partners with God in creating new life, and they accept children as "the supreme gift of marriage" (*Gaudium et Spes* 50; see *CCC* 1664).

Just as God expressed his love in creating the world and all its creatures,

so the Sacrament of Matrimony calls a husband and wife to go beyond their love for one another *to love others as God loves*. Through their love, they are to create new life. For this reason, the Church teaches the evils of **abortion**, the use of **contraception**, and deliberate **sterilization**. Instead, the Church teaches married couples to be open to the gift of children and that "it is necessary that each and every marriage act remain ordered per se to the procreation of human life" (*Humanae Vitae* 11). Married couples who wish to space the birth of their children for just reasons can practice **Natural Family Planning**, which uses the natural fertile and infertile times in the woman's monthly reproductive cycle and the woman's cervical mucus to plan or postpone a pregnancy.

Not all Christian marriages are blessed with children. Some couples, for various physical reasons, are unable to have children. Despite this situation, the Sacrament of Matrimony still calls these couples to engage in a love that is fruitful. Childless couples can still "radiate a fruitfulness of charity, of hospitality, and of sacrifice" (*CCC* 1654). "Physical sterility in fact can be for spouses the occasion for other important services to the life of the human person, for example, adoption, various

forms of educational work, and assistance to other families and to poor or handicapped children" (*Familiaris Consortio* 14).

The Unity of Marriage

The purpose of sacramental marriage is not just the procreation of children. Its additional purpose is the mutual growth of husband and wife in holiness, through their incarnated (the union of physical and spiritual) love (see *Gaudium et Spes* 50). Sacramental marriage recalls the great mystery of the Incarnation: that God chose to make his love visible in human flesh. Likewise, husband and wife express and find God's love through their sexual intimacy with one another. They are to love one another unconditionally and completely, body and soul. "In marriage the physical intimacy of the spouses becomes a sign and pledge of spiritual communion" (*CCC* 2360).

The two purposes of sex in marriage—unitive and procreative—help achieve the twofold end of Matrimony: the joy and pleasure of the couple and the transmission of life. Sex not only fosters intimacy, it provides a sense of emotional security and reduces stress and anxiety. Sex helps the couple point to the love between God and humankind.

Jesus' presence at the wedding at Cana (see John 2:1–11) is of great significance. The Church understands that he performed his first sign, or miracle, at a wedding (at his Mother's request) to indicate the goodness of marriage along with the promise that "marriage will be an efficacious sign of Christ's presence" (*CCC* 1613). Both Sacred Scripture and Sacred Tradition use the analogy of marriage to describe Jesus' relationship with the Church. The Church is "the Bride of Christ"

(see *CCC* 796), "the spotless *spouse* of the spotless lamb (Rev 19:7; 21:2, 9; 22:17) whom Christ 'loved'" (*Lumen Gentium* 6). Jesus himself is the perfect Bridegroom (see Matthew 9:15; Mark 2:19; Luke 5:34) who will be with his Church always (see Matthew 28:20).

Sacramental marriage is an efficacious sign of Christ's presence; it is the "sacrament of the covenant of Christ and the Church" (*CCC* 1617). For this reason, St. Paul wrote, "Husbands, love your wives, even as Christ loved the church and handed himself over for her" (Eph 5:25). The revised Rite of Marriage reminds us of this profound unity:

> Father, you have made the bond of marriage a holy mystery, a symbol of Christ's love for his Church. Hear our prayers for N. and N. With faith in you and in each other they pledge their love today. May their lives always bear witness to the reality of that love. (Opening Prayer, *Mass of Marriage*, 106)

DID YOU KNOW?

The Church teaches that a Catholic who enters into a *mixed marriage* (a marriage with a baptized non-Catholic) first needs "the express permission of Church authorities" (*Code of Canon Law* 1124). A Catholic who enters into a marriage that involves a *disparity of cult* (a marriage with a non-baptized person) first needs express dispensation from Church authorities (*Code of Canon Law* 1086).

Sacramental marriage is also a sign of the future union between God and humans that is to take place at the Second Coming:

> "Alleluia!
> The Lord has established his reign,
>   [our] God, the almighty.
> Let us rejoice and be glad

and give him glory.
For the wedding day of the Lamb has come,
     his bride has made herself ready." (Rev 19:6–7)

Sacramental marriage, then, is both a present reality (a sign of Christ's love with us now) and a reminder of the glorious future that awaits all the faithful.

For Review

1. In what ways is a Christian marriage a covenant?
2. What are the two purposes of sex in marriage?
3. How is sacramental marriage to be both procreative and unitive?
4. What was significant about Jesus' attendance at the wedding at Cana?

For Reflection

At your age and state in life, how can you be faithful to the covenant of marriage?

CHAPTER QUICK VIEW

Main Ideas

- The effects of Matrimony, as a Sacrament at the Service of Communion, are primarily directed on the spouse and children. (p. 237)
- The Sacrament of Matrimony gives men and women the grace to overcome some of the effects of Original Sin while glimpsing the love and unity of the Blessed Trinity. (p. 238)
- The Sacrament of Matrimony adds a whole new dimension to natural marriage; the couple loves each other in Christ. (p. 238)
- Marriage came from the "hand of the Creator"; it has existed since the beginning of time. (p. 239)
- Marriage was afflicted by the sin of humankind; the Law of Moses ruled against some of the abuses of marriage, including polygamy and adultery. (pp. 239-240)
- Jesus Christ restored marriage to its original state and raised it to a sacrament among the baptized. (p. 240)
- The priest or deacon serves as the official Church witness to the sacrament. The man and woman are the ministers of the sacrament. (p. 240 and p. 242)
- The Second Vatican Council taught more about the purpose of marriage, including the procreation of children, growth in spiritual perfection, and ways to serve the common good of the Church and society. (pp. 241-242)
- The free consent of the couple and the accompanying recitation of marriage vows is the essential rite of the sacrament. (p. 243)
- A symbolic ring, a nuptial blessing, reception of Holy Communion, and a final blessing are other elements of the sacrament.(pp. 244-245)

- The graces of married life have to do with communion between the husband and wife and with their children, Church, and society. (pp. 245-247)
- The domestic church—the "Church in miniature"—is a product of the union of husband and wife. (p. 248)
- Christian families transform their love into outward action that includes service in the Church and in society. (pp. 248-250)
- Christian marriage is a covenant of love that is indissoluble until the death of a spouse. (pp. 251-252)
- Fruitful love in marriage describes a mutual love between husband and wife that is productive and open to the creation of children. (p. 252)
- The two purposes of sex in marriage are procreative and unitive and help achieve the twofold purpose of Matrimony: the joy and pleasure of the couple and the transmission of life. (p. 253)
- The love of the husband for his wife mirrors the love Christ has for the Church. (p. 253)

TERMS, PEOPLE, PLACES

Chose the italicized word that best completes each sentence.

1. The (*papal blessing*/*nuptial blessing*) takes place at a wedding after the couple give their consent to be married.
2. A (*decree of nullity*/*divorce*) ends a civil marriage contract.
3. The (*domestic church*/*parochial school*) is often called the "Church in miniature."
4. The promise made by the bride and groom to honor one another during their marriage is known as (*marriage consent*/*fidelity*).
5. (*Abortion*/*Sterilization*) is a surgical procedure that prevents conception.

Famous Catholics and the Sacraments:

ST. MARGARET OF SCOTLAND

An outstanding example of a wife and mother who understood that marriage is a Sacrament at the Service of Communion is St. Margaret, queen consort and patroness of Scotland. To understand Margaret's holiness and selfless generosity in serving others both inside and outside her family, it is necessary to review a bit of British history.

Margaret's grandfather, King Edmund Ironside, ruled England for seven months and one week in 1016. His reign and life ended abruptly in 1016, and his rival King Canute of Denmark became the king of all of England per the terms of a treaty between the two. King Edmund's surviving family was exiled to the European continent, winding up in Hungary. About thirty years later, Margaret was born to Edward the Exile (son of King Edmund) and his wife, Agatha. Margaret grew up in Hungary and was raised a Catholic. She was very pious and took her religion seriously.

The royal family did not return to England until Margaret's uncle, St. Edward the Confessor, ruled as king. Shortly after he died in 1066, William the Conqueror of Normandy attacked England and took over the government. Agatha (now the widow of Edward the Exile) and her children were forced to flee for their lives from England. Bound for the European continent, their ship was driven to Scotland by a storm, and they received refuge in the Royal Scots Court.

Margaret was now a beautiful, gracious, highly cultured, and well-educated young woman. In about 1070, she married her family's protector, Scottish King Malcolm III, at the castle of Dunfermline. This marriage gave her the title of queen consort. Margaret's marriage was, by all accounts, exceptionally happy. She and Malcolm had eight children,

six sons and two daughters. The eldest son, Edward, was killed in 1093. Edmund, the second son, grew up to become King Edmund I of Scotland in 1094. The third son, Ethelred, became abbot of Dunkeld. The fourth son, Edgar, became King Edgar of Scotland from 1097 to 1107. Alexander, the fifth son, succeeded Edgar as king of Scotland from 1107 to his death in 1124. The youngest son, David, ruled as king of Scotland from 1124 to 1153. The Church also canonized him as a saint. Edith, the older daughter, married King Henry I of England. Mary of Scotland, the younger daughter, married Count Eustace III of Boulogne.

In addition to being a good wife and mother, Margaret took seriously her responsibility to serve both the nation and the Church. She did this primarily in two ways: as a social worker and as a Church reformer. Margaret had a passionate love for the poor in her kingdom and went out of her way to provide for their needs. She used her own money to promote the arts and education throughout Scotland. Although she had more than enough wealth to live in luxury, she chose to live austerely as a form of penance and religious devotion. In addition to the usual Church fasts during Advent and Lent, Margaret also fasted in almost every other season of the year. She allowed herself little sleep so that she could rise each night for midnight Mass and also have time each day for prayer and Scripture reading. She also spent a great deal of time helping the poor in her husband's kingdom, even inviting them to dinner at the castle during Lent. One biographer says she never refused alms to the many beggars who surrounded her in public. She became known for her unusual charity, especially for visiting the sick and nursing them back to health.

Margaret also had a great love for the Church and believed she had an important role to play as a Church reformer. During Margaret's life, there was talk of the Church in Scotland, because of its Celtic roots, seceding from the Roman Catholic Church. The Church in Scotland did not always do things the way the rest of the universal Church did them, and Margaret was determined to prevent a rift with Rome. She instigated synods that voted to follow the rest of the Church in promoting marriage. These synods also promoted Easter communion and abstinence from servile work on Sundays, two practices found in the Church outside Scotland. The synods also ruled that Mass should be celebrated in Latin, rather than in the Celtic language, to show union with other Catholics throughout Europe. During her reign as queen consort, Margaret commissioned the building of churches, founded Benedictine monasteries, and established safe hostels for pilgrims who visited the shrine of St. Andrew.

In 1093, William the Conqueror's son William Rufus attacked the Scottish castle and killed both King Malcolm and his oldest son, Edward. Margaret, upon hearing of their deaths, is reported to have prayed, "I thank you, Almighty God, for sending me so great a sorrow to purify me from my sins." She died four days later from illness at the age of forty-seven. She is buried in Dunfermline Abbey. Those who have visited her tomb have reported several miracles.

Pope Innocent IV canonized Margaret in 1249. In 1673 she became the patron saint of Scotland. Today her feast day is celebrated on November 16.

- In Margaret's time, marriages were often arranged to foster political alliances. Research the connection, through marriage, between Margaret and the characters in Shakespeare's *Macbeth*.
- Research more on the life of St. Margaret. Write a report showing how she can be a role model to married couples today in living their vocation of service in the Church.
- St. Gianna Molla is a recently canonized saint who was married. Research and report on her life and the cause of her sainthood.

ST. MARGARET OF SCOTLAND

ONGOING ASSIGNMENTS

As you cover the material in this chapter, choose and complete at least three of these assignments.

1. Research the laws of your state regarding marriage. What is the minimum age requirement? What must someone younger than the minimum age do if he or she wants to get married? What is the closest blood relationship that may exist between a husband and wife?
2. Research and report on the requirements of your diocese or parish for couples who want to get married in the Church.
3. In the United States today, about one in every two marriages ends in divorce. Using the library or the Internet, find out what main reasons couples give for seeking to end their marriage. Report your findings to the class.
4. Find out what happens at a Cana Conference (a marriage preparation program). Prepare a short report on it. How do you think this program could benefit Catholic engaged couples?
5. Find out more about Engaged Encounter (another marriage preparation program). Prepare a short report on it. How do you think this program could benefit Catholic engaged couples?
6. Many parishes have a wedding planner or coordinator to help a bride and groom with their wedding. Find out if your parish has such a person. Interview the person, either by phone, by e-mail, or in person, to see what he or she does. Prepare a short report on your findings.
7. Imagine your future wedding. Select three Scripture readings for the Mass, including one Gospel reading, that are related in theme to one another and the occasion.
8. If you could design a matching set of wedding rings for use at your wedding, what would the rings look like? Draw and describe in words what the rings look like.
9. Using the library or the Internet, research the life of St. Elizabeth of Hungary or St. Elizabeth Ann Seton. Imagine yourself as a son or daughter of that saint. How do her actions and values shape your daily life? How does she help you grow in faith? Is it easy or difficult for you to have such a mother? Be prepared to share your findings and thoughts with the class.
10. Using the library or the Internet, find out about families living in another country whose rights are being threatened today. Choose one right found on page 250 and write a one-page report why this right is so important to families in your chosen country.
11. Using the library or the Internet, research a situation in the United States that is problematic for families (a situation that threatens one of the rights found on page 250). Write a one-page report on why this right is so important to these families in America.

PRAYER SERVICE

Theme: Our Call to Be a Holy Family

Leader: The Church celebrates the Feast of the Holy Family on the Sunday between Christmas and New Year's Day. The Sacrament of Matrimony itself makes every day a feast of the Holy Family, for it calls all family members to act like Jesus, Mary, and Joseph toward one another. Let us pray today for the grace to grow in holiness and help transform our own families into the family of Jesus.

Reader 1: Sirach 3:2-6, 12-14

All: Happy are you who love the Lord and walk in his ways.

Side 1: Happy are the families who love the Lord,
Who walk in his ways.

Side 2: They shall eat the fruit of their handiwork;
Happy shall they be, and favored.

All: Happy are you who love the Lord and walk in his ways.

Side 1: A wife shall be like a fruitful vine
In the recesses of the home.
A husband will be happy and feel blessed.

Side 2: Children will be like olive plants
Around the table.

All: Happy are you who love the Lord and walk in his ways. (*Adapted from Psalm 128*)

Reader 2: Colossians 3:12-21

Reader 3: Luke 2:22, 39-40

Leader: (*Invite students to offer spontaneous petitions for their own families and for other families in need throughout the world.*)

Closing Prayer:

All: Father in Heaven, Creator of all, you ordered the earth to bring forth life and crowned its goodness by creating the human family. In history's moment when all was ready, you sent your Son to dwell in time, obedient to the laws of life in our world. Teach us the sanctity of human love, show us the value of family life, and help us to live in peace with all people, that we may share in your life forever. Amen.

(Adapted from the Opening Prayer, Feast of the Holy Family, *Sacramentary*, 120)

Epilogue:
The Sacraments *and* You

At the Last Supper, the Apostle Thomas said to Jesus: "Master, we do not know where you are going; how can we know the way?" (Jn 14:5). Jesus said in response:

"I am the way and the truth and the life. No one comes to the Father except through me. If you know me, then you will also know my Father. From now on you do know him and have seen him." (Jn 14:6–7)

The sacraments allow us to know Jesus today. By knowing Jesus in the sacraments, we are put in relationship with the Blessed Trinity—Father, Son, and Holy Spirit. By encountering Christ in the sacraments, we have a clear road map, a vehicle, and the necessary fuel to help us live as God's People. The sacraments help us become "the salt of the earth" (Mt 5:13) and "the light of the world" (Mt 5:14). They help us follow Christ and become temples of the Holy Spirit. Most important, however, the sacraments are about the mystery of love—the Father's redeeming love for us and our love for him and others. St. Paul's famous description of love in his First Letter to the Corinthians (often chosen as a Scripture reading for a wedding liturgy) offers the best description of our call to love:

If I speak in human and angelic tongues but do not have love, I am a resounding gong or a clashing cymbal. And if I have the gift of prophecy and comprehend all mysteries and all knowledge; if I have all faith so as to move mountains but do not have love, I am nothing. If I give away everything I own, and if I hand my body over so that I may boast but do not have love, I gain nothing.

Love is patient, love is kind. It is not jealous, [love] is not pompous, it is not inflated, it is not rude, it does not seek its own interests, it is not quick-tempered, it does not brood over injury. It does not rejoice over wrongdoing but rejoices with the truth. It bears all things, believes all things, hopes all things, endures all things.

Love never fails. If there are prophecies, they will be brought to nothing; if tongues, they will cease; if knowledge, it will be brought to nothing. For we know partially and we prophesy partially, but when the perfect comes, the partial will pass away. When I was a child, I used to talk as a child, think as a child, reason as a child; when I became a man, I put aside childish things. At present we see indistinctly, as in a mirror, but then face to face. At present I know partially; then I shall know fully, as I am fully known. So faith, hope, love remain, these three; but the greatest of these is love. (1 Cor 13:1–13)

In your own life—whether you choose to enter the priesthood, become a religious brother or sister, get married, or remain single—may the sacraments continue to bless and assist you on your journey. In the words from the Rite of Marriage: "May you always bear witness to the love of God in this world so that the afflicted and the needy will find in you generous friends, and welcome you into the joys of heaven" (Final Blessing, *Mass of Marriage* 125).

Appendix: Catholic Handbook *for* Faith

A. BELIEFS

Apostles' Creed

I believe in God,
the Father almighty,
Creator of heaven and earth,
and in Jesus Christ, his only Son, our Lord,
who was conceived by the Holy Spirit,
born of the Virgin Mary,
suffered under Pontius Pilate,
was crucified, died and was buried;
he descended into hell;
on the third day he rose again from the dead;
he ascended into heaven,
and is seated at the right hand of God the Father
almighty;
from there he will come to judge the living and the
dead.

I believe in the Holy Spirit,
the holy catholic Church,
the communion of saints,
the forgiveness of sins,
the resurrection of the body,
and life everlasting. Amen.

Nicene Creed

I believe in one God,
the Father almighty,
maker of heaven and earth,
of all things visible and invisible.

I believe in one Lord Jesus Christ,
the Only Begotten Son of God,
born of the Father before all ages.
God from God, Light from Light,
true God from true God,
begotten, not made, consubstantial with the Father;

through him all things were made.
For us men and for our salvation
he came down from heaven,
and by the Holy Spirit was incarnate of the Virgin Mary,
and became man.

For our sake he was crucified under Pontius Pilate,
he suffered death and was buried,
and rose again on the third day
in accordance with the Scriptures.
He ascended into heaven
and is seated at the right hand of the Father.
He will come again in glory
to judge the living and the dead
and his kingdom will have no end.

I believe in the Holy Spirit, the Lord, the giver of life,
who proceeds from the Father and the Son,
who with the Father and the Son is adored and glorified,
who has spoken through the prophets.

I believe in one, holy, catholic and apostolic Church.
I confess one Baptism for the forgiveness of sins
and I look forward to the resurrection of the dead
and the life of the world to come. Amen.

Gifts of the Holy Spirit

1. Wisdom
2. Understanding
3. Counsel
4. Fortitude
5. Knowledge
6. Piety
7. Fear of the Lord

Fruits of the Holy Spirit

1. Charity
2. Joy
3. Peace
4. Patience
5. Kindness
6. Goodness
7. Generosity
8. Gentleness
9. Faithfulness
10. Modesty
11. Self-control
12. Chastity

The Symbol of Chalcedon

Following therefore the holy Fathers, we unanimously teach to confess one and the same Son, our Lord Jesus Christ, the same perfect in divinity and perfect in humanity, the same truly God and truly man composed of rational soul and body, the same one in being (*homoousios*) with the Father as to the divinity and one in being with us as to the humanity, like unto us in all things but sin (cf. Heb 4:15). The same was begotten from the Father before the ages as to the divinity and in the later days for us and our Salvation was born as to his humanity from Mary the Virgin Mother of God.

We confess that one and the same Lord Jesus Christ, the only-begotten Son, must be acknowledged in two natures, without confusion or change, without division or separation. Their union never abolished the distinction between the natures but rather the character proper to each of the two natures was preserved as they came together in one person (*prosôpon*) and one hypostasis. He is not split or divided into two persons, but he is one and the same only-begotten, God the Word, the Lord Jesus Christ, as formerly the prophets and later Jesus Christ himself have taught us about him and as has been handed down to us by the Symbol of the Fathers.

—From the General Council of Chalcedon (451)

B. GOD AND JESUS CHRIST

Attributes of God

St. Thomas Aquinas named nine attributes that seem to tell us some things about God's nature. They are:

1. *God is eternal.* He has no beginning and no end. Or, to put it another way, God always was, always is, and always will be.
2. *God is unique.* God is the designer of a one and only world. Even the people he creates are one-of-a-kind.
3. *God is infinite and omnipotent.* This reminds us of a lesson we learned early in life: God sees everything. There are no limits to God. *Omnipotence* is a word that refers to God's supreme power and authority over all of creation.
4. *God is omnipresent.* God is not limited to space. He is everywhere. You can never be away from God.
5. *God contains all things.* All of creation is under God's care and jurisdiction.
6. *God is immutable.* God does not evolve. God does not change. God is the same God now as he always was and always will be.
7. *God is pure spirit.* Though God has been described with human attributes, God is not a material creation. God's image cannot be made. God is a pure spirit who cannot be divided into parts. God is simple but complex.
8. *God is alive.* We believe in a living God, a God who acts in the lives of people. Most concretely, he came to this world in the incarnate form of Jesus Christ.
9. *God is holy.* God is pure goodness. God is pure love.

The Holy Trinity

The Trinity is the mystery of one God in Three Persons—Father, Son, and Holy Spirit. The mystery is impossible for human minds to understand. Some of the Church dogmas, or beliefs, can help:

- *The Trinity is One.* There are not three Gods, but one God in Three Persons. Each one of them—Father, Son, and Holy Spirit—is God whole and entire.
- *The Three Persons are distinct from one another.* For example, the Father is not the Son, nor is the Son the Holy Spirit. Rather, the Father is Creator, the Son is begotten of the Father, and the Holy Spirit proceeds from the Father and Son.
- *The divine persons are related to one another.* Though they are related to one another, the Three Persons have one nature or substance.

St. John Damascus used two analogies to describe the doctrine of the Blessed Trinity:

Think of the Father as a root,
of the Son as a branch,
and of the Spirit as a fruit,
for the substance of these is one.

The Father is a sun
with the Son as rays
and the Holy Spirit as heat.

Read the *Catechism of the Catholic Church* (232–260) on the Holy Trinity.

Faith in One God

There are several implications for those who love God and believe in him with their entire heart and soul (see *CCC* 222–227):

- It means knowing God's greatness and majesty.
- It means living in thanksgiving.
- It means knowing the unity and dignity of all people.
- It means making good use of created things.
- It means trusting God in every circumstance.

C. SCRIPTURE AND TRADITION

Canon of the Bible

There are seventy-three books in the canon of the Bible—that is, the official list of books the Church accepts as divinely inspired writings: forty-six Old Testament books and twenty-seven New Testament books. Protestant Bibles do not include seven Old Testament books (Tobit, Judith, 1 and 2 Maccabees, Wisdom, Sirach, and Baruch). Why the difference? Catholics rely on the version of the Bible that the earliest Christians used, the *Septuagint*. This was the first Greek translation of the Hebrew Scriptures begun in the third century BC. Protestants rely on an official list of Hebrew Scriptures compiled in the Holy Land by Jewish scholars at the end of the first century AD. Today, most Protestant Bibles print the disputed books in a separate section at the back of the Bible, called the *Apocrypha*.

The twenty-seven books of the New Testament are divided into three categories: the Gospels, the letters written to local Christian communities or individuals, and the letters intended for the entire Church. The heart of the New Testament, in fact all of Scripture, is the Gospels. The New Testament is central to our knowledge of Jesus Christ. He is the focus of all Scripture.

There are forty-six books in the Old Testament canon. The Old Testament is the foundation for God's self-revelation in Christ. Christians honor the Old Testament as God's word. It contains the writings of prophets and other inspired authors who recorded God's teaching to the Chosen People and his interaction in their history. For example, the Old Testament recounts how God delivered the Jews from Egypt (the Exodus), led them to the Promised Land, formed them into a nation under his care, and taught them in knowledge and worship.

The stories, prayers, sacred histories, and other writings of the Old Testament reveal what God is like and tell much about human nature, too. In brief, the Chosen People sinned repeatedly by turning their backs on their loving God; they were weak and easily tempted away from God. Yahweh, on the other hand, *always* remained faithful. He promised to send a Messiah to humanity.

Listed below are the categories and books of the Old Testament:

THE OLD TESTAMENT

The Pentateuch

Genesis	Gn
Exodus	Ex
Leviticus	Lv
Numbers	Nm
Deuteronomy	Dt

The Historical Books

Joshua	Jos
Judges	Jgs
Ruth	Ru
1 Samuel	1 Sm
2 Samuel	2 Sm
1 Kings	1 Kgs
2 Kings	2 Kgs
1 Chronicles	1 Chr
2 Chronicles	2 Chr
Ezra	Ezr
Nehemiah	Neh
Tobit	Tb
Judith	Jdt
Esther	Est
1 Maccabees	1 Mc
2 Maccabees	2 Mc

The Wisdom Books

Job	Jb
Psalms	Ps(s)
Proverbs	Prv
Ecclesiastes	Eccl
Song of Songs	Sg
Wisdom	Wis
Sirach	Sir

The Prophetic Books

Isaiah	Is
Jeremiah	Jer
Lamentations	Lam
Baruch	Bar
Ezekiel	Ez
Daniel	Dn
Hosea	Hos
Joel	Jl
Amos	Am
Obadiah	Ob
Jonah	Jon
Micah	Mi
Nahum	Na
Habakkuk	Hb
Zephaniah	Zep
Haggai	Hg
Zechariah	Zec
Malachi	Mal

THE NEW TESTAMENT

The Gospels

Matthew	Mt
Mark	Mk
Luke	Lk
John	Jn
Acts of the Apostles	Acts

The New Testament Letters

Romans	Rom
1 Corinthians	1 Cor
2 Corinthians	2 Cor
Galatians	Gal
Ephesians	Eph
Philippians	Phil
Colossians	Col
1 Thessalonians	1 Thes
2 Thessalonians	2 Thes
1 Timothy	1 Tm
2 Timothy	2 Tm
Titus	Ti
Philemon	Phlm
Hebrews	Heb

The Catholic Letters

James	Jas
1 Peter	1 Pt
2 Peter	2 Pt
1 John	1 Jn
2 John	2 Jn
3 John	3 Jn
Jude	Jude
Revelation	Rv

How to Locate a Scripture Passage

Example: 2 Tm 3:16–17

1. *Determine the name of the book.*
   The abbreviation "2 Tm" stands for the Second Book of Timothy.
2. *Determine whether the book is in the Old Testament or New Testament.*
   The Second Book of Timothy is one of the New Testament letters.
3. *Locate the chapter where the passage occurs.*
   The first number before the colon—3—indicates the chapter. The larger numbers that divide a book set off chapters in the Bible.
4. *Locate the verses of the passage.*
   The numbers after the colon indicate the verses. In this case, verses 16 and 17 of chapter 3.
5. *Read the passage.*

For example: "All scripture is inspired by God and is useful for teaching, for refutation, for correction, and for training in righteousness, so that one who belongs to God may be competent, equipped for every good work."

D. CHURCH

Marks of the Church

1. *The Church is one.* The Church remains one because of its source: the unity in the Trinity of the Father, Son, and Spirit in one God. The Church's unity can never be broken and lost because this foundation is itself unbreakable.
2. *The Church is holy.* The Church is holy because Jesus, the founder of the Church, is holy, and he joined the Church to himself as his body and gave the Church the gift of the Holy Spirit. Together, Christ and the Church make up the "whole Christ" (*Christus totus* in Latin).
3. *The Church is catholic.* The Church is catholic ("universal" or "for everyone") in two ways. First, it is catholic because Christ is present in the Church in the fullness of his body, with the fullness of the means of Salvation, the fullness of faith, sacraments, and the ordained ministry that comes from the Apostles. The Church is also catholic because it takes its message of Salvation to all people.
4. *The Church is apostolic.* The Church's apostolic mission comes from Jesus: "Go, therefore, and make disciples of all nations" (Mt 28:19). The Church remains apostolic because it still teaches the same things the Apostles taught. Also, the Church is led by leaders who are successors to the Apostles and who help guide us until Jesus returns.

THE APOSTLES AND THEIR EMBLEMS

St. Andrew

Tradition holds that Andrew was crucified on a bent cross, called a *saltire*.

St. Bartholomew

Bartholomew was flayed alive before being crucified. He was then beheaded.

St. James the Greater

James the Greater, the brother of John, was beheaded by Herod Agrippa. It is the only death of an Apostle mentioned in Scripture (Acts 12:2). The shell indicates James's missionary work by sea in Spain. The sword is representative of martyrdom.

St. James the Less

James the Less is traditionally known as the first bishop of Jerusalem. The saw for his emblem is connected with the tradition of his body's being sawed into pieces after he was pushed from the pinnacle of the Temple.

St. John the Evangelist

John was the first bishop of Ephesus. He is the only Apostle believed to have died a natural death, in spite of many attempts by his enemies to murder him. One attempt included his miraculous survival of drinking a poisoned drink.

St. Jude

Some traditions have Jude and St. Peter martyred together. It is thought he traveled throughout the Roman Empire with Peter.

St. Matthew

Matthew's shield depicts three purses, reflecting his original occupation as tax collector.

St. Matthias

Matthias was the Apostle chosen by lot to replace Judas. Tradition holds that Matthias was stoned to death and then beheaded with an ax.

St. Peter

Simon Peter was the brother of Andrew. The first bishop of Rome, Peter was crucified under Nero, asking to be hung upside down because he felt unworthy to die as Jesus did. The keys represent Jesus' giving to Peter the keys to the Kingdom of Heaven.

St. Philip

Philip may have been bound to a cross and stoned to death. The two loaves of bread at the side of the cross refer to Philip's comment to Jesus about the possibility of feeding the multitudes of people (Jn 6:7).

St. Simon

The book with fish depicts Simon as a "fisher of men" who preached the Gospel. He was also known as Simon the Zealot.

St. Thomas

Thomas is thought to have been a missionary in India, where he is thought to have built a church. Hence, the carpenter's square. He may have died by arrows and stones. It is thought that he then had a lance run through his body.

The Pope

The bishop of Rome has carried the title "pope" since the ninth century. *Pope* means "papa" or "father." St. Peter was the first bishop of Rome and, hence, the first pope. He was commissioned directly by Jesus:

> And so I say to you, you are Peter, and upon this rock I will build my church, and the gates of the netherworld shall not prevail against it. I will give you the keys to the kingdom of heaven. Whatever you bind on earth shall be bound in heaven; and whatever you loose on earth shall be loosed in heaven. (Mt 16:18–19)

Because Peter was the first bishop of Rome, the succeeding bishops of Rome have had primacy in the Church. The entire succession of popes since St. Peter can be traced directly to the Apostle.

The pope is in communion with the bishops of the world as part of the Magisterium, which is the Church's teaching authority. The pope can also define doctrine in faith or morals for the Church. When he does so, he is infallible and cannot be in error.

The pope is elected by the College of Cardinals by a two-thirds plus one majority vote in secret balloting. Cardinals younger than the age of eighty are eligible to vote. If the necessary majority is not achieved, the ballots are burned in a small stove inside the council chambers along with straw that makes dark smoke. The sign of dark smoke announces to the crowds waiting outside St. Peter's Basilica that a new pope has not been chosen. When a new pope has been voted in with the necessary majority, the ballots are burned without the straw, producing white smoke signifying the election of a pope.

Recent Popes

Since 1900 and through the pontificate of Pope Pope Benedict XVI, there were ten popes. Pope John Paul II was the first non-Italian pope since Dutchman Pope Adrian VI (1522–1523). The popes of the twentieth century through John Paul II with their original names, place of origin, and years as pope are as follows:

- Pope Leo XIII (Giocchino Pecci): Carpineto, Italy, February 20, 1878–July 20, 1903
- Pope St. Pius X (Giuseppe Sarto): Riese, Italy, August 4, 1903–August 20, 1914
- Pope Benedict XV (Giacomo della Chiesa): Genoa, Italy, September 3, 1914–January 22, 1922
- Pope Pius XI (Achille Ratti): Desio, Italy, February 6, 1922–February 10, 1939
- Pope Pius XII (Eugenio Pacelli): Rome, Italy, March 2, 1939–October 9, 1958
- Pope John XXIII (Angelo Giuseppe Roncalli), Sotto il Monte, Italy, October 28, 1958–June 3, 1963
- Pope Paul VI (Giovanni Battista Montini): Concessio, Italy, June 21, 1963–August 6, 1978
- Pope John Paul I (Albino Luciani): Forno di Canale, Italy, August 26, 1978–September 28, 1978
- Pope John Paul II (Karol Wojtyla): Wadowice, Poland, October 16, 1978–April 2, 2005
- Pope Benedict XVI (Joseph Ratzinger): Marktl am Inn, Germany, April 19, 2005–February 28, 2013.
- Pope Francis (Jorge Mario Bergoglio): Buenos Aires, Argentina, March 13, 2013–present

Pope Benedict XVI

Fathers of the Church

Church Fathers, or Fathers of the Church, is a traditional title that was given to theologians of the first eight centuries whose teachings made a lasting mark on the Church. The Church Fathers developed a significant amount of doctrine that has great authority in the Church. The Church Fathers are named as either Latin Fathers (West) or Greek Fathers (East). Among the greatest Fathers of the Church are:

Latin Fathers	Greek Fathers
St. Ambrose	St. John Chrysostom
St. Augustine	St. Basil the Great
St. Jerome	St. Gregory of Nazianzen
St. Gregory the Great	St. Athanasius

Doctors of the Church

The Doctors of the Church are men and women honored by the Church for their writings, preaching, and holiness. Originally the Doctors of the Church were considered to be Church Fathers Augustine, Ambrose, Jerome, and Gregory the Great, but others were added over the centuries. St. Teresa of Avila was the first woman Doctor (1970). St. Catherine of Siena was named a Doctor of the Church the same year. The Doctors of the Church are listed on page 269.

NAME	LIFE SPAN	DESIGNATION
St. Athanasius	296-373	1568 by Pius V
St. Ephraem the Syrian	306-373	1920 by Benedict XV
St. Hilary of Poitiers	315-367	1851 by Pius IX
St. Cyril of Jerusalem	315-386	1882 by Leo XIII
St. Gregory of Nazianzus	325-389	1568 by Pius V
St. Basil the Great	329-379	1568 by Pius V
St. Ambrose	339-397	1295 by Boniface VIII
St. John Chrysostom	347-407	1568 by Pius V
St. Jerome	347-419	1295 by Boniface XIII
St. Augustine	354-430	1295 by Boniface XIII
St. Cyril of Alexandria	376-444	1882 by Leo XIII
St. Peter Chrysologous	400-450	1729 by Benedict XIII
St. Leo the Great	400-461	1754 by Benedict XIV
St. Gregory the Great	540-604	1295 by Boniface XIII
St. Isidore of Seville	560-636	1722 by Innocent XIII
St. John of Damascus	645-749	1890 by Leo XIII
St. Bede the Venerable	672-735	1899 by Leo XIII
St. Peter Damian	1007-1072	1828 by Leo XII
St. Anselm	1033-1109	1720 by Clement XI
St. Bernard of Clairvaux	1090-1153	1830 by Pius VIII
St. Hildegard of Bingen	1098-1179	2012 by Pope Benedict XVI
St. Anthony of Padua	1195-1231	1946 by Pius XII
St. Albert the Great	1206-1280	1931 by Pius XI
St. Bonaventure	1221-1274	1588 by Sixtus V
St. Thomas Aquinas	1226-1274	1567 by Pius V
St. Catherine of Siena	1347-1380	1970 by Paul VI
St. John of Avila	1500-1569	2012 by Pope Benedict XVI
St. Teresa of Avila	1515-1582	1970 by Paul VI
St. Peter Canisius	1521-1597	1925 by Pius XI
St. John of the Cross	1542-1591	1926 by Pius XI
St. Robert Bellarmine	1542-1621	1931 by Pius XI
St. Lawrence of Brindisi	1559-1619	1959 by John XXIII
St. Francis de Sales	1567-1622	1871 by Pius IX
St. Alphonsus Ligouri	1696-1787	1871 by Pius IX
St. Thérèse of Lisieux	1873-1897	1997 by John Paul II

Ecumenical Councils

An ecumenical council is a worldwide assembly of bishops under direction of the pope. There have been twenty-one ecumenical councils, the most recent being the Second Vatican Council (1962–1965). A complete list of the Church's ecumenical councils with the years each met:

Nicaea I	325
Constantinople I	381
Ephesus	431
Chalcedon	451
Constantinople II	553
Constantinople III	680
Nicaea II	787
Constantinople IV	869-870
Lateran I	1123
Lateran II	1139
Lateran III	1179
Lateran IV	1215
Lyons I	1245
Lyons II	1274
Vienne	1311-1312
Constance	1414-1418
Florence	1431-1445
Lateran V	1512-1517
Trent	1545-1563
Vatican Council I	1869-1870
Vatican Council II	1962-1965

E. MORALITY

The Ten Commandments

The Ten Commandments are a main source for Christian morality. God revealed the Ten Commandments to Moses. Jesus himself acknowledged them. He told the rich young man, "If you wish to enter into life, keep the commandments" (Mt 19:17). Since the time of St. Augustine (fourth century), the Ten Commandments have been used as a source for teaching baptismal candidates.

I. I, the Lord am your God: you shall not have other gods besides me.

II. You shall not take the name of the Lord, your God, in vain.

III. Remember to keep holy the sabbath day.

IV. Honor your father and your mother.

V. You shall not kill.

VI. You shall not commit adultery.

VII. You shall not steal.

VIII. You shall not bear false witness against your neighbor.

IX. You shall not covet your neighbor's wife.

X. You shall not covet your neighbor's goods.

The Beatitudes

The word *beatitude* means "happiness." Jesus preached the Beatitudes in his Sermon on the Mount. They are:

Blessed are the poor in spirit, for theirs is the kingdom of God.
Blessed are they who mourn, for they will be comforted.
Blessed are the meek, for they will inherit the land.
Blessed are they who hunger and thirst for righteousness, for they will be satisfied.
Blessed are the merciful, for they will be shown mercy.
Blessed are the clean of heart, for they will see God.
Blessed are the peacemakers, for they will be called children of God.
Blessed are they who are persecuted for the sake of righteousness, for theirs is the kingdom of heaven.

Cardinal Virtues

Virtues—habits that help in leading a moral life—that are acquired by human effort are known as moral or human virtues. Four of these are the cardinal virtues as they form the hinge that connects all the others. They are:

- Prudence
- Fortitude
- Justice
- Temperance

Theological Virtues

The theological virtues are the foundation for moral life. They are related directly to God.

- Faith
- Hope
- Love

Corporal (Bodily) Works of Mercy

1. Feed the hungry.
2. Give drink to the thirsty.
3. Clothe the naked.
4. Visit the imprisoned.
5. Shelter the homeless.
6. Visit the sick.
7. Bury the dead.

Spiritual Works of Mercy

1. Counsel the doubtful.
2. Instruct the ignorant.
3. Admonish sinners.
4. Comfort the afflicted.
5. Forgive offenses.
6. Bear wrongs patiently.
7. Pray for the living and the dead.

Precepts of the Church

1. You shall attend Mass on Sundays and on holy days of obligation and rest from servile labor.
2. You shall confess your sins at least once a year.
3. You shall receive the Sacrament of Eucharist at least during the Easter season.
4. You shall observe the days of fasting and abstinence established by the Church.
5. You shall help to provide for the needs of the Church.

Catholic Social Teaching: Major Themes

The 1998 document *Sharing Catholic Social Teaching: Challenges and Directions—Reflections of the U.S. Catholic Bishops* highlighted seven principles of the Church's social teaching. They are:

1. Life and dignity of the human person
2. Call to family, community, and participation
3. Rights and responsibilities
4. Option for the poor and vulnerable
5. The dignity of work and the rights of workers
6. Solidarity
7. God's care for creation

Sin

Sin is an offense against God.

Mortal sin is the most serious kind of sin. Mortal sin destroys or kills a person's relationship with God. To be a mortal sin, three conditions must exist:

- The moral object must be of grave or serious matter. Grave matter is specified in the Ten Commandments (e.g., do not kill, do not commit adultery, do not steal, etc.).
- The person must have full knowledge of the gravity of the sinful action.
- The person must completely consent to the action. It must be a personal choice.

Venial sin is less serious sin. Examples of venial sins are petty jealousy, disobedience, and "borrowing" a small amount of money from a parent without the intention of repaying it. Venial sins, when not repented, can lead a person to commit mortal sins.

Vices are bad habits linked to sins. The seven capital vices are pride, avarice, envy, wrath, lust, gluttony, and sloth.

F. LITURGY AND SACRAMENTS

Church Year

The cycle of seasons and feasts that Catholics celebrate is called the Church Year or Liturgical Year. The Church Year is divided into five main parts: Advent, Christmas, Lent, Easter, and Ordinary Time.

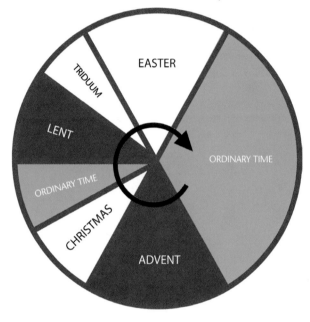

Holy Days of Obligation in the United States

1. Immaculate Conception of Mary, December 8
2. Christmas, December 25
3. Solemnity of Mary, Mother of God, January 1
4. Ascension of the Lord, Forty days after Easter
5. Assumption of Mary, August 15
6. All Saints Day, November 1

The Seven Sacraments

1. Baptism
2. Confirmation
3. Eucharist
4. Penance and Reconciliation
5. Anointing of the Sick
6. Matrimony
7. Holy Orders

How to Go to Confession

1. Spend time examining your conscience. Consider your actions and attitudes in each area of your life (e.g., Faith, family, school/work, social life, relationships). Ask yourself, "Is this area of my life pleasing to God? What needs to be reconciled with God? With others? With myself?"
2. Sincerely tell God you are sorry for your sins. Ask God for forgiveness and for the grace you will need to change what needs changing in your life. Promise God you will try to live according to his will for you.
3. Approach the area for confession. Wait an appropriate distance until it is your turn.
4. Make the Sign of the Cross with the priest. He may say: "May God, who has enlightened every heart, help you to know your sins and trust his mercy." You reply: "Amen."
5. Confess your sins to the priest. Simply and directly talk to him about the areas of sinfulness in your life that need God's healing touch.
6. The priest will ask you to pray an Act of Contrition. Pray an Act of Contrition you have committed to memory. Or, say something in your own words, like: "Dear God, I am sorry for my sins. I ask for your forgiveness, and I promise to do better in the future."
7. The priest will talk to you about your life, encourage you to be more faithful to God in the future, and help you decide what to do to make up for your sins—your penance.
8. The priest will then extend his hands over your head and pray the Church's official prayer of absolution:

   > God, the Father of mercies, through the death and resurrection of his Son, has reconciled the world to himself and sent the Holy Spirit among us for the forgiveness of sins; through the ministry of the Church may God give you pardon and peace, and I absolve you from your sins in the name of the Father, and of the Son, and of the Holy Spirit.

   You respond: "Amen."
9. The priest will wish you peace. Thank him and leave.
10. Go to a quiet place in church and pray your prayer of penance. Then spend time quietly thanking God for the gift of forgiveness.

Order of Mass

There are two main parts of the Mass, the Liturgy of the Word and the Liturgy of the Eucharist. The complete order of Mass:

The Introductory Rites

The Entrance
Greeting of the Altar and of the People Gathered
The Act of Penitence
The *Kyrie Eleison*
The *Gloria*
The Collect (Opening Prayer)

The Liturgy of the Word

Silence
The Biblical Readings (the reading of the Gospel is the high point of the Liturgy of the Word)
The Responsorial Psalm
The Homily
The Profession of Faith (Creed)
The Prayer of the Faithful

The Liturgy of the Eucharist

The Preparation of the Gifts
The Prayer over the Offerings
The Eucharistic Prayer
The Communion Rite
The Lord's Prayer
The Rite of Peace
The Fraction (Breaking of the Bread)
Communion
Prayer after Communion

The Concluding Rites

Communion Regulations

To receive Holy Communion properly, a person must be in the state of grace (free from mortal sin), have the right intention (only for the purpose of pleasing God), and observe the Communion fast.

The fast means that a person may not eat anything or drink any liquid (other than water) one hour before the reception of Communion. Exceptions are made to this fast only for the sick and aged.

Three Degrees of the Sacrament of Orders

There are three degrees of the Sacrament of Holy Orders: the ministries of bishop, priest, and deacon.

The bishop receives the fullness of the Sacrament of Holy Orders. He is the successor to the Apostles. When he celebrates the sacraments, the bishop is given the grace to act in the person of Christ, who is the head of the body of the Church.

Priests are ordained as coworkers of the bishop. They too are configured to Christ so that they may act in his person during the Sacraments of the Eucharist, Baptism, and the Anointing of the Sick. They may bless marriages in the name of Christ and, under the authority of the bishop, share in Christ's ministry of forgiveness in the Sacrament of Penance and Reconciliation.

Deacons are ordained for service and are configured to Christ the servant. Deacons are ordained to help and serve the priests and bishops in their work. While bishops and priests are configured to Christ to act as the head of Christ's body, deacons are configured to Christ in order to serve as he served. Deacons may baptize, preach the Gospel and homily, and bless marriages.

G. MARY AND THE SAINTS

Mother of God

Mary, the Mother of Jesus, is the closest human to cooperate with her Son's work of Redemption. For this reason, the Church holds her in a special place. Of her many titles, the most significant is that she is the Mother of God.

The Church teaches several truths about Mary.

First, she was conceived immaculately. This means from the very first moment of her existence she was without sin and "full of grace." This belief is called the Immaculate Conception. The Feast of the Immaculate Conception is celebrated on December 8.

Second, Mary was ever-virgin. She was a virgin before, in, and after the birth of Jesus. As his Mother, she cared for him in infancy and raised him to adulthood with the help of her husband, Joseph. She witnessed Jesus' preaching and ministry, was at the foot of his cross at his crucifixion, and was present with the Apostles as they awaited the coming of the Holy Spirit at Pentecost.

Third, at the time of her death, Mary was assumed body and soul into Heaven. This dogma was proclaimed as a matter of faith by Pope Pius XII in 1950. The Feast of the Assumption is celebrated on August 15.

The Church has always been devoted to the Blessed Virgin. This devotion is different from that given to God—Father, Son, and Holy Spirit. Rather, the Church is devoted to Mary as her first disciple, the Queen of all saints, and her own Mother. Quoting the fathers of the Second Vatican Council:

> In the meantime the Mother of Jesus, in the glory which she possesses in body and soul in heaven, is the image and the beginning of the Church as it is to be perfected in the world to come. Likewise she shines forth on earth, until the day of the Lord shall come, a sign of certain hope and comfort to the pilgrim People of God. (*Lumen Gentium* 68)

Marian Feasts Throughout the Year
(see also page 51)

January 1	Solemnity of Mary, Mother of God
March 25	Annunciation of the Lord
May 13	Our Lady of Fatima
May 31	Visitation
August 15	Assumption
August 22	Queenship of Mary
September 8	Birth of Mary
September 12	Most Holy Name of Mary
September 15	Our Lady of Sorrows
October 7	Our Lady of the Rosary
November 21	Presentation of Mary
December 8	Immaculate Conception
December 12	Our Lady of Guadalupe

Canonization of Saints

Saints are those who are in glory with God in Heaven. *Canonization* refers to a solemn declaration by the pope that a person who either died a martyr or lived an exemplary Christian life is in Heaven and may be honored and imitated by all Christians. The canonization process first involves a process of beatification that includes a thorough investigation of the person's life and certification of miracles that can be attributed to the candidate's intercession.

The first official canonization of the universal Church on record was St. Ulrich of Augsburg by Pope John XV in 993.

Some non-Catholics criticize Catholics for "praying to saints." Catholics *honor* saints for their holy lives, but we do not pray to them as if they were God. We ask the saints to pray with us and for us as part of the Church in glory. We can ask them to do this because we know that their lives have been spent in close communion with God. We also ask the saints for their friendship so that we can follow the example they have left for us.

Patron Saints

A patron is a saint who is designated for places (nations, regions, dioceses) or organizations. Many saints have also become patrons of jobs and professional groups and intercessors for special needs. Listed below are patron saints for several nations and some special patrons:

Patrons of Places

Americas	Our Lady of Guadalupe, St. Rose of Lima
Argentina	Our Lady of Lujan
Australia	Our Lady Help of Christians
Canada	St. Joseph, St. Anne
China	St. Joseph
England	St. George
Finland	St. Henry
France	Our Lady of the Assumption, St. Joan of Arc, St. Thérèse of Lisieux
Germany	St. Boniface
India	Our Lady of the Assumption
Ireland	St. Patrick, St. Brigid, St. Columba
Italy	St. Francis of Assisi, St. Catherine of Siena
Japan	St. Peter
Mexico	Our Lady of Guadalupe
New Zealand	Our Lady Help of Christians
Poland	St. Casmir, St. Stanislaus, Our Lady of Czestochowa
Russia	St. Andrew, St. Nicholas of Myra, St. Thérèse of Lisieux
Scotland	St. Andrew, St. Columba
Spain	St. James, St. Teresa of Ávila
United States	Immaculate Conception

Special Patrons

Accountants	St. Matthew
Actors	St. Genesius
Animals	St. Francis of Assisi
Athletes	St. Sebastian
Beggars	St. Martin of Tours
Boy Scouts	St. George
Dentists	St. Apollonia
Farmers	St. Isidore
Grocers	St. Michael
Journalists	St. Francis de Sales
Maids	St. Zita
Motorcyclists	Our Lady of Grace
Painters	St. Luke
Pawnbrokers	St. Nicholas
Police Officers	St. Michael
Priests	St. John Vianney
Scientists	St. Albert
Tailors	St. Homobonus
Teachers	St. Gregory the Great, St. John Baptist de la Salle
Wine Merchants	St. Amand

H. DEVOTIONS
The Mysteries of the Rosary

Joyful Mysteries

1. The Annunciation
2. The Visitation
3. The Nativity
4. The Presentation in the Temple
5. The Finding of Jesus in the Temple

Mysteries of Light

1. Jesus' Baptism in the Jordan River
2. Jesus Self-manifestation at the Wedding of Cana
3. The Proclamation of the Kingdom of God and Jesus' Call to Conversion
4. The Transfiguration
5. The Institution of the Eucharist at the Last Supper

Sorrowful Mysteries

1. The Agony in the Garden
2. The Scourging at the Pillar
3. The Crowning with Thorns
4. The Carrying of the Cross
5. The Crucifixion

Glorious Mysteries

1. The Resurrection
2. The Ascension
3. The Descent of the Holy Spirit
4. The Assumption of Mary
5. The Crowning of Mary as the Queen of Heaven and Earth

How to Pray the Rosary

Opening

1. Begin on the crucifix and pray the Apostles' Creed.
2. On the first bead, pray the Our Father.
3. On the next three beads, pray the Hail Mary. (Some people meditate on the virtues of faith, hope, and charity on these beads.)
4. On the fifth bead, pray the Glory Be.

The Body

Each decade (set of ten beads) is organized as follows:

1. On the larger bead that comes before each set of ten, announce the mystery to be prayed (see above) and pray one Our Father.
2. On each of the ten smaller beads, pray one Hail Mary while meditating on the mystery.
3. Pray one Glory Be at the end of the decade. (There is no bead for the Glory Be.)

Conclusion

Pray the following prayer at the end of the Rosary:

Hail, Holy Queen
Hail, holy Queen, Mother of Mercy,
our life, our sweetness, and our hope.
To thee do we cry,
poor banished children of Eve.
To thee do we send up our sighs,
mourning and weeping in the valley of tears.

Turn then, most gracious advocate,
thine eyes of mercy toward us;
and after this our exile,
show unto us the blessed fruit of thy womb, Jesus.
O clement, O loving, O sweet Virgin Mary.

Pray for us, O holy Mother of God,
that we may be made worthy of the promises of Christ.
Amen.

Stations of the Cross

The Stations of the Cross is a devotion and also a sacramental. (A sacramental is a sacred object, blessing, or devotion.) The Stations of the Cross are individual pictures or symbols hung on the interior walls of most Catholic churches depicting fourteen steps along Jesus' Way of the Cross. Praying the stations means meditating on each of the following scenes:

1. Jesus is condemned to death.
2. Jesus takes up his cross.
3. Jesus falls the first time.
4. Jesus meets his mother.
5. Simon of Cyrene helps Jesus carry his cross.
6. Veronica wipes the face of Jesus.
7. Jesus falls the second time.
8. Jesus consoles the women of Jerusalem.
9. Jesus falls the third time.
10. Jesus is stripped of his garments.
11. Jesus is nailed to the cross.
12. Jesus dies on the cross.
13. Jesus is taken down from the cross.
14. Jesus is laid in the tomb.

Some churches also include a fifteenth station, the Resurrection of the Lord.

Novenas

A novena consists of the recitation of certain prayers over a period of nine days. The symbolism of nine days refers to the time Mary and the Apostles spent in prayer between Jesus' Ascension into Heaven and Pentecost.

Many novenas are dedicated to Mary or to a saint with the faith and hope that she or he will intercede for the one making the novena. Novenas to St. Jude, St. Anthony, Our Lady of Perpetual Help, and Our Lady of Lourdes remain popular in the Church today.

Liturgy of the Hours

The Liturgy of the Hours is part of the official, public prayer of the Church. Along with the celebration of the sacraments, the recitation of the Liturgy of the Hours, or Divine Office (*office* means "duty" or "obligation"), allows for constant praise and thanksgiving to God throughout the day and night.

The Liturgy of Hours consists of five major divisions:

1. An hour of readings
2. Morning praises
3. Midday prayers
4. Vespers (evening prayers)
5. Compline (a short night prayer)

Scriptural prayer, especially the psalms, is at the heart of the Liturgy of the Hours. Each day follows a separate pattern of prayer with themes closely tied in with the liturgical year and feasts of the saints.

The Divine Praises

These praises are traditionally recited after the Benediction of the Blessed Sacrament.

Blessed be God.
Blessed be his holy name.
Blessed be Jesus Christ, true God and true man.
Blessed be the name of Jesus.
Blessed be his most Sacred Heart.
Blessed be his most Precious Blood.
Blessed be Jesus in the most holy sacrament of the altar.
Blessed be the Holy Spirit, the Paraclete.
Blessed be the great Mother of God, Mary most holy.
Blessed be her holy and Immaculate Conception.
Blessed be her glorious Assumption.
Blessed be the name of Mary, Virgin and Mother.
Blessed be St. Joseph, her most chaste spouse.
Blessed be God in his angels and his saints.

I. PRAYERS

Sign of the Cross

In the name of the Father,
and of the Son,
and of the Holy Spirit. Amen.

In nómine Patris,
et Filii,
et Spíritus Sancti.
Amen.

Our Father

Our Father
who art in heaven,
hallowed be thy name.
Thy kingdom come;
thy will be done on earth as it is in heaven.
Give us this day our daily bread
and forgive us our trespasses
as we forgive those who trespass against us.
And lead us not into temptation,
but deliver us from evil.
Amen.

Pater Noster qui es in caelis:
sanctificétur Nomen Tuum;
advéniat Regnum Tuum;
fiat volúntas Tua,
sicut in caelo, et in terra.
Panem nostrum
cuotidiánum da nobis hódie;
et dimítte nobis débita nostra,
sicut et nos
dimíttimus debitóribus nostris;
Et ne nos inducas in tentatiónem,
sed libera nos a Malo.
Amen.

Glory Be

Glory be to the Father
and to the Son
and to the Holy Spirit,
as it was in the beginning,
is now,
and ever shall be,
world without end. Amen.

Glória Patri
et Filio
et Spiritui Sancto.
Sicut erat in princípio,
et nunc et semper,
et in saecula saeculórum.
Amen.

Hail Mary

Hail Mary, full of grace,
the Lord is with thee.
Blessed art thou among women
and blessed is the fruit of thy womb, Jesus.
Holy Mary, Mother of God,
pray for us sinners now
and at the hour of our death. Amen.

Ave, María, grátia plena,
Dóminus tecum.
Benedicta tu in muliéribus,
et benedíctus fructus ventris
    tui, Iesus.
Sancta María, Mater Dei,
ora pro nobis peccatoribus
nunc et in hora mortis nostrae.
Amen.

Memorare

Remember, O most gracious Virgin Mary,
that never was it known
that anyone who fled to your protection,
implored your help,
or sought your intercession was left unaided.
Inspired by this confidence,
I fly unto you,
O virgin of virgins, my mother,
To you I come, before you I stand,
sinful and sorrowful.
O Mother of the word incarnate,
despise not my petitions,
but in your mercy hear and answer me. Amen.

The Angelus

V.   The angel spoke God's message to Mary.

R.   And she conceived by the Holy Spirit.

Hail Mary . . .

V.   Behold the handmaid of the Lord.

R.   May it be done unto me according to your word.

Hail Mary . . .

V.   And the Word was made flesh.

R.   And dwelled among us.

Hail Mary . . .

V.   Pray for us, O holy mother of God.

R.   That we may be made worthy of the promises of Christ.

Let us pray:

We beseech you, O Lord, to pour out your grace into our hearts. By the message of an angel we have learned of the incarnation of Christ, your son; lead us by his passion and cross, to the glory of the resurrection. Through the same Christ our Lord. Amen.

Regina Caeli

Queen of heaven, rejoice, alleluia.
The Son you merited to bear, alleluia,
has risen as he said, alleluia.
Pray to God for us, alleluia.

V.   Rejoice and be glad, O Virgin Mary, alleluia.

R.   For the Lord has truly risen, alleluia.

Let us pray.

God of life, you have given joy to the world by the resurrection of your son, our Lord Jesus Christ. Through the prayers of his mother, the Virgin Mary, bring us to the happiness of eternal life We ask this through Christ our Lord. Amen.

Grace at Meals

Before Meals

Bless us, O Lord,
and these your gifts,
which we are about to receive from your bounty,
through Christ our Lord. Amen.

After Meals

We give you thanks, almighty God,
for these and all the gifts
which we have received
from your goodness
through Christ our Lord. Amen.

Guardian Angel Prayer

Angel of God, my guardian dear, to whom God's love entrust me here, ever this day be at my side, to light and guard, to rule and guide. Amen.

Prayer for the Faithful Departed

Eternal rest grant unto them, O Lord.
R: And let perpetual light shine upon them.
May their souls and the souls of all faithful departed,
through the mercy of God, rest in peace.
R: Amen.

Morning Offering

O Jesus, through the immaculate heart of Mary, I offer you my prayers, works, joys, and sufferings of this day in union with the Holy Sacrifice of the Mass throughout the world. I offer them for all the intentions of your Sacred Heart: the salvation of souls, reparation for sin, the reunion of all Christians. I offer them for the intentions of our bishops and all members of the apostleship of prayer and in particular for those recommended by your Holy Father this month. Amen.

Act of Faith

O God,
I firmly believe all the truths that you have revealed
and that you teach us through your Church,
for you are truth itself
and can neither deceive nor be deceived.
Amen.

Act of Hope

O God,
I hope with complete trust that you will give me,
through the merits of Jesus Christ, all necessary grace
in this world
and everlasting life in the world to come,
for this is what you have promised
and you always keep your promises.
Amen.

Act of Love

O my God, I love you above all things, with my whole heart and soul, because you are all good and worthy of all my love. I love my neighbor as myself for the love of you. I forgive all who have injured me, and I ask pardon of all whom I have injured. Amen.

Prayer for Peace (St. Francis of Assisi)

Lord, make me an instrument of your peace.
Where there is hatred, let me sow love;
where there is injury, pardon;
where there is doubt, faith;
where there is despair, hope;
where there is darkness, light;
where there is sadness, joy.
O Divine Master,
grant that I may not seek so much to be consoled as
to console;
to be understood, as to understand,
to be loved, as to love.
For it is in giving that we receive,
it is in pardoning that we are pardoned,
and it is in dying that we are born to eternal life.

Glossary

abortion

The direct and deliberate ending of a pregnancy by killing the unborn child. Direct abortion, willed either as a means or an end, gravely contradicts moral law.

absolution

The prayer by which a priest, by the power given to the Church by Jesus Christ, pardons a repentant sinner in the Sacrament of Penance.

Act of Contrition

A prayer, either formal or informal, penitents pray at the Sacrament of Penance to express sorrow for their sins.

adultery

Infidelity in marriage whereby a married person has sexual intercourse with someone who is not the person's spouse.

Advocate

A name for the Holy Spirit. The Advocate is the "Paraclete" or "helper" who will live in us and guide us to truth.

age of discretion

Also called the "age of reason," it is the age (typically the end of the seventh year) at which a person becomes capable of moral reasoning.

almsgiving

The act of giving money or material goods to anyone who is needy.

apocalyptic

A genre of writing that assigns the enactment of God's justice to after death or to an end time when good people will be rewarded and evil people will be punished. In the Bible, the Books of Daniel and Revelation contain examples of apocalyptic writing.

apostasy

The denial of Christ and the repudiation of the Christian faith by a baptized person.

apostolate

The mission, focus, or duties of a religious community.

apostolic succession

An unbroken chain of power and authority connecting the pope and bishops to St. Peter and the Twelve Apostles of Jesus.

balsam

An oily, resinous substance that flows from certain plants, like pine, and which the Church usually mixes with olive oil for use as chrism. Another term for balsam is the "balm of Gilead."

Baptism of blood

The belief that martyrs—people who die for their faith in Jesus—receive forgiveness for their sins and experience God's saving mercy if they had not yet been baptized by water.

Baptism of desire

The belief that catechumens who die before receiving the Sacrament of Baptism receive forgiveness for their sins and experience God's saving mercy.

baptistery

A separately planned structure around the Baptism font.

basilica

A long, narrow church building based on the architecture of public Roman assembly halls. The term is also an honorary one to describe churches that have special importance.

bishops

Successors to the Apostles. A bishop governs the local Church in a given diocese and governs the universal Church with the pope and college of bishops. A bishop receives the fullness of the Sacrament of Holy Orders.

blaspheming

The act of insulting or contempt of God, holy people, or holy things.

Blessed Sacrament

The consecrated species of bread from Mass that is reserved in the tabernacle in church. The Blessed Sacrament is the Real Presence of Jesus.

blessings

Divine life-giving actions that originate from God the Father. His blessing is both word and gift.

breviary

A common name for a liturgical book from which priests pray the Liturgy of the Hours each day.

catechists

Teachers of the faith. They are ordained ministers and laypeople who help make Christian disciples.

catechumenate

A Greek word that means "study or instruction." In the early Church, the catechumenate was a period of study about Jesus and the Christian faith. Celebration of the Sacraments of Initiation did not occur until after the catechumenate.

catechumens

Unbaptized people who are preparing to receive all of the Sacraments of Christian Initiation.

cathedra

The chair or throne in a bishop's cathedral from which he presides over special functions. The earliest type of bishop's throne consisted of a high-backed armchair rounded at the top and made out of a single block of marble.

celibacy

The renunciation of marriage made by those who receive the Sacrament of Holy Orders for more perfect observance of chastity. Celibacy also extends to consecrated life and to those who forego marriage for some honorable end.

charism

A God-given talent, gift, skill, or ability that is given to each person for the good of everyone in the Church.

chasuble

The outer vestment worn by a priest at liturgy. Its color follows the liturgical seasons—purple for Advent or Lent; white for Christmas, Easter, and other feasts of Christ; red for Good Friday and Pentecost; and green for Ordinary Time.

Chrism Mass

An annual Mass celebrated in a diocesan cathedral on or near Holy Thursday in which the bishop consecrates the Sacred Chrism that will be used in the diocese throughout the year.

Chrismation

The name in the Eastern rites for the Sacrament of Confirmation. It comes from the chrism used as part of the sacrament.

Christ

A Hebrew name that means "anointed one." This name, when applied to Jesus, means he is the Son of the living God.

Church Year

Also known as the liturgical year, it organizes the major events of Jesus' life around the seasons of Advent, Christmas, Ordinary Time 1, Lent, Triduum, Easter, and Ordinary Time 2.

clergy

A term for ordained men; it comes from a Greek word for "lot."

Collect

The opening prayer of the Mass. It concludes the Introductory Rites and precedes the Liturgy of the Word.

common priesthood

The priesthood of the faithful. Christ has made the Church a "kingdom of priests" who share in his priesthood through the Sacraments of Baptism and Confirmation.

Communion of Saints

The unity of all those living on earth (the pilgrim Church), those being purified in Purgatory (the Church suffering), and those enjoying the blessings of Heaven (the Church in glory).

concupiscence

An inclination to commit sin that can be found in human desires and appetites as a result of Original Sin.

confession

Acknowledging and telling one's sins to a priest. Honest confession of sins is an essential part of the Sacrament of Penance.

GLOSSARY

confirmand
A candidate for Confirmation.

Confiteor
A term that means "I confess," it is used at the beginning of Mass and at other times to prepare to receive grace.

contraception
Any artificial means (e.g., pills, condoms, diaphragms, surgeries) that deliberately and directly has as an outcome closing off one of the aims of sexual intercourse—the sharing of life. Contraception also opposes the unitive aspect of the conjugal act by not allowing for the total self-giving of the couple to one another.

contrition
Heartfelt sorrow and aversion for sins committed, along with the intention of sinning no more. Contrition is the most important act of penitents and is necessary for receiving absolution in the Sacrament of Penance.

conversion
The first step of a sinner to repentance and returning in love to God the Father.

dalmatic
The outer liturgical vestment of a deacon. It may also be worn by bishops under the chasuble and certain solemn liturgies.

declaration of nullity
The Church's declaration that a particular marriage—whether presumed as a sacramental bond or simply a natural bond—was never valid.

Deposit of Faith
The body of saving truth entrusted by Christ to the Apostles and handed on by them to be preserved and proclaimed by the Church's Magisterium.

diocese
A geographic section of the Church, made up of parishes, that is headed by a bishop.

discern
To perceive differences between more than one option.

divorce
The ending of a civil marriage contract. Church law forbids divorced Catholics from remarrying unless their first marriage has been declared null. It also forbids a Catholic from marrying a divorced person of any faith unless that marriage has been declared null.

domestic church
A term for the family, the Church in miniature.

doxology
A prayer of praise to the Blessed Trinity. The Eucharistic Prayer ends in a doxology.

Easter Triduum
The three-day liturgy that is the Church's most solemn celebration of the Paschal Mystery. It begins with the Mass of the Lord's Supper on Holy Thursday, continues through the Good Friday service, and concludes with the evening prayer on Easter Sunday. Although it takes place over three days, the Triduum is considered one single liturgy.

Ecumenical Council
An assembly of all (or most) bishops from throughout the world in union with the pope. Such a council is the highest authority in the universal Church.

efficacious
A term that means "capable of producing a desired effect." This means that the sacraments actually confer the grace they signify.

Epiclesis
The prayer that petitions God to send the Holy Spirit to transform the bread and wine offered at the Eucharistic liturgy into the Body and Blood of Jesus Christ. This term also applies to the prayer said in every sacrament that asks for the sanctifying power of the Holy Spirit.

episcopal college
The unity of all ordained bishops in the worldwide Church, in both the East and the West. The pope heads the episcopal college.

eschatological
A term to describe the "last things" (death, judgment, Heaven, Hell, Purgatory, the Second Coming of Christ, and the resurrection of the body).

Eucharistic Prayer
The Church's great prayer of praise and thanksgiving to God that takes place during the Liturgy of the Eucharist. There are four Eucharistic Prayers in the Roman Rite.

evangelists
The writers of the four Gospels in the New Testament. According to tradition, the four evangelists are Matthew, Mark, Luke, and John.

evangelization
The act of bringing the Good News of Jesus Christ to others.

evangelize
To bring the Good News of Jesus Christ to others.

examination of conscience
An honest assessment of how well we have lived God's covenant of love. This examination leads us to accept responsibility for our sins and to realize our need of God's merciful forgiveness.

excommunication
A serious penalty that means a baptized person is no longer "in communion" with the Catholic Church. Some excommunications are automatic, including for the sins of apostasy, heresy, and schism.

exorcisms
Prayerful rites in preparation for Baptism that invoke God's help in overcoming the power of Satan and the spirit of evil.

extreme unction
A term that means "last anointing." It once referred to the time that the Sacrament of the Anointing of the Sick is received just before death. It is accompanied by a final reception of Holy Communion called *Viaticum.*

Feast of Tabernacles
Also known as the Sukkot or Feast of Booths, the Feast of Tabernacles begins five days after Yom Kippur and lasts for eight days. It commemorates the forty years the Jews spent in the desert when they had to protect themselves by constructing huts or booths.

fidelity
An attribute of God that describes his eternal faithfulness to his promises.

forgiveness
God's merciful pardon for our sins. God forgives our sins in the Sacrament of Penance and welcomes us back into communion with him.

fornication
Sexual intercourse between an unmarried man and an unmarried woman.

Fraction Rite
The time during the Communion Rite when the priest breaks the Body of Christ. He puts a piece of the consecrated bread into the chalice containing the Blood of Christ to signify the unity of the Body and Blood of Christ.

fruits of the Spirit
Perfections that result from living in union with the Holy Spirit.

General Intercessions
Also called the Prayers of the Faithful, these are prayers of petition for the sake of others.

Gifts of the Holy Spirit
Outpourings of God's gifts to help us live a Christian life. The traditional seven Gifts of the Holy Spirit are wisdom, understanding, counsel, fortitude, knowledge, piety, and fear of the Lord.

Great Amen
The affirmation by the faithful to the entire Eucharistic Prayer.

heresy
False teaching that denies essential truths of the Catholic faith.

holy day of obligation
One of several special days in the Church Year when all Catholics are obliged to participate in Mass.

Holy Trinity
The central mystery of the Christian faith and of Christian life that there are three Divine Persons in one God. God alone can make it known to us by revealing himself as Father, Son, and Holy Spirit.

homily

A reflection given by a bishop, priest, or deacon that reflects on the Scripture readings during Mass or the sacraments. The homily helps us hear God's Word and apply it to our lives today.

human solidarity

The virtue of social charity, friendship, and responsible sharing whereby we recognize our interdependence on others and that we are all brothers and sisters of one family under a loving Father.

humility

The virtue by which Christians acknowledge that God is the author of all that is good.

hypostatic union

The doctrine of faith that recognizes two natures (one human and one divine) in the one divine Person of Jesus Christ.

icons

From a Greek word meaning "image," icons are religious images or paintings.

imprimatur

A bishop's approval to print a religion textbook because its contents agree with Church teaching.

Incarnation

A word that means "taking on human flesh." Jesus is the Incarnation of God. In Jesus, God took human form.

indifference

Selflessness that is open to going wherever one is most needed and to doing whatever seems best. God's will takes precedence over an individual's will.

infallibility

The charism or gift of the Church offered by Christ whereby she is protected from error in matters of faith and morals. The pope or an Ecumenical Council most exclusively exercises the gift.

Introit

A part of a psalm that is sung when the priest enters the church and approaches the altar.

invocation

A call, request, or supplication for God's help.

Jesus

A Hebrew name that means "God saves." This name explains the purpose of Jesus' life—to save all people from sin.

L'Arche community

Family- and faith-based homes where people with disabilities live together. The name is French for "the Ark," as in Noah's Ark. L'Arche was founded in 1964 when Jean and Pauline Vanier welcomed two men with disabilities into their home in France.

laity

All the members of the Church who have been initiated into the Church through Baptism and who are not ordained (the clergy) or in consecrated life. The laity participate in Jesus' prophetic, priestly, and kingly ministries.

laying on of hands

A gesture that is a main rite and origin of the Sacrament of Confirmation. Acts 19:1-6 tells the story of a new group of disciples who, after being baptized, received the Holy Spirit when St. Paul laid hands on them.

lectio divina

Literally, "divine reading." This is a prayerful way to read the Bible or any other sacred reading.

Liturgy of the Hours

The public prayer of the Church that makes holy the entire course of the day and night. It is also called the Divine Office.

Liturgy of the Word

The part of the Mass that includes the "writings of the prophets" (the Old Testament reading and psalm) and the "memoirs of the Apostles" (the New Testament Epistles and the Gospel), the homily, the profession of faith, and the intercessions for the world.

liturgy

The official public worship of the Church. The sacraments and the Divine Office constitute the Church's liturgy. Mass is the most important liturgical celebration.

mandate

An official appointment from the pope that says a certain priest has been chosen to be a bishop.

marks of the Church
Four essential signs or characteristics of Christ's Church that mark her as his true Church. The Church is one, holy, catholic, and apostolic.

marriage consent
The promises made by the bride and groom to honor one another and to be faithful in good times and in bad, in sickness and in health throughout their lives. By their consent to one another, the couple establish a permanent covenant in love.

martyrs
Literally "witnesses." A martyr is someone who has been killed because of his or her faith.

Mass of the Catechumens
The first part of the Mass that was attended by catechumens along with baptized Catholics. The prayers, Scripture readings, and homily were meant to be a form of instruction for the catechumens. Today this part of the Mass is called the Liturgy of the Word.

Messiah
The long-prophesied Savior that God would send to save people from their sins. Some Jews in the time of Jesus thought this Messiah would be a political figure, someone who would rescue them from domination by the Romans.

ministerial priesthood
The priesthood of Christ received in the Sacrament of Holy Orders. Its purpose is to serve the common priesthood by building up and guiding the Church in the name of Christ.

moral object
Either good moral actions or evil actions; it answers the "what" question of morality and can objectively determine if an action is right or wrong.

moral virtues
Virtues acquired through human effort and with the help of God's grace.

mortal sins
Serious violations of God's law of love that result in the loss of God's life (sanctifying grace) in the soul of the sinner. To commit mortal sins, there must be grave matter, full knowledge of the evil done, and full consent of the will.

moto propio
Means "of his own accord." It signifies words in papal documents that were decided by the pope personally.

mystagogia
A Greek term that means "unfolding of the mystery." It is named for the period following the Baptism of adults. During this time, the newly baptized are to open themselves more fully to the graces received in Baptism.

Natural Family Planning
A Church-approved method for regulating births in a marriage that is in accord with God's will because it is pursued by spouses without external pressure nor motives of selfishness and is practiced through natural means of periodic continence and use of infertile periods.

neophytes
Those newly received into the Church through the Sacraments of Initiation at the Easter Vigil.

Nicene Creed
The formal Profession of Faith recited at Mass. It came from the first two Ecumenical Councils, at Nicaea in 325 and Constantinople in 381.

novena
A nine-day prayer for a certain intention.

nuncio
An archbishop who acts as the official Vatican delegate for a nation. He is also called the Apostolic Delegate.

nuptial blessing
Nuptial is a Latin-derived word that means "wedding." The nuptial blessing sanctifies the marriage covenant of the bride and groom. It takes place after the couple gives their consent to be married.

Oil of Catechumens
Olive oil or another plant oil that is blessed by a bishop at the Chrism Mass on or around Holy Thursday. This blessed oil is used to anoint catechumens, giving them wisdom and strength in their journey toward Baptism.

Oil of the Sick
Olive or another plant oil that is blessed by a bishop either at a Chrism Mass or at the time of anointing. The Oil of the Sick is an efficacious sign of healing and strength that is part of the Sacrament of the Anointing of the Sick.

ordinand
A person receiving the Sacrament of Holy Orders at any level: episcopate, presbyterate, or diaconate.

ordinary bishop
The name for the diocesan bishop. He is the pastoral and legal representative of his diocese.

original holiness and justice
The state of man and woman before sin. "From their friendship with God flowed the happiness of their existence in paradise" (*CCC* 384).

Original Sin
The fallen state of human nature into which all generations of people are born. Christ Jesus came to save us from Original Sin.

Paraclete
Another name for the Holy Spirit that means advocate, defender, or consoler.

parish
A diocesan subdivision headed by a pastor. A parish is a local Church community.

parochial school
A private school sponsored by a parish. Catholics and other Christian denominations run parochial schools to educate children in the Faith.

penance
A sign of our true sorrow for the sins we have committed. Among other actions, penance may be a prayer, an offering, a work of mercy, an act of service to neighbor, or a voluntary act of self-denial.

penitential rite
Part of the introductory rite at Mass when the priest invites people to repent of their sins and prepare themselves to encounter Christ in the Eucharist.

penitentiaries
Books for confessors in the past that listed all possible sins and the appropriate penance that should be given for each one.

penitents
People who admit their sins, are truly sorry for having sinned, and wish to be restored to the good graces of God and the Church.

Pentecost
A Greek word that means "fiftieth day." On this day, the Church celebrates the descent of the Holy Spirit upon Mary and the Apostles. It is often called the "birthday of the Church."

personal sins
Any sins committed by an individual. Mental sin includes our thoughts and attitudes. Actual sin includes our words and actions.

polygamy
Being married to two or more people at the same time. It is contrary to conjugal love, which is undivided and exclusive.

Precepts of the Church
Basic rules that bind Catholics who belong to Christ's Body.

presbyters
Priests or members of the order of priesthood who are coworkers with the bishops and are servants to God's People, especially in celebrating the Eucharist.

primordial sacrament
A reference to Jesus as the "prime sacrament" because he points to God's love while at the same time he is God's love for us as he reconciles the world to his Father.

Purgatory
Purification after death for those who died in God's friendship but still need to be purified because of past sins before entering Heaven. It is also called "the Church suffering."

Real Presence
The doctrine that Jesus Christ is truly present in his Body and Blood under the form of bread and wine in the Eucharist.

reconciliation

Being reunited in peace and friendship with someone we have hurt by our sins—especially God, the Church, and ourselves.

Responsorial Psalm

A psalm sung or said at Mass afer the first Scripture reading.

restitution

The act of repairing, restoring, or paying for any damage our sins have inflicted on others or their property.

resuscitation

Reviving a person who is dead or seems to be dead. Jesus performed at least three resuscitation miracles.

righteousness

The status of sinners who have been forgiven. Jesus suffered and died so that humans could be made righteous—that is, saved from sin and restored to a loving relationship with the Father.

Rite of Baptism of Children (RBC)

The process by which infants are initiated into the Church and after which catechesis takes place gradually as the person grows.

Rite of Christian Initiation for Adults (RCIA)

The process by which anyone of catechetical age is initiated into the Catholic Church.

Sabbath

From the Hebrew word *Shabbat*, "to cease," the Sabbath is a weekly day of rest and worship in the Jewish faith. Jews observe the Sabbath on the seventh day of the week. Christians have replaced the Sabbath with observance of the Lord's Day on Sunday, the first day of the week and the day Christ rose from the dead.

sacrament

An outward (visible) sign of an invisible grace. An "efficacious" symbol that brings about the spiritual reality to which it points. This term applies to Christ Jesus, the great sign of God's love for us; to the Church, his continuing presence in our world; and to the Seven Sacraments.

sacramental

A sacred sign (for example, objects, places, and actions) that resemble the sacraments. Through the prayers of the Church, spiritual effects are signified and obtained.

sacramental character

An indelible spiritual mark which is the permanent effect of the Sacraments of Baptism, Confirmation, and Holy Orders. The mark is a permanent configuration to Jesus Christ and a specific standing in the Church. The reception of these sacraments is never repeated.

sacramental economy

an expression that means the communication or dispensation of the fruits of Christ's Paschal Mystery through the celebration of the sacramental liturgy.

sacramental grace

A participation in the life and love of the Trinity that comes to us through the sacraments. Each sacrament brings us a different dimension of God's life and love.

sacramental seal

The secrecy priests are bound to keep regarding any sins confessed to them.

Sacred Chrism

Blessed by a bishop, this perfumed oil is used for anointing in the Sacraments of Baptism, Confirmation, and Holy Orders. It represents the gift of the Holy Spirit.

Sacred Tradition

The living transmission of the Church's Gospel message found in the Church's teaching, life, and worship. It is faithfully preserved, handed on, and interpreted by the Church's Magisterium.

sanctoral cycle

The feasts of saints found throughout the year on the Church's liturgical calendar.

schism

A break in Church unity from the failure to accept the pope as the Vicar of Christ.

scrutinies

Prayer services in which the Church prays for and over the elect. The prayers ask God to forgive the elected people's sins and to strengthen them with grace.

Second Coming of Christ

Also known as the Parousia, this is the time when the Kingdom of God will be fully established and victory over evil will be complete.

Secret

A prayer from the Tridentine Mass said by the celebrant in a low voice at the end of the Offertory. It was said in a low voice because it occurred at the same time the choir sang the Offertory hymn.

seminary

The place where the training of candidates for the priesthood takes place. The Council of Trent instructed the bishops in each diocese to set up a seminary college to train men for the priesthood.

social justice

A form of justice that treats all people fairly and equally, according to their due. Social justice involves fair treatment of individuals. It also involves the structures of society that protect or oppress the rights of certain people.

Society of Jesus

A religious order established in the sixteenth century by St. Ignatius of Loyola to help with the reform of the Church. Popularly known as the Jesuits, the order is especially engaged in preaching, teaching, writing, and the ministering of schools and colleges.

Son of Man

A title Jesus frequently used in speaking of himself. It meant two things: Jesus' association with all of humanity and his identity as the righteous one who will usher in God's Kingdom at the end of time (see Daniel 7:13ff).

Stations of the Cross

A meditative prayer based on the Passion of Jesus. The devotion grew out of the custom of Holy Land pilgrims who retraced the last steps of Jesus on the way to Calvary.

sterilization

Any surgical procedure that prevents conception. Some sterilization procedures in women include tied or cut fallopian tubes, removal of ovaries, and/or removal of the uterus. Sterilization procedures in men include vasectomy (cutting tubes carrying sperm from the testicles) or castration (removing the testicles). Deliberate sterilization is contrary to one of the characteristics of sacramental marriage, the openness to children.

stole

A long, narrow band of fabric, like a scarf. A deacon's stole is worn diagonally from one shoulder. A priest's stole is worn straight from the shoulders.

synod of bishops

A group of bishops, usually chosen from throughout the world, who come together to advise the pope on certain issues.

Ten Commandments

Ten rules God gave to the Israelites through Moses. These commandments told the people how they were to live in relation to God and to one another.

theodicy

The theological question that tries to connect belief in God's justice with the reality that sometimes good people suffer unjustly and die.

theological virtues

Three important virtues bestowed on us at Baptism that relate us to God: faith (belief in and personal knowledge of God), hope (trust in God's Salvation and his bestowal of graces needed to attain it), and charity (love of God and love of neighbor).

Transfiguration

The occasion when Jesus revealed his glory before Peter, James, and John on a high mountain. His face "shone like the sun and his clothes became white as light" (Mt 17:2).

transubstantiation

What happens at the consecration of the bread and wine at Mass when their entire substance is turned into the entire substance of the Body and Blood of Christ, even though the appearances of bread and wine remain. The Eucharistic presence of Christ begins at the moment of consecration and endures as long as the Eucharistic species subsist.

venial sins
Sins that weaken and wound our relationship with God but do not destroy divine life in our souls.

vicar
One who serves as a substitute, an agent, or a representative of another. Bishops are vicars of Christ; they take his place in the Church. The pope is the Supreme Vicar of Christ.

Words of Institution
The words said by Jesus over the bread and wine at the Last Supper. The priest repeats these words over the bread and wine at Mass as they are changed into the Body and Blood of Christ.

Scripture Index

CCC Index

Photo Index